The Psychosocial Implications of Disney Movies

The Psychosocial Implications of Disney Movies

Special Issue Editor

Lauren Dundes

MDPI • Basel • Beijing • Wuhan • Barcelona • Belgrade

MDPI

Special Issue Editor
Lauren Dundes
Department of Sociology, McDaniel College
USA

Editorial Office
MDPI
St. Alban-Anlage 66
4052 Basel, Switzerland

This is a reprint of articles from the Special Issue published online in the open access journal *Social Sciences* (ISSN 2076-0760) from 2018 to 2019 (available at: https://www.mdpi.com/journal/socsci/special_issues/Disney_Movies_Psychosocial_Implications)

For citation purposes, cite each article independently as indicated on the article page online and as indicated below:

LastName, A.A.; LastName, B.B.; LastName, C.C. Article Title. *Journal Name* **Year**, *Article Number*, Page Range.

ISBN 978-3-03897-848-0 (Pbk)
ISBN 978-3-03897-849-7 (PDF)

Cover image courtesy of Hsun-yuan Hsu.

Contents

About the Special Issue Editor

Lauren Dundes received her undergraduate degree from Stanford University and her doctoral degree from Johns Hopkins University. She has been a professor of sociology at McDaniel College in Westminster, Maryland, USA, since 1996. She has published more than 60 articles, including eight about Disney movies. In the fall of 2018, she taught a seminar called Decoding Disney.

Preface to "The Psychosocial Implications of Disney Movies"

With its widespread and sustained influence, the Walt Disney Company has achieved iconic status. Its products are a mainstay of popular culture, salient in the everyday lives of people in many countries around the globe. In fact, MDPI data documenting the countries in which readers have accessed the articles in this volume attest to the cross-cultural interest in the Disney megabrand (see these articles below, mentioned parenthetically by author name).

The power of the Disney brand has heightened the need for academics to question whether Disney films and music function as a tool of the Western elite that shapes the views of those less empowered (Anjirbag; Armstrong; Hodge). Given its global reach, how the Walt Disney Company handles the role of race, gender, and sexuality in social structural inequality merits serious reflection according to a number of the articles in this volume (Harris; Hine, Ivanovic, and England; Perea; Uppal). On the other hand, some academics argue that Disney productions can help individuals cope with difficult situations or embrace progressive thinking (Brydon; Graham, Yuhas, and Roman; Hine, England, Lopreore, Horgan, and Hartwell; Zurcher, Webb, and Robinson). The different approaches to the assessment of Disney films as cultural artifacts also vary according to the theoretical perspectives guiding the interpretation of both overt and latent symbolic meaning in the movies (Dundes, Streiff Buitelaar, and Streiff; Koushik and Reed; Macaluso; Primo).

Regardless of discrepant views about the significance of Disney fare, its films simultaneously mirror societal trends and reshape them. Yet, audience buy-in also governs this interplay. For example, in late summer 2018, a pre-release image from Disney's *Ralph Breaks the Internet: Wreck-It Ralph 2* depicted Disney "princesses" assembled in a group, showcasing their new, updated look. Although most were still recognizable, Princess Tiana, Disney's only Black princess, was not. Her new biracial appearance provoked an outcry, prompting Disney to revise the animation to make Princess Tiana more closely resemble her original appearance in the *Princess and the Frog* (2009). Disney's decision to incur the extra expense necessary to make the changes indicates the power of public reactions in the production of media fare.

The increasingly dynamic creation of entertainment media has both expanded the opportunity for audience input and galvanized academics from a variety of disciplines. The 15 studies of Disney films comprising this volume were written by authors from a number of different fields, including the following: education, schooling, and society; sociology; psychology; communications; music; musical theater; business communication; children's literature; human development and family studies; and geography, media, and communication. The multidisciplinary perspectives presented in this volume are based on a range of methodologies, such as content analysis, interview data, census data tallies, children's drawings, and Reddit data.

The Collection of 15 Articles in the Special Issue

In the first article in this volume, Zurcher et al. use a census analysis of 85 Disney animated films from 1937–2018 to examine the portrayal of family dynamics. The authors studied this topic in light of children's ability to gain insight into their own conflicts by bonding with fictional characters (through so-called parasocial relationships). The authors laud the opportunity for children in single-parent families, disproportionately represented in Disney movies, to model the resiliency of characters facing familial challenges they themselves experience.

The second article in the volume also discusses how Disney films can model healthy responses to challenging life circumstances and events. In an extension of previous work on the same topic, Graham et al. assess death depictions in Disney films by comparing concepts of death in 23 death scenes from 10 Disney animated films from 1937 to 2003 with 10 death scenes from eight full-length Disney and Pixar animated films from 2003 to 2016. The authors find that increasingly realistic portrayals of death exemplify ways to cope and express emotions when individuals face the demise of a loved one. In particular, characters that turned to family or friends when they were upset modeled the importance of support systems in building connections that facilitate healthy grieving.

In the next article, Perea also explores connections to characters in Disney films, including how they may be relatable to viewers who experience outsider status. Perea identifies the representation of otherness as it relates to queer identity by elucidating both overt and latent markers in the title characters of *Dumbo* and *Lilo & Stitch*. For example, to avoid eliciting consternation in others, Stitch hides his extra limbs and tentacles, while Dumbo pins his ears to disguise nonconformity. Perea illustrates the range of interpreted meanings embedded within Disney characters, noting that violations of normative codes can occur even within the very industry that perpetuates them.

Disney's involvement in distributing stories that resonate with marginalized groups was also evidenced by its hit, *Black Panther* (produced by Marvel Studios and distributed by Walt Disney Studios Motion Pictures). Harris analyzes the film along with Disney's *The Queen of Katwe*, a live-action film based on the true story of a girl from the slum of Katwe in Kampala, Uganda, who becomes a chess champion. Harris applauds Disney for breaking new ground in these portrayals of "Africana royalty" that rise above the legacy of colonialization, capitalism, and globalization. Harris nevertheless asserts that to dismantle the matrix of domination, depictions of non-dominant groups cannot be mere "cinematic bumps in the road".

This matrix of domination paradigm that encompasses the role of race, class, and gender in oppression also applies to the article by Uppal. Uppal used interview data and drawings to study girls in India and Fiji after they watched clips of Jasmine (from Disney's Aladdin), Mulan, and Pocahontas (that is, nonwhite Disney princess characters). Compared with girls from Sweden, those in India and Fiji believed they lacked the qualities to be a princess, especially white skin color. Uppal's research connects widespread Disney princess imagery with a "white" beauty standard, especially in countries with less media exposure to ethnically similar characters.

In the next article, Hine et al. (2018a) also report entrenched notions of traits associated with princesses. Their study of 131 eight- and nine-year-old children in the United Kingdom documents how children attributed feminine and masculine characteristics to "princesses" both before and after watching an older princess movie (*Sleeping Beauty*, 1959) and a newer Disney princess movie (*Moana*, 2016). While the children recognized that Moana had a more androgynous gender profile than that of Aurora of *Sleeping Beauty*, nearly half of them did not identify Moana as a princess at all. The authors argue that although the traditional conceptualization of princesses appears resistant to change, increasing examples of characters that depart from gender stereotypes may alter these views.

The subsequent paper by Anjirbag also analyzes *Moana*. In her article, Anjirbag suggests that the presentation of Moana is neither culturally authentic nor a significant improvement over Mulan. Anjirbag explores potential barriers between the characters and viewers, distance communicated through stereotypical visual and musical aesthetics. These flat representations of diversity not only depart from authentic portrayals of these cultures, but also contribute to colonial erasure that reinforces current hegemonic power structures.

The next paper offers a detailed critique of the music in *Moana*. In this paper, Armstrong argues that the songs in *Moana* reflect imperialism and the appropriation of Polynesian musical traits. She notes that while audiences do hear the influence of cultural insider and Polynesian composer Opetaia Foa'i, who was involved in the film, those sounds are framed or accompanied by those used in the music of American Broadway and film. Armstrong raises concerns about Disney's self-appointment as an authority in its presentation of a culture likely to be associated with its "Disneyfied" version.

Hodge finds similar ethnocentrism in EPCOT's 13-minute nighttime show "IllumiNations: Reflections of Earth", which is designed to transport audiences to other "worlds" using culturally thematic music. Hodge explains that the show presents Euro-American music as the end point of a musical evolutionary process—a demonstration of musical supremacy of sorts. He argues that "IllumiNations" showcases traditional Western musical sounds that American consumers expect while reinforcing their superiority.

Modernized Disney franchises such as *Star Wars: The Last Jedi* and the live-action version of *Beauty and the Beast* also express traditional hierarchies as consumer friendly. In the next article in the volume, Koushik and Reed argue that despite placing more females in prominent roles in these films, men are still portrayed as wiser, less emotional, and more experienced. The authors attribute these surface-level post-feminist reboots to Disney's financial goals: commodity feminism that allows women to identify with their femininity and feel empowered by consumerism. They argue that ultimately, the films operate within an established capitalist system that protects the dominant patriarchy.

The role of gender stereotypes in creating characters that are marketable commodities also relates to Disney's *Hercules*. In the next article, Primo explores this topic in assessing whether the title character's lack of resonance is related to Disney's modification of traditional masculinity in the film. Primo examines Hercules' non-cohesive male identity, including the female-associated trait of selflessness. She argues that the title character's deviation from alpha male traits did not appear to have encouraged subsequent portrayals of more progressive masculinity.

Despite concerns about the lack of progress in gender equality in Disney films, Hine et al. (2018b) argue that modern Disney princesses have become more androgynous in their behavioral profiles and are increasingly involved in handling dangerous situations, while male leads demonstrate an increasing number of feminine traits. In addition, they report that the sexes are equal in the number of rescue behaviors depicted. The authors argue that this trend could promote healthier and more inclusive attitudes consistent with increasing gender role flexibility.

Brydon shares with Hine et al. (2018b) a certain amount of optimism about increasing gender role equity. In her analysis of the *Incredibles 2*, Brydon argues that a different model of masculinity exists within the empowered and collaborative parenting shown in the film. She applauds role fluidity especially as it is embraced and engaged in by a stereotypically gendered man, Mr. Incredible. His wife, Mrs. Incredible, is able to bridge the gap between third-wave and matricentric feminists in finding strength in oneself versus strength in the village; Mrs. Incredible achieves both, modeling gender role flexibility.

Macaluso offers a view of the *Incredibles 2* that differs from that of Brydon, as he argues that the humorous role reversal of Mr. and Mrs. Incredible constitutes a postfeminist spin on the gains of women. In ridiculing men, women's progress occurs at the expense of males, inciting backlash that Macaluso documents with online Reddit data that capture viewers' reactions to the film. Macaluso calls for more egalitarian progress of spouses as partners advancing together.

According to Dundes, Streiff Buitelaar, and Streiff, progress towards gender equality is complicated by discomfort with powerful women as illustrated by Elsa, a powerful queen in *Frozen*. Elsa embraces the storm power of Zeus over romance—a decision facilitated by her ability to independently produce two snowman sons, Olaf and Marshmallow. The fact that these two characters are gender nonconforming reflects fears surrounding the maelstrom of societal changes, including expanding fertility options and the re-conceptualization of gender identity. Despite the outward progressiveness of the plot, the normalcy of male dominance drives the resolution of the story, in which Elsa learns to wield power in a non-threatening manner.

In Gratitude

The Special Issue guest editor wishes to express her appreciation for the contributions by all of the authors whose articles comprise this volume. She also is grateful to the editors of Social Sciences, especially Dragana Oborina, as well as the many anonymous reviewers whose time and expertise made this volume possible. The cover art by Hsun-yuan Hsu (www.hsunyuanart.com), created specifically for this volume, is also greatly appreciated.

Lauren Dundes
Special Issue Editor

social sciences

MDPI

Article

The Portrayal of Families across Generations in Disney Animated Films

Jessica D. Zurcher *, Sarah M. Webb and Tom Robinson

School of Communications, Brigham Young University, Brimhall Building, #360, Provo, UT 84604, USA;
sare.b.webb@gmail.com (S.M.W.); thomas_robinson@byu.edu (T.R.)
* Correspondence: jessica_zurcher@byu.edu

Received: 5 February 2018; Accepted: 14 March 2018; Published: 18 March 2018

Abstract: Disney animated films continue to serve as an influential form of media that shapes children's development of beliefs about the world surrounding them, including the construct of the family. However, a census analysis as to how Disney animated films represent depictions of families has yet to be conducted. To fill this gap, we assessed the qualities of family demographics, structure, and function in a census analysis of 85 Disney animated films from the years 1937–2018. Results indicated that single parent families (41.3%) was the most predominantly represented family structure, followed by nuclear (25%) and guardian (19.2%). We also observed that the first depiction of a non-Caucasian family was presented in the 1990s, with a growing number of ethnically diverse families since that time. However, minimal interactions between families of differing ethnicities are noted. Overall, over 75% of all Disney animated films depicted warm and supportive familial interactions, with 78.8% of the films illustrating a positive relationship between the protagonist and his/her family. Analysis and implications are offered for parents and educators who wish to further understand the content Disney animated films offer in depicting families.

Keywords: content analysis; cultivation; Disney; family; family structure; family function

1. Introduction and Literature Review

Media representations of the family to younger audiences have been of interest since the emergence of television (Morgan et al. 1999, p. 47). Singer and Singer (1984) equated the degree of influence of media families to children's real-life interactions with parents and family environment. Indeed, media family portrayals provide children with exemplars that offer information about family construction, home environment, parent-child interactions, and family roles. Thus, children may identify with and experience emotional bonds to certain characters to the extent to which they develop parasocial relationships, draw comparisons between media families and real-life interactions, and imitate behavioral practices (Callister et al. 2007; Robinson and Skill 2001).

Whereas past research has moderately explored family portrayals on prime-time television (Butsch 1992; Callister et al. 2007; Dates and Stroman 2001; Douglas and Olson 1995; Greenberg and Collette 1997; Heintz-Knowles 2001; Mastro and Greenberg 2000; Merritt and Stroman 1993; Moore 1992; Pohan and Mathison 2007; Power et al. 1993; Robinson and Skill 2001; Skill and Robinson 1994), it is important to examine similar depictions in film. Black and Bevan (1992) argued that film's lengthier format and freedom from commercial breaks may elevate movies to a more powerful medium than television. Yet, research that investigates family portrayals in film is somewhat sparse, particularly regarding media content that appeals to children (Holcomb et al. 2015; Callister et al. 2007).

Some scholars propose Disney films as key influencers of children's perceptions due to their ubiquitous presence and repetitive consumption (Giroux and Pollock 2010; Holcomb et al. 2015). For over eighty years, Disney has continued to entertain young audiences with a wide array of content.

From films and video games to lunch boxes, the Disney characters and their stories have been recurring cultural motifs in modern society. Yet, greater exploration is needed in understanding the patterns and themes of such a widely distributed entertainment source. Consequently, the following examination explores portrayals of the family within Disney animated films from 1937 to 2018. We offer an analysis of the general representation, construction, and function of families within Disney animated films over time in retrospect to a discussion of the effects of media on children.

1.1. Media Effects of Family Portrayals on Children

Turner and West (1998) purported that film and other forms of visual media offer possible modeling influences through increased accessibility and repeated audience consumption. In a national study, Leon and Angst (2005) found that 99% of children aged two to eighteen live in a home containing at least one television and noted that children watch close to 4 h of television daily. Moreover, McDonough (2009) asserted that media viewing among children was at an eight-year high, with two to five-year-olds watching visual content about thirty-two hours a week and six to eleven-year-olds watching about twenty-eight hours. More recent research suggests that some of this time has transitioned to other screen formats, such as browsing websites, using social media and/or playing video, computer, or mobile games. In a nationally representative sample of US adolescents (n = 2658), Rideout (2016) reported that children ages eight to twelveyear-olds spent close to 2 and half hours (2:26) daily watching TV/DVDs/videos with a total daily screen media time of 4 h, 36 min.

Extensive media use suggests a further exploration for not only the types of content children consume but also the possible effects of repeated consumption. Specific to family portrayals, Callister et al. (2007) outlined three potential media effect factors. First, media family depictions can be perceived as reality—particularly as children may struggle to distinguish between portrayed reality and reality (Douglas 2003; Mazur and Emmers-Sommer 2003). As Callister et al. (2007) explained, children may look to family media portrayals as "a type of touchstone for evaluating their own experiences" (p. 147). Similarly, the research of Dorr et al. (1989) argued that children often associate qualities of television families with real-life families.

Callister, Robinson, and Clark further identified the amount of consumed visual media as an important variable related to media effects. For instance, Buerkel-Rothfuss et al. (1982) observed a significant increase in children's estimates of the number of conflicts real-life families experience among heavy consumers of family situation comedies versus light viewers. Moreover, Morgan et al. (1999) assessed the acceptance of traditional versus nontraditional family values and found that heavy viewers of television more often aligned with nontraditional values portrayed on many prime-time television series in comparison to light viewers.

A third factor explores the comparisons children make between other families and their own family. Bandura (1994) suggested that "during the course of their daily lives, people have direct contact with only a small sector of the physical and social environment. They generally travel the same routes, visit the same places, and see the same group of associates" (p. 66). This sector of people often narrows for preschoolers and pre-adolescents (Buerkel-Rothfuss et al. 1982). As such, children may rely on media portrayals for information regarding typical family function and structure. For example, Douglas (2003) proposed that through media consumption, some children develop ideas that reinforce negative stereotypes concerning minority families, particularly among children who experience limited contact with minority groups. Additionally, some studies observed that children as young as three-years-old convey ageist attitudes towards older adults (Aday et al. 1996a; Aday et al. 1996b; Rich et al. 1983). Such findings are intriguing in comparison to studies that revealed that 44% of older characters in Disney animated films from 2004 to 2016 (Zurcher and Robinson 2017) and 38% of older characters in children's cartoons (Robinson and Anderson 2006) are portrayed as negative.

Related Media Effects Theories: Cultivation Analysis and Social Learning Theory

Two communication theories that provide insight into the possible effects associated with repeated media exposure are cultivation analysis and social learning theory. Cultivation analysis examines media's role in shaping or "cultivating" individual perceptions of social reality (Gerbner et al. 2002). The theory asserts that the greater exposure one experiences to media content, the greater the likelihood that individuals may perceive their reality as similar. Consequently, cultivation analysis centers on aggregated messaging, or the enduring thematic patterns that viewers encounter, rather than on the influence of a single episode or program (Signorielli and Morgan 2001).

Central to cultivation analysis is the distinction between light and heavy viewers of media (Gerbner et al. 2002). Buerkel-Rothfuss et al. (1982) conducted an examination of what children learn from TV families. Greenberg and colleagues found that heavy viewers were more likely to form the belief that real-world families show greater support and concern for one another. A more recent study examined beliefs about fathers, gendered roles, and television viewing habits among first-time expectant parents (Kuo and Ward 2016). Results suggested that an increased attribution of realism to televised content predicted belief in gendered family roles; additionally, heavy television viewers were more likely to downplay the role of the father as it relates to a child's development. Kuo and Ward argued that first-time expectant fathers may be "especially vulnerable to media messages about father roles" (p. 1).

Another theory that evaluates possible effects related to media consumption is social learning theory (SLT, Bandura 1994). SLT differs from cultivation analysis, as it directs attention from the influence of repeated exposure on individual perceptions to observational learning through modeling. SLT posits that learning is not merely derived from real-life encounters, but that individuals further observe, evaluate, are instructed from, and possibly imitate various forms of models surrounding them—including mass media models. As Mayes and Valentine (1979) described, next to parents, mass media forms such as television, movies, and books are children's most influential sources of behavioral modeling.

The media effects literature provides the foreground for studying portrayals of families in media. Given that children's learning is a vicarious experience and that many children encounter visual media regularly, it stands to reason that repeated exposure to portrayed modeled behavior can influence children's perceptions of social norms. Thus, in light of both cultivation analysis and SLT, assessment of the types of messages that children encounter regularly is important for understanding possible related effects.

1.2. Media Portrayals of the Family

1.2.1. General Family Representations

The majority of the family portrayals literature examines depictions on prime-time television; minimal research has applied this focus to film. Additionally, a gap exists within the literature, with most prime-time television studies conducted between the early 1990s to mid-2000s.

Family qualities most often explored of prime-time television include constructs such as family demographics, family structure, and family function. Regarding demographic portrayals, several scholars note a deficiency in the representation of minority families within popular media (Douglas 2003; Moore 1992; Robinson and Skill 2001). Moore (1992), for instance, argued that there was a lack of minority family representation on prime-time television from 1950 to 1990. Robinson and Skill (2001) echoed similar findings to Moore, suggesting that families portrayed from 1990–1995 on prime-time television were 80.5% Caucasian, 13.5% African American, 5.3% racially mixed, less than 1% Asian, and 0% Hispanic. Some scholars assert improvements to ethnic representation percentages in later years. For instance, Romine (cited in Lisotta 2005) reported ethnic representations on prime-time television during the 2005 to 2006 season as the following: 76% Caucasian, 14% African American, 6% Hispanic, and less than 3% Asian/Pacific Islanders.

1.2.2. Family Structure and Function

In addition to family ethnic representations, media portrayals often provide children with exemplars of family composition and interactions (Levy 1991). In assessing these exemplars, Morgan et al. (1999) proposed that family portrayal investigations must consider two distinct characteristics of families: structure and function. Family structure refers to the formation of the family (e.g., total number of individuals, the number of children) and the presentation of divorce, single parents, or stepfamily members. Family function examines family member interactions and the family relationship climate (e.g., love and supporting versus hostile and non-binding environments).

Family structure. Two basic family structures are traditional and nontraditional families. The traditional or nuclear family structure includes two parents with dependent children in the home. Other types of family structures include single parent, extended, guardian, and reconstituted (or blended) families.

Some social critics link the "decay of the conventional family configuration with the rise of television" (Skill et al. 1987, p. 361). Indeed, several scholars noted a decrease in "conventional" family configurations, or families constituted of parents and married couples without children from the 1950s–1990s within prime-time television (Moore 1992; Skill and Robinson 1994). Divorce and remarriage, blended families, cultural intermixing, and gay and lesbian couples have played a part in forming "contemporary families" (Mazur and Emmers-Sommer 2003, p. 159). The definition of the family diverged from the traditional family in the 1990s and into the early twenty-first century as it began to include a greater array of structures (Staricek 2011). Thus, the definition of the traditional family experienced a shift as families began to be defined as entities that "agreed upon societal rules and expectations specifying appropriate and inappropriate ways to behave in a particular society" (Abu-Laban and Abu-Laban 1999, p. 53).

Other explorations highlight an increased number of traditional family depictions in children's media in comparison to other media. For instance, when exploring family portrayals on children's programing during the 2005–2006 season, Callister et al. (2007) observed 85% two parent families, with 8% single parents (82.3% single mothers and 17% single fathers), 4% other relatives, and 3% non-relatives only. Of the depicted nuclear families, 89% included biological parents, whereas 9% were blended families, and 2.3% had adoptive parents. Callister et al. asserted that the representation of nuclear families in children's prime-time television was above the U.S. national average. Similarly, portrayals of children living with a single mother or a single father were lower than national averages, whereas children who lived with extended family or non-relatives were higher than average.

Dissonance between media exemplars and reality may create tension between children's perceptions and expectations. As Mazur and Emmers-Sommer (2003) summarized, "exposure to more nontraditional views of the family might aid in individuals' understanding, acceptance, and comfort with alternative ways of viewing and defining the family" (p. 160). However, Robinson and Skill (2001) argued that divergence from traditional family structures may, in turn, implicate the precedent that nontraditional family structures are normative.

Family function. Bryant and Alison Bryant (2001) compiled an extensive overview of the family portrayals literature in their book, *Television and the American Family*. In their examination of 258 prime-time episodes from the 1990s, Bryant et al. (2001) argued that prime-time television families in the 1990s appeared to be psychologically healthy—emphasizing depictions of cohesion within family units, adaptability, and good communication skills. Bryant and colleagues further noted that positive depictions within family prime-time television portrayals from the 1990s increased over time. Their results revealed that families from 1999 were "were better connected emotionally, more suited to change, and better in communication skills than those of the 1991 and 1996 samples" (p. 267).

The research of Callister et al. (2007) presented a more mixed depiction of family function. Specific to portrayals of primary caregivers in children's prime-time television shows, Callister et al. observed that whereas female caregivers were often portrayed as competent and mature, nearly 40% of male caregivers were depicted as buffoons. Moreover, 25% of male caregivers were depicted as immature.

Callister and colleagues commented that observations of American culture in which children disrespect parents are reinforced, to some degree, on prime-time television.

Related to general family portrayals, Larson (2001) assessed sibling interactions in situation comedies from the 1950s to the 1990s. She asserted that sibling engagements on television presented a predominately positive image, with 63% of communication interactions coded as positive or affiliative. However, Larson observed an absence of sibling identity development and that family portrayals were often devoid of siblings working with one another to negotiate with parents. Again, continued analysis of the role media plays in shaping perceptions of the family is needed for a greater understanding of the possible implications for mass audiences.

1.2.3. Family Portrayals in Disney Animated Films

The role of Disney in the lives of millions around the world is momentous. As a 169-billion-dollar industry, the Disney Corporation serves as a global leader with respect to media creation and product distribution (Forbes 2017). Furthermore, Lin (2001) asserted that once a movie is purchased, children view Disney films repeatedly—even to the same extent that they view children's television series.

Parallel to the wide dissemination of the Disney brand, storylines, and characters, examination of Disney film content depictions is also of large interest. Such investigations include gender portrayals and the modeling of gender (Coyne et al. 2016; Davis 2006; Davis 2015; England et al. 2011; Gillam and Wooden 2008; Hoerrner 1996), feminism (Downey 1996; Sawyer 2011), race and diversity (Cheu 2013; Faherty 2001; Lacroix 2004; Towbin et al. 2004), aggressive behaviors (Coyne and Whitehead 2008), the portrayal of older characters (Robinson et al. 2007; Zurcher and Robinson 2017), and pro-social behaviors (Padilla-Walker et al. 2013).

Assessment of family portrayals within Disney films have, comparatively, been minimally explored. To date, most investigations explore specific qualities related to family portrayals (e.g., the presence and role of single parents, themes related to couples and families in Disney princess films, etc.) in comparison to broader representations of the family and family structures. For instance, Junn (1997) observed that when lead characters suffered the loss of a parent, this absence often featured the loss of a mother rather than the father. Moreover, DiPirro (2007) observed that 63% of Disney princesses had fathers and only 25% had mothers. Others posited that it is through Disney's portrayal of marginalized women and elevated men within the nuclear family that the need for a princess to find love and a marriage for herself surfaced (Hecht 2011). Similarly, Garlen and Sandlin (2017) asserted that audiences may create unrealistic expectations of family, love, and marriage that are "socially harmful to women" through the repetitive consumption of Disney princess films (p. 960). Garlen and Sandlin further declared that a consistent emphasis on true love partners, marriage, and the romantic ideal perpetuates the belief that the highest degree of happiness can only be achieved by finding one's "true love" and marital success. Such precedence within Disney princess films, may, in turn, set individuals up for failure and is labeled by the researchers as a "cruel optimism" (p. 958).

A few investigations explore Disney family-related themes in smaller samples of Disney animated films. To illustrate, Tanner et al. (2003) identified four overarching thematic patterns regarding family portrayals within 26 Disney animated films: patterns included (1) "family relationships are a strong priority"; (2) "families are diverse, but the diversity is often simplified"; (3) "fathers are elevated while mothers are marginalized"; and (4) "couple relationships are created by 'love at first sight', are easily maintained, and are often characterized by gender-based power differentials" (p. 355).

A comprehensive analysis of the portrayal of families in Disney animated films has yet be undertaken. Junn (1997) called attention to a gap in the family portrayals literature, suggesting the need for further research of Disney films. She stated:

> Future research must examine the relation between media depictions and children's perceptions, in addition to further study of the other variables that may influence children's developing concepts of love, marriage, and sexuality (e.g., age, gender, ethnicity, culture, media, family structure). [...] while the Disney name and traditions are without a doubt

beloved by many around the world as symbolizing 'wholesome, family entertainment', this study reinforces the fact that the media, including the film industry, also represents a social and cultural institution that ultimately creates, produces, and disseminates ideological constructs in the form of a commercial mass product (Levy 1991). Armed with this economic and political perspective, both researchers and the public might be better equipped to demand accountability and high quality programming from the media industries.

We are not aware of any research that has conducted a broad, comprehensive analysis of the portrayal of families within Disney animated films. As Disney animated films are repeatedly watched and offer possible cultivated and learning implications, this investigation seeks to provide a greater understanding of the portrayals of families within Disney animated films from 1937 to 2018. The following research questions served as a guide in this inquiry:

RQ1: What are the predominant family structures that appear within Disney animated films?
RQ2: How are families represented in terms of ethnicity?
RQ3: What is the composition of families in terms of the number of children and siblings?
RQ4: Are families supportive or unsupportive of one another?
RQ5: Are the relationships between the protagonist and their families positive, negative, or neutral?
RQ6: What is the predominant family relationship climate?
RQ7: Have any of the aforementioned qualities changed over time?

2. Materials and Methods

2.1. Film Selection Procedures

The present investigation evaluated a census of 85 Disney animated feature films through content analysis. To create this census, we integrated two Disney animated film census lists from previous explorations beginning with *Snow White* in 1937 and ending with *Coco* in 2017.

The first film list was constructed by Robinson et al. (2007) in their assessment of older characters in Disney animated films. This list was comprised of a census of 34 Disney animated films from 1937 to 2004. The research of Robinson and colleagues excluded computer animated films, as their original intent was to only evaluate animated films. As computer animated films have increased in popularity and production, the present analysis added 6 computer animated films that were released during 1937–2004, including *The Nightmare Before Christmas*, *Toy Story*, *A Bug's Life*, *Dinosaur*, *Monsters Inc.*, and *Finding Nemo*.

The second census film list was constructed by Zurcher and Robinson (2017) as a follow-up examination to the research of Robinson et al. (2007). This list included a total of 42 films from 2004 to 2016 and was comprised of both animated and computer animated films. Additionally, two animated Disney films (*Cars 3* and *Coco*) have premiered since the publication of Zurcher and Robinson (2017) and were added.

2.2. Coding Procedures

A modified version of the coding sheet developed by Callister et al. (2007) that assessed family portrayals on children's programing was used; this coding sheet evaluates general family representations and relationships, including family composition, ethnic representation, structure, support, and general familial relationship environment.

Two independent coders received approximately 5 h of training prior to commencing the study. Coding instruction included training in (1) family identification and composition; (2) extended family identification and composition; (3) family ethnic representations; (4) overall family relationship and support; and (5) overall relationship quality between the protagonist and his/her family.

The inclusion of a family was identified through at least one of the following qualities: (1) married or unmarried adults with dependent or adult children; (2) homeowner(s) with dependent children; and/or (3) characters that performed parent-like duties and were depicted as genetically or legally related (Callister et al. 2007; Skill and Robinson 1994). Additionally, we coded for predominant family structures or families that maintained an influential role to the film's central plot. Family structures or members that were featured briefly (usually less than 5 s on-screen) or that did not offer general character information (such as the names of characters) were excluded. Surrogate families, or other organizational structures that featured strong relationships (e.g., workplace members, sports teams), were also excluded (Douglas and Olson 1995)

Cohen's (1960) Kappa was used to establish inter-coder reliability. Coders evaluated 10% of the total number of included animated films separately and discussed variances. All reliabilities achieved 85% or higher. Coding discrepancies were discussed and resolved by both coders.

2.3. Variables of Interest

Operational definitions as identified by the research of Callister et al. (2007) regarding family structure and function were used. Definitions for variables of interest are provided below.

Family configuration. Structural classifications of family configuration mirrored definitions provided by the US Census. *Nuclear families* included families in which both parents (either biological, stepparents, or adoptive) were present with dependent children. *Single-parent families* involved only one parent present with dependent children. *Reconstituted families*, or blended families, were defined as a nuclear family in which families are joined through a new marriage from a previous marriage. *Empty-nest families* were defined as married couples who have adult children who no longer live in the home. *Childless families* included married couples who do not have children. *Extended families* were households that encompassed family members other than parents and their children (such as cousins, uncles, aunts, and grandparents, etc.). Finally, *guardian families* were defined as families led by individuals who are not the legal parents of children but who assumed responsibility for the involved child or children (Skill and Robinson 1994).

Family support. Family support was categorized through the variables of *supportive, unsupportive,* and *mixed support*. *Supportive families* displayed instances in which family members assisted one another through affection, emotional support, and/or positive parent-child interactions. A clear example of this is Simba's father, Mufasa, in *The Lion King*. *Unsupportive families* illustrated negative parent-child relationships in which parents were uninvolved, reckless, cruel, and/or uncaring towards children, such as the relationships between Cinderella, her stepmother, and her stepsisters in *Cinderella*. Families that contained both supportive and unsupportive family members were coded as *mixed support*. For instance, the film *Peter Pan* portrays an unsupportive father with a supportive mother. The relationship between the siblings of John, Michael, and Wendy depict both instances of being supportive and unsupportive. Consequently, this family organization was categorized as mixed support.

Family relationship climate. Family support was related to an assessment of the general family relationship climate. Family relationship climates were coded as either warm, cold, or mixed climate. *Warm relationship* climates included qualities such as family support, love, kindness, and/or positive parent-child interactions. For instance, the Robinson family in *Meet the Robinsons* depicts numerous instances in which the entire family shows love, support, and sincere care towards each family member. Contrastingly, *cold relationship* climates displayed familial interactions that are unsupportive, unkind, and/or illustrate negative parent-child interactions. The relationship between Snow White and her stepmother, The Queen, in the film *Snow White*, for example, depicts a cold family relationship.

In instances that showed interactions of both warm and cold family interactions, the family climate was coded as *mixed climate*. A strong example of this occurs in the film *Tarzan* among the relationships between Tarzan, his gorilla father, Kerchak, and gorilla mother, Kala. Whereas Kala illustrates love, support, and affection towards Tarzan, Kerchak portrays a predominately unsupportive, detached relationship with Tarzan. Consequently, this family portrayal was coded as mixed climate.

Protagonist to family relations. The relationship between a protagonist and his or her family was also assessed. A protagonist was defined as the film's central character, or the character that drives the main storyline (e.g., Mulan in *Mulan*, Belle in *Beauty and the Beast*). Once a protagonist was identified, the relationship that he or she held with family members was coded as either positive, negative, or mixed relationship. *Positive* protagonist-family relationships involved interactions in which family members treated one another with kindness, love, and respect. Belle from *Beauty and the Beast* and her relationship with her father, for example, illustrated a positive relationship. *Negative* depictions displayed protagonist-family interactions in which members were mean, unkind, hateful, and/or cold. For instance, the relationship between Rapunzel and Mother Gothel in *Tangled* was coded as negative. In films that illustrate a character's transition from negative to positive or vice-versa, coders accounted for the predominant portrayal or the depiction that was illustrated through the majority of the film. Additionally, families that illustrated both positive and negative interactions with the protagonist were coded as mixed relationships.

3. Results

A total of 85 films created a census of Disney animated films from 1937 to 2018. Of the 85 Disney animated film census, 12 films did not depict family representations that met our family identification criteria (see materials and methods section). These films included *Robin Hood*, *The Rescuers*, *Home on the Range*, *Monsters Inc.*, *Cars*, *Wall-E*, *Tinkerbell and the Lost Treasure*, *Cars 2*, *Wreck-It Ralph*, *Planes*, *Planes Fire and Rescue*, and *Cars 3*. Seventy-three films included portrayals of families that met the identified criteria for a total of 104 families. The film, *Elena of Avelor*, contained the highest number of family depictions with three portrayals. Twenty-nine films portrayed two families, and 43 films portrayed only one family depiction.

3.1. General Representations of Families

RQ1 explored predominant family structures that appeared within Disney animated films. Representations of family structure were observed as follows: 43 (41.3%) single parent, 26 (25%) nuclear, 20 (19.2%) guardian, 6 (5.8%) extended, 4 (3.8%) other, 3 (2.9%) childless, and 2 (1.9%) reconstituted. In terms of the caretaker role, 31 (29.8%) of the depicted families included a married couple, followed by 25 (24%) single father, 20 (19.2%) single mother, 9 (8.7%) guardian female, 7 (6.7%) guardian male, 5 (4.8%) other, 4 (3.8%) guardian couples, and 3 (2.9%) married without children.

RQ2 examined how families are represented in terms of ethnicity. Only human characters were coded for ethnicity, which decreased the total number of families (n = 104) to 65 human families. Ethnicity was depicted as follows: 45 (69.2%) Caucasian, 5 (7.7%) Hispanic, 4 (6.2%) mixed race, 4 (6.2%) Asian, 2 (3.1%) Islander, 2 (3.1%) African American, 2 (3.1%) Native American, and 1 (1.5%) Arab. The top five films that diverged from a majority representation of Caucasian ethnic portrayal included *Aladdin*, *Mulan*, *Brother Bear*, *Moana*, and *Coco*.

3.2. Family Composition

RQ3 assessed the composition of families based on the total number of children and sibling portrayals. Sixty-nine families (66.3%) were portrayed with one child, with 20 families (19.2%) that depicted two children, 8 families (7.7%) with three children, 2 families (1.9%) with zero children, 3 families (2.9%) with four children, 1 family (1%) with six children, and 1 family (1%) with seven children. Regarding the sex of children, 52.2% of children were portrayed as male and 47.8% of children portrayed were female.

3.3. Family Function

RQ4 through RQ6 evaluated family function and relationship climates. RQ4 inquired if families illustrated supportive, unsupportive, or mixed support. Seventy-nine families (76.0%) were portrayed as supportive, with 14 families (13.5%) as unsupportive and eleven families (10.6%) as mixed support.

RQ5 investigated the relationship between the protagonist and his or her family. Eighty-two (78.8%) of the films portrayed a positive relationship between the protagonist and his/her family. Thirteen families (12.5%) portrayed a negative relationship, and nine (8.7%) of the films were coded as a mixed relationships.

RQ6 examined the overall family relationship climate. The majority of family portrayals, or 80 families (76.9%), were depicted as positive, with fifteen families (14.4%) as negative and 9 families (8.7%) as mixed climates.

3.4. Family Portrayals over Time

The final research question evaluated patterns and changes of the data over time. The data were organized into two decade periods and included the following: 1930–1949, 1950–1969, 1970–1989, 1990–2009, and 2010–2018. Frequency analysis was calculated by period to provide an overarching comparative framework (see Table 1). Noteworthy findings included variation from traditional family structures over time, with clear dominance in the representation of single parent family structures throughout. The representation of families with only one child also predominant in each time period. Moreover, all family structures were represented as Caucasian until the 1990s. Finally, Disney animated film families portrayed an overwhelming degree of family support, warmth, and general positivity, with each of these variables above 70% in each time period. Further evaluation of these data is provided in the discussion section.

Table 1. Comparative Analysis of Variables by every Two Decades (1937–2017).

Assessed Characteristic	1930/40s	1950/60s	1970/80s	1990/2000s	2010s
Family Type					
Nuclear	1 (25%)	3 (27.3%)	0	9 (18.8%)	13 (38.2%)
Extended	0	0	0	3 (6.3%)	3 (8.8%)
Single Parent	3 (75%)	3 (27.3%)	3 (42.9%)	23 (47.9%)	11 (32.4%)
Childless	0	1 (9.1%)	0	1 (2.1%)	1 (2.9%)
Reconstituted	0	0	0	0	1 (2.9%)
Guardian	0	1 (9.1%)	4 (57.1%)	10 (20.8%)	3 (8.8%)
Other	0	3 (27.3%)	0	2 (4.2%)	2 (5.9%)
Total: 104 (100%)	4 (100%)	11 (100%)	7 (100%)	48 (100%)	34 (100%)
Caretaker(s)					
Married Couple w/Children	1 (25%)	3 (27.3%)	0	11 (22.9%)	16 (47.1%)
Married Couple w/o Children	0	1 (9.1%)	0	1 (2.1%)	1 (2.9%)
Single Father	1 (25%)	2 (18.2%)	2 (28.6%)	15 (31.3%)	5 (14.7%)
Single Mother	2 (50%)	2 (18.2%)	1 (14.3%)	9 (18.8%)	6 (17.6%)
Guardian Couple	0	2 (18.2%)	0	2 (4.2%)	0
Guardian Male	0	0	2 (28.6%)	4 (8.3%)	1 (2.9%)
Guardian Female	0	1 (9.1%)	2 (28.6%)	4 (8.3%)	2 (5.9%)
Other	0	0	0	2 (4.2%)	3 (8.8%)
Total: 104 (100%)	4 (100%)	11 (100%)	7 (100%)	48 (100%)	34 (100%)
Family Ethnicity					
Caucasian	2 (100%)	7 (100%)	2 (100%)	19 (63.3%)	15 (62.5%)
Hispanic	0	0	0	1 (3.3%)	4 (16.7%)
Afr. American	0	0	0	2 (6.7%)	0
Asian	0	0	0	2 (6.7%)	2 (8.3%)
Islander	0	0	0	1 (3.3%)	1 (4.1%)
Amer. Indian	0	0	0	2 (6.7%)	0
Arab	0	0	0	1 (3.3%)	0
Mixed Race	0	0	0	2 (6.7%)	2 (8.3%)
Total: 65 (100%)	2 (100%)	7 (100%)	2 (100%)	30 (100%)	24 (100%)

Table 1. *Cont.*

Assessed Characteristic	1930/40s	1950/60s	1970/80s	1990/2000s	2010s
Number of Children Per Family					
0	0	0	0	1 (2.1%)	1 (2.9%)
1	4 (100%)	6 (54.5%)	4 (57.1%)	35 (72.9%)	20 (58.8%)
2	0	1 (9.1%)	1 (14.3%)	8 (16.7%)	10 (29.4%)
3	0	2 (18.2%)	1 (14.3%)	3 (6.3%)	2 (5.9%)
4	0	2 (18.2%)	0	0	1 (2.9%)
6	0	0	0	1 (2.1%)	0
7	0	0	1 (14.3%)	0	0
Total: 104 (100%)	4 (100%)	11 (100%)	7 (100%)	48 (100%)	34 (100%)
Number of Male Children Per Family					
0	1 (25%)	5 (45.5%)	2 (28.6%)	16 (33.3%)	16 (47.1%)
1	3 (75%)	3 (27.3%)	4 (57.1%)	26 (54.2%)	15 (44.1%)
2	0	1 (9.1%)	1 (14.3%)	4 (8.3%)	2 (5.9%)
3	0	2 (18.2%)	0	2 (4.2%)	1 (2.9%)
Total: 104 (100%)	4 (100%)	11 (100%)	7 (100%)	48 (100%)	34 (100%)
Number of Female Children Per Family					
0	3 (75%)	2 (18.2%)	3 (42.9%)	27 (56.3%)	12 (35.3%)
1	1 (25%)	8 (72.7%)	3 (42.9%)	17 (35.4%)	16 (47.1%)
2	0	0	0	3 (6.3%)	6 (17.6%)
3	0	1 (9.1%)	0	1 (2.1%)	0
6	0	0	1 (14.3%)	0	0
Total: 104 (100%)	4 (100%)	11 (100%)	7 (100%)	48 (100%)	34 (100%)
Number of Boys and Girls Represented Per Family					
Boys (82)	3 (75%)	11 (50%)	6 (40%)	40 (60.6%)	22 (44%)
Girls (75)	1 (25%)	11 (50%)	9 (60%)	26 (39.4%)	28 (56%)
Total: 157 (100%)	4 (100%)	22 (100%)	15 (100%)	66 (100%)	50 (100%)
Family Support					
Supportive	3 (75%)	8 (72.7%)	6 (85.7%)	34 (70.8%)	28 (82.4%)
Mixed Support	0	2 (18.2%)	0	7 (14.6%)	3 (8.8%)
Unsupportive	1 (25%)	1 (9.1%)	1 (14.3%)	7 (14.6%)	3 (8.8%)
Total: 104 (100%)	4 (100%)	11 (100%)	7 (100%)	48 (100%)	34 (100%)
Protagonist's Relationship with Family					
Positive	3 (75%)	9 (81.8%)	6 (85.7%)	37 (77.1%)	28 (82.4%)
Mixed Relationship	0	1 (9.1%)	1 (14.3%)	6 (12.5%)	5 (14.7%)
Negative	1 (25%)	1 (9.1%)	0	5 (10.4%)	1 (2.9%)
Total: 104 (100%)	4 (100%)	11 (100%)	7 (100%)	48 (100%)	34 (100%)
Family Climate					
Warm	3 (75%)	8 (72.7%)	6 (85.7%)	35 (72.9%)	28 (82.4%)
Mixed Climate	0	2 (18.2%)	1 (14.3%)	7 (14.6%)	5 (14.7%)
Cold	1 (25%)	1 (9.1%)	0	6 (12.5%)	1 (2.9%)
Total: 104 (100%)	4 (100%)	11 (100%)	7 (100%)	48 (100%)	34 (100%)

4. Discussion

This investigation sought to provide greater understanding of the predominant messages children receive about the general representation, structure, and function of families within Disney animated films from 1937 to 2018. As younger audiences often watch these films repeatedly, it becomes imperative to understand the messages children encounter from this medium. Specifically, we assessed representations of family structure, ethnicity, family composition, family support, and the familial relationship climate. The final research question provided assessment of how each of these areas is represented over time through the organization of variables by every two decades.

Although our analysis specifically examines representation and not direct effects, we highlight several content patterns and possible implications that may be helpful for future effects research designs. First, regarding family structure, the data revealed single parents as the predominant structure (41.3%), followed by nuclear families (25%) and guardian families (19.2%). These results support previous scholarship contending that Disney often selects fictional storylines that integrate the absence of a parental figure as a driving plot element (Junn 1997). However, nuclear family portrayals within

Disney animated films were less often depicted in comparison to other forms of children's media. For instance, Callister et al. (2007) asserted that "the traditional, nuclear family clearly dominates the landscape of children's programing" (p. 155).

Family structure representations within Disney animated films were also incongruent with US census data. Data that evaluated family structures of children under the age of 18 suggest that nuclear families are the most predominant family arrangement (69%), followed by single mother households (23%) (Porter 2016). Comparison of US census data to Disney animated film representations are close to polar opposites (Disney nuclear families = 25%/US census nuclear families = 69%; Disney single parent families = 41.3%/US census data with single parent families = 27.5%).

Implications related to incongruent representations of Disney animated families to real-world families are twofold: particularly for children who experience nontraditional family arrangements, diversity within family depictions may promote a broader perspective regarding the constitution of family and, accordingly, assist in promoting social norms that do not marginalize and/or present nontraditional structures as inferior. However, as Skill and Robinson (1994) asserted, an over-representation of nontraditional family structures may perpetuate ideals of "antifamily"—or the notion that unconventional family structures are normative and conventional structures are possibly unattainable. Interestingly, recent US census data documented a 19% decrease in nuclear families between the years of 1960–2016 (Porter). Future research should explore these two phenomena in greater detail. Specifically, understanding the viewing habits of various audiences (e.g., light versus heavy viewers of Disney animated films) relative to beliefs about family structures may provide greater insight into the influence of prevalent children's media on social norms and behavior.

Another observation relates to an over-representation of single parents. Our results indicated that close to half (41.3%) of Disney animated films depicted a single parent family. Don Hahn, an executive producer for some of the most well-known Disney animated films (including *Beauty and the Beast* and *The Lion King*), provided commentary for this storyline selection:

> I never talk about this, but I will. One reason is practical because the movies are 80 or 90 min long, and Disney films are about growing up. They're about that day in your life when you have to accept responsibility. Simba ran away from home but had to come back. In shorthand, it's much quicker to have characters grow up when you bump off their parents. Bambi's mother gets killed, so he has to grow up. Belle only has a father, but he gets lost, so she has to step into that position. It's a story shorthand. (Radloff 2014)

Hahn refers to the use of single parent family structures as a "story shorthand." Yet, an over-representation of single parents within children's media holds several implications. For one, Signorielli and Morgan (2001) argued that "single parents, contrary to what we see on television, do not live comfortably; most are young, single mothers, often women of color, who do not have the luxury of high paying jobs or a comfortable lifestyle complete with live-in help" (p. 347). Signorielli and Morgan further asserted that positive depictions of single parents can influence societal perceptions, and, in turn, perpetuate policies that provide insufficient resources offered to single-parent families. Other scholars argue that positive representations may offer hope to negative single-parent stereotypes (Pistole and Marson 2005). To illustrate, if a child consumes messaging that depicts film characters from single-parent homes overcoming difficulties and achieving their goals, such messaging may be productive in building children's resiliency.

Depicting young protagonists who evolve and mature within a film may also provide a rationale for our findings of a predominance of single child families. Although Disney pulls many of their storylines from traditional fairytales, the choice to portray single child families further supports a "coming of age" character journey. "Coming of age" protagonist portrayals are useful in exposing children to exemplars of resiliency, courage, and pro-social behaviors with unfamiliar others. Examples of these qualities can be seen in films such as *Mulan*, *Tangled*, *Beauty and the Beast*, and *The Lion King*. Nonetheless, such depictions often remove characters from one of their most valuable support systems—the family. As Davis (2006) observed,

> When the mother is alive and present, she is as good a mother as she possibly can be. However, she is powerless, for whatever reason, to really help her child, thus forcing the child to save him- or herself. Most often, however, she is not only dead, she is never even mentioned. Fathers are a little luckier in Disney. They are rarely killed [. . .] Granted, where there are fathers, they are often just as incapable of protecting their offspring as are the mothers [. . .]. (pp. 103–104)

The removal of key family members may lessen the perception that families are relevant to children and their abilities to overcome obstacles. In particular, when parents are removed from storylines, parent-child interactions that illustrate parental protection, support, and safety become nonexistent. Future research should more deeply explore implications to storylines in which traditional family structures are removed or absent.

Related to only-child families are the lack of sibling portrayals. In many instances, Disney animated films do not use siblings as primary characters but rather as introductions to the protagonist. For instance, in the film *Zootopia*, the rabbit protagonist Judy Hopps is shown with hundreds of siblings, even though these siblings play a minimal role in Judy's adventure of becoming a police officer. Such portrayals de-emphasize the role of siblings and may create friction within a familial setting. Nevertheless, we observed that films that do overtly portray sibling interactions usually involve siblings journeying together. Instances of these types of portrayals include *Peter Pan* and *The Incredibles*. Although these depictions are more of a rarity, such illustrations may inspire positive sibling interactions as siblings work together to achieve a common objective.

A third insight regards ethnic representation. Disney animated films' first depiction of a non-Caucasian family structure was *Aladdin* in 1992, followed by *Pocahontas* in 1995 and *Mulan* in 1998. Since the 1990s, diversity in ethnic family portrayals has comparatively increased. Although awareness of ethnic diversity and inclusion of varying cultures may be on the rise for Disney creations, it is important to address possible psychosocial implications for the Disney animated genre as a whole. First, some Disney animated films—particularly those created prior to 1990—may perpetuate ethnocentrism through depictions of centrally Caucasian family structures. In other genres of children's media, older content may not be considered as relevant or influential as compared to recent content. Yet, as older Disney animated films are often regarded as family classics in which generations of children, parents, and grandchild continue to watch these films, the possible influence of older Disney animated films should not be disregarded.

Ignorance about strong ethnic predominance may also perpetuate cultivated beliefs that view a singular race as superior, which belies the complexity of modern family structures. Awareness of the limited racial representation in some Disney animated films may be helpful for parents, educators, and practitioners seeking to promote greater respect and acceptance of ethnic diversity. Such an awareness can lead to greater discussions about ethnicity among parents and children. As Towbin et al. (2004) stated, "[. . .] Disney movies can serve as an example of society in microcosm: there are embedded messages of racism in many of the movies. Learning to find them and bringing the messages into the open can be educational and empowering for children" (p. 41).

Additionally, although representations of various family ethnicities emerged in the 1990s, we further noted minimal interaction of families with differing ethnic backgrounds. Such observations echo one of the four central themes established by Tanner et al. (2003): "Families are diverse, but the diversity is often simplified" (p. 355). For instance, the film *Moana* (2016) illustrated several Polynesian families; however, these families do not engage with families of other ethnicities. A similar pattern holds true in other films, including *Aladdin*, *Mulan*, *The Emperor's New Groove*, and *Coco*.

One explanation for minimal cross-racial interactions involves the contextually bound nature of the types of stories Disney animated films portray. For example, the film *Mulan* centers on a geographically defined Asian culture and remains consistent with this depiction throughout the film. Interestingly, however, ethnic representations have somewhat shifted in more recent Disney live action films. For instance, the recent releases of the live action films *Cinderella* in 2015 and *Beauty and the*

Beast in 2017 depict a much more racially diverse cast, presenting a stark contrast to the films' earlier animated counterparts. Indeed, some critics suggest that Disney has entered into an "inclusive third golden age" beginning with the film *The Princess and the Frog*—with Disney creatives going to great lengths to "avoid gross stereotyping" (Harris 2016). Such transitions may encourage storylines that illustrate characters of various racial backgrounds, thus promoting greater diversity in animated depictions. Again, educators and parents may use these insights to better discern and discuss with children the messages Disney animated films share about ethnicity and interacting with diverse groups of individuals.

The final insight relates to family function within Disney animated films. Douglas (2003) observed divergent findings in the literature, suggesting that some media portrayals of the family highlight loving, warm, and affectionate depictions, whereas others illustrate families that are uninvolved, cold, and distant. Overall, the present census analysis overwhelming supported the first supposition: Disney animated films provide example after example of family support, warm familial relational climates, and overall general positivity. This finding parallels the theme identified by Tanner et al. (2003) in their analysis of 26 Disney films, in which they commented that "family relationships are a strong priority" (p. 355). Positive depictions of family function are of great interest, particularly as cultivation analysis and social learning theory posit that children may learn from and imitate interactions they view in media. Hence, the value of children's media that illustrate instances of family members working through conflicts and showing love and support for one another is noteworthy.

Author Contributions: Jessica D. Zurcher conceived and designed the study. She oversaw the training of coders and the analysis of data. She wrote the majority of the paper and served as the study lead. Sarah M. Webb conceived and designed the study. She served as a main coder for data collection and was responsible for the input of all data. She helped to revise sections of the paper. Tom Robinson conceived and designed the study. He oversaw the training of coders and the analysis of data. He contributed materials/analysis tools. He helped to revise sections of the paper.

Conflicts of Interest: The authors declare no conflict of interest.

References

Abu-Laban, Sharon McIrvin, and A. Abu-Laban. 1999. Culture, society, and change. In *An Introduction to Sociology*. Edited by W. A. Meloff and W. D. Pierce. Scarborough: Nelson Canada.

Aday, Ronald H., Cyndee Rice Sims, Winni McDuffie, and Emilie Evans. 1996. Changing children's attitudes toward the elderly: The longitudinal effects of an intergenerational partners program. *Journal of Research in Childhood Education* 10: 143–51. [CrossRef]

Aday, Ronald H., Kathryn L. Aday, Josephine L. Arnold, and Susan L. Bendix. 1996. Changing children's perceptions of the elderly: The effects of intergenerational contact. *Gerontology and Geriatrics Education* 16: 37–51. [CrossRef] [PubMed]

Bandura, Albert. 1994. Social cognitive theory of mass communication. In *Media Effects: Advances in Theory and Research*. Edited by Jennings Bryant and Dolf Zillmann. Hillsdale: Lawrence Erlbaum Associates, Inc., pp. 61–90.

Black, Stephen L., and Susan Bevan. 1992. At the movies with Buss and Durkee: A natural experiment on film violence. *Aggressive Behavior* 18: 37–45. [CrossRef]

Bryant, Jennings, and J. Alison Bryant. 2001. *Television and the American Family*. Mahwah: Lawrence Erlbaum Associates.

Bryant, Jennings, Charles F. Aust, J. Alison Bryant, and Gautham Venugopalan. 2001. How psychologically healthy are America's prime-time television families? In *Television and the American Family*, 2nd ed. Edited by Jennings Bryant and J. Alison Bryant. Mahaway: Erlbaum, pp. 207–28.

Buerkel-Rothfuss, Nancy L., Bradley S. Greenberg, Charles K. Atkin, and Kimberly Neuendorf. 1982. Learning about the family from television. *Journal of Communication* 32: 191–201. [CrossRef]

Butsch, Richard. 1992. Class and gender in four decades of television situation comedy: Plus change. *Critical Studies in Mass Communications* 9: 387–99. [CrossRef]

Callister, Mark A., Tom Robinson, and Bradley R. Clark. 2007. Media portrayals of the family in children's television programming during the 2005–2006 season in the US. *Journal of Children and Media* 1: 142–61. [CrossRef]

Cheu, Johnson. 2013. *Diversity in Disney Films: Critical Essays on Race, Ethnicity, Gender, Sexuality and Disability*. Jefferson: McFarland and Company.

Cohen, Jacob. 1960. A coefficient of agreement for nominal scales. *Educational and Psychological Measurement* 20: 37–46. [CrossRef]

Coyne, Sarah M., and Emily Whitehead. 2008. Indirect aggression in animated Disney films. *Journal of Communication* 58: 382–95. [CrossRef]

Coyne, Sarah M., Jennifer Ruh Linder, Eric E. Rasmussen, David A. Nelson, and Victoria Birkbeck. 2016. Pretty as a princess: Longitudinal effects of engagement with Disney princesses on gender stereotypes, body esteem, and prosocial behavior in children. *Child Development* 87: 1909–25. [CrossRef] [PubMed]

Dates, Jannette L., and Carolyn A. Stroman. 2001. Portrayals of families of color on television. In *Television and the American Family*, 2nd ed. Edited by Jennings Bryant and J. Alison Bryant. Mahaway: Erlbaum, pp. 207–28.

Davis, Amy M. 2006. *Good Girls and Wicked Witches: Women in Disney's Feature Animation*. Eastleigh: John Libbey Publishing.

Davis, Amy M. 2015. *Handsome Heroes and Vile Villains: Masculinity in Disney's Feature Films*. Eastleigh: John Libbey Publishing.

DiPirro, Danielle Marie. 2007. From Biting the Apple to Breaking the Spell: Analyzing Love in the Disney Princess Collection. Master thesis, California State University, Los Angeles, CA, USA.

Dorr, Aimee, Peter Kovaric, and Catherine Doubleday. 1989. Parent-child coviewing of television. *Journal of Broadcasting and Electronic Media* 33: 35–51. [CrossRef]

Douglas, William. 2003. *Television Families: Is Something Wrong in Suburbia?* Mahwah: Erlbaum.

Douglas, William, and Beth M. Olson. 1995. Beyond family structure: The family in domestic comedy. *Journal of Broadcasting and Electronic Media* 39: 236–61. [CrossRef]

Downey, Sharon D. 1996. Feminine empowerment in Disney's Beauty and the Beast. *Women's Studies in Communication* 19: 185–212. [CrossRef]

England, Dawn Elizabeth, Lara Descartes, and Melissa A. Collier-Meek. 2011. Gender role portrayal and the Disney princesses. *Sex Roles* 64: 555–67. [CrossRef]

Faherty, Vincent E. 2001. Is the mouse sensitive? A study of race, gender, and social vulnerability in Disney animated films. *Studies in Media and Information Literacy Education* 1: 1–8. [CrossRef]

Forbes. 2017. Global 2000: Top Regarded Companies. Forbes. Available online: http://www.forbes.com/companies/walt-disney/ (accessed on 28 December 2017).

Garlen, Julie C., and Jennifer A. Sandlin. 2017. Happily (n)ever after: The cruel optimism of Disney's romantic ideal. *Feminist Media Studies* 17: 957–71. [CrossRef]

Gerbner, George, Larry Gross, Michael Morgan, Nancy Signorielli, and James Shanahan. 2002. Growing up with television: Cultivation processes. *Media Effects: Advances in Theory and Research* 2: 43–67.

Gillam, Ken, and Shannon R. Wooden. 2008. Post-princess models of gender: The new man in Disney/Pixar. *Journal of Popular Film and Television* 36: 2–8. [CrossRef]

Giroux, Henry A., and Grace Pollock. 2010. *The Mouse that Roared: Disney and the End of Innocence*. Lanham: Rowman & Littlefield.

Greenberg, Bradley S., and Larry Collette. 1997. The changing faces on TV: A demographic analysis of network television's new seasons, 1966–1992. *Journal of Broadcasting and Electronic Media* 41: 1–13. [CrossRef]

Harris, Aisha. 2016. Moana Makes It Official. Disney Has Entered a Progressive, Inclusive Third Golden Age. Slate. Available online: http://www.slate.com/blogs/browbeat/2016/11/21/with_moana_frozen_big_hero_6_and_zootopia_disney_has_entered_an_inclusive.html (accessed on 16 March 2018).

Hecht, Jennifer. 2011. Happily ever after: Construction of Family in Disney Princess Collection Films. Master's thesis, San Jose State University, San Jose, CA, USA.

Heintz-Knowles, Katherine E. 2001. Balancing acts: Work-family issues on prime-time TV. In *Television and the American Family*, 2nd ed. Edited by Jennings Bryant and J. Alison Bryant. Mahway: Erlbaum, pp. 177–206.

Hoerrner, Keisha L. 1996. Gender roles in Disney films: Analyzing behaviors from Snow White to Simba. *Women's Studies in Communication* 19: 213–28. [CrossRef]

Holcomb, Jeanne, Kenzie Latham, and Daniel Fernandez-Baca. 2015. Who cares for the kids? Caregiving and parenting in Disney films. *Journal of Family Issues* 36: 1957–81. [CrossRef]

Junn, Ellen N. 1997. Media Portrayals of Love, Marriage and Sexuality for Child Audiences: A Select Content Analysis of Walt Disney Animated Family Films. ERIC. Available online: https://eric.ed.gov/?id=ED407118 (accessed on 16 March 2018).

Kuo, Patty X., and L. Monique Ward. 2016. Contributions of television use to beliefs about fathers and gendered family roles among first-time expectant parents. *Psychology of Men and Masculinity* 17: 352–62. [CrossRef]

Lacroix, Celeste. 2004. Images of animated others: The orientalization of Disney's cartoon heroines from The Little Mermaid to The Hunchback of Notre Dame. *Popular Communication* 2: 213–229. [CrossRef]

Larson, Margali Sarfatti. 2001. Sibling interaction in situation comedies over the years. In *Television and the American Family*, 2nd ed. Edited by Jennings Bryant and J. Alison Bryant. Mahaway: Erlbaum, pp. 207–28.

Leon, Kim, and Erin Angst. 2005. Portrayals of stepfamilies in film: Using media images in remarriage education. *Family Relations* 54: 3–23. [CrossRef]

Levy, Emanuel. 1991. The American dream of family in film: From decline to comeback. *Journal of Comparative Family Studies* 22: 187–204.

Lin, Carolyn A. 2001. The VCR, home video culture, and new video technologies. In *Television and the American Family*, 2nd ed. Edited by Jennings Bryant and J. Alison Bryant. Mahwah: Lawrence Erlbaum, pp. 91–107.

Lisotta, C. 2005. TV continues to lag on diversity. *Television Week* 24: 3–19.

Mastro, Dana E., and Bradley S. Greenberg. 2000. The portrayal of racial minorities on prime time television. *Journal of Broadcasting and Electronic Media* 44: 690–703. [CrossRef]

Mayes, Sandra L., and K. B. Valentine. 1979. Sex role stereotyping in Saturday morning cartoon shows. *Journal of Broadcasting and Electronic Media* 23: 41–50. [CrossRef]

Mazur, Michelle A., and Tara M. Emmers-Sommer. 2003. The effect of movie portrayals on audience attitudes about nontraditional families and sexual orientation. *Journal of Homosexuality* 44: 157–81. [CrossRef]

McDonough, Patricia. 2009. TV Viewing among Kids at an Eight-Year High. Nielsen. Available online: http://www.nielsen.com/us/en/insights/news/2009/tv-viewing-among-kids-at-an-eight-year-high.html (accessed on 16 March 2018).

Merritt, Bishetta, and Carolyn A. Stroman. 1993. Black family imagery and interactions on television. *Journal of Black Studies* 23: 492–99. [CrossRef]

Moore, Marvin L. 1992. The family as portrayed on prime-time television, 1947–1990: Structure and characteristics. *Sex Roles* 26: 41–61. [CrossRef]

Morgan, Michael, Susan Leggett, and James Shanahan. 1999. Television and family values: Was Dan Quayle right? *Mass Communication and Society* 2: 47–63. [CrossRef]

Padilla-Walker, Laura M., Sarah M. Coyne, Ashley M. Fraser, and Laura A. Stockdale. 2013. Is Disney the nicest place on earth? A content analysis of prosocial behavior in animated Disney films. *Journal of Communication* 63: 393–412. [CrossRef]

Pistole, Carole M., and Gia Marson. 2005. Commentary on the family's vitality: Diverse structures with TV illustrations. *The Family Journal* 13: 10–18. [CrossRef]

Pohan, Cathy A., and Carla Mathison. 2007. Television: Providing powerful multicultural lessons inside and outside school. *Multicultural Perspectives* 9: 19–25. [CrossRef]

Porter, Jenny. 2016. The Majority of Children Live with Two Parents, Census Bureau Reports. United States Census Bureau. Available online: https://census.gov/newsroom/press-releases/2016/cb16-192.html (accessed on 30 January 2018).

Power, Stephen P., David J. Rothman, and Stanley Rothman. 1993. Transformation of gender roles in Hollywood movies: 1946–1990. *Political Communication* 10: 259–83. [CrossRef]

Radloff, Jessica. 2014. Why Most Disney Heroines Don'T Have Mothers and So Many More Secrets from the Disney Archives. Glamour. Available online: https://www.glamour.com/story/disney-secrets-beauty-and-the-beast (accessed on 28 February 2018).

Rich, Pamela E., Robert D. Myrick, and Chari Campbell. 1983. Changing children's perceptions of the elderly. *Educational Gerontology* 9: 483–91. [CrossRef]

Rideout, Vicky. 2016. Measuring time spent with media: The Common Sense census of media use by US 8-to 18-year-olds. *Journal of Children and Media* 10: 138–44. [CrossRef]

Robinson, James D., and Thomas Skill. 2001. Five decades of families on television: From the 1950s through the 1990s. In *Television and the American Family*, 2nd ed. Edited by Jennings Bryant and J. Alison Bryant. Mahway: Erlbaum, pp. 177–206.

Robinson, Tom, and Caitlin Anderson. 2006. Older characters in children's animated television programs: A content analysis of their portrayal. *Journal of Broadcasting & Electronic Media* 50: 287–304. [CrossRef]

Robinson, Tom, Mark Callister, Dawn Magoffin, and Jennifer Moore. 2007. The portrayal of older characters in Disney animated films. *Journal of Aging Studies* 21: 203–13. [CrossRef]

Sawyer, Nicole. 2011. Feminist Outlooks at Disney Princess's. Journal of James Madison University. Available online: https://www.scribd.com/document/347296420/Feminist-Outlooks-at-Disney-Princess-s-pdf (accessed on 14 March 2018).

Signorielli, Nancy, and Michael Morgan. 2001. Television and the family: The cultivation perspective. In *Television and the American Family*, 2nd ed. Edited by Jennings Bryant and J. Alison Bryant. Mahway: Erlbaum, pp. 177–206.

Singer, Jerome L., and Dorothy G. Singer. 1984. Family patterns and television viewing as predictors of children's beliefs and aggression. *Journal of Communication* 34: 73–89. [CrossRef]

Skill, Thomas, and James D. Robinson. 1994. Four decades of families on television: A demographic profile, 1950–1989. *Journal of Broadcasting and Electronic Media* 38: 449–65. [CrossRef]

Skill, Thomas, James D. Robinson, and Samuel P. Wallace. 1987. Portrayal of families on prime-time TV: Structure, type and frequency. *Journalism Quarterly* 64: 360–98. [CrossRef]

Staricek, Nicole Catherine. 2011. "Today's "Modern Family": A Textual Analysis of Gender in the Domestic Sitcom". Ph.D. dissertation, Auburn University, Auburn, AL, USA.

Tanner, Litsa Renee, Shelley A. Haddock, Toni Schindler Zimmerman, and Lori K. Lund. 2003. Images of couples and families in Disney feature-length animated films. *The American Journal of Family Therapy* 31: 355–73. [CrossRef]

Towbin, Mia Adessa, Shelley A. Haddock, Toni Schindler Zimmerman, Lori K. Lund, and Litsa Renee Tanner. 2004. Images of gender, race, age, and sexual orientation in disney feature-length animated films. *Journal of Feminist Family Therapy* 15: 19–44. [CrossRef]

Turner, Lynne H., and Richard L. West. 1998. *Perspectives on Family Communication*. Mountain View: Mayfield Publishing.

Zurcher, Jessica D., and Tom Robinson. 2017. From "Bibbid-Bobbidi-Boo" to Scrooge: An update and comparative analysis of the portrayal of older characters in recent Disney animated films. *Journal of Children and Media*, 1–15. [CrossRef]

social sciences

MDPI

Article

Death and Coping Mechanisms in Animated Disney Movies: A Content Analysis of Disney Films (1937–2003) and Disney/Pixar Films (2003–2016)

James A. Graham *, Hope Yuhas and Jessica L. Roman

Department of Psychology, The College of New Jersey, Ewing Township, NJ 08628, USA;
yuhash1@tcnj.edu (H.Y.); jsscrmn@yahoo.com (J.L.R.)
* Correspondence: jgraham@tcnj.edu; Tel.: +1-609-771-2638

Received: 11 September 2018; Accepted: 12 October 2018; Published: 16 October 2018

Abstract: The purpose of this content analysis was to examine how death depictions in animated Disney films have changed in the past 14 years and the coping mechanisms used to process death within these films. A content analysis from 2005 was used to investigate the influence of Disney films on children's concepts of death based on 23 death scenes from 10 full-length Disney Classic animated films from 1937 to 2003 and 10 death scenes from 8 selected full-length Disney and Pixar animated films from 2003 to 2016. Our goal was to compare the findings across the two studies. Similar to the original study, the portrayal of death focused on five categories: character status; depiction of death; death status; emotional reaction; and causality. We expanded on the original study and more research by examining coping mechanisms used to process death within a selection of these films. Our findings indicated that some scenes from animated Disney and Pixar films obscure the permanence and irreversibility of death and often fail to acknowledge deaths emotionally. Our conclusions showed that Disney's and Pixar's portrayal of death in newer films might have more positive implications for children's understanding of death than Disney Classic animated films.

Keywords: death; children; Disney; coping mechanisms

---

1. Introduction

Death is a painful but unavoidable part of life. For children between 2–11 years of age, death is a complex topic to grapple with and can have a significant impact on their lives. Specifically, if we assume that if children think differently and are constrained by cognitive limitations, then they need adult protection. A contrasting view is that children are increasingly sophisticated as they encounter a greater variety of media content (Livingstone 2002). Children's media repertoires are increasingly independent of their parents' influence. The availability of media, in children's lives, as well as parents' lack of knowledge about modern digital media allow children to decide independently what media they use and what they acquire from it (Bovill and Livingstone 2001). This leads to fewer opportunities for shared media experiences of parents and children (Bovill and Livingstone 2001). Some media scholars attach more significance to the independence or agency of children rather than the idea of childhood as a preparatory stage for adult life.

While some media scholars have taken a more modern "agency" approach to development, the dominant approach in developmental psychology has been a more protectionist stance (Buckingham 2000). There are indeed pros and cons of both approaches in the field of death education, but this is not the focus of this study. We assume that children and adult's knowledge or experience with death differ from each other.

The current content analysis expands upon the previous research by Cox et al. (2005). Specifically, our goal was to compare how the top 10 grossing Disney films from 1937–2003 compared to the top 8 grossing Disney and Pixar films from 2003–2016. Similar to the original study, the portrayal of death focused on five categories: character status; depiction of death; death status; emotional reaction; and causality. A more recent study by Tenzek and Nickels (2017) describes and analyzes the portrayal of end-of-life (EOL) or death across a more comprehensive list of animated Disney and Pixar films. Unlike Tenzek and Nickels (2017), we included coping mechanisms displayed by characters dealing with death within a selection of these films. In the current study, we argue that children who watch Disney and Pixar films might learn about ways to cope with death. To examine the possible influence that animated cinema might have for children's processing and coping with death, it is necessary to provide some theoretical perspectives on how they conceive death. Specifically, we include literature related to children's comprehension of death, developmental level, life experiences, parental involvement and emotional coping mechanisms related to death.

1.1. Theoretical Perspectives on Children's Understanding of Death

1.1.1. Developmental Age

The Dougy Center, a United States national center for grieving children and families that provides support groups, education, and training (https://www.dougy.org), reported that two main factors contribute to a child's understanding of death: developmental level and experience. According to a 2009 Dougy Center table (as cited in Favazza and Munson 2010), children's understanding of death changes at different developmental stages. At the egocentric stage (i.e., 2–4 years), children see death as reversible, will notice changes in how they are cared for and may ask many questions. They may perceive death as abandonment. When in the developmental stage where they begin to gain a sense of autonomy (i.e., 4–7 years), children still see death as reversible, but questions begin to focus on how and why the death happened. Some children at this age may try to act as though nothing has happened. At the concrete thinking stage (i.e., 7–11 years), children begin to realize death is irreversible and become concerned with other people's reactions to understand what an appropriate response to death is (Favazza and Munson 2010). Willis (2002) noted four aspects of death that children and adults view differently: reversibility, finality, inevitability, and causality. According to Brent et al. (1996), children may not understand the permanence of death, the fact that death is inevitable for all living beings, and, because young children cannot think abstractly, they may not understand the causality of death. However, children who are older than eleven may still not believe death is permanent due to religious beliefs. Beliefs about death based on religious values may indicate a more mature mindset because abstract thinking is required (Brent et al. 1996).

1.1.2. Experience—Grieving Process

Baker et al. (1992) identified three stages of children's grieving process after a death. In the first stage, the child gathers a basic understanding of death. It is important for a child to understand that just because someone they know has died does not mean they are in any imminent danger. They must feel safe and secure. In the second stage, a child accepts the death as a reality and accepts any accompanying emotional response to death. In this stage, a child may reflect on happy memories with their deceased loved one. Adults should have an honest conversation with the child about death and allow the child to process any emotions they have. In the third stage, a child re-examines their concept of identity and their relationships with others after a death. The child should know that though someone they loved has died, other people in their lives are not in danger of dying. Ultimately, this final stage should culminate in healthy coping skills. Some scholars believe that children take longer to complete the grieving process than adults, as they tend to have less experience with death and developmentally have a limited understanding of death (Baker et al. 1992).

1.1.3. Experience—Parent Role in Children's Comprehension of Death

Many parents use confusing language when talking about death with children. Some parents may try to protect young children from such a complex topic by using phrases such as, "sleeping for a long time" or "taken a long trip." Though intentions are good, phrases like this may confuse children as to what death is. A child may believe that a deceased loved one will wake up or return from a trip someday (Willis 2002). A child may also become frightened about sleeping, for fear that they will not wake up (Grollman 1990).

In addition to language, parents should be mindful of their reactions to death, as, according to a 2009 Dougy Center table as displayed in Favazza and Munson (2010), children will look to and possibly mimic them to understand appropriate responses to death. If a parent is uncomfortable with the concept of death themselves, they may restrict their children's comprehension of death and their ability to cope effectively (Favazza and Munson 2010). Most adults do not believe children have the mental and emotional capacity to cope with death and therefore attempt to avoid representations of death. Specifically, many parents try to shield their children from death in film and television programs (Gutiérrez et al. 2014). Gutiérrez et al. (2014) found that twice as many parents tried to shield their children from death representations in films than books, in part because it is easier to modify literature than movies.

1.2. Emotional and Behavioral Coping Mechanisms in Films

Sedney (1999) studied the grieving process of characters in children's movies in reaction to a death. Children's films generally maintained a positive outlook on life after death wherein characters could move forward and still be happy after the death of a loved one but in some films, deaths went unacknowledged. The lack of acknowledgment was particularly prevalent in cinema with missing parents (Sedney 1999, 2002).

Schultz and Huet (2001) found that most portrayals of death in the highest grossing American films and Academy Award nominees were dramatic and implausible. A lot of children's movies mimicked protective parental language. The films were indirect in acknowledging death and the reality of life after a death, which is in part due to social stigma around conversations about death (Schultz and Huet 2001).

Some researchers describe coping as the way a person regulates behavior and emotion under stressful circumstances (Skinner and Zimmer-Gembeck 2007). Children's stress reactions include cognitive and behavioral coping (De Boo and Wicherts 2007). Children begin to develop coping mechanisms in infancy and evolve their strategies as they advance through different stages of life (Skinner and Zimmer-Gembeck 2007). The development of healthy coping mechanisms in childhood is important to overall emotional, mental and physical wellbeing. Skinner and Zimmer-Gembeck (2007) identified 12 families of coping strategies: problem-solving, information-seeking, helplessness, escape, self-reliance, support-seeking, delegation, social isolation, accommodation, negotiation, submission, and opposition. These families are present in developmentally appropriate ways at different stages of life. Skinner and Zimmer-Gembeck (2007) found of the 12 families; children tended to use support-seeking, problem-solving, escape and distraction the most.

When children do not learn healthy, effective coping mechanisms, they may be incapable of adequately managing their stress levels. Higher levels of stress in children have been linked to unhealthy eating styles (Michels et al. 2015) and inadequate coping mechanisms related to psychological harm and stunted maturation (Corr 2010). Naturally, coping is not just an individual task. Family and support systems influence children's ability to cope (Corr 2010).

Especially in modern times, children cannot easily ignore the topic of death, due to both direct experiences with death and indirect through the media. Many children's books directly address death and attempt to model different coping mechanisms through characters. The primary purpose of the story in these books is to address the realities of death or serve as a guide to grieving children (Webb 2010). Though they are fictional and not involved in the real-life aftermath of a death a child has experienced, children can identify with characters who have also experienced loss and learn practical and ineffective coping strategies from them (Corr 2004). These characters can also show children ways to release negative emotions healthily. For example, in one story Corr (2004) examined, a young boy continually asked questions about his father's death, leading to his older brother to release some anger he had been holding in. After expressing his anger, the older brother was able to engage in conversations about happy memories with their father (Vogel 2002, as cited in Corr 2004).

1.3. The Current Study

Cox et al. (2005) conducted a study of how Disney films portrayed death and grieving, and the potential influence of films on children's concepts of death. A more recent study by Tenzek and Nickels (2017) expanded upon Cox et al. (2005) by examining 71 EOL portrayals in Disney and Pixar animated films. We hope to contribute to the extant literature on portrayals of death in animated Disney and Pixar films by examining two research questions. First, we are interested in seeing if the portrayal of death in Disney films had changed in the past 14 years compared to Cox et al. (2005), and Tenzek and Nickels (2017). For our current research, we consider the Cox et al. (2005) study as Disney Film Analysis (1937–2003). We refer to the current study as Disney and Pixar Film Analysis (2003–2016). Our second research question extends the previous work (i.e., Cox et al. 2005; Tenzek and Nickels 2017) by addressing the relationship between film and behavioral/emotional regulation processes. Specifically, what types of coping mechanisms do characters dealing with death display within these films?

2. Materials and Methods

2.1. Sampling Strategy

We used a content analysis to examine how death depictions in animated Disney films have changed in the past 14 years, and the coping mechanisms used to process death within these films. We did not choose the films haphazardly; instead, the researchers carefully reviewed the plot outlines of all animated Disney Classic and Pixar films. We chose from that list 8–10 top grossing films over the two-time frames (i.e., 1937–2003; and 2003–2016) being careful to select films that children are familiar with today. The original analyzed content from 1937–2003 consisted of 10 Disney Classic animated full-length feature films. We selected movies in which a death occurred or was a theme in the plotline. The films included in this study were: *Snow White and the Seven Dwarfs* (1937), *Bambi* (1942), *Sleeping Beauty* (1959), *The Little Mermaid* (1989), *Beauty and the Beast* (1991), *The Lion King* (1994), *The Hunchback of Notre Dame* (1996), *Hercules* (1997), *Mulan* (1998) and *Tarzan* (1999). No full-length feature Disney films from 2000–2003 included death scenes.

The analysis of the current study (i.e., 2003–2016) consists of 8 Disney and Pixar modern animated full-length feature films. In our selection of movies, we included both animated Disney and animated Disney/Pixar films, but the movies were also only selected if they occurred after 2002 because we wanted to focus on the modern, 21st-century depiction of death. The films examined for this study were: *Finding Nemo* (2003), *The Incredibles* (2004), *Up* (2009), *The Princess and the Frog* (2009), *Tangled* (2010), *Frozen* (2013), *Big Hero 6* (2014) and *Moana* (2016).

2.2. Coding Categories

In the original study by Cox et al. (2005) and the current study, two coders viewed all the movies and coded the data individually. The following five coding criteria analyzed each character's death in both studies. The coding categories are identical across the two studies. As noted in Cox et al. (2005), the data was analyzed using the following categories and operational definitions.

2.2.1. Character Status

This category refers to the role the character that died played in the plot. We coded as either a protagonist or an antagonist. First, a *protagonist* is a character seen as the "good guy," hero/heroine of the movie, or the main character whom the story revolves around. An *antagonist* is a character seen as the "bad guy," villain, nemesis, or enemy of the protagonist.

2.2.2. Depiction of Death

This category refers to how the character dies in the film. An *explicit death* would be when the audience sees that the character is dead because the body is physically damaged/killed or the dead, motionless body is on screen. An *implicit death* refers to one in which the audience can only assume that the death of a character because they do not appear again in the film or that they have encountered something that would presumably result in death. Examples include seeing a shadow of a dead body or a character falling off a cliff. Sleep death refers to an instance in which a character falls into a state of prolonged sleep.

2.2.3. Death Status

This category refers to if a death was a real end of life or if it was something negotiable that does not necessarily represent the absolute end of life. A *permanent/final death* is one in which the character does not return in any form. A *reversible death* is one where a character returns in one of two ways. A *reversible-same form of death* is one in which the character seemingly comes back from a dead or seemingly dead state in his or her original body. In a *reversible-altered form of death*, the character returns either in a physically transformed state or the form of a spirit.

2.2.4. Emotional Reaction

This category refers to how the other characters in the movie responded to or dealt with the death. *Positive emotion* refers to a character or characters being visibly happy (e.g., smiling, cheering) or showing signs of relief. *Negative emotion* refers to a character or characters reacting with frustration, remorse, anger, or general signs of sadness (e.g., crying). *Lacking emotion* refers to characters reacting to death as if it is inconsequential or the death is not dealt with or acknowledged by all characters.

2.2.5. Causality

Causality refers to what led to or caused the death and whether the death portrayed as justified or unjustified. In a *purposeful death,* a character dies as the result of another character's intent to harm or kill him or her. An *accidental death* refers to one where the death was unintentional and was the result of an unplanned event. In addition to being either purposeful or accidental, we coded death events as being either justified or unjustified. *Justified deaths* were ones in which the character who died had done something that warranted punishment; the general message conveyed was that they "deserved" to die. *Unjustified deaths* were ones in which the character did not do anything wrong; there was a sense that they did not deserve to die.

2.2.6. Coping Mechanisms

Unlike previous studies, the original study, we also consider the coping mechanisms used by the characters after a death. Families who displayed *positive coping skills* included support-seeking, self-reliance, and accommodation. Specific positive coping mechanisms included getting support from friends and loved ones, allowing oneself to express sadness, hugging and trying to accomplish positive goals that a loved one who has passed would encourage. Families who displayed *negative coping skills* in movies included escape, social isolation, and opposition Specific negative coping mechanisms included isolation, seeking revenge, and being overly cautious to the point of restricting oneself from opportunities and experiences.

2.3. Intercoder Reliability

In the original study, two coders rated the selected films. Intercoder reliability was judged as acceptable if the raters achieved more than 70% agreement on all categories, using Cohen's Kappa. We tested the reliability between coders on a subsample of four films (40% of the sample). Intercoder reliability was computed for each of the five categories of interest: character status (K = 1.00), depiction of death (K = 0.92), death status (K = 1.00), emotional reaction (K = 1.00) and causality (K = 0.87).

In the current study, two coders rated the selected films and we computed intercoder reliability for each of the five categories of interest: character status (K = 1.00), depiction of death (K = 1.00), death status (K = 1.00), emotional reaction (K = 1.00) and causality (K = 1.00).

3. Results

3.1. Character Status: 1937–2003 (Disney) and 2003–2016 (Disney/Pixar)

In the 10 Disney films from 1937–2003, a total of 23 death scenes were analyzed. There were nearly balanced portrayals of death for protagonists, main characters depicted as the "good guy" (52%; n = 12) and antagonists, depicted as villainous (48%; n = 11) in those scenes. From 2003–2016, a total of 10 death scenes occurred in the 8 Disney films used in our investigation. The majority of these deaths were of protagonists. Out of the 10 characters who died, 70% were protagonists (n = 7) and 30% (n = 3) were antagonists (see Table 1). Films, where a protagonist died, included *Finding Nemo*, *Up*, *The Princess and the Frog*, *Frozen*, *Big Hero 6* and *Moana*. Films, where an antagonist died, included *The Incredibles*, *The Princess and the Frog* and *Tangled*.

3.2. Depiction of Death: 1937–2003 (Disney) and 2003–2016 (Disney/Pixar)

From Disney films (1937–2003), implicit death, wherein death or a dead body was directly shown resulted in 43% of total deaths (n = 10) and explicit death, wherein death was implied and not shown accounted for 48% (n = 11). Based upon character status, implicit deaths was more common among antagonists (70%; n = 7) than protagonists (30%; n = 3). For explicit deaths, a total of 64% occurred among protagonists (n = 7) and 36% were of antagonists (n = 4). Sleep death represented a smaller percentage of death instances (9%; n = 2) in which both occurred among protagonists.

We found that there was a much higher prevalence of implicit deaths than explicit deaths in Disney films from 2003–2016. Implicit death represented 80% of total deaths (n = 8), while only 20% of deaths were explicit (n = 2). There was an equal amount of explicit deaths between a protagonist (50%; n = 1) and an antagonist (50%; n = 1). In contrast, implicit deaths occurred more among protagonists (75%; n = 6), than antagonists (25%; n = 2) in implicit death scenes. Sleep death did not occur in any of selected films (see Table 1).

Table 1. Depiction of Death by Character Type (2003–2016).

Depiction of Death	Protagonist	%	Antagonist	%	Total
Explicit death	1	50%	1	50%	2
Implicit death	6	75%	2	25%	8
Sleep death	0	0%	0	0%	0
Total	7	70%	3	30%	10

Note: Percentages are row percentages. Films containing explicit death included *The Princess and the Frog* and *Tangled*. Films containing implicit death included *Finding Nemo*, *The Incredibles*, *Up*, *The Princess and the Frog*, *Frozen*, *Big Hero 6* and *Moana*.

3.3. Death Status: 1937–2003 (Disney) and 2003–2016 (Disney/Pixar)

Most deaths depicted in Disney films from 1937–2003 were permanent, final and irreversible (74%; n = 17). For permanent deaths, the number was higher among antagonists (59%; n = 10) than protagonists (41%; n = 7). Reversible deaths (n = 6; all protagonists) accounted for 26% of death scenes. Four of the characters (i.e., 67%) returned in their same form and two (i.e., 33%) reappeared in altered forms.

Like Disney films from 1937–2003, most deaths depicted in films from 2003–2016 were permanent, final and irreversible (90%; $n = 9$). For permanent deaths, the number was higher among protagonists (67%; $n = 6$) than antagonists (33%; $n = 3$). Reversible deaths ($n = 1$; protagonist; altered form) accounted for 10% of death scenes. None of the reversible deaths were same form reversible deaths (see Table 2).

Table 2. Death Status by Character Type (2003–2016).

Death Status	Protagonist	%	Antagonist	%	Total
Reversible/Same	0	0%	0	0%	0
Reversible/Altered	1	100%	0	0%	1
Permanent/Final	6	66.66%	3	33.33%	9
Total	7	70%	3	30%	10

Note: Percentages are row percentages. The film that included reversible/altered death was *Moana*. Films containing permanent/final death included *Finding Nemo*, *The Incredibles*, *Up*, *The Princess and the Frog*, *Tangled*, *Frozen* and *Big Hero 6*.

3.4. Emotional Reaction: 1937–2003 (Disney) and 2003–2016 (Disney/Pixar)

The most prevalent type of emotional reaction in the original study was negative emotions (i.e., sadness or anger,), which occurred in 48% of death scenes ($n = 11$). The deaths of protagonists accounted for 91% ($n = 10$) of the negative emotional responses compared to only 9% ($n = 1$) from the death of an antagonist. The deaths of antagonists solely accounted for 13% ($n = 3$) of the positive emotional responses. In the original study, neutral or lacking emotion accounted for 39% of death scenes ($n = 9$) and the clear majority were connected to antagonists deaths (78%; $n = 7$) compared to protagonist deaths (22%; $n = 2$).

Negative emotional responses were observed for most death scenes (70%; $n = 7$) in Disney and Pixar films from 2003–2016. All of the negative emotional responses (100%; $n = 7$) were for protagonists deaths rather than antagonists deaths. Positive emotion occurred in only 10% of deaths ($n = 1$) and resulted from the death of an antagonist. Neutral or lacking emotion occurred in 20% of death scenes ($n = 2$) and associated with the deaths of antagonists ($n = 2$) (see Table 3).

Table 3. Emotional Reactions by Character Type (2003–2016).

Emotional Reaction	Protagonist	%	Antagonist	%	Total
Positive emotion	0	0%	1	100%	1
Negative emotion	7	100%	0	0%	7
Lacking emotion	0	0%	2	100%	2
Total	7	70%	3	30%	10

Note: Percentages are row percentages. The film that included positive emotional reaction was *The Incredibles*. Films containing negative emotional reaction included *Finding Nemo*, *Up*, *The Princess and the Frog*, *Frozen*, *Big Hero 6* and *Moana*. Films lacking emotion included *The Princess and the Frog* and *Tangled*.

3.5. Causality: 1937–2003 (Disney) and 2003–2016 (Disney/Pixar)

From Disney films (1937–2003), purposeful deaths, wherein a character was intentionally killed, resulted in 70% ($n = 16$) of all deaths compared to accidental deaths (30%; $n = 7$). For purposeful deaths, 38% of deaths were justified ($n = 6$) and 62% of deaths were unjustified ($n = 10$). For accidental deaths, 71% ($n = 5$) were justified and 29% ($n = 2$) were unjustified. The frequency of justified deaths (48%, $n = 11$), wherein the character who died had done something that warranted punishment, and unjustified deaths (52%; $n = 12$), wherein the character who died did nothing wrong, was nearly equal. When the interactions of the causality categories were examined together (i.e., purposeful-justified, purposeful-unjustified, accidental-justified, and accidental-unjustified), the findings indicated: all purposeful-justified deaths ended with the death of an antagonist ($n = 6$), and all purposeful-unjustified deaths were among protagonists (n = 10). Furthermore, all the accidental-justified deaths were antagonists (n = 5) compared to accidental-unjustified deaths were protagonists (n = 2).

In the Disney/Pixar analysis from 2003–2016, accidental deaths occurred most frequently, that is, 70% (n = 7) of all deaths compared to purposeful deaths (30%; n = 3). For accidental deaths, 14% (n = 1) were justified and 86% (n = 6) were unjustified. Out of accidental deaths, 67% (n = 2) were justified and 33% (n = 1) was unjustified. The frequency of unjustified deaths (70%, n = 7) was more prevalent than justified deaths (30%; n = 3). When the interactions of the causality categories were examined together (i.e., purposeful-justified, purposeful-unjustified, accidental-justified, and accidental-unjustified), we found the following: all purposeful-justified deaths resulted in the death of antagonists (n = 2) and all purposeful- unjustified deaths was a protagonist (n = 1). The accidental-justified death was an antagonist (n = 1), and the accidental-unjustified deaths were protagonists (n = 6) (see Table 4).

Table 4. Cause of Death by Character Type (2003–2016).

Depiction of Death	Protagonist	%	Antagonist	%	Total
Accidental-justified	0	0%	1	100%	1
Accidental-unjustified	6	100%	0	0%	6
Purposeful-justified	0	0%	2	100%	2
Purposeful-unjustified	1	100%	0	0%	1
Total	7	70%	3	30%	10

Note: Percentages are row percentages. The film that included accidental-justified death was *The Incredibles*. Films that included accidental-unjustified death included *Finding Nemo, Up, The Princess and the Frog, Frozen, Big Hero 6 and Moana*. Films that included purposeful-justified death included *The Princess and the Frog* and *Tangled*. The film that included purposeful-unjustified death was *The Princess and the Frog*.

4. Discussion

The primary goals of the current study were to compare the representation of death in full-length animated Disney Classic films (1937–2003) to full-length animated Disney/Pixar films (2003–2016). Based on the updated content analysis, several trends supported our first primary research objectives and confirmed the findings of previous work by Cox et al. (2005), and Tenzek and Nickels (2017). After analyzing these trends, we will also discuss how the portrayal of death in these films might influence children's understanding of death.

4.1. Character Status

In the Disney Film Analysis (1937–2003), there were almost equal numbers of protagonist and antagonist deaths. The similar numbers demonstrated that both "good" and "bad" character types are susceptible to death and that positive characters may also die (Brent et al. 1996; Willis 2002). In Disney and Pixar full-length feature films from 2003–2016, there was not an equal distribution of characters. Surprisingly, there were more protagonist deaths than antagonist deaths. The unequal distribution, even more so, shows that all characters are vulnerable.

4.2. Depiction of Death

In their original study, Cox et al. (2005) noted that explicit deaths were more prevalent in scenes where protagonists died. They argue that it could be positive because the scenes demonstrate real, explicit deaths of characters to whom the viewer has developed an attachment, but that it could be potentially traumatic for some children. Throwing Mufasa to his death in *The Lion King* is an example of a death that could be traumatic. Overall, the Disney Film Analysis (1937–2003) had a relatively equal amount of explicit and implicit deaths, while the Disney Film Analysis (2003–2016) had very few explicit deaths. These results show how the depiction of death has changed over time to less direct and less traumatic representations.

Animated Disney and Pixar films have not stopped showing death, but it does seem that they are beginning to move away from scenes that may be especially distressing, such as explicit death, like findings by Tenzek and Nickels (2017). Implicit deaths occurred mostly among antagonists in the Disney Film Analysis (1937–2003). Cox et al. (2005) discussed how this might send the message that their deaths were inconsequential in comparison to those of the protagonists. This trend was not evident in the current investigation, and most deaths were implicit regardless of the protagonist or antagonist status. However, the increase in implicit deaths could make all deaths, even those of protagonists, seem incidental.

Lastly, Cox et al. (2005) discussed the sleep deaths that occurred in films from 1937–2003. Two sleep deaths occurred in two movies that came out before the 1970s: *Sleeping Beauty* and *Snow White*. They explained that the fact that sleep deaths did not occur in Disney films released post-1970s may be a trend that there is an increase in children's exposure to death and is now a more acceptable issue in American culture. This idea seems to have continued through the 2000s since there were no sleep deaths in any of the films examined in the current study.

4.3. Death Status

Most deaths as noted in the original study were permanent. Cox et al. (2005) asserted that this was positive because it enforced the idea of the finality of death. Witnessing death in Disney films might help some children experience and comprehend the complexities of death sooner. They further contended that it is essential that parents and teachers guide children through the processes of learning about death; otherwise, they might be upset at the permanence of death. Most deaths in the Disney Film Analysis (2003–2016) and Tenzek and Nickels (2017) were also permanent deaths. Renaud et al. (2015) discussed how it is possible that the irreversibility of death is a concept learned through experience, rather than an explanation. They continued to say that parents may want to explore ways to remember those who pass away, rather than focusing on the end of the physical relationship that we experience when someone dies.

In the Disney Film Analysis (1937–2003), six deaths were reversible, and all of them occurred among protagonists. The authors discussed how this implies that antagonists do not get a second chance at life, while protagonists are more likely to have this chance. Half of the protagonists "came back" in some form or fashion. Cox et al. (2005) used the example of a scene in *The Lion King* where Mufasa returns from the grave to communicate with his son Simba. The authors concluded that was meant to show children that loved ones can always be a part of them, even after death. However, young children may misinterpret this scene with the idea that their loved one may return (Worden and Silverman 1996).

In the current investigation, the film *Moana* had a very similar example of this where Moana's grandmother comes back in the form of a stingray to help guide Moana on her journey through the ocean. This scene was very similar to the intent behind Mufasa's return in *The Lion King*, but one could easily misinterpret the intent. *Moana* is the one and the only film where there is any reversible death in the Disney Film Analysis (2003–2016), which is a reversible altered form of death. This finding highlights one of the most significant changes among studies on the topic of death status (e.g., Cox et al. 2005; Tenzek and Nickels 2017). Also, the direction of change indicates that Disney and Pixar films might be moving away from these ideas of reversible death. This finding also goes back to the thoughts about the positives of permanent deaths in children's movies.

It is worth reiterating that cultural and religious differences impact beliefs about death status. In some belief systems, death is not considered permanent. Beliefs about death may include reincarnation of a person; the body dies but, the soul lives on and many more beliefs that do not promote the idea that death is final. As a large corporation, Disney has viewers all over the world who may view films differently due to their religion. While some researchers may suggest that children who do not believe death is permanent are in a lower stage of development, this notion does not consider cultural differences. Instead, children who subscribe to a belief system wherein death is not considered permanent and espouse these views may be more developmentally mature because they have demonstrated abstract thinking (Brent et al. 1996).

4.4. Emotional Reaction

In the Disney Film Analysis (1937–2003), most of the negative emotion resulted as a reaction to a protagonist's death. This might serve as a model of grieving to some children who lack the knowledge or experience with death (Baker et al. 1992). This finding paralleled the Disney Film Analysis (2003–2016), where the emotional reactions to all protagonist deaths were negative.

In both studies, positive emotion occurred only in reaction to antagonist deaths. However, this was not very common and happened only three times in the Disney Film Analysis (1937–2003) and only once in the Disney Film Analysis (2003–2016). In both studies, all the deaths lacking emotional reactions were antagonists' deaths. These results continue to show the portrayal of antagonists' deaths as unacknowledged However, the few antagonists deaths that are acknowledged, are portrayed positively and jubilantly. In the Disney Film Analysis (2003–2016), only the death of Syndrome, the antagonist in *The Incredibles*, has a response of relief and celebration. This finding shows that fewer deaths are being reacted to positively in these films. This finding has promise, as it teaches children that it is appropriate and entirely reasonable to feel negative emotions surrounding death.

4.5. Causality

In both studies, we found that all justified deaths were antagonist deaths. Similarly, all unjustified deaths were among protagonists. These results further demonstrate the trend to denounce the antagonists to a point where viewers perceive them as deserving death in Disney and Pixar full-length animated films. The deaths of antagonists often result from accidents; however, many animated films portray that the antagonists have done harmful things, so they deserve to die. Their accidental death allows them to "get what they deserve" while still permitting the protagonists to look good. It reinforces the idea that the protagonists are too good to kill others, which is why the antagonists must die accidentally. Cox et al. (2005) use a scene from *Beauty and the Beast* to illustrate this idea between Gaston (the antagonist) and the Beast (the protagonist). In the scene, Gaston purposefully stabs the Beast who "accidentally" causes Gaston to lose his balance on the castle tower and fall to his death.

A similar example can be seen in *The Incredibles* when Syndrome (the antagonist) is escaping in his plane. Mr. Incredible (the protagonist) throws a car up at the plane to try and stop it. This action does not directly kill Syndrome, but it results in Syndrome being sucked up into the engine. Mr. Incredible does not directly kill him and continues in his "good guy" image, but it still results in the death of the "bad guy." In the Disney Film Analysis (1937–2003), protagonists were most often purposely killed by antagonists. The direct intent to kill further demonstrated the evil of the antagonists. In the Disney Film Analysis (2003–2016), almost all protagonists died because of an accident (i.e., illness, a fire, war, etc.). There was also only a total of 3 purposeful deaths overall, which is the biggest change from the Disney Film Analysis (1937–2003). It seems that children's films, specifically Disney films, are starting to move away from purposeful deaths where one character purposely kills another and toward more "realistic" and common causes of death. A universal portrayal of death is not only more relatable for children, but it moves away from fatalities that may make it seem like it is okay to take another life. The reasons for this shift are notable, but they are not the focus of the current investigation. We encourage future research to examine the economic, brand, marketing, or other factors related to this apparent shift with Disney and Pixar.

4.6. Behavioral and Emotional Regulation

Unlike previous studies, the original study, we also consider the coping mechanisms used by the characters after a death. Incorporation of coping mechanisms in a storyline that includes death is essential, as characters can serve as models for children on how to cope with death in their own lives (Corr 2010). Characters could demonstrate which coping mechanisms are positive and effective versus which mechanisms are negative and unhelpful. Families who displayed positive coping skills included support-seeking, self-reliance, and accommodation (Skinner and Zimmer-Gembeck 2007). Specific positive coping mechanisms included getting support from friends and loved ones, allowing oneself to express sadness, hugging and trying to accomplish positive goals that a loved one who has passed would encourage. At least three movies included a character trying to achieve a goal that their passed loved one encouraged. One example was in *Moana*, wherein Moana's grandmother helped her to retrieve a magical stone that would save their island, even as the grandmother was dying. Though she faces trials and tribulations, Moana is determined to accomplish this goal and finds motivation through her grandmother's spirit. In doing so, she becomes more confident and happier.

Families who displayed negative coping skills in movies included escape, social isolation, and opposition (Skinner and Zimmer-Gembeck 2007). Specific negative coping mechanisms included isolation, seeking revenge and being overly cautious to the point of restricting oneself from opportunities and experiences. Characters in the films stopped using these coping strategies after realizing they did not feel better. For example, in *Big Hero 6*, the protagonist Hiro attempted to avenge his brother Tadashi's death by ordering a robot to kill the man who set the fire that killed Tadashi. However, Hiro's friends discouraged his malicious intent, and the robot questioned if killing this man would improve Hiro's emotional state. Hiro realized hurting other people would not make him feel better. While of course, this was an exaggerated version of events that would happen in a child's life after losing a loved one, the child may understand that taking out anger on other people after a death is never the answer. It is worth noting that coping mechanisms were not utilized after the death of an antagonist, because characters' lives were either unchanged or improved by an antagonist death. Therefore, *The Incredibles* and *Tangled* did not contain coping mechanisms.

Family and friend support were crucial to the characters' coping styles. In the film *Up*, without any support system, Carl, once vibrant and full of life, turned into a grumpy, aggressive person following the death of his wife. He became isolated from the world. However, once Carl made a true connection with Russell, Carl began to appreciate happy memories with his wife and regained a more positive outlook on the world. In all films, if a protagonist at first employed a negative coping strategy, they at some point came to understand this strategy did not work or was unhealthy. By all of the films' ends, characters found healthier ways to cope and express emotions. Each film ended with the protagonist happy and in positive surroundings.

4.7. Emerging Trends in the Disney Film Analysis (2003–2016) Films

Of the films in the current study, only *Finding Nemo* and *The Princess and the Frog* depicted non-human deaths, incorporating the death of a fish and the death of a bug, respectively. Both characters were protagonists. Though the characters were not human, they were humanized through abstract concepts like having aspirations and fears as well as concrete concepts like having a family and talking. Because the non-human characters were protagonists and were humanized, their deaths were treated no different than those of human characters and both deaths were met with negative emotion. It is worth exploring if the death of a non-humanized character would be met with the same level of emotion as a human character.

Another trend of the deaths in the current study was familial ties to the main character. Of the seven protagonists who died in these films, six were related to the main character either through blood or marriage. This could be an intentional mechanism to make the death more relatable and understandable to children who may encounter the death of a close relative. No antagonists were technically related to the main character. In *Tangled*, Mother Gothel attempted to portray herself as Rapunzel's mother, but she was her kidnapper. In simple terms, the bad guys were never related to the main character, who was always portrayed as good.

Of the ten total deaths, only two deaths seem to occur in old age. In *Up*, though Ellie's actual cause of death is not disclosed, she is an old woman when she dies. Likewise, in *Moana*, Moana's grandmother's cause of death is not disclosed, but she is also an old woman. All other characters are at least in early adulthood at the time of their death. Ray's age at the time of his death in *The Princess and the Frog* is not entirely clear. It is interesting that the films do not depict the death of young characters and that there is only a small number of old characters who die.

5. Conclusions

The primary goal of this study was to examine how the depiction of death in animated Disney and Pixar films has changed in the past 14 years, keeping in mind past research on children's perceptions of death. We also examined the inclusion of coping mechanisms within these films. This study serves to gain more knowledge surrounding the findings of Cox et al. (2005), Tenzek and Nickels (2017) and to suggest areas worth further examination. These are not conclusive statements but observations of trends over time.

Developmental level and experience with death contribute to a child's ability to comprehend death (Favazza and Munson 2010). Experience with death can be direct, like the death of a relative, or indirect, like through media. Characters in media who have experienced loss might serve as models for grieving children by employing different coping mechanisms. Whether coping skills included in children's media are healthy or unhealthy, children could learn from them (Corr 2004). Coping mechanisms begin to develop in infancy and evolve as children mature (Skinner and Zimmer-Gembeck 2007). This underscores the importance of fostering healthy, effective coping styles in children as early as possible.

Our findings indicate that Disney and Pixar films seem to be moving toward less explicit, more familiar and realistic displays of death. Many characters died as a result of illness, old age and tragic accidents (i.e., shipwreck, building catching on fire, war). These are more common scenarios that many children may hear about in real life. The films show most of these deaths partially, and almost all the deaths are made clear that they are irreversible. Many of these aspects seem to be pointing toward a more realistic portrayal of death. As discussed in Cox et al. (2005), Tenzek and Nickels (2017), these films may give children something to relate to when they are facing a loss.

The addition of identifying coping mechanisms also adds to this idea of helping children learn how to grieve and deal with a death. Films included in the Disney and Pixar Film Analysis (2003–2016) employed at least two of the four most common coping styles families use with children: support-seeking and escape (Skinner and Zimmer-Gembeck 2007). This finding suggests that Disney characters' coping styles on-screen could be relatable to young viewers. Therefore, the fact that characters in these films replace ineffective coping mechanisms with healthy coping skills is a step in the right direction, as characters can serve as role models to children (Corr 2004). Further, the fact that characters who had or sought support from family or friends coped more healthily is positive for viewers, as it may demonstrate the influence of support systems in children's abilities to cope (Corr 2010). Overall, the coping skills related to death portrayed in Disney films are realistic and convey a message of importance about learning to cope healthily and effectively.

Though our content analysis provides compelling insight into changes over time in the portrayal of death and coping mechanisms related to death in Disney and Pixar films, there are some limitations of this study. First, like Cox et al. (2005), we used a convenience sample because the current study focused solely on Disney and Pixar movies that were known to contain death. Second, due to the small sample of films, the results may not generalize to other animated features. Third, our research focused on the idea that death is permanent, but many children may not agree with that idea, due to different belief systems.

Continuing studies in this field can focus on different types of animated films besides Disney or Pixar movies, as well as children's films that are not animated. Further, continuing studies could delve more into different trends in children's films, like how human versus non-human characters are treated or trends in characters' ages at time of death. Future studies could incorporate actual children as viewers into the study to analyze the actual impact these films have on their understanding of death, as opposed to researchers' interpretations of children's perceptions of death from animated films. Future research in this area should approach this topic from a more updated and empowering perspective, which moves away from viewing children as cognitively limited to sophisticated media

Soc. Sci. **2018**, 7, 199

consumers. Finally, there is a pressing need for future research with an emphasis on cultural beliefs about death and how this relates to the depiction of death in children's media.

Through our research, we can begin to answer questions we previously posed: Do Disney and Pixar's depiction of death impact children's understanding of it? At some point in their lives, children will inevitably be exposed to death. If children are educated at a developmentally appropriate level, they can build on their understanding of death as they grow older. Media can tackle the realities of death and act as an example to grieving children (Webb 2010). The younger children begin this education, the more prepared they may be to cope with it in their life. Though we cannot definitively claim Disney and Pixar's portrayals of death have an impact on children's comprehension of death, we can state that we found examples of several coping mechanisms modeled by characters in these films. We assert that children could potentially learn what coping mechanisms are productive and healthy by watching characters enact different strategies and seeing the outcome of those strategies. While we can only speak to our specific study, we believe this is an excellent start to a complex concept.

Author Contributions: Conceptualization, Writing, Review, & Editing: J.A.G.; Methodology, Data Curation, Writing-Original Draft Preparation, H.Y.; Methodology, Data Curation, Writing, Review, & Editing, J.L.R.

Funding: This research received no external funding.

Conflicts of Interest: The authors declare no conflict of interest.

References

Baker, John E., Mary Ann Sedney, and Esther Gross. 1992. Psychological tasks for bereaved children. *American Journal of Orthopsychiatry* 62: 105–16. [CrossRef] [PubMed]

Bovill, Moira, and Sonia Livingstone. 2001. Bedroom Culture and the Privatization of Media Use. In *Children and Their Changing Media Environment. A European Comparative Study*. Edited by Sonia Livingstone and Moira Bovill. Mahwah: Lawrence Erlbaum, pp. 179–200.

Brent, Sandor B., Mark W. Speece, Chongede Lin, Qi Dong, and Chongming Yang. 1996. The development of the concept of death among Chinese and U.S. children 3–17 years of age: From binary to "fuzzy" concepts? *Omega: The Journal of Death and Dying* 33: 67–83. [CrossRef]

Buckingham, David. 2000. *After the Death of Childhood*. Cambridge: Polity Press.

Corr, Charles A. 2004. Bereavement, grief and mourning in death-related literature for children. *Omega: The Journal of Death and Dying* 48: 337–63. [CrossRef]

Corr, Charles A. 2010. *Children's Encounters with Death, Bereavement and Coping*. New York: Springer, pp. 21–37.

Cox, Meredith, Erin Garrett, and James A. Graham. 2005. Death in Disney films: Implications for children's understanding of death. *Omega: The Journal of Death and Dying* 50: 267–80. [CrossRef]

De Boo, Gerly M., and Jelte M. Wicherts. 2007. Assessing cognitive and behavioral coping strategies in children. *Cognitive Therapy and Research* 33: 1–20. [CrossRef]

Favazza, Paddy Cronin, and Leslie J. Munson. 2010. Loss and grief in young children. *Young Exceptional Children* 13: 86–99. [CrossRef]

Grollman, Earl A. 1990. *Talking about Death: A Dialogue between Parent and Child*, 3rd ed. Boston: Beacon Press.

Gutiérrez, Isabel T., Peggy J. Miller, Karl S. Rosengren, and Stevis S. Schein. 2014. III. Affective dimensions of death: Children's books, questions and understandings. *Monographs of the Society for Research in Child Development* 79: 43–61. [CrossRef] [PubMed]

Livingstone, Sonia. 2002. *Young People and New Media: Childhood and the Changing Media Environment*. London: Sage.

Michels, Nathalie, Isabelle Sioen, Liesbet Boone, Caroline Braet, Barbara Vanaelst, Inge Huybrechts, and Stefaan De Henauw. 2015. Longitudinal association between child stress and lifestyle. *Health Psychology* 34: 40–50. [CrossRef] [PubMed]

Renaud, Sarah-Jane, Paraskevi Engarhos, Michael Schleifer, and Victoria Talwar. 2015. Children's earliest experiences with death: Circumstances, conversations, explanations and parental satisfaction. *Infant and Child Development* 24: 157–74. [CrossRef]

Schultz, Ned W., and Lisa M. Huet. 2001. Sensational! Violent! Popular! Death in American movies. *Omega: The Journal of Death and Dying* 42: 137–49. [CrossRef]

Sedney, Mary Anne. 1999. Children's grief narratives in popular films. *Omega: The Journal of Death and Dying* 39: 315–25. [CrossRef]

Sedney, Mary Anne. 2002. Maintaining connections in children's grief narratives in popular film. *American Journal of Orthopsychiatry* 72: 279–88. [CrossRef] [PubMed]

Skinner, Ellen A., and Melanie J. Zimmer-Gembeck. 2007. The development of coping. *Annual Review of Psychology* 58: 119–44. [CrossRef] [PubMed]

Tenzek, Kelly E., and Bonnie M. Nickels. 2017. End-of-Life (EOL) in Disney and Pixar films: An opportunity for engaging in difficult conversation. *Omega: Journal of Death and Dying*. [CrossRef]

Vogel, Robin Helen. 2002. *The Snowman*, rev. ed. Omaha, NE: Centering Corp.

Webb, Nancy Boyd. 2010. Helping bereaved children: A handbook for practitioners. In *Social Work Practice with Children and Families*. Edited by N. B. Webb. New York, NY, USA: Guilford Press, pp. 3–21.

Willis, Clarissa A. 2002. The grieving process in children: Strategies for understanding, educating and reconciling children's perceptions of death. *Early Childhood Education Journal* 29: 221–26. [CrossRef]

Worden, J. William, and Phyllis R. Silverman. 1996. Parental death and the adjustment of school-age children. *Omega: The Journal of Death and Dying* 33: 91–102. [CrossRef]

social sciences

MDPI

Article

Touching Queerness in Disney Films *Dumbo* and *Lilo & Stitch*

Katia Perea

Department of Sociology, City University New York, 2001 Oriental Blvd., Brooklyn, NY 11235, USA;
Katia.Perea@kbcc.cuny.edu; Tel.: +1-718-368-5679

Received: 26 September 2018; Accepted: 1 November 2018; Published: 7 November 2018

Abstract: Disney's influence as a cultural purveyor is difficult to overstate. From cinema screen to television programming, vacation theme parks to wardrobe, toys and books, Disney's consistent ability to entertain children as well as adults has made it a mainstay of popular culture. This research will look at two Disney films, *Dumbo* (1941)[1] and *Lilo & Stitch* (2002),[2] both from distinctly different eras, and analyze the similarities in artistic styling, studio financial climate, and their narrative representation of otherness as it relates to Queer identity.

Keywords: *Dumbo*; *Lilo & Stitch*; Disney; queer; mean girls; boobs and boyfriends; girl cartoon; gender; pink elephants; commodification; Walter Benjamin

1. Introduction

As a Cuban-American child growing up in Miami during *el exilio*,[3] my experience as an other meant my cultural heritage was tied to an island diaspora. Learning about Cuban identity was easy because everyone around me was Cuban; we all read, wrote and spoke in Spanish. Cuban identity was our heritage; American identity was learned. Though television programs like *Sesame Street* and *Captain Kangaroo* were instrumental in helping me learn to speak English, my strongest personal connection to what identified American culture was Disney. I loved everything Disney and happily consumed all kinds of Disney cultural products—I loved wearing Disney clothes, having Disney-themed birthday parties, reading Disney books, watching *The Wonderful World of Disney* on television every weekend and taking yearly family trips to Walt Disney World. Within its pantheon of cultural products, it was Disney animation that cemented my fandom, and among all the loveable Disney characters, my strongest association was with the baby elephant, Dumbo. Dumbo was my favorite stuffed animal, Dumbo the Flying Elephant was my favorite Disney World ride, and Sharpsteen (1941) was my all-time favorite Disney movie, until I saw Sanders and DeBlois (2002).

This article will explore the similarities of these two films' artistic styling, the financial landscape of Disney Studios at the time of production, and the use of othering as a narrative drive. Much has been written about Disney's hegemonic representation of a world represented by the ruling elite (Seiter 1993; Bell et al. 1995; Ortega 1998). White characters are in power and are good and pure hearted, while dark-skinned characters are subservient, dim-witted, and often villainous. Christian undertones and the battle of good versus evil are the norm in Disney productions (Cholodenko 1991; Bell et al. 1995; Leslie 2002) as well as heterosexual romance and

---

1   Director Ben Sharpsteen, artist Joe Grant and Dick Huemer.
2   Directors Dean DeBlois and Chris Sanders.
3   Beginning in 1960 and spanning nearly a decade, *El Exilio* is the era where roughly half a million Cubans, predominantly educated professionals, emigrated to the US seeking political asylum after the Cuban Revolution and were predominantly settled in Miami.

women's subservient positioning (Zipes 1995). This research will draw upon the existing cultural critique of each individual film as well as present a coding system of Queer signifiers represented throughout each film, in order to draw a comparative analysis of how outsider identity presents itself. The research will add insight to how these identities touch Queerness and create new portals for Queer critique from within a Disney culture industry product.

2. Cartoon Theory and Methodology

Cartoons can present a counter-hegemonic potential to the culture industry, particularly because the medium lubricates deviation from the dominant paradigms of thought. Walter Benjamin expressed in his writings on Mickey Mouse (Leslie 2002, p. 105) that he believed in the potential that popular media, particularly early Disney cartoons, could have in countering bourgeois sensibilities. He believed the masses could internalize the images of the animations' abdication of mental laws and as a result begin to question the rules of society. Sergei Eisenstein described this ability to express the revolutionary and convey any idea, however outlandish, "morphing [any shape] without apparent regard for narrative logic that could at any moment transform into anything else", as cartoons' 'plasmaticness' (Sammond 2012, p. 153). Siegfried Kracauer wrote similarly in his review of *Dumbo* in The Nation, suggesting that "[cartoons tend towards] the dissolution rather than the reinforcement of conventional reality" (Kracauer 1941). Because of this potential to deviate from the dominant paradigms of thought, cartoons facilitate playful transgressions on normative coding. Benjamin lamented the loss of this potential upon the release of *Snow White* (1937). The Disney film set the standard for gendered representation in children's motion picture production (Seiter 1993) and created an animation standard of narrative and realism, moving it away from its initial presentation of alternative, surrealistic imagery and subversive, socio-cultural perspectives (Cholodenko 1991; Benshoff 1992; Leslie 2002) which Benjamin claimed brought moralistic values and sexual repression, making cartoons into a respectable consumption for bourgeois sensibilities (Leslie 2002, p. 121).

This critique is exemplified best through Disney's own attempt to repackage *Lilo & Stitch* and *Dumbo*'s Pink Elephants scene. After the success of *Lilo & Stitch*, Disney released several franchise movies, the first of which was titled *Stitch! The Movie* (2003), followed by *Lilo & Stitch 2: Stitch has a Glitch* (2005) and *Leroy and Stitch* (2006). Disney's attempt to repackage the films as a recommodifiable product meant the downplay of Lilo herself, the girl character, emphasizing the focus on Stitch, the boy character, presumably to follow the industry's old gendered adage that girls will watch a boy character but boys will not watch a girl character, even though the success of the original film had already proven otherwise. Not since *Alice in Wonderland* (1951) had there been a lead girl character that was not a princess; the focus onto Stitch removed the gendered counter-hegemonic potential of the film franchise.

The repackaging of *Dumbo*'s Pink elephant scene (46:30) into the Heffalump scene (12:05) in Disney's *Winnie the Pooh and the Blustery Day* (1968) is a more pronounced example of this. It is a perfect specimen for the description that represents an innate resistance to counter-hegemonic potential simply by attempting to make it for everyone, making it less sensibly marginal. What troubles me most is that the watering down, the dumbing down, is conditional in creating a children's product. Shot by shot, the Heffalump scene is almost an identical reproduction of the Pink Elephants scene, yet since it is intended for children to consume, it is made softer, cuter, and especially gendered, whereas the Pink Elephants scene was gender neutral. While some of the changes are subtle, such as the music change of minor key in Pink Elephants to major key in Heffalumps (Bohn 2017), other changes are a bit more obvious. Actively undoing the Queer signifiers, the androgynous pink elephants (29:02) are now wearing gendered clothing (14:03), creating a heteronormative identity. Winnie the Pooh's Heffalump scene and the removal of Lilo's name from the title of the franchise films are evidence of this mechanism of how capitalism stays current and yet retains bourgeoisie sensibilities. This occurs through the removal of aspects of dissent from the culturally innovated product, in this case, the counter-hegemonic gender signifiers, that involves feeding it back to the same population as a watered down version.

The methodology used in this research initiated a thematic coding scheme by textually analyzing the films, documenting what is occurring both verbally and visually to identify markers of Queer identity both overt and naturally transgressive, traditional performative traits and subtle, counter-normative characteristics. This includes, but is not limited to, dialogue, behaviors, images, songs, clothing, jokes, background design, secondary characters, and friendship dynamics. It is a difficult hurdle for Disney scholars to publish with accompanying images from Disney films because the company is very protective of its images as enforced by property infringement restrictions. As such, these occurrences of identifiable markers, as well as descriptive moments in both films are identified by the film's time code to facilitate the reader's finding the scenes referenced on their own.

3. Similarities in Studio Economics and Artistic Choices

The two films, Sharpsteen (1941) and Sanders and DeBlois (2002), were released in very different eras, more than half a century apart, yet the two films share some interesting similarities. *Dumbo* and *Lilo & Stitch* are both the studios' 'little picture that could'. Both these films had been shelved projects that were produced as Disney studios' cost-efficient attempts for financial stability. When Sharpsteen (1941) came out in theaters, it was preceded by two major financial failures for Disney studios (Barrier 1999), *Pinocchio* (1940) and *Fantasia* (1940), and followed by the financial failure of *Bambi* (1942); the studio at the time was also in the midst of labor disputes (Barrier 2007, p. 176). Walt Disney was able to physically distance himself from the labor strikes at his studio under the guise of traveling as research for upcoming film projects, *Saludos Amigos* (1942) and *Los Tres Caballeros* (1944). He had departed in August of that year as a representative for the South American Goodwill Tour, sponsored by Nelson Rockefeller for the newly established US State Department office of the Coordination of Inter-American Affairs in an attempt to build propaganda with Latin America to counter-act the penetration of pro-Nazi influences in those countries and create a defensive super-bloc (Langer 1990, p. 310; Leslie 2002, p. 212). Sanders and DeBlois (2002) had a similar fiscal landscape at Disney Studios, preceded by the financial failures of *The Emperor's New Groove* (2000) and *Atlantis: The Lost Empire* (2001) and like *Dumbo*, was soon followed by another financial failure, *Treasure Planet* (2002) (Corliss 2002). Although they were not in strikes, in 2002 "Disney animation studios shed 500 jobs because of escalating production and labor costs and slashed animators' salaries by 30% to 50%" (Eller and Verrier 2002).

Aside from the similarities in their financial landscape, these two films also share the aesthetic similarity of being painted in watercolor. Watercolor was being used regularly in Disney shorts but feature narratives were painstakingly created in time-consuming hand-painted cells that drove up the labor costs. For *Dumbo*, the use of watercolor was to ensure that production was not cost-prohibitive. When *Lilo & Stitch* was made, the use of watercolor background had not been used since the 1940s (Turan 2002; Fischer 2002; Vincent 2002). Because the film was released in the era of CGI (computer-generated images)-dominated feature narratives, and *Lilo & Stitch*'s return to watercolor was not motivated by cost but rather an intentional aesthetic choice. As co-creator Dean DeBlois points out, "Watercolor seemed to complement [the film] so much with the residual line that gets left behind in the tracedowns, and the fact that it's a transparent medium left a glow. It's perfect for portraying Hawaii, with its organic volumes of light. It's so lush and overgrown" (Desowitz 2002, p. 5).

The production of *Dumbo* also had the unique predicament of being a 'hands-off' film for Walt Disney, who was on his South American tour. Production control was chiefly exercised by storymen Joe Grant and Dick Huemer who rewrote the story and added the unique Pink Elephants sequence to the film, a segment that Disney scholar Mark Langer feels would not have been added had Walt Disney been overseeing the project. Langer explains,

> "While West Coast animation was more consistent with the codes of classic Hollywood cinema, the New Yorker style violated those codes through its emphasis on the artificial quality of animation. ... motivation and causality tended to be discarded in favor of dreamlike connections between events". (Langer 1990, p. 310)

The East Coast animators' style had the expositional feel that Benjamin claimed helped the audience recognize the constructions of the world, whereas West Coast style exemplifies Benjamin's critique of a tamed, naturalistic Disney product.

Though the use of watercolor was not a financially driven decision for *Lilo & Stitch*, changing production style was. Then President of Walt Disney Animation Tom Schumacher granted writing and storyboard direction to co-creators Dean DeBlois and Chris Sanders, who had just worked together on *Mulan* (1998), with the intention of creating a personalized artist driven project. DeBlois said of the process, "we thought if we had the freedom, we could probably lop a whole year off the production time of the film—just by maintaining a consistency from the people who wrote the screenplay pages to the people who storyboarded it and cut it together into story reels and the oversaw its production" (Fischer 2002, p. 7). *Lilo & Stitch*'s release was a presumed a studio risk by industry watchers when its weekend release coincided with the Steven Spielberg film *Minority Report* (2002) starring Tom Cruise. The financial risk of these first-time directors versus one of Hollywood's most celebrated directors was a success; *Lilo & Stitch* tied *Minority Report* in the box-office tally (Vincent 2002). The studio had made the right choice.

4. Otherness, Commodification and the Body

The other similarity I would like to acknowledge is how the two films share a particular sense of identifying otherness as the central storyline. The idea of other I associated with as a child watching *Dumbo* was reawakened when I watched the out-spoken, native Hawaiian, seven-year-old, Lilo.

While there had already been non-white female characters represented in Disney Animation prior to *Lilo & Stitch*, the identifier of girl needs to be addressed in that Lilo is seven years old whereas Pocahontas is animated as an adult with a curvaceous adult body and the rest, Mulan, Tiana and Moana have young adult bodies.[4] As a seven-year-old, Lilo is a girl, not a woman, represented without any overt sexualization, such as breast, curves, sexually suggestive clothing, or romantic interest. In my research, I find twelve to be the age where animators portray girl characters with "boobs and boyfriends", a sexually objectifiable body for the gaze usually accompanied by a heteronormative romantic interest (Perea 2015). As a seven-year-old, Lilo's Queerness is free from these sexualized representations.

Much has been written about Dumbo's resonated difference (Glassmeyer 2014; Harrington 2014; Langer 1990; Sammond 2012). I have no doubt that this difference is why I associated with him so strongly. As a Queer adult, I often look to where I touched Queer as a child (Moñoz 2009, p. 1); what were my earliest moments of identifying who I was and what I wanted to be. When I saw *Dumbo* as a child, I identified with that little elephant because he was an outcast for being different. Dumbo's confidence as he becomes self-actualized, identifying his difference as his strength, is to me his Queerness touched. Lilo is Queer when we meet her.

Upon meeting her, Lilo quickly reveals to us that she is not your typical little girl. In the first nine minutes of meeting Lilo, as a result she we get to see her swim in the Pacific ocean by herself next to a hammerhead shark, feed a peanut butter sandwich to her fish friend Pudge (10:22), navigate her breath in the big waves (10:50), skillfully take a photo of an obese tourist (11:12), get into a fist fight (13:22), describe her doll as having head parasites (14:33), listen to Elvis (15:35), and perform voodoo (19:30). In the opening scenes of *Lilo & Stitch*, scientist Jumba is on trial for creating an alien monster, experiment number 626. The Galactic Council is mortified by the monstrosity and gasp. In transport to exile, he escapes to Earth and lands at a dog pound in Kauai, Hawaii. He is named Stitch when adopted by Lilo, and her nineteen-year-old sister Nani. Much like many Disney stories, Lilo's parents

---

[4] *Pocahontas* (1995) is the first Disney non-white female protagonist. As a native Hawaiian girl, Lilo is the third non-white female character to be given a lead role in a Disney animated film, Mulan being the second, four years prior in *Mulan* (1998), and repeated seven years later with Tiana in *The Princess and the Frog* (2009) and another seven years later with Moana in *Moana* (2016).

are deceased and as a result, she is being raised by her older sister Nani, who works full time to support the household. This is woven in as a central plotline to the narrative conflict. If Nani, Lilo, and Stitch do not learn how to create a stable household, their family will be separated; Lilo will be sent to the foster care system and Stitch will be exiled on an abandoned asteroid. After shootings, chasings, and kidnappings, Lilo manages to rehabilitate Stitch into a best friend and convince the Galactic Councilwoman that he is *Ohana*. *"Ohana means family. No one gets left behind or forgotten"* (36:15).

The narrative format of outsider identity is similar in *Dumbo*. Dumbo is a happy baby elephant that is shunned by his community because his large ears make him different and unique. Though never discussed by other Disney scholars, I believe Dumbo's ears reveal that he is presumably a child of bicontinental origins. All the elephants in the circus, including Mrs. Jumbo, are identifiable as Indian elephants, *Elephas maxius indicus*, which have much smaller ears than African elephants, *Loxodonta africana*. It can be deduced that Mr. Jumbo is of African ancestry and that Dumbo's ears are physical markers of this.[5] Within the first minute of meeting baby Dumbo, the other elephants ridicule him because of his ears, "Jumbo, more like Dumbo" (09:50). "The ridicule is aggressive and cunning; Dumbo is oblivious and his absent doe-eyed reaction only furthers the viewers' sympathy and idealization of his position" (Harrington 2014, p. 125). This harshness is quickly wiped away by Dumbo's mother as she shuts the mean ladies out and playfully gives her baby loving affection; we quickly fall in love with his gentle sweetness and recognize the love of an affirming mother (11:30). Queer kids are disproportionately kicked out of their homes for their difference; Dumbo is loved and accepted by his mother with his Queerness seen. Speaking volumes with his feelings, baby Dumbo never utters a word the entire film, with the exception of a happy squeak he lets out while bathing (17:40). *Dumbo* is the only Disney animated feature in which the title character never talks.

When Dumbo's mother spanks the bully human child that assaulted baby Dumbo, she is swiftly and violently beaten, restrained with chains, and jailed (20:00) A new mother protecting her child is incarcerated and the child is left in negligent, emotionally abusive foster care. "For every child under ten who sees the movie, the chaining and imprisoning of Mrs. Jumbo must be a nearly traumatic experience" (Willmington 1980, p. 77). "This moment in the film is indulgently sentimental and gratuitously manipulative" (Harrington 2014, p. 129). Claiming to be of "a proud race" (21:50), the other elephants shun Dumbo, who is subsequently befriended by a circus mouse, similarly modeled after Jiminy Cricket from the preceding year's Disney film *Pinocchio* (1940). Timothy openly claims that there is nothing wrong with Dumbo's ears, "in fact, I think they are quite decorative" (24:45). Following a night of accidental intoxication with his workplace buddy, Dumbo meets some free-flying crows that live in the trees close to the circus camp.

> [This scene] has usually been perceived as Disney's first major use of characters that are racially marked as black. The crows who find it hard to believe Dumbo can fly inhabit a set of codes that are readily recognizable as performance of blackness which conform to white audience expectations in the 1940s, drawing on the codes current in music hall and short cartoons for supposedly 'obvious' character traits". (Byrne and McQuillian 1999, p. 96)

When we meet the crows, they are hanging out and sporting super cool fashion: spats with a vest, pink sunglasses, striped turtlenecks, even enjoying a cigar (51:51). Some scholars refer to the lead crow as Jim Crow, though there is no indication that he was named that in the original script nor production notes. However, though it was honestly not creator Dick Huemer's intention, made evident by how easily he dismissed it when addressed, and I would add that the basis for the critique is not in the characters but the minstrel-style portrayal in the art itself. These crows are all painted the same shade of black; along with their white eyes, this bears a strong resemblance to a minstrel's black

---

5   This interpretation mirrors a natural uniqueness due to the ineffectiveness of cross-breeding the two types of elephants. The one recorded birth was baby elephant Motty in the Cleveland Zoo in 1978 who sadly did not survive past two months (Rees 2001).

face. This portrayal is a glaring oversight when compared to the animated elephants who are all painted different shades of grey tones. This same artistic choice could easily have been made with the crows. Some purple could have been added around the neckline where crows have iridescent feathers, or simply different tones of black ink. With the understanding that intention is different from impact, the artistic decision to paint them all the same shade demonstrates an application of minstrel-type imagery, albiet self-identified by Huemer as unintentional. When asked about the crows' racial critique, Huemer was surprised to hear it because he remembers that the film makers went out of their way to ensure that black voice actors were hired to voice the crows, an uncommon practice during a time that was difficult for black voice actors to find work.

> "[W]hen veteran Disney animator Dick Huemer was confronted years later, in 1978, with the suggestion that the crows were racist, he bridled, suggesting that the 'colored choir who had sung "When I See an Elephant Fly" and voiced some of the crows' voices had liked it very much and enjoyed doing it hugely. They even offered suggestions, and we used some of their ideas, lines of dialogue or words, little touches . . . I don't think the crow sequence is derogatory. In fact, when someone mentioned the possibility to me, I was quite taken aback. I never gave the angle a thought and I still don't". (Sammond 2012, p. 161)

After some playful teasing, the crows help Dumbo believe in his ability to fly by giving him one of their own black feathers as a talisman; the Magic Feather (59:05). Believing in himself and the power of his otherness, Dumbo triumphs as a celebrated wonder. In the end, though, he chose to stay in the circus with his mother (1:03:07), a decision I never felt comfortable with, particularly because the ringmaster had violently whipped his mother and the other elephants ridiculed him with amused contempt. This observation is also shared by film analyst Siegfried Kracauer who reviewed *Dumbo* upon its theatrical release and noted that,

> "[Y]oung Dumbo, instead of flying off toward some unknown paradise, chooses wealth and security and so ends as the highly paid star of the same circus director who once flogged his mother Jumbo". (Kracauer 1941, p. 2)

Although there is similar emancipation in both narratives- Dumbo flies free from his abusive fate as a clown and his mother is freed from jail—Lilo stays out of the foster care system and Stitch is freed from his role of child weapon[6]-Timothy mouse portrays a confident, optimistic personality to help guide a distraught Dumbo, yet Lilo and Stitch are both equally marked by outsider identity. To the aliens, Stitch is an outlaw, sentenced to exile in isolation as his only safe alternative because he's a dangerous agent of chaos. Lilo herself is quickly revealed as a perceived trouble maker when the hula instructor realizes she is late and exclaims "Ay-yi-yi" (11:53). Basically, he is not surprised that she is late. She cements this outsider identity when she explains her lateness to him.

> [Lilo] "Every Thursday I take Pudge the fish a peanut butter sandwich". [Instructor] "Pudge is a fish?" [Lilo] "And today we were out of peanut butter! So I asked my sister what to give him and she said a tuna sandwich. I can't give Pudge tuna! Do you know what tuna is?" [Instructor] "Fish?" [Lilo] "It's fish! If I gave Pudge tuna, I'd be an abomyou're ination! I'm late because I had to go to the store and get peanut butter 'cause all we have is stinkin' tuna!" [Instructor] "Lilo, Lilo, why is this so important?" [Lilo] "Pudge controls the weather". (12:45)

When Lilo asks the instructor "do you know what tuna is?" she reveals that this is a new concept for her and she assumes that others may not have yet figured it out. This is an existential awareness for Lilo, making the connection of a food to the animal of its source and its perceived insensitivity to her

---

[6] As he has presumably newly been created by Jumba, Stitch is a baby monster.

friend Pudge. Damian Alexander points out that of course Lilo is invested in a friendship with a fish that controls the weather because we later learn that her parents' fatal car crash was during a rainstorm (Alexander 2017). At this explanation, Mertle Emmonds, the leader of the other little girls, says to Lilo, "you're crazy" (13:22), to which Lilo responds by punching her in the face and biting her.

In my cartoon research I have found the archetype of mean girl to represent a constructed, normative aspect of femininity that can be used to challenge the empowerment of girl characters like Lilo (Perea 2015). Mertle Edmunds is a mean girl. Though Lilo is strong and defies 'girly' stereotypes, Mertle reinforces that those 'girly' stereotypes are accurate. The mean girl presents a constructed boundary to the protagonist girl's empowered transgressions. The mean girl is gendered with characteristics that are intentionally absent in the main character. She is superficial, snobby, manipulative; she is not nice and is often popular. While Lilo is potentially transgressing gender normative coding, the portrayal of what is considered a normative girl, Mertle, makes Lilo into an exception, an other, and thus her Queer signifiers remain as outsider identities.

In their own way, the supporting characters of Lilo and Stitch's *ohana* are all outsiders. Nani is suddenly thrust into single parent head of household, which prevents her from having a normal young adult social life (33:38). Outsiderness also accompanies Stitch's potential capturers, Jumba, a self-identified evil genius, now a disgraced scientist (08:42), and Pleekley, who is gendered as an alien male in clothing and pronouns, decides upon arriving in Kauai to don women's clothing as a disguise and finds himself quite comfortable "looking pretty" in his wig, dress, purse, and makeup (38:30).

Dumbo's Timothy is also an outsider of sorts; the archetypical hustler character that welcomes the new stranger, "hey kid, you're all alone, let me show you the ropes. Here, have a peanut." However, Timothy is in a uniform. He is part of the industry, presumably part of an unseen 'mouse circus' act in the Casey Jr. circus. Timothy sees Dumbo's ears as a way into circus stardom and commodifies Dumbo's otherness as a means to raise their class status and qualify them both as celebrated participants of industry. Stitch and Lilo's otherness is not packaged for consumption. Though at the end of the film both protagonists remain outcasts, they are no longer trying to find the place where they belong because they belong together. This is representational of what the Queer community refers to as 'chosen family'- the fellow Queer weirdos that join together to give each other the love and support that is denied to them because of their outsider status.

As outsiders, Dumbo, Stitch, and Lilo are all gasped at in some point of the films. Stitch proclaims some sort of alien profanity that causes the Galactic Council to gasp and one robot member to vomit nuts and bolts (2:30). Dumbo receives a resounding gasp from the other elephants when his ears are revealed (10:38), yet he smiles at them, and later he happily wiggles his ears to the boys in the circus before they physically assault him. Lilo's gasp is not directed at her but her handmade doll Scrump who has a misshapen, oversized head (14:33).

Dumbo's smile and Lilo's attempts to play dolls show that neither is anti-social. Lilo's interests in dolls is a girl gender marker; she is revealed as desirous for the world. "I made her, but her head is too big. So I pretend a bug laid eggs in her ears, and she's upset because she only has a few more days to ... " (14:35). As she realizes that the girls have walked away and abandoned her, she throws Scrump on the ground and stomps away, only to return and pick her up and give her a loving, affectionate embrace. Lilo initially faults Scrump for her weirdness and throws her out, only to return with the affirmation that she truly loves her and embraces her with deep affection. This quality of Lilo, to love Scrump with Queerness seen, is what facilitates Lilo's connection to Stitch.

This outsider connection between Stitch and Lilo is intentionally shown early on through dialogue initiated by Gantu asking his command crew "does this look infected to you?" (04:00), after a restrained Stitch manages to bite him. The exact line is repeated ten minutes later by Mertle Evans after Lilo bites her and she asks the other little girls "does this look infected to you?" (14:11). Lilo is self-aware of her outsider identity when she explains to Nani, "people treat me differently". (22:35). After Nani comforts Lilo and the sisters make up, Lilo gives Nani a roll of film to develop. We see her body of work on the wall by her bed. A photo essay on what we saw earlier, that even though she was running late for hula practice, she did not compromise her artistic integrity, taking a step back to fit the colossal tourist body into the frame. She runs her hand over her art and says to Nani, "aren't they beautiful?" (22:58).

Lilo is affirming of bodies that are otherwise seen as unattractive by the presumed viewer; it is never mentioned by Lilo nor Nani who are both native Hawaiians that those bodies are not normative. It is not that Lilo does not see these bodies as fat, in the way of 'I don't see fat', like the problematic 'I don't see color'. She does see the difference yet does not perceive this as a social stigma. Lilo's perception of outsider bodies deviates from the dominant paradigms of thought that often expects that Queer bodies have to conform. Much like Stitch has to tuck his extra set of limbs and tentacles, Dumbo attempts to bind his ears so as to hide the freak inside. Both Dumbo and Stich need to conform their Queer bodies in order to fit into normative standards of bodily acceptability.[7]

Lilo is accepting of oddities. It is her own outsider identity that allows her to have the space in her life to welcome an alien outcast, which in turn allows Stich to gain freedom from incarceration, Pleakley from his bureaucratic servitude, and Jumba from intellectual disgrace; yet it is not an entry point into the status quo. This is revealed in the end of the film when the Galactic Councilwoman advises that Stitch is serving his life sentence in exile on Kauai: "We will check in from time to time" (1:16:47), and advises her ship's crew that Jumba and Pleakley are not welcome: "don't let those two get on my ship" (1:17:03). Whereas Dumbo is recognized as a celebrity amongst those that previously shunned him, the end credits of *Lilo & Stitch* reveal that the new *ohana*, composed of Nani, Lilo, Stitch, Jumba, and Pleekly, all live in the same house with little gain in social or economic status.

5. Conclusions

"*This is my family. I found it all on my own. It is little, and broken, but still good*" (1:15:05). In the Queer community we use the term "chosen family" to refer to the Queer folks we surround ourselves with as adults, primarily because so many of us have been rejected by our birth families. These associations with each other help form the definitions of our Queer identities and in turn, our vision of the future of Queer: our Queer future has a gay past. We use a shared recollection of the past, a past accessed by us through avenues such as films, poems, novels, historical writings, photography, art, and oral histories. These access points to our Queer past are tied to homosexual and transgender people—historical cultural purveyors who performed Queerness. Yet Queerness is not exclusively about details surrounding sexual relations, or how you present your gender. It is about many other things—outsider identity markers that change with time in a social structure that shapes our identities through performativity.

The outsider identity signifiers of *Dumbo* and *Lilo & Stitch* are relatable to all who have experienced otherness. My Queer read on these films does not claim these signifiers as exclusively Queer, nor does it claim Queer identity on all who experience outsiderness. I am reading the Queer experience of the signifiers, showing up the Queer performativity of the characters, and the Queer realness of the narrative to demonstrate how these identities touch Queerness and create new portals for Queer critique from within a Disney culture industry product.

After the success of *Snow White* (1937), Disney's film set the standard for gendered representation in children's motion picture production and created an animation standard of not just how cartoons were to look but also what messages they were allowed to deliver, moving cartoons away from their initial presentation of alternative, surrealistic imagery and subversive, socio-cultural perspectives (Cholodenko 1991; Benshoff 1992; Leslie 2002; Seiter 1993; Wells 2002). Disney scholar Mark Langer points out that "the tendency among scholars [is] to ignore discontinuities within the Disney opus [to] confirm the existence of an internally unified style or vision" (Langer 1990, p. 305). These two films, *Dumbo* and *Lilo & Stitch*, reveal that transgressions of these Disney standard normative codes are

---

[7] Though not explored here, it is valuable to note that much has been written on how Native people, people with disabilities, immigrants, and People of Color have to alter their appearance to fit into dominant society.

Soc. Sci. **2018**, *7*, 225

possible from within the very cultural industry that creates them, and not in an emphatic display of gender non-conforming, like Mulan (Ortega 1998), but rather in a playful transgression, like the androgynous coupling of the pink elephants or Lilo performing Voodoo and listening to Elvis. Disney products can also be used to display Queerness; it is for us to find that magic feather.

Funding: This research received no external funding.

Conflicts of Interest: The authors declare no conflicts of interest.

References

Alexander, Damian. 2017. *Lilo & Stitch* Meant the World to My Gay, Parentless 10-Year-Old Self. *Teen Vogue*, June 21.

Barrier, Michael. 1999. *Hollywood Cartoons: American Animation in its Golden Age.* New York: Oxford University Press.

Barrier, Michael. 2007. *The Animated Man: A Life of Walt Disney*. Berkeley: University of California Press.

Bell, Elizabeth, Lynda Haas, and Laura Sells, eds. 1995. *From Mouse to Mermaid: The Politics of Film, Gender, and Culture*. Bloomington: Indiana University Press.

Benshoff, Harry M. 1992. Heigh-Ho, Heigh-Ho, is Disney High or Low? From Silly Cartoons to Postmodern Politics. *Animation Journal* 2: 62–85.

Bohn, James. 2017. *Music in Disney's Animated Features: Snow White and the Seven Dwarfs to the Jungle Book*. Jackson: University Press of Mississippi.

Byrne, Eleanor J., and Martin McQuillian. 1999. *Deconstructing Disney*. London: Pluto Press.

Cholodenko, Alan. 1991. *The Illusions of Life: Essays on Animation*. Sydney: Powers Publication.

Corliss, Richard. 2002. Stitch in Time. *Time Magazine*, June 24, vol. 159.

Desowitz, Bill. 2002. Swept Away: The Making of Lilo & Stitch. *Animation Magazine*, June.

Dumbo, 1941. Directed by Ben Sharpsteen. Burbank: Walt Disney Production.

Eller, Claudia, and Richard Verrier. 2002. Disney Confirms Animation Cuts. *Los Angeles Times*, March 19.

Fischer, Lawrence. 2002. Lilo & Stitch. *Cinefantastique* 34: 102.

Glassmeyer, Danielle. 2014. Fighting the Cold War with Pinocchio, Bambi and Dumbo. In *Diversity in Disney Films: Critical Essays on Race, Ethnicity, Gender, Sexuality, and Disability*. Edited by Johnson Cheu. London: McFarland & Company, Incorporated Publishers, pp. 99–114.

Harrington, Sean. 2014. *The Disney Fetish*. Eastleigh: John Libbey Publishing.

Kracauer, Siegfried. 1941. Dumbo. *The Nation*, November 8.

Langer, Mark. 1990. Regionalism in Disney Animation: Pink Elephants and Dumbo. *Film History* 4: 305–21.

Leslie, Esther. 2002. *Hollywood Flatlands: Animation, Critical Theory and the Avant Garde*. London and New York: Verso.

Lilo & Stitch, 2002. Directed by Chris Sanders, and Dean DeBlois. Burbank: Walt Disney Production.

Moñoz, Jose. 2009. *Cruising Utopia: The Then and There of Queer Futurity*. New York: New York University Press.

Ortega, Teresa. 1998. Cartoon cross-dresser: Disney's Mulan joins a long line of women who dress like men on-screen. *The Advocate* 763: 57.

Perea, Katia. 2015. Girl Cartoons Second Wave: Transforming the Genre. *Animation Journal* 10: 189–204. [CrossRef]

Rees, P. A. 2001. A History of the National Elephant Center, Chester Zoo. *International Zoo News* 48: 170–83.

Sammond, Nicholas. 2012. Dumbo, Disney, and Difference: Walt Disney Productions and Film as Children's Literature. In *The Oxford Handbook of Children's Literature*. Edited by Lynne Vallone and Julia Mickenberg. Oxford: Oxford University Press.

Seiter, Ellen. 1993. *Sold Separately: Children and Parents in Consumer Culture*. New Brunswick: Rutgers University Press.

Turan, Kenneth. 2002. A Welcome Break from Disney Formula. *Los Angeles Times*, June 1, p. 21.

Vincent, Mal. 2002. Lilo is a Stitch with Razor-Sharp Teeth, Six Legs, Antennae and Back Spikes, Stitch is an Unlikely Disney Hero, But He's a Hit at the Box Office. *Virginian Pilot*, June 28, p. E1.

Wells. 2002. *Animation and America*. New Brunswick: Rutgers University Press.

Willmington, Michael. 1980. Dumbo. In *The American Animated Cartoon: A Critical Anthology.* Edited by Danny Peary and Gerald Peary. New York: E.P. Dutton, pp. 76–81.

Zipes, Jack. 1995. Breaking the Disney Spell. In *From Mouse to Mermaid: The Politics of Film, Gender, and Culture.* Edited by Elizabeth Bell, Lynda Haas and Laura Sells. Bloomington: Indiana University Press, pp. 21–42.

social sciences

MDPI

Article

Queen Phiona and Princess Shuri—Alternative Africana "Royalty" in Disney's Royal Realm: An Intersectional Analysis

Heather E. Harris

Department of Business Communication, Stevenson University, 11200 Ted Herget Way, Owings Mills, MD 21117-6254, USA; hharris@stevenson.edu

Received: 30 September 2018; Accepted: 15 October 2018; Published: 20 October 2018

Abstract: This paper explores the representations of two of Disney's Africana royals, Phiona from the Queen of Katwe and Princess Shuri from Black Panther. Taking into consideration the pedagogical impact of media to reinforce ideologies of White supremacy and privilege, the depictions of these alternative royals in Disney's royal realm are analyzed using intersectionality theory. The girls' intersecting identities are juxtaposed with Collins' matrix of domination concept. The analysis revealed that, while both Phiona and Shuri are challenged by the legacy of colonialization, capitalism, and globalization that constitute the matrix of domination, their approaches to these challenges are different as a result of the unique ways that their identities intersect. The author stresses that while it is commendable of Disney, and Hollywood, to allow for the affirming portrayals of these Africana girls on screen, the gesture is baseless unless a tipping point is reached where such films, and those depicting other non-dominant groups, become the norm rather than the exceptions. In other words, the challenge for those in the industry is not to resist the matrix of domination that stymies the creation of films that reflect the spectrum of the lived and fantastical experiences of Africana, and people of color; rather, the challenge is to dismantle it.

Keywords: Africana; alternative royals; intersectionality; matrix of domination

1. Introduction

Perceived as strong without super powers, Africana (African diaspora) women are also viewed, and often view themselves, as queens without crowns. Perhaps this is what renders us truly magical in our own eyes, as well as in eyes of a conglomerate like Disney. Notably, in the last decade, Disney has seen it as profitable, both in finances and in terms of an expanded audience demographic, to mingle its magic with ours in such films as *The Princess and the Frog* (2009), *Queen of Katwe* (2016), and *Black Panther* (2018). Yet, although The Princess and the Frog was much anticipated prior to its release in 2009, once screened, the animated feature film resulted in animus from some segments of the Black community. Some of the reasons for the dismay included but were not limited to the following: the film's erasure of Tiana by a frog for the majority of the feature; the fact that she was not a princess from birth; her ambiguously ethnic and unambitious prince; and the presence of her spoiled White friend, Charlotte, appearing in big and bold contrast to the hardworking and sacrificing Tiana—all served to sour the highly anticipated cinematic experience for many. Rather than debunking the stereotypes connected with Africana women, and Blacks generally, the film served to reinforce them in creative and not so creative ways (Gregory 2010; Lester 2010; Moffitt and Harris 2014; Parasecoli 2010). Nevertheless, Disney has made progress in subsequent films featuring Africana women. Hence, while Tiana was the first Africana princess in Disney's official royal realm, she has not been the last Africana female to hold a title, and she will also not be the focus of this paper. Rather, alternative Africana royalty will be examined in the form of 10-year-old Phiona Mutesi from the

Queen of Katwe (2016), and 16-year-old Princess Shuri from *Black Panther* (2018). These two girls not only improve on the representations of Africana females on the big screen, they also lend themselves to the creation of a new trope—noble Africana genius girls—that the writer defines as Africana girls who are intelligent and innovative, and who apply their knowledge and skills to advance themselves as well as their communities. Furthermore, even though one story is based on fact, Phiona's, and one on fiction, Shuri's, both girls serve as exemplars for all girls, and Africana girls especially. Needless to say, their images go beyond those usually seen in film.

According to hooks (2009, p. 255), when Blacks partake in cinematic images, it is with the understanding that those representations are designed to uphold and reproduce White supremacy. " ... Cinema assumes a pedagogical role in the lives of many people ... I began to realize that my students learned more about race, sex, and class from movies than from all of the theoretical literature" (hooks 2009, p. 3). Sandlin and Maudlin (2015, p. 2) spoke specifically to the power of Disney's pedagogical practices, "from parks to movies to deluxe cruise line vacations, The Walt Disney Company goes to great lengths to create intricately fabricated fantasies of pleasure and fulfillment that promise an escape from the realities of our everyday lives". They described what they refer to as the Disneyverse as being an integral part of the affective economy, and a perpetuator of Whiteness in the form of heteropatriarchal privilege. Sandlin and Maudlin also stressed that " ... we cannot rely on comfort or pleasure as a means of escaping the ubiquity of racist/colonialist/imperialist Disney narratives, there is a certain relief that comes with the relinquishment of Disney's impossible dream" (Sandlin and Maudlin 2015, p. 14). The perniciousness and the destructive impact of ideologies of Whiteness, and White supremacy in Western societies is also affirmed by the literature (Ayisi and Brylla 2013, p. 126; Lester 2010, p. 295; Pellerin 2012, p. 78). Lester (2010, p. 295) identified "beauty, fame, fortune, and desire" as being conflated with Whiteness as it relates to American media. Furthermore, when the concepts of Whiteness and White supremacy are expanded to include representations of the continent of Africa and its peoples, little shifts. Ayisi and Brylla (2013, p. 125) asserted that the media output of Western societies "consistently constructed cinematic images of African life and society that are reductive and even offensive". They added that as a result of Africans being perceived and portrayed as inferior to Whites, there tended to be an absence of culturally affirming representations. They said there is a need to move beyond the breathtaking landscapes, where the images of war, misery, and poverty remain. Pellerin (2012, p. 76) added that most of the images related to Africana women specifically contribute to the "assault of African humanity". Africana women are shaped by the experiences that result from their resistance (Alinia 2015, p. 2337). For Cartier (2014, p. 151), that resistance may take the form of a more expansive representation of Blackness on screen along the lines of Alondra Nelson's concept of future texts—namely a reconfiguration of Blackness that borrows from the past as it seeks to shift images in the present, while also envisioning novel representations of how Black women might appear on screen in the future. Cartier (2014, p. 151–52) posited that it is necessary to move beyond " ... accepting blackness as a spectrum and refusing the primacy of the politics of respectability and the culture of dissemblance as the most effective weapons black women wield against the intersecting oppressions of patriarchy, racism, and the prejudices that arise from class and sexuality". She added that there is still work to be done for Blackness and Africana women in order to be seen across the experiences spectrum on screen, as they exist in life. According to her, our Blackness is mined for its cool, while our full humanity is denied. Perhaps the future is now and a shift in the representations of gender and race ideologies as they pertain to Africana women on screen, as espoused by Collins (2005, p. 212) may be at hand, to a degree, in the films *Queen of Katwe* (2016) and *Black Panther* (2018).

In a sampling of reviews about the films, there was praise for the representations. Iyer (2017, p. 42) referred to *Queen of Katwe* (2016) as remarkable and an improbable Disney film. She appeared to credit Disney's new direction in the film to the insider's gaze of its director Mira Nair, who lived in the film's location, Uganda, for nearly three decades. According to Iyer (2017, p. 43), Nair refrains from using the West as a standard for Uganda, but rather tells the story from Uganda's perspective, without whitewashing the complexities of that country. Shattuck (2017, p. 9) heralded *Queen of Katwe* (2016) as a film of female empowerment. Abraham (2017, p. 70) said that Disney had decidedly challenged its unenlightened representations of race and gender in the film, "Unlike most Disney and other Western films set in Africa and focused on Black people, this film does not employ lazy racist, heteronormative tropes. There is no White savior." (Abraham 2017, p. 71). The same can be said for *Black Panther* (2018), particularly for the character of Princess Shuri. Framke (2018) described Shuri as " ... The feisty Disney princess we need and deserve". According to Finley (2018), Hickey (2018), and Thompson (2018), it is roles like that of Princess Shuri that provide role models in technology and other areas for Africana women. She is a multidimensional character.

The film reviews show that these two Disney productions may have the potential to be representation changers. In this paper, the extent of that change will be explored using intersectionality theory, as outlined by Windsong (2016, p. 136). The term intersectionality was coined by Kimberlé Crenshaw. In a recent Washington Post piece she stated, "Intersectionality, then, was my attempt to make feminism, anti-racist activism, and anti-discrimination law do what I thought they should—highlight the multiple avenues through which racial and gender oppression were experienced ... " (Crenshaw 2015). Intersectionality, as defined by Collins (2015, p. 2), is " ... the critical insight that race, class, gender, sexuality, ethnicity, nation, ability, and age operate not as unitary, mutually exclusive entities, but as reciprocally constructing phenomena that in turn shape complex social inequities". This paper's analysis is intended to provide a multidimensional understanding of the ways in which Phiona and Shuri are represented, and the oppressions and privilege that they participate in. Rather than engaging their identities and oppressions as additive, the theory will enable the writer to present the girls in their wholeness as they navigate what Collins, as cited in Windsong (2016), labels as the matrix of domination—namely the varied types of oppression faced by women in general, but particularly women of color. Alinia (2015, p. 2336) states "The struggle of resistance shaped around struggles of colonialism, racism, and foreign occupations has often been male dominated and patriarchal." According to Veenstra (2013, p. 648), intersecting disadvantaged identities experience oppression in a multiplicative fashion. In other words, one form of oppression is not added and/or ranked but becomes more oppressive than what would be expected "by double, triple, or quadruple jeopardy". When Windsong (2016, p. 136) speaks of shifting from an additive analysis, she cites Collins noting that one's intersecting identities do not exist discreetly and cannot be ranked in terms of privileged or oppressed, but rather one's identities intersect with one's oppressions and privileges resulting in an individual being capable of being both oppressed and the oppressor. " ... The matrix of domination does not contain many pure victims or pure oppressors but instead each person experiences different forms of domination and privilege from the multiple systems of oppression" (Windsong 2016, p. 136).

Citing McCall, Windsong (2016, p. 138) would describe the forthcoming analysis as intracategorical in that the focus is on Africana women. The aspect of intersectionality theory, namely moving beyond an additive analysis perspective, as outlined by Windsong (2016, p. 136), will be applied as a means to unveil Phiona's and Shuri's cinematic representations as Africana females in *Queen of Katwe* (2016) and *Black Panther* (2018), respectively. It is important to note that Windsong (2016, p. 136) acknowledges that intersectionality theory does not dictate a design for incorporating and analyzing texts such as the films under discussion.

2. Film Summaries

Adapted from an ESPN news story, *Queen of Katwe* (2016) is set in the Kampala city slum of Katwe in Uganda. Filled with compassion and hope, the film depicts the extraordinary challenges faced by a 10-year-old Phiona over a four-year period as she strives to become an unlikely chess champion. Prior to a fortuitous meeting with the sports ministry's part-time employee, Robert Katende, also known as Coach, her days consisted of selling maize in order to supplement the family's (her mother, sister, and two brothers) finances rather than schooling. By happenstance, she meets Coach while he is in the process of feeding children, his Pioneers, porridge in a room belonging to the ministry. He invites her to join them, and to learn an unfamiliar game. Initially rebuffed by the other children because of her offensive smell and dirty clothes, Phiona is drawn to the game. Indeed, Coach realizes that she is a chess prodigy, and highly intelligent. With his chess and life tutoring; reading lessons from his wife, Sara; the support of her mother, Harriet; and eventual formal schooling, Phiona literally rises from the poverty-stricken Katwe to compete, and win, in chess championships on the continent of Africa and in Europe.

Black Panther (2018) tells the story of the technologically and intellectually advanced fictional African kingdom of Wakanda, and its new king T'Challa—also known as the Black Panther. T'Challa and the people of Wakanda find themselves grappling with whether to share their nation's alien element vibranium to help others of the African diaspora advance and prosper. In the past, Wakandans believed that the key to their progress was best kept secret, but upon his ascension to the throne after his father's murder, King T'Challa finds himself challenged both physically and ideologically by his cousin, Killmonger. In the midst of T'Challa's crisis of conscious and country, it is his sister, Princess Shuri, a 16-year-old genius, who is instrumental in assisting him through the crisis. Shuri, in addition to being his younger sister, is also one of his greatest supporters and protectors. Everything she does is for her country; her family; and, after her father's death, her brother. Through experiments, creations, and innovations in her laboratory, she transforms vibranium, seemingly single-handedly, into time traveling holograms, technologies such as the Black Panther's suit, military armour, radio devices, and cures for previously mortal wounds. She is Wakandan royalty, its chief scientist, and a fierce warrior. Hence, when the nation comes under threat from her cousin Killmonger, she simultaneously "womans" the technology while also holding her own on the battlefield alongside the all-female Dora Milaje.

3. Film Analyses Using Intersectionality Theory

When examining the operationalization of intersectionality theory, as outlined by Windsong (2016), in terms of moving beyond the additive analysis of the identities, multiple layers of the girls are revealed. This section will begin with an analysis of the Queen of Katwe's Phiona, followed by one of Black Panther's Princess, Shuri, in order to gain an understanding of how their identities synergistically operate with Collins' matrix of domination—namely intersecting oppressions—to manifest the young women's realities.

"Use your minds, follow your plans, and you will all find safe spaces"—Coach speaking to his chess Pioneers in the film *Queen of Katwe* (2016). This quote can be said to provide an umbrella for Phiona's journey in the film. Her knowledge and application of the game of chess also becomes a chessboard for her life. At first glance, it would appear that Phiona's life is one without privilege, based on her life conditions. She is poor, female, Christian, and Black. Yet, with all of these seeming disadvantages, Phiona is able-bodied and relatively healthy. As the hardest worker in her family, next to her mother, she enables them to eke out a fragile existence. She does not have to beg, but she suffers nevertheless.

In the film, it can be said that Phiona's major intersecting identities were her class, her gender, her Christian faith, and her race. How the identities shifted in their nexus depended on her circumstances, as well as the gaze (dominant or oppositional) being applied. Her identities pushed against the legacy of colonialism, capitalism, and globalization, which made up her opposing matrix of domination. The legacy of colonialism and its partner, capitalism, is what oppresses people like Phiona in the film; for people like her, while they are seen, are simultaneously invisible amidst the hustle and bustle of Kampala life. They are nuisance people. Fortunately, in her case, she is seen by someone who was once like her, but who managed to change his life through education. Yet, as an educated man, he is initially unable to land a coveted engineering job because of his low class status and lack of familial connections. Nevertheless, rather than despairing, he helped his Pioneers using his part-time job with the sports ministry, and his wife's teacher's salary.

Phiona's class and gender under the legacy of colonialism and capitalism are felt most acutely as she competes in tournaments at schools now occupied by the beneficiaries of the colonial past. There, she and her fellow Pioneers are scorned, and are tellingly out of place due to their lack of exposure to such environments. However, it is in these environments, and her overcoming gender stereotypes that she further awakens to the matrix of domination and her power to question and surpass her circumstances. Even when she wins a trophy for "Best Boy" in a tournament, because they had no prizes for girls, she realizes the power of the queen piece to better her life on the chessboard as well as in general.

Although now in full recognition of the matrix's impact on her life, when she traveled to Russia to play at a chess Olympiad, she forgets her skill and questions her very presence in such a space. As she played a White Canadian teenager, she lost her focus and her fortitude and resigned the match. Perhaps her meltdown was due to the pressure of globalization that affirms certain bodies in certain spaces. She seemingly felt out of place not because of her skill, but because of her experiences with class, gender, and now first-hand contact with the global negative perception of Blackness. It is a subtle but powerful scene. The messages of globalization—what one watches on film, the advertisements that one is exposed to, and the education canon—all contribute to the ideologies that promote White supremacy and Western superiority.

Back home in Katwe, Phiona recognized, through the experiences of her mother and older sister, Night, that her class, gender, and faith can make her the prey of some men, and the target of jealousy of some women. For example, after one of her brothers is hit by a car and requires stitches and hospitalization, her mother sneaks him out of the hospital just before she is to pay the bill. When she returns to her one room shack, she finds her family locked out by the landlady because the rent has not been paid. Phiona's mother explains that the money for rent was used to pay someone to drive them to the hospital after the accident, but the landlady is merciless. Before she throws their belongings into the street, she chastises Phiona's mother for being too good to sell her body to fulfill her financial needs. Harriet, a praying woman, continued to maintain her faith in God even as she walked the slum with her children and belongings in search of shelter. In another scene, Night, the sister, against her mother's warnings and tired of being destitute, becomes the girlfriend of a bad boy in order to get money, food, flashy clothes, and synthetic hair. Once she becomes pregnant, he dumps her. Phiona sees this and wonders if such a fate is inevitable for her. She asks Night if God is mad at them, and her sister responds that she does not believe God even thinks of them. Then, Phiona tells Coach that because she is poor and female, she fears that soon the boys will come for her. That nightmare never happens for Phiona. Coach and Sara's provision of a safe space for Phiona in their home, as well as schooling and chess tutoring, enable her to fight her oppressions in ways that her sister and mother could not. For while Harriet did not sell her body, she did sell a prized and beautiful garment given to her by Phiona's grandmother, so that Phiona would be able to study. In the end, although at times feeling beaten down by life, Phiona learned the aforementioned lessons vicariously, and with Coach's advice, "Do not be quick to tip your king" *Queen of Katwe* (2016), she was able to simultaneously affirm her gender, transcend her class, maintain her faith in a Christian god, and pull her family out of Katwe.

"We have watched with disgust as your technological advancements have been overseen by a child who scoffs at tradition" *Black Panther* (2018)—M'Baku speaking about Princess Shuri and to Wakandans before he challenges T'Challa for the throne. Princess Shuri's matrix of domination is similar to that of Phiona's with the legacy of colonization, and the presence of capitalism, and globalization. However, Shuri's intersecting identities, namely class, nationality, gender, race, and age manifest themselves differently in that she perceives her agency in interacting with the matrix of domination. Shuri is a supporting character in *Black Panther* (2018), she appears several times throughout the film. We are first introduced to her upon her brother's return to Wakanda after their father's death. Although she is solemn in the presence of her mother, the banter between her and her brother provides a clue to a mischievous side to her that is confirmed throughout the film. She is fully immersed in her royal status, but does not take it for granted. She knows that her responsibility is to Wakanda, and based on the challenges for the throne, she knows that her status may not be for life. Nevertheless, being royalty does have its privileges, and in the Marvel universe, she is among the most intelligent—woman or man. Shuri knows she is also a young woman and Black. Although the matrix of domination is very real for Shuri, her identities appear to cause her no pain when pushed against the matrix. Her class alone gave her access to education, warrior training, and exposure to the global affairs that she monitors from her laboratory. And while she is taken aback by M'Baku's pronouncement about a child running the kingdom, perhaps it is due more to the sting of his words than to his menacing presence as he moved towards her at the Challenge Day ceremony. There is an African term "nommo" that means the power of the word. No doubt she is aware of this and may have momentarily felt convicted by his verbal venom.

Throughout the film her identities seem to operate seamlessly in Wakanda and in her laboratory. She creates and innovates using all of her identities. Her inventions are useful, humorous, reflective of African traditions and surroundings, and are internationally influenced. Her progress is by no means stymied by any of her identities, as long as she is dealing with Wakandans—even M'Baku. Beyond Wakanda, the story is different one. For example, once when she was called upon to assist her brother, Black Panther, through a hologram connection to Korea, she is undoubtedly aware of how Wakandans; Black Africans; and, by extension, Africana people, are perceived globally when Claw, a White Western villain, refers to them as savages undeserving of the power provided them by vibranium. Additionally, in spite of her healing him from a mortal wound to his back, CIA agent, Everett Ross, does not appear to thank Shuri for saving his life. Instead, nonplussed, he questions her expertise in disbelief. Rather than express gratitude for his life, he, as liberal as he appears to be earlier in the film, cannot prevent the dissonance from rising within him when he realizes that the fabled Wakanda exists. Shuri, on the other hand, is unimpressed by his Eurocentric arrogance and sarcastically calls him out for who he is when she says, "Do not scare me like that colonizer" (*Black Panther* 2018). She then shows her privilege and power by telling Ross who he is, without revealing her identity. When he asks for confirmation of being in Wakanda, she tells him he is in Kansas.

In another example, M'Baku silences Shuri when she, her mother Ramonda, and the spy Nakia, sought the help of the Jabari so as to defeat Killmonger. M'Baku cut her off when she spoke. He would not entertain the child he perceived her to be to have voice in his territory. Yet it was in Jabari Land where Shuri watched and learned from the Queen Mother—a tradition M'Baku believed her to be disinterested in, namely how to formulate the herb that gives Black Panther his power. Shuri was not a flouter of tradition, and she did not allow M'Baku's perception of her as a child or his silencing to thwart her acquisition of ancient and sacred knowledge. Not to mention, it was the same "child" who encouraged Nakia to don the armour of the Dora Milaje to fight for Wakanda against Killmonger and Wakanda's traitors. Then, while in battle, she guided the confused Ross to pilot a fighter plane to shoot down cargo planes with vibranium that was destined for sale globally by Killmonger. Shuri saw herself holistically, each identity necessary, but not all defining. It can be argued that her privileged position as a Wakandan royal first and foremost permitted this self-evaluation, and cushioned her from the often vicious impact of White supremacy and privilege that serve as the foundation of the legacy of colonialism, capitalism, and globalization.

4. Discussion

What constitutes the stark differences in how the analysis of the films using intersectionality theory differed for the alternative royals? One film is based on fact and the other on fantasy. While there may be more leeway given to fantasy, all Hollywood productions serve to replicate patterns and images of the dominant ideologies of White supremacy and privilege (Ayisi and Brylla 2013, p. 126; Lester 2010, p. 295; Pellerin 2012, p. 78; Sandlin and Maudlin 2015, p. 14). *Queen of Katwe* (2016) and *Black Panther* (2018) are not exceptions. We witness the films' directors, Mira Nair and Ryan Coogler, being able to challenge the cinematic tension between what (Kellner 2003) refers to as the modes of production and political economy. Furthermore, the directors' oppositional gazes enabled these alternative royals to exist on celluloid. According to Kellner, "The system of production often determines what sort of artifacts will be produced, what structural limits there will be as to what can and cannot be said and shown" (Kellner 2003, p. 12). Hence, it is undoubtedly due to Nair and Coogler that viewers are able to see affirming Africana images like Phiona and Shuri on screen. As mentioned previously, Nair had an intimacy with Uganda, having lived there for several years. This appears to have enabled her to transcend the dictates that Kellner writes about, and use an oppositional gaze to tell Phiona's story in an affirming fashion. The same is true for Coogler, who gathered a predominately Africana team to tell Wakanda's story. He was so successful in his interpretation of the African jewel of the Marvel universe that some people of the African diaspora wished for Wakanda to be real. Like the alternative Africana Disney royals, Nair and Coogler recognized the matrix of domination, and resisted it—Nair in the form of a "cinematically" authentic Ugandan experience, and Coogler in terms of unequivocal box office success.

5. Conclusions

In both movies, steps were made to move beyond the stale tropes used to describe and erroneously define Africana women and people in general. Disney made room for alternative royals to exist, albeit outside of their official royal realm. Cognizant of it, the directors resisted the matrix of domination to excellent effect. They used their position to leverage their privilege in an industry with a pedagogical agenda to produce stereotypes in the representations of people of color. And while one can appreciate Disney's support for these films, resistance to the matrix of domination cannot be the focus in the quest for films that are reflective of the spectrum of experiences of Africana and other non-dominant groups on screen. The provision of a smattering of films featuring people of color borders on corrupt. More big budget feature films depicting both the lived and fantastical experiences of people of color must be produced and directed within and outside of Hollywood. Anything less relegates Phiona and Shuri to no more than diverse cinematic bumps in the road, and their royalty to the realm of illegitimacy. Box office receipts continue to indicate that audiences are ready to see, and are able to relate to, people of color on screen, as evidenced by *Black Panther* (2018) and *Crazy Rich Asians* (2018). These films, and others produced in Hollywood, show, without question, that a foundation exists. The time is now to stop adding to it, and to actually build upon it with images that reflect and challenge us as human beings. Africana peoples, and others of non-dominant groups can create, in spite of the oppressions at every level of the production process; but should this be our challenge? Our challenge should be to dismantle the matrix of domination and its effects, rather than resist it. Imagine those films, and the box office receipts.

Funding: This research received no external funding.

Conflicts of Interest: The author declares no conflict of interest.

References and Notes

Abraham, Stephanie. 2017. Queen of Katwe. *Bitch Media*, September 11, pp. 70–71. Available online: https://www.bitchmedia.org/article/queen-katwe/director-mira-nair (accessed on 10 September 2018).

Alinia, Minoo. 2015. On Black feminist thought: Thinking oppression and resistance through intersectional paradigm. *Ethnic and Race Studies* 38: 2334–40. [CrossRef]

Ayisi, Florence, and Catalin Brylla. 2013. The politics of representation and audience reception: Alternative visions of Africa. *Research in African Literatures* 44: 125–41. [CrossRef]

Cartier, Nina. 2014. Black women on-screen as future texts: A new look at Black pop culture representations. *Cinema Journal* 53: 150–57. [CrossRef]

Directed by Jon M. Chu. Produced by Nina Jacobson, Brad Simpson, and John Penotti. Screenplay by Peter Chiarelli and Adele Lim. Burbank: Warner Bros.

Directed by Ron Clements and John Musker. Produced by Peter Del Vecho and John Lasseter. Screenplay by Ron Clements, John Musker, and Rob Edwards. Burbank: Walt Disney Pictures.

Collins, Patricia Hill. 2005. *Black Sexual Politics: African Americans, Gender, and the New Racism.* New York: Routledge Classics.

Collins, Patricia Hill. 2015. Intersectionality's definitional dilemmas. *Annual Review of Sociology* 41: 1–20. [CrossRef]

Directed by Ryan Coogler. Produced by Kevin Feige. Written by Ryan Coogler and Joe Robert Cole. Burbank: Walt Disney Pictures.

Crenshaw, Kimberlé. 2015. Why Intersectionality Can't Wait. *Washington Post*, September 24. Available online: https://www.washingtonpost.com/news/in-theory/wp/2015/09/24/why-intersectionality-cant-wait/?noredirect=on&utm_term=.6d15a9176a9e (accessed on 10 September 2018).

Finley, Taryn. 2018. "Black Panther" Actress Letitia Wright Hopes Shuri Inspires More Girls to Pursue STEM. Available online: https://www.huffingtonpost.com/entry/black-panther-actress-letitia-wright-hopes-shuri-inspires-more-girls-in-stem_us_5a8ba183e4b09fc01e02b764 (accessed on 10 September 2018).

Framke, Caroline. 2018. Why Shuri, Black Panther's Teen Girl Genius is Marvel's Most Promising Character in Ages. Available online: https://www.vox.com/culture/2018/2/20/17030266/black-panther-shuri-letitia-wright-best (accessed on 10 September 2018).

Gregory, Sarita. 2010. Disney's second line: New Orleans, racial masquerade, and the reproduction of whiteness in the princess and the frog. *Journal of African American Studies* 14: 432–49. [CrossRef]

Hickey, Walt. 2018. 'Black Panther' Is Groundbreaking, But It's Shuri Who Could Change the World. Available online: https://fivethirtyeight.com/features/black-panther-is-groundbreaking-but-its-shuri-who-could-change-the-world/ (accessed on 10 September 2018).

hooks, Bell. 2009. *Reel to real.* New York: Routledge Classics.

Iyer, Niranjana. 2017. Queen of Katwe. *Herizons.* pp. 42–43. Available online: https://www.questia.com/magazine/1P4-1991944384/queen-of-katwe (accessed on 10 September 2018).

Kellner, Douglas. 2003. Cultural studies, multiculturalism, and media culture. In *Gender, Race, and Class in Media: A Text Reader*, 2nd ed. Edited by Gail Dines and Jean. M. Humez. Thousand Oaks: Sage Publications, pp. 9–20.

Lester, Neal A. 2010. Disney's the princess and the frog: The pride, the pressure, and the politics of being a first. *The Journal of American Culture* 33: 294–308. [CrossRef]

Moffitt, Kimberly R., and Heather E. Harris. 2014. Of negation, princesses, beauty, and work: Black mothers reflect on Disney's the princess and the frog. *Howard Journal of Communications* 25: 56–76. [CrossRef]

Directed by Mira Nair. Produced by John Carls and Lydia Dean Pilcher. Screenplay by William Wheeler. Burbank: Walt Disney Pictures.

Parasecoli, Fabio. 2010. A taste of Louisiana: Mainstreaming Blackness through food in the princess and the frog. *Journal of African American Studies* 14: 450–68. [CrossRef]

Pellerin, Marquita. 2012. Defining Africana womanhood: Developing an Africana womanism methodology. *The Western Journal of Black Studies* 36: 76–85.

Sandlin, Jennifer A., and Julie G. Maudlin. 2015. Disney's pedagogies of pleasure and the eternal recurrence of whiteness. *Journal of Consumer Culture.* [CrossRef]

Shattuck, Kathryn. 2017. Queen of Katwe. *New York Times*, April 25, p. C9.

Thompson, Rachel. 2018. How Shuri from 'Black Panther' Is Inspiring Young Women in STEM, 29 June 2018. Available online: https://mashable.com/article/letitia-wright-interview/#k7npVCi2cmqP (accessed on 10 September 2018).

Veenstra, Gerry. 2013. The gendered nature of discriminatory experiences by race, class, and sexuality: A comparison of intersectionality theory and the subordinate male target hypothesis. *Sex Roles* 68: 646–59. [CrossRef]

Windsong, Elena A. 2016. Incorporating intersectionality into research design: An example using qualitative interviews. *International Journal of Social Research Methodology* 21: 135–47. [CrossRef]

social sciences

MDPI

Article

Over Time and Beyond Disney—Visualizing Princesses through a Comparative Study in India, Fiji, and Sweden

Charu Uppal

Department of Geography, Media and Communication, Karlstad University, 65188 Karlstad, Sweden;
charu.uppal@kau.se

Received: 24 December 2018; Accepted: 23 March 2019; Published: 31 March 2019

Abstract: Disney animated princesses are broadcasted around the world through Disney Channel and its global affiliates as well as through numerous other networks that purchase distribution rights. In an attempt to provide diversity in the last 25 years, Disney has featured nonwestern princesses such as those in *Aladdin* (1992), *Pocahontas* (1995), *Mulan* (1998), and *Moana* (2016). This study examines how princesses in animated Disney movies are perceived and understood by girls (8–15 years) in three different countries, over two time-periods with a gap of nearly a decade (2009 and 2018). The primary research question, considering Disney's global reach, is how race, culture, and presence of a royal family interact with transnational access to the same media content in the perception of the princess concept and about being a girl. The selected countries provide an opportunity to explore differences in perception of Disney princesses between girls raised in countries with and without a royal family, and between girls in nonwestern and western countries. Differences in the perception are attributed to local and national cultures that allow a different lens to view the same content. A mixed method combining interviews, focus groups, and participant-generated images was used to gather data in India, Fiji, and Sweden. Results indicate Disney princesses, with their ubiquitous presence in various formats, e.g., media content, costumes and school stationery, have created a uniform idea of beauty across countries. Princesses in Disney were perceived by participants as being Caucasian and American, regardless of the race or country they represented. Girls in India and Fiji did not identify with Jasmine or Mulan, whom they considered 'American', whereas girls in Sweden considered Jasmine and Mulan as princesses of nonwestern origin. Girls in India and Fiji did not think they could be princesses because of their skin color, and did not want to lead a life 'restricted with responsibilities', but girls in Sweden considered the same question from the place of a choice, i.e., they preferred not to lead a 'boring' and regulated life like that of a princess. Participants from Fiji, with the least access to domestic programming that showed girls of their same Fijian origin, were least likely to consider themselves capable of being a princess.

Keywords: Disney; girls; beauty; transnational media; princess

1. Introduction

The 'Disney Universe'[1] has captured audiences and consumers around the world for nearly a century. On its international website[2], the company that appeals mostly to children and young adults, lists nine online destinations, seven of which are regions or continents—Asia, Africa, Australia, Europe, North America, Latin America, and Middle East, and two of which are countries with large populations,

---

[1] As used in J. Wasko, 2001.
[2] http://www.disneyinternational.com.

India and Russia. The website lists India, a country of 1.3 billion people, with a growing market that consumes much media in English, as a separate market from Asia[3]. Each tab has a drop-down menu that takes the viewer to country and language-specific content. Each region is further divided into many subregions and countries. In essence, Disney is everywhere. If not in theatres, then it can be found on electronic screens that are omnipresent, or as logos and images, posters and book covers, theme designs for birthday cakes, and even professionally painted onto the walls of young children's rooms[4] (Figure 1).

Figure 1. Scenes from *Little Mermaid* on a wall in a house in India.

This study illustrates how Disney's global presence mainstreams views on being a girl. Disney's global presence has been critiqued both for perpetuating stereotypical images (England et al. 2011) and its potential impact on cultures, especially in countries lacking domestic programming that relies on western media content (Forman-Brunell and Hains 2014). Ubiquity of American media including Disney, and the absence of media rooted in native cultures can hamper young girls' identification with and taking pride in their own culture. Domestic audio-visual programming focusing on culturally relevant stories and folklore can potentially empower young girls to counter Disney's transnational but monocultural narrative (Nastasia and Uppal 2014). Countries that do not have a thriving domestic media industry present no competition to transnational media content. Not surprisingly, Fiji, a country which lacks domestic industry,[5] does not attract Disney's interest, and is missing from its international website, possibly because it is a small market and Disney is aware that lack of competition in the country ensures viewership.

Sweden, India, and Fiji, the locales of research for this study, provide a complex intertwining of variables which allow examining the role of Disney princesses on young girls' perceptions about being a girl. The three countries, as described in detail in the following sections, vary in culture, ethnicity, and use of transnational media.

---

[3] http://www.disneyinternational.com/#panel1i, accessed September 2018.
[4] The researcher had seen one such wall-painting in India.
[5] While Bollywood, the Hindi film industry of India, is prominent in Fiji, it is consumed mainly by Indo-Fijians who constitute less than 40% of the population, due to language constraints.

This comparative study examines data gathered through a participatory study on girls between 8 and 15 years of age in three different countries over two time periods nearly a decade apart—India and Fiji, in 2009, and Sweden in 2018. All three countries are democracies[6] with considerable differences, that function as variables. Sweden, a constitutional monarchy, has a modest media industry and leads in the use of internet and social media among the three countries. India, the largest democracy, has possibly the largest media industry, but without the same international appeal or reach as Disney. Fiji consumes mostly western media, with the exception of Indian media products mostly consumed by people of Indian diaspora. While India, a democracy since 1947, only opened its audiences to foreign media since economic liberalization in the 1990s, Sweden is a much older democracy that has a royal family and real-life princesses. Fiji, the smallest in population among the three, also has the least robust domestic media industry, where television was introduced as late as 1991. In addition, Sweden is largely a Caucasian country, whereas India has ethnic diversity that is known more by lingual and cultural rather than racial differences. Fiji, a multicultural country, constitutes several ethnicities of which Fijian and Indo-Fijans form over eighty percent.

By comparing data from two time periods and on three different continents, the study critically analyzes the intricate link between location/geography, exposure to Disney animated princesses, visualization of the concept of princess, and whether domestic cultures are articulated despite Disney's popularity and allow culturally representative images of princesses, a concept which is an important component of playtime for girls (Wohlwend 2009; Pollen 2011).

In creating brands and homogenizing appearances, Disney's depiction, bound by western ways of looking at the world, molds even the princesses of Chinese, Pacific, and Middle Eastern descent such that they are perceived to be western. For example, though Disney's *Pochahantas* and *Mulan* are considered atypical princesses that challenge stereotypical images in Disney, research suggests that nonwestern girls consider them western/American and do not identify with them (Lemish 2010; Nastasia and Uppal 2014, 2010). In comparison to Disney, a historically girl-oriented channel, Nickelodeon, is considered more balanced in providing programming for both girls and boys (Lemish 2010) with regard to screen time.[7]

Beyond catering to one gender over the other, scholars have argued that Disney's programming creates misconceptions of the real world. Schickel (1997) argued that Disney animated films in creating a world with dichotomous characters that can be divided into villains and heroes, promoted the values of upper class, and supported commercial enterprises. Scholars have likened the magical realm created in Disney movies to that of capitalism where labor and work remain hidden, and most do not seem to work for the 'necessities of life' (Dorfman and Mattelart 1975, p. 68), nor do they reflect realities of life (Wasko 2001). Furthermore, scholars have demonstrated a hierarchy in Disney, where masculinity and whiteness are presented as positive, strong, and central to the plots, and female characters are shown to be frail and shy (Lawrence 1986). Western values of individualism are upheld, as opposed to community and duty to the extent that nonwestern stories are altered to suit Disney's narrative (Limbach 2013). For example, in the ballad of Hua Mulan, the basis for Disney version of the story, the protagonist cross-dresses as a man with the help of her parents, but in the Disney rendition, she does so by breaking 'away from her family to find her identity' (p. 115); and while in the actual story, Mulan spends twelve years in training and fights several battles, in the movie, her screen time dressed as a man is comparatively short (Limbach 2013). Disney, wary of blurring the lines between male and female, not only limits Mulan's screen time dressed as a man, which could counteract concepts of gender as binary, but also portrays being a man as a more 'active' process in comparison to being a woman/girl (Limbach 2013, p. 119).

---

6   Although Fiji had its fourth coup in 2006, since then there have been two elections.
7   Although scholars have argued that even on Nickoldean shows featuring 'girls' often struggle between 'strong' vs. 'feminine' portrayal of girls (Hains 2007).

While Disney's universe is inhabited by diverse characters, Disney princesses have created a world that has captured girls' imagination around the world and now command their own website as a Disney brand[8]. Now worth over four billion USD, the brand was created in 2000, by the then- CEO after observing young girls dressed as princesses in homemade costumes when attending shows such as Disney on Ice (Pollen 2011). Stories of Disney princesses are woven into young girls' play and fantasy world, often supplemented with costumes referring to Disney princesses (Wohlwend 2009; Pollen 2011; Garabedian 2015). As Forman-Brunell and Hains (2014) state, "Princesses are everywhere there are girls" (p. xi), and Disney's multiple ventures supplement the princess culture with costumes and accessories to manifest a fantasy world. Childhood, suggest some scholars, is threatened by the 'childhood culture industry' (Pollen 2011), which now mass manufactures clothing, toys, and accessories connected with fantasy play, limiting options available for imaginative and performative play. While young girls dressing up is a practice as old as fairy tales, mass production and growth of the children's clothing market that manufactures fantasy costumes have driven demand for princess costumes. This trend of using costumes in play is also accompanied by a 'pinkification' of outfits and objects aimed at young girls (Pollen 2011). Pollen (2011) argues that though associating pink with girls is fairly recent, the trend towards 'pinkification' is so prominent that it is even considered to be an indicator of a biological imperative. In a survey conducted to understand the link between available fantasy (dressing-up) outfits for girls and the issue of agency in performative play and creation/performance of femininity, Pollen (2011) establishes that limits on playing/performing being a girl are woven into the fabrics, colors, and the designs of the costumes available to the girls, which are often purchased and promoted by parents themselves. Whether or not young girls perform femininity normatively (as outlined by Judith Butler), girls practicing agency during playtime can challenge stereotypical concepts of girlhood (Pollen 2011) and is considered 'appealing and confining' at the same time (Wohlwend 2009, p. 80). However, the motives for wearing pink or glittery outfits is an indication that the girls associate it with being pretty and with popular characters whom they want to emulate (Pollen 2011). Although childhood theorists stress that a child uses his/her agency just as much as an adult and is not always passively imitative (James et al. 1998; Clarke 2007; Wohlwend 2009), Pollen (2011) through her study demonstrates that designs, colors, and fabrics used for fantasy costumes limit that agency. For example, in the sample used to study various outfits used for play by young girls, 14 of 52 outfits were based on princess characters, where 12 out of 52 costumes were Disney characters (Pollen 2011). Disney's popularity has standardized the appearance of Disney princesses, unlike original story books with more imaginative and varied princess content. Merchandise then facilitates the emulation of Disney images e.g., wearing the appropriate outfit along with tiaras or wands, etc. (Pollen 2011). In fact, Disney's popularity is so prevalent that a study found no correlation between screen time spent watching Disney princess films and owning Disney Princesses products, implying that ownership of princesses merchandise was not dependent on exposure to Disney films (Golden and Jacoby 2018).

1.1. Standardization of the Princess Concept

The idea of royalty is embedded in the human psyche. 'Once there was a King' as several fables, fairy tales and historic stories begin in many cultures, usually evokes images of riches and luxury, even as it narrates trials and tribulations of a royal family. Addressing children as a prince or princess in most cultures is a form of endearment and a way of showing affection, although it can also imply someone who is pampered. Though the concept is universal, an authentic presentation of royalty must vary with culture, e.g., a crown, seen frequently in Disney movies featuring princesses, is not a universal marker of royalty. Similarly, long gowns, as featured in Disney, do not represent royal attire in many cultures. Famous princess tales such as Snow White and Cinderella, despite retaining plot and character names, were not uniformly drawn in picture books, which allowed for variation in the

---

8   https://princess.disney.com.

visualization of these princesses. Disney's portrayal of princesses has standardized their skin color, behavior, and appearance. Other than shaping the characterization of princesses, usually depicted as young girls with long hair, Disney's uniform presentation of princesses restricts a child's imagination and behavior. Scholars argue that Disney princesses in movies such as Frozen (Elsa), despite being acclaimed as a norm-breaker for being independent (Garabedian 2015) have not learnt the value of interconnectedness of human relationships (Stehn 2018). Elsa, while embracing her authentic self, does so at the expense of personal relationships, which can be equally detrimental as forgoing self for relationships (Stehn 2018). Princess stories and fairytales are also usually connected to being Caucasian since historically 'power and privilege' are linked to being white (Dundes and Streiff 2016). Since white princesses fare better and are more successful in Disney princesses' movies than princesses of color (Dundes and Streiff 2016) young audiences associate princesses with being white. Young girls often translate what they see on screen into their playtime by enacting the scenes with the figurines sold by Disney (Wohlwend 2009; Garabedian 2015) and therefore, the appearance and behavior of Disney princesses are a significant influence on young girls.

1.2. Sweden, Royal Family, Princesses, Media, and Disney

Sweden, the largest among the Nordic countries, and the third largest country in Western Europe, combines a constitutional monarchy and a parliamentary form of government, although since 1975, the royal family only serves a ceremonial role and has no executive powers (Rehmann 2010; Åse 2013; Jönsson and Lundell 2009). Although until recently, the queen was recognized for her beauty and her role of providing a male heir, since 1980, the imperative of a male heir has been removed and made gender neutral, implying that it is the first born and not the first male who is the heir to the throne (Åse 2013).

Often ranked quite high in media freedom, until the mid-1980s, Swedish TV and radio were a government monopoly with strict policies against commercialization. The policies that protected Swedish airwaves from an onslaught of foreign programming have gradually been relaxed and currently the majority of content on television, including the public television, is imported. Just as with any other country, despite reservations, the majority of programming on Swedish screens, other than public broadcasting, is American. Sweden's national Donaldist society, simply called the 'Duck' (Wasko 2001), has incorporated Disney into mainstream entertainment for decades; for example, *Kalle Anke* (Donald Duck) is staple viewing for families on Christmas eve.

Sweden, a country that prides keeping its traditions alive, often celebrates the royal family by covering it in their media. Some scholars argue that royal families, including that of Sweden, function like a 'corporate heritage brand' (Balmer 2011) where consumers, i.e., commoners, are linked to observances that connect them to a sense of continuity and a collective past (Otnes and Maclaran 2015). Media plays an increasingly significant role in how royal weddings reach the public and maintain the myth of centrality of royal family in the lives of Swedes (Widestedt 2009). How royal families are mediated also impacts the way gender, nation, and family life are defined in the country (Åse 2013). In the last decade, Sweden has witnessed three royal weddings, all of which were highly anticipated and nationally televised (Åse 2013). However, a significant change from royal weddings of previous generations is that all the three royals—two princesses and one prince—married commoners, as has also happened in some Disney films. One of the variables explored in the study is influence of exposure to a real-life royal family in perceiving the princess concept. Would growing up in a country with a royal family bring a more realistic understanding of princesses and their lives?

1.3. India, Fiji, Royal Families, and Disney

Though historically both India and Fiji[9] have had princesses, or similar entities, both countries have chosen to be democracies with multiparty systems, thereby passing the role for playing princesses to celebrities. Although both India and Fiji have in the past had royal families, the tradition has been discontinued, as India became independent and Fiji ceded power to the British. Any mention of royalty or monarchy therefore happens in folktales, history, and textbooks. Disney princesses, however, have a strong presence in both the countries, where movies are released regularly, and images of Disney princesses are found in objects of everyday use for young girls such as stationery and notebooks. While India has a thriving domestic media industry, Fiji is mostly dependent on transnational media, which often originates in nonwestern countries and primarily comes from the US. However, the Indian media industry has taken a turn towards westernization as well as seen a proliferation of domestic programming in the 1980s, while Indian television has also featured several series with princesses and royalty. Disney India Limited began as a joint venture with Modi enterprises in 1993 and a decade later became an independent channel broadcasting in three Indian languages, as well as English. Relaxed rules for media and broadcasting since the liberalization of the Indian economy made it possible for Disney movies to be released at the same time as in the United States, which earlier were either never released on screens in India[10] or screened years after their original release. A content analysis conducted in 2007 based on 102 hours of recorded programming established that 84% of India's children programming was imported and only 16% was local/domestic (Götz and Lemish 2012). By 2009, when the data were collected in India and Fiji, Disney movies featuring princesses and royalty, such as *Aladdin, Little Mermaid, Pocahontas,* and *Mulan,* had been released. When the study was conducted in 2009, both Indian and Fijian children had been exposed to Disney princesses for several years.

2. Media Use Among Children and Youth

Any study conducted today with regard to potential influence of media viewing must also consider the many ways the same content can be accessed. With the increased access to media, and ubiquity of mobile media, even in remote corners of the world, Disney's reach has increased multifold in the last decade. Since social media's affordances, i.e., forwarding, customizing media messages, and instant interaction, encourage increased screen time, parents and teens alike are concerned about their screen time and have taken measures to reduce it (Jiang 2018).

Scholars have long commented that the use of technology among young girls has become so common that it is central to expression of their identities (Turkle 2011). Even though by the early 2000s, young girls in urban India were already using the Internet to explore the world (Verma and Sharma 2003), smart phones were not yet prevalent. Participants in India and Fiji shared that they watched Disney movies either on a playback system or television.

Sweden, a country of nearly ten million, has over ninety-five percent penetration of smart phones in the 16–24 age range (Statistics Sweden 2018). Furthermore, in Sweden, where access to media is almost universal, as opposed to India and Fiji, there is little or no difference in the amount spent on various media platforms (International Data on Youth and Media 2017). A youth and media survey suggests that for ages between 13 and 29, smart phones are the most common mode of accessing media, followed by personal computers and television (International Data on Youth and Media 2017). Data suggest that although the frequency of using smart phones increased with age between 8 and 15 years, until 2014, neither smart phones nor tablets were used every day and stationary TV was more

---

9 Fiji has a history of coups, having gone through four coups as of 2006. However, in September of 2014, Fiji held a democratic election, which was deemed fair by international observers. Although the data in Fiji were gathered in 2009, it is important to note that the coup had no impact on reception and distribution of entertainment media.
10 Pirated versions only in English were usually available.

prevalent than WebTV (International Data on Youth and Media 2017), making this study significant in providing information on viewing habits and preferences of young girls. While animation remained the most watched programs worldwide, in Sweden by 2014, factual entertainment was preferred over animation and live TV was the most popular among children and youth (br.online.de).

The Internet, iPads, and laptops were well in use in 2009 when smart phones had not yet penetrated the market in both India and Fiji; therefore, movie viewing was restricted to VCRs, DVD, and television.

3. Main Research Question and Rationale

Considering Disney's global reach, the overarching research question for this study, is 'How do race, culture, and presence of a royal family interact with transnational access to the same media content (Disney Princesses) to influence the perception of being a girl?' The selected countries provide an opportunity to explore if there is a difference in perception of Disney princesses between girls raised in a country with and without a royal family, and between girls in nonwestern and western countries. Differences in the perception are attributed to local and national cultures that allow a different lens to view the same content. This paper compares the data collected in 2018 in Sweden with that from India and Fiji in 2009 to understand the shifts that have occurred in the way young girls perceive and consume princesses in animated Disney movies.

The rationale for comparison of data that is nearly a decade apart and in countries in with different cultures can be understood first by the global presence of Disney and its impact, as explained in the previous section, and by the use of a visual method in the study, i.e., drawing pictures of princesses, as explained in detail in the following section. By comparing research done in two time periods and on three different continents, the study critically analyzes the intricate links between location/geography, exposure to Disney animated princesses, and their perception. Culture, presence/absence of domestic media industry, presence/absence of a royal family are considered variables that may influence perception of Disney princesses. Analyzing data across time, the study attempts to understand the shifts that have occurred in the way young girls understand and consume princesses in animated Disney movies.

A secondary purpose of the study was to gather information on the viewing practices and way of accessing Disney princesses by young girls in 2018. Data from Fiji and India were collected at the cusp of the mobile media revolution, especially smart phones, so extra questions about media viewing were added for data collected in 2018.

4. Methodology: Mixed Method, Intersecting Factors, and Research Questions

4.1. Mixed Method

Data were gathered by combining three methodologies that complemented each other and compensate for the difference between cultures and ability to express. All the participants were asked to draw their version of a princess, followed by individual interviews and focus group discussions. This study, which compares data from 2009 to data gathered in 2018, conducts an in-depth analysis of drawings, and adds Sweden, as opposed to the US, as a representative of a western country. The 2009 study was conducted in India, Fiji, China, and the US did include drawings, but the final analysis focused more on participant interviews (Nastasia and Uppal 2010, 2014). The 2018 study which uses data collected in India and Fiji, replaces the US with Sweden, making the language variant a constant by only including countries that have languages other than English as their national language.

Participant-generated images: Considering the age range and culture differences in the sample, which can influence levels of articulation and methods of expression, participant-generated images (drawings) were included to allow expression without using language. Using this visual method is especially significant for working with young people because it empowers them by 'placing the agency literally in their own hands' (Literat 2013, p. 12) and increasing access to data without depending on language proficiency of the participants (Guillemin and Drew 2010). As an activity that is both playful and conducive to group activity, drawing is an efficient method that is ethically sound and can be applied across cultures (Literat 2013). In this particular study, drawings were used to transcend cultural differences and allow manifestation of local, culturally-appropriate images. A systematic analysis of drawings, can reveal a layered description of concepts, both emotional and cognitive, in a personally relevant manner (Literat 2013), which may be difficult to elicit if language were the only mode of communication.

4.2. Intersecting Factors

Considering the diversity of data, factors considered in analysis were identified before categorization and coding. The following factors were identified before data collection for comparing and contrasting: presence/absence of a royal family, geography, culture and dominant racial group in the country, language and presence of Disney and access to domestic and international media (Table 1).

Table 1. Variables considered in the study.

	Sweden	India	Fiji
Ethnicity and Culture	Mostly Caucasian	Indian—Indians are a mix of ethnicities and are not classified as one single race.	Fijian, Indo-Fijian, Other Pacific Islanders, Chinese and other minorities.
Domestic Media	Modest Domestic Industry	Robust domestic media industry, but present media products are highly influenced by western media norms. By mid 2000s, over 80% of children's programming was imported	Minimal domestic media industry
Transnational Media	All media directed at children is either in Swedish or dubbed in Swedish	Media for children is available in a variety of Indian languages, including English.	Most of the content for children is imported and broadcasted in English without any subtitles. There is a small amount of local programming for children in three national languages English, Fijian and Hindi.
Form of Government	A democracy since 1917	A parliamentary democracy since 1947	Fiji has had four coups since 1987. Since its last election in 2014 was deemed credible by international media, it currently classifies itself as a democracy.

Presence/Absence of Royal family: Royal families both in India and Fiji have been discontinued but Sweden maintains a Royal family which is regularly featured in the national media. Exposure to a real-life royal family in media was considered a factor of consequence in how girls between 8 and 15 perceived Disney princesses. Would the real-life experience allow for more realistic understanding of the princess concept?

Ethnicity, race, and culture: Geography was a significant consideration in this study. Ethnicity and race are autogenerated factors as a result of location of the three countries. Race, although not categorically defined in Fiji, India, and Sweden, all of which are multiethnic, varies in predominance.

Participants from Fiji had the least access to programming in their native language as compared to participants from India and Sweden. Sweden, although a multiethnic nation, is predominantly a Caucasian country, which makes it easy for the majority to identity with programming from western countries. In addition, since all the non-Swedish programming in Sweden is subtitled in Swedish, it provides a semblance of watching programming that is culturally similar. Although 'Indian' is not a race, it does present a different ethnicity from that of Fiji and Sweden, in addition to having access to domestic programming in several Indian languages featuring people of Indian descent. Disney has released several princess of color in the last 25 years. How does diversity in Disney's princess movies influence perception of princesses in countries that vary in production of domestic and culturally relevant programming? Do Disney's attempts at diversity empower girls to isolate their culture from global/transnational culture? Does that empowerment vary with ethnicity and race? Is the local/national culture reflected in the participant-generated images?

Language & Presence of Disney: Access to Disney princesses in native language is another factor that can influence perception of Disney princesses. Fijian participants, who spoke both Fijian and English, could watch Disney only in English. Indian participants in this study were conversant in Hindi and English and had access to Disney princess movies in both languages. In Sweden, where all programming for children is dubbed in Swedish, participants had watched Disney princesses only in Swedish. Fiji was the only country in the study where Disney animated films were not dubbed into Fijian or Hindi, the two widely spoken languages in the country, other than English. Does watching Disney movies in one's own language make a difference in how being a girl is perceived?

Access to media/technology: Compared to Sweden, both in India and Fiji, access to technology is not uniformly distributed. To ensure access to transnational media, participants were limited to the middle class who had access to a home play-back system and cable. While the concept of middle class is relative, participants in India and Fiji were from families that had stable income, both parents were college-educated, and lived in capitals. While Disney's popularity is not restricted to any class, selecting a sample from the middle class ensured that the participants had consumed both Disney movies and products bearing the Disney brand. Data for Sweden, gathered in 2018, where rural–urban divide in media access is not as prominent, were gathered in Karlstad, a town of about 100,000 people, a three hour train-ride from the capital. The population in Sweden[11] not only has near universal media access, but also more purchasing power for media technology, such as smartphones, laptops, tablets, etc.

4.3. Research Questions

The following secondary research questions were isolated from the overarching research question, which were then explored through data gathered for the study.

- **RQ#1:** Considering Disney princesses are a global presence, how do the girls from countries that have had traditions of royalty (India and Fiji) in the past imagine princesses today? (drawings and interviews).
- **RQ#2:** Does Disney's way of coloring and drawing the world of princesses (young girls drawn in primary colors, smiles, long dresses, and other accessories) influence young girls in their imagination and visualization of princesses? Does that vary in countries with different histories and cultures? (via drawings). Does that influence concepts of girlhood? (via interviews).
- **RQ#3:** How do girls between 8 and 15 receive Disney princesses in a country that has a real-life royal family (Sweden)? (drawings) What roles do girls in a country with a real-life monarchy see princesses playing in real life, as compared to Disney princesses? (interviews).
- **RQ#4:** Has young girls' way of visualizing princesses changed over time, since Disney has released several nonwestern princesses in the last decade?
- **RQ#5:** How do girls (8–15) visualize princesses in the age of social media? Has the introduction of digital media influenced how the concept of a princess is consumed, understood, and applied?

5. Sample and Data Collection

The sample, in all the countries, was divided into three subgroups of 8–10, 11–12, and 13–15, each with a minimum of five participants to allow for homogeneity of cognitive and expressive abilities in each group. In Fiji, where Fijians are the majority, the selected sample was restricted to girls of Fijian descent to allow a dataset least exposed to culturally relevant programming depicting characters with

---

[11] Sweden, among the three countries has the least wage and wealth gap between professions.

racial and cultural similarities. Girls of Fijian descent among all the three countries were also most exposed to transnational media, and characters who neither looked Fijian nor reflected Fijian culture.

Recruitment and Data Collection: Participants were recruited through personal contacts. Legal guardians of the participants were informed about the study through a written document. Those who volunteered to participate were invited to sign the consent forms. On the day of the study, participants and their guardians were invited to the research venue, offered light snacks, and encouraged to clear any doubts. Thereafter, participants were invited to a large meeting room, provided with pencils, plain sheets, and colors and asked to draw their version of a princess. No special instructions were given except, 'Draw what you think a princess looks like'. Only in Sweden, where the participants had reference to national princesses, were participants asked to give a name and age to the drawing, whereas in India and Fiji, the question was incorporated in focus groups. Since the participants were allowed to draw as many images they wished, the final number of drawings was greater than the number of participants, and the total number of drawings in each country was different. A total of 63 drawings, 16 from India, 26 from Fiji, and 21 from Sweden, were analyzed. One participant at a time was invited for an individual interview in a separate room to allow privacy, while the rest of the group continued drawing. Once all the individual interviews were complete, a focus group with all the participants was conducted. In all countries, the author was present at all the interviews. Research associates fluent in Fijian, Swedish, and Hindi were hired and were present at all the interviews. In addition to English, the author is fluent in Hindi and has intermediate fluency in Swedish.

In India and Fiji, where media access is not universal, the study began with a short viewing of clips of Mulan, Jasmine, and Pocahontas[12], to ensure fresh memories of the Disney princesses with nonwestern heritage and the critical events they go through in the movies.

Interviews and focus groups: A standard set of questions was used in all the countries, with some added questions on access to technology and use of mobile media in Sweden. The age group 8–15 is impressionable, when both peers and media can have significance influence on self-perception (Blowers et al. 2003). Studying this age group can reveal how the princess concept is accepted, rejected, or critiqued by different age groups. Since 8–15 are crucial years when gender roles are learnt and a self-image is developing, it was important to ask questions about how the concept 'princess' was perceived by the participants. Individual interviews began with questions that could be broadly categorized into three: What do the participants understand by being a girl (Who is a princess? What does a princess grow up to be? Does a princess have friends?) How do girls perceive Disney princess (How does a princess appear, and behave with other people?) Does the girls' perception of princesses influence identifying with them? (What age did you start watching Disney princess films? Does a princess go to school? What kind of a school does a princess go to? How does she behave at school? Who is your favorite princess? Why/Why not? What do you like/dislike about a princess? Would you like to change anything about any of the Disney princesses? Would you like to be or have you ever wanted to be a princess? Do you think you could be a princess?').

Questions for focus group discussions were altered in the context of each country. In India and Fiji, where a movie clip-screening was held, participants were prompted to compare nonwestern princess, i.e., Mulan, Pocahontas, and Jasmine, to explore how nonwestern girls viewed Disney's representation of nonwestern princesses. In Sweden, where participants were not exposed to Disney movie clips, girls were asked if they knew of any nonwestern or ethnic Disney princess. Culture-specific follow-up questions were asked in each country, e.g., How do you compare real life princesses to Disney princesses (Sweden), Can you name a princesses from your country (India and Fiji). Since data from Sweden was gathered in 2018 in a different technological environment than 2009, an added

---

[12] Moana, the first ever princess from the South Pacific was not released until 2016.

emphasis was placed on the use of technology, viewing experience, reasons for preference of a platform such as computer, phone, TV, iPad etc. to access media during focus groups.

During the recordings, the primary researcher confirmed with the research associate to ensure that the correct follow-up questions were being asked. Both individual interviews and focus groups were recorded and transcribed. Transcriptions of interviews were tabulated after analyzing patterns, themes, and trends, within the context of geography, culture, and access to media. Images were subjected to a similar analysis, coding, and categorization which is explained in the following section.

6. Coding and Categorization

Drawings: To analyze sketches and gather images conjured up by the word 'princess', it was necessary to create categories that would compensate for differences in drawing abilities of the participants, while revealing meaningful patterns and themes that answered research questions, without requiring explanation from participants. Categories were created and the data were tabulated, after a systematic examination. Primary categories were: *main colors* used in the drawings—to examine what colors stand out prominent for the participants when conceiving a princess; *outfit* that the princess was wearing—categorized as long/medium/short dress that went down to the ankles, knees, or above the knees, respectively: to examine how a princess is depicted as formal, semiformal, or informal; the *color of hair*, black, brown, yellow (blonde), orange/red, or other. Artificial color such as green or blue, was put into the 'other' category; *Facial expression*—whether or not the princesses had a smile on her face, to investigate how happy a princess was perceived: coded with two values, yes/no; *skin color*, which was coded with four values, no color (wherever skin was left empty) and light (usually pink), yellow, brown/black, and other (tanned, orange, red, etc.): this was to assess if any race had been assigned to the princess. In the final analysis, light and no color were combined as portraying 'light skin'; *crown/headdress/head-jewelry*, evaluated by three values, yes or no and somewhat (clips, bows, decoration in hair). The category 'somewhat', a value given to head jewelry, received half the value of either crown or head-dress: to associate a certain position that made a princess stand out from civilians; and *accessories*: to study if any special accessories were presented with the drawing, e.g., wand, sash, extra jewelry, or similar objects. Finally, notes were taken about anything extra that was drawn. Since no specific instructions for drawing were given, each detail drawn also indicated an association with being a princess and assigning a status to the figure in the drawing. Two girls in Sweden drew cats, when asked to draw princesses, which, although included in the analyses, could not be judged on some aspects such as facial expression.

7. Results and Analysis

At this juncture, it is important to emphasize that the study is not implying a causal connection. However, since the study focuses on the concept of princesses, and specifically asked the participants about Disney princesses, the analysis thus concentrates on Disney's portrayals of princesses in particular, and examines how it is reflected in the drawings. Interviews and focus groups are used to further delve into the issue to explore any transference of, embodiment of, preference for values and characteristics represented by Disney princesses and explore new insights into the use of technology and access to Disney princesses.

Drawings: Despite the geographical diversity of the participants, and data that were collected nearly a decade apart, drawings from participants not only resembled Disney princesses, but also were more similar than different from each other (Figures 2–5). There was a noticeable commonality in drawings between data sets from 2009 and 2018, a period during which Disney released several movies with a princess of color with light skin (RQ#2 & RQ#4). The consistent increase in the number of nonwhite princesses since Jasmine (Aladdin, 1992), however, has not replaced images of popular white princesses in Disney, that have a much older and global presence. The majority of participants from all countries drew princesses either with light skin or no skin color, leaving the skin as 'white', the color of the sheet provided during the study, with no noticeable difference between the data collected in 2009 and 2018 (Table 2, Figures 2, 3 and 6 (2009), Figures 4 and 5 (2018)). Of all the participants, across all age groups in India and Fiji, two countries where light skin, akin to many Disney princesses such as Snow White or Cinderella, is rare, only two participants in India and none in Fiji, drew princesses with brown skin. In Sweden, where the majority of the population is Caucasian, even the mixed-race/nonwhite participants drew princesses with light skin color Figures 4, 5, 7 and 8 (2018). Participants in Fiji, a country with negligible domestic media content in Fijian, did not visualize princesses as people of color (Figures 2 and 9–12 (2009); Table 2; Figures 6 and 13), and some participants shared in interviews that they were too dark to be a princess themselves.

In Fiji, despite viewing movie clips of nonwestern princesses, six of the 11 girls in the 8–10 years group and three of ten in the 13–15 years group drew the Little Mermaid with long red hair, two participants in the 11–12 age group titled their drawing Sleeping beauty, and one in the same age group called hers a Cinderella, indicating the popularity of these movies (Figure 2) (RQ#2). None of the participants in Fiji, where straight hair is rare among Fijian girls, drew princesses with curly hair (Figures 11 and 12). Instead, medium to long straight hair was common, three of 26 drawings had blonde hair and eight of the nine mermaids drawn had red hair, none of which are Fijian traits (Figures 9 and 10) (RQ#2). One image in Fiji (Figure 11) had long blonde hair that almost covered the whole image. Similarly, Figure 3 from India and Figure 7 from Sweden show similarly prominent yellow hair. Although only one of 16 drawings of princesses from India had blonde hair, seven of 16 were drawn with auburn or brown hair, rather than black, the more common hair color in India (Figures 6 and 13) (RQ#2).

Figure 2. Fiji Sleeping Beauty 8–10.

Figure 3. India Crown Blonde 8–10.

Figure 4. Sweden 8–10.

Figure 5. Sweden 8–10.

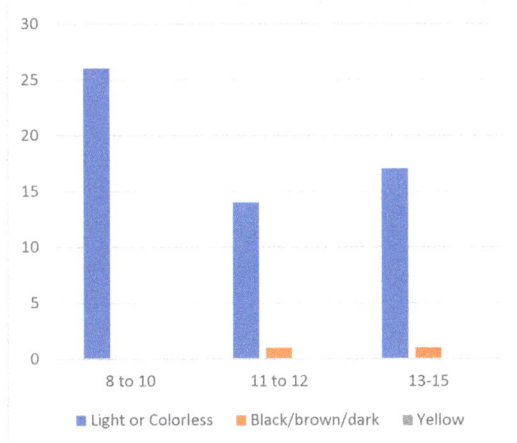

Figure 6. An overwhelmingly large number of girls across cultures drew princesses with light skin color. (The following table that was created after adding all data points from three countries, illustrates how across all age groups and in all countries, light colored princesses outnumbered tan or dark princesses.).

Table 2. Despite the fact that between 2009 and 2018, several Disney princesses of color were released, participants in 2018 drew more princesses with light than dark skin color. Following table shows the percentage of light-colored princesses drawn across countries, age, and years.

	Year 2009 Fiji	Year 2009 India	Year 2018 Sweden
8 to 10	100	67	83
11 to 12	100	83	100
13 to 15	100	83	88

Notes: The percent of princesses that were drawn with light skin by country.

Figure 7. Sweden, Business wear & Crown 13–15.

Figure 8. Sweden 8–10 Business Wear & Crown.

Transnational media is critiqued for mainstreaming western beauty ideals, and aiding in deracinating young girls from their own culture. None of the participants in nonwestern countries, i.e., India and Fiji, drew princesses wearing traditional outfits, or with any cultural accessories such as anklets or nose ring for India and shell or flower jewelry in Fiji, that represented their respective national cultures (RQ#1). Both in India and Fiji, not only were all the princesses drawn in western outfits or as mermaids, indicating a trend towards deracination and westernization, but also many drawings were made with long formal gowns, similar to the ones that Disney princesses wear (Figures 2, 9–11, 14 and 15) (RQ#1&2). No drawing in India, a country where wearing a saree is still an everyday affair, and many shows on TV portray princesses and queens in sarees, was drawn with a saree. No drawing from Fiji represented sulu-chamba, the traditional attire for Fijian women, indicating that the girls equated princesses with being western. In Sweden, where participants were exposed to real life princesses, about half of the total selected sample drew princesses in dresses categorized as 'medium dress' that were not formal gowns, but with a crown, indicating participants' experience with the princesses who follow a dress code for the length of dresses worn for business (Figures 7 and 8) (RQ#2 & RQ#3). However, participants in Sweden also conceived of princesses as being much younger than the both of the current princesses in Sweden. When asked to give an age and a name for the princess drawn, only one participant (from the 11–12-year group) stated 30, whereas most participants placed princesses between 10 and 20 years of age. About half of the participants identified their princesses as a teenager, closer to how Disney princesses are presented. Even the 'cat princesses', drawn with a youthful look of flowers on their head (Figure 16) were given 'two animal' years, making them teenagers. At the time of this study, Swedish princesses, Princess Victoria and Princess Madeline, who are regularly featured in Swedish media were 41 and 36, respectively. None of the princesses were given the same name as either of the Swedish princesses, and none except one was given a name from a Disney princess, Belle (RQ #3). Possibly taking a cue from the Swedish word 'Kronprincessa' crown princess—crowns featured more prominently in drawings by Swedish participants than in India and Fiji. Even though during the interviews several participants stated that the princesses usually feel restricted by the rules they have to follow, out of 63 drawings in total, forty were drawn with a clearly visible smile (Figures 3, 7, 9, 10 and 14), indicating a sign of happiness and prosperity as Disney princesses are usually shown by the end of a movie. Distribution of the four categories of long gowns, smile, crown, and light skin, as shown in Figure 13, illustrates that girls in Fiji, who had least amount of access to media in Fijian, drew princesses far removed from their lived experience, mostly with light skin.

Figure 9. Fiji Mermaid 8–10.

Figure 10. Fiji Mermaid 13–15.

Figure 11. Fiji Long Hair 13–15.

Figure 12. Fiji Straight Hair 11–12.

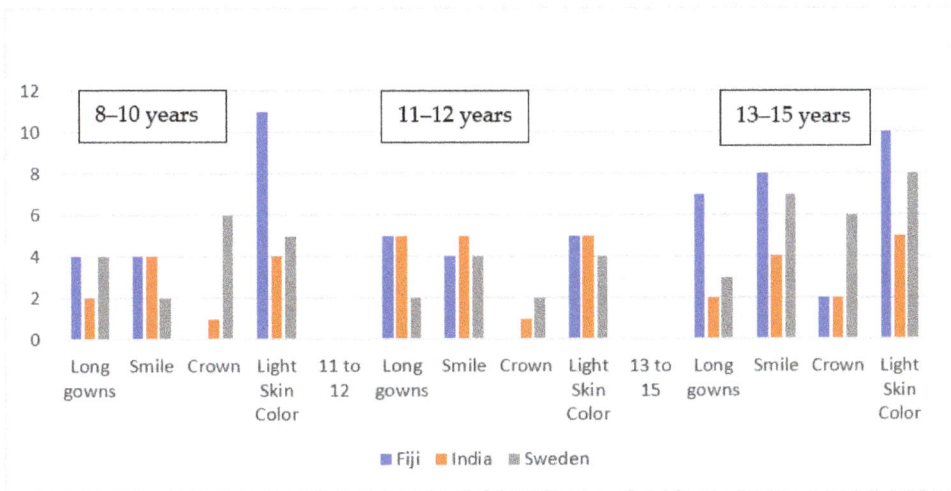

Figure 13. The distribution of four categories across drawings. (Long gowns, Smile, Crown, and Light Skin.).

Figure 14. India, Gown & Wand 13–15.

Figure 15. India, Gown 13–15.

Figure 16. Sweden Cat Princesses 8–10.

Many participants in Fiji and India were not familiar with *Aladdin*, *Mulan*, and *Pocahontas* before the study, but almost all had seen classic Disney princess, namely Cinderella and Snow White, which explains why heels and wands were the most common accessories drawn in both the countries. The three main colors used across the countries were pink, red, and blue, followed by yellow and green (RQ#2). Black, a color often used in Disney movies to depict evil, was used the least in dresses or accessories. No princess was drawn wearing trousers, even in India, where loose trousers are both casual and formal wear.

Interviews and focus groups: Participants in all three countries shared that Disney princess viewing had been a part of their childhood viewing from before they could remember. Both in India and Fiji, girls between 13 and 15 stated that they were slightly old for discussion on Disney princesses. In Sweden, girls of all age groups (2018) expressed that Disney princess movies were for girls in preschool, indicating an increase in availability of diversified age-specific media. Analysis of focus group and individual interviews identified popularity of Disney, and certain assumptions and trends, related to idea of princesses and being a girl, and media viewing, respectively.

Disney's popularity: Disney was equally popular in the three countries. Classic Disney princesses, such as Snow White, Cinderella, Sleeping Beauty, and the Little Mermaid, were more popular in all the three countries than Mulan, Pocahontas, or Jasmine. Snow White, Cinderella, and Sleeping Beauty were mentioned by participants of all age groups in the three countries. It is important to note that several girls in India and Fiji had not watched Mulan or Pocahontas. However, most participants were familiar with other princesses not mentioned in the briefing, e.g., Cinderella, Snow White, and

Sleeping Beauty, which have been part of popular culture much longer and before the creation of Disney movies. Princesses of color, such as Mulan, Jasmine, and Pocahontas, were not as popular in any of the countries as Cinderella and Snow White (RQ#1). Since 2009, Disney princesses have also been released as feature films, which participants of all age groups in Sweden preferred over animated versions ('I like to watch real people' (8–10, Sweden)).

Beauty, luxury, and youth: The most common feature in defining a princess in the three countries in all age groups was beauty and luxury. Princesses were defined as belonging to royalty, being the daughter of a King and a Queen, who lived in palaces, had expensive things, and wore fine and expensive dresses. Responses such as 'They will marry a prince' (13–15, India), 'They are waiting to be saved by a prince' (13–15, Sweden), 'They like boys, because they are always with a prince' (13–15, Fiji) indicated how girls in the 13–15 age group in all countries considered a prince and marriage being significant to princess's identity. A reflection of age (13–15) when the participants interest in the opposite sex is increasing, the need for a prince was expressed differently in each country. In India, the focus was on marriage, in Sweden on princesses' helplessness in Disney movies, and in Fiji, the focus was on socialization. This difference also reflects cultural differences; for example, Sweden's commitment to gender equality encourages girls to be self-reliant, weddings and marital status are significant in India, where many Bollywood movies use wedding as a plot, and in Fiji culture, social standing is significant in everyday socialization. This, however, does not imply that no girls in Sweden wish for a marriage/long term commitment, or that girls in India and Fiji are not encouraged to be self-reliant.

Consistent with drawings, girls in all countries associated princesses to be young girls, no more than 21 years of age, with the exception of one participant in Sweden who listed a princess age of 30.

Being a girl: When asked which princess they thought represented their country, most participants in India and Fiji did not have a response, although some pointed at Jasmine being relatable. Girls in Sweden (8–11) said that Elsa from Frozen seemed like a Nordic princess because she was surrounded by snow and fjords. Responses to question about learning from a Disney princess varied by age, despite several common factors. Age groups 8–10 and 11–12 in all countries stated they could learn to be kind, polite, and brave. However, both in India and Fiji, girls added qualities of learning how to dress up and look nice. A participant in Fiji stated (after viewing Disney princesses) 'now I ask my parents to buy me more dresses' (8–10 year, Fiji). Both 11–12 and 13–15 age groups in all the countries were critical of princesses and stated that they were not real people, 'only cartoons, only stories'. Both the age groups in all the countries also recognized that princesses had little freedom, and their lives seemed boring. When asked if princesses go to school, some girls in India and Fiji stated that 'princess do not need to learn anything because they would have servants for everything'. Indicating a low media profile kept by the Swedish Royal family, participants in Sweden in all age groups stated that they were not sure which school princesses attended but 'they are likely to attend a 'private or special schools or even be homeschooled' (11–12 Sweden).

Most participants across age groups and in all three countries denied wanting to be a princess, but reasons were different across age groups and between the countries. Some reasons, reflected even in drawings, seemed to coincide with images perpetuated by Disney movies, such as princesses being beautiful and light skinned. Standardization of beauty in Disney princess movies was reflected in responses and drawings from all countries. As many participants stated, 'princesses are beautiful, wear long dresses and have long hair'. Lived experience of participants was reflected in some of the responses. For example, girls in Sweden mentioned being 'blonde', as one of the qualities, more so than in India and Fiji. However, since beauty and wealth in nonwestern countries that were colonized is usually associated with being light-skinned (Ralson 1997; Glenn 2008), participants in India and Fiji, both colonized by the British, stated 'fair skin and long straight hair' as being princess traits. The most common responses in Fiji were 'I do not belong to a royal family, am not light skinned, and not as polite, so cannot be a princess.' (across all age groups in Fiji) Girls in both nonwestern countries emphasized skin color more than those in Sweden as a prerequisite for being beautiful (and how a princess was envisioned). In addition, girls in Fiji always had someone they knew was prettier than they, and more likely to be a princess, because she was 'slim, tall or long haired'. Disney's representation of princesses reinforces the same beauty ideals of the west and caucasianizes their lead characters in features, body traits, and mannerisms, even when they are not Caucasian. A participant in Fiji (11–12) stated 'Pocahontas is *palangi* (white), because of the way she talks'. Another participant in India (8–10) said that 'only Jasmine was Indian' among the three princesses they watched in the movie clips and 'Mulan and Pocahontas were American'.

In comparison, participants in Sweden, stated not wanting to be a princess because their lives would be boring. The concept of a royal's life being 'boring' may result from seeing real princesses' in official gatherings where they perform a merely ceremonial function, i.e., cutting a ribbon, shaking hands, etc. In many televised events, such as the Nobel Prize Ceremony, the royal family has a minimal role to play. However, one participant in Sweden (11–12) lamented that 'it was not fair that the media gets to talk about princesses' birthdays, while ordinary girls never have their birthdays celebrated on television.'

Girls in all countries, especially between the ages of 11 and 15, stated lack of freedom as one of the reasons for not wanting to be a princess; however, there was a sense of agency in participants from Sweden. The word 'beauty' was used more often in India and Fiji than in Sweden. Although characteristics identified for princesses were the same in all the three countries, e.g., long hair, dresses, and expensive jewelry, girls in Sweden did not label those characteristics as being 'beautiful'. Being Caucasian removed the pressure to be someone else in order to be labelled attractive, which is a colonial residue for many post-colonial states, where beauty is equated with having light skin.

Language and Culture: In countries with colonial history, the language of colonizers is associated with being sophisticated and well-educated. Participants in India preferred to speak in English during the interview.

Participants in India and Fiji, who watched movies in English, did not see much difference between Jasmine, Pocahontas, and Mulan, all of whom looked 'American'. 'Because they look, behave and talk like an American', was a common explanation, but they were considered different from 'Snow White, and Cinderella' because of their skin color.

Consistent with findings of an earlier study (Nastasia and Uppal 2014; Nastasia and Uppal 2010), girls in both the nonwestern countries, who watched movies in English considered all the nonwestern princesses as American, indicating that young girls did not recognize any Indian or Fijian or nonwestern traits in princesses of color. The earlier study that included participants from three nonwestern countries—India, China, and Fiji—and the US, established that princesses were considered synonymous with beauty in all four countries and across all age groups (Nastasia and Uppal 2010, 2014). However, participants from all three nonwestern countries considered Mulan and Pocahontas as American and not Chinese or Native American. Participants from the US, who were divided into four racial groups to explore how race and nationality influence participants' perception of Disney princesses[13], were 'color blind' and identified with Jasmine, Pocahontas, and Mulan regardless of race (Nastasia and Uppal 2010, 2014). This identification may be attributed to the participants being American and identifying with language, accent, and mannerisms, the same attributes that distanced girls in China, India, and Fiji from princesses of color, indicating that Disney princesses, regardless of their ethnicity, are perceived to be western and American. Girls both in India and Fiji stated that princesses of color such as Jasmine or Mulan were actually American. 'Jasmine's skin is like an American, but hair and face is like an Indian', said a Fijian participant (8–10) who watched the movie in English, and indicated that 'Jasmine behaved like an American'. A participant from India (8–10) stated that 'only Jasmine was Indian, but others (Mulan and Pocahontas) were American. In comparison,

---

[13] Participants in the US were chosen to represent Caucasian Americans, Native Americans, African Americans, and Chinese Americans.

girls in Sweden who watched the movies in Swedish considered Jasmine to be from Egypt and could pronounce 'Aladdin' appropriately, rather than with American pronunciation, as it is in the English version. The language in which movies are viewed seems to have had an influence, because viewing movies in English, for girls whose first language was not English, made the girls feel the characters were American and distant from them. Disney movies have been critiqued for using accents inconsistently and inappropriately, e.g., several negative characters have non-American accents, and orthodox or old-fashioned characters such as the Sultan in Aladdin are depicted with a non-American accent, even though his daughter, the lead in the movie, talks with an American accent. Such creative liberties use accents to label characters as progressive, evil, or orthodox, can be confusing for young viewers.

When asked to name princesses from their culture, girls from Fiji and India either had no response or took a long time to come up with historical names like 'Jhansi Ki Raani' (India). Girls in India, where stories of several princesses have been made into TV series, did not consider Disney princesses and 'Indian' princess in the same category, because 'Indian princesses are always related to war, Disney princesses have their personal issues' (13–15, India) (RQ #1). One girl in Fiji named 'Princess Ruby' that she said she had read about in a book.

Responsibilities and Rights: Participants in all the countries articulated that princesses, despite being rich and leading a luxurious life, had responsibilities towards their 'people'. Girls in all countries emphasized kindness and responsibilities of a princess, but those in Sweden emphasized 'real work', e.g., attending meetings, representing the country to other countries, taking care of animals, etc. (RQ# 3). Understanding of princesses and their responsibilities both in India and Fiji were consistent with Disney's portrayal. However, participants in Sweden derived their understanding from coverage of the Swedish Royal family.

New media, New interaction, New princesses: Data from Statistics Sweden (2018) indicated new trends and directions in media viewing and media consumption. Participants in all age groups stated being too old for Disney movies; however, they shared their interest in the Disney princesses in feature films such as the recent Cinderella and Beauty and the Beast. 'They look like real people'. However, girls in the age group of 11–15 mentioned following several YouTubers, such as Terese Lindgren, who is also 'blonde, has many things, loves animals, and has nice things'. (RQ #5). When asked in the focus group, 'but don't you think that they have the same qualities you mentioned in Disney princesses?', the girls (13–15), responded, 'maybe, have not thought about it', but they considered the YouTubers to be 'real people' An earlier study (Lövheim 2011) has established popularity of young girl bloggers in Sweden, where bloggers conduct themselves with a certain distance and provide limited access to their blogs, much like royalty or celebrities, resulting in their popularity. Other shows mentioned by girls in Sweden, such as High School Musical and Soy Luna are also Disney productions and perpetuate the same concepts of being a girl, such as being beautiful and independent (RQ#5). Despite the change in media viewing, from TV and DVD playback in Fiji and India at the time of data collection (2009) to mobile media, such as iPads, Laptops, and smartphones, as the primary viewing platform in Statistics Sweden (2018) the concept of beauty and how a princess looks has not altered with time (RQ#5).

All age groups in Sweden indicated having access to mobile media and the internet. Girls in the 13–15 age group in Sweden stated that they had owned smart phones for four to six years and accessed media mostly on their phones. Multitasking, viewing several programs simultaneously while using snapchat was common among 13–15-year-olds. Most girls had access to Netflix on their phones and there was no restriction on screen time by their parents, but some participants indicated that they had school and house work-related chores that they needed to complete, which limited their screen time, indicating the role parents can play in regulating media usage.

8. Conclusions

Even though a causal connection between watching Disney and a specific way of viewing and organizing the world for its young viewers is not indicated, the ubiquity of and replication of images produced by Disney products clearly matters. In various media and materials in daily lives, e.g., movie characters, school supplies, outfits, wall hangings, bed-linen, toys, etc. and the drawings made by the participants, may provide alternative images of girlhood in many countries, especially in those with a paucity of domestic programming. What features constituted beauty, the visualization of princesses and factors seen as integral to being a girl were consistent between 2009 and 2018. Most prominently indicated as representing beauty were youth and light skin color. Being white and young was considered to be the norm of beauty, especially for nonwhite, nonwestern participants. Whiteness intertwined with girlhood in both Disney and other media and its use (by media) gets reinforced in the public with repetitive use, e.g., Projansky (2014) cites the use of a single image of a blonde girl to evoke sympathy about the Connecticut shooting in 2012, while both girls and boys, white and nonwhite children were affected by the incident. Even though it impacts both whites and nonwhites, whiteness, as perpetuated by media, becomes the face of an event/tragedy, making alternative faces/races invisible in the media, and therefore less likely to be recognized and able to evoke empathy. In 2014, Disney released the song 'Let it Go' from *Frozen* in 25 languages, and was critiqued for the fact that none of the Indian or African languages were included in the release.[14] Disney's portrayal of princesses, even princesses of color, seems be through a western lens, which does not allow girls of color to identify with the characters. Instead, girls in Fiji and India, despite having watched clips of Mulan, Jasmine, and Pocahontas, indicated that they did not possess the right qualities for being a princess, especially skin color, nor did they identify with any of the princesses, nor could they correctly place the countries to which the princesses belonged. Disney's depiction of princesses only provides surface diversity, which upholds norms of western beauty (light skin, long-straight-blonde hair) and western values (independence and self-reliance at the expense of personal relationships) (Limbach 2013; Garabedian 2015).

Presence of domestic media provided some alternative images from the home culture, e.g., participants in India who had access to images of young women who looked like them more than the participants in Fiji, drew more nonwhite princesses. Girls in Fiji, who were exposed to the most nondomestic media, expressed their inadequacy at being a princess the most. Beyond the language in which Disney movies are viewed, participants both in India and Fiji stated that they did not identify with Disney princesses. However, a significant impact of Disney movies was reflected in association of royalty/princesses with western outfits, as none of the participants from India and Fiji drew princesses in traditional Indian or Fijian outfits. Significance of culturally similar images and use of native languages in media products in building a positive self-image was reflected in responses and drawings by participants in Sweden who did not associate having light skin with being beautiful, modern or stylish as did girls in India and Fiji.

Disney's impact is not restricted to Disney animated princesses, because the company also creates celebrities who are presented as princesses for young girls to emulate, through shows such as Hanna Montana (Projansky 2014). The characteristics once identified with princesses are embodied by new, young, and technologically hip personalities on social media. These 'princess-like characters' who are 'kind, nice to animals, and want to share the things they have' are the new bloggers and YouTubers who personify the princess characteristics and become role models for young girls. The ideas of beauty and being a girl, perpetuated by Disney animated princesses, are now demonstrated by many vloggers, who are the new princesses sitting in their home studios talking directly to young girls on their personal phones. Disney has, over the last century, standardized beauty ideals, which are copied even by domestic media industries, as is evident in Indian media industry.

Today, media have an intimate presence in the lives of the young. As media scholars and critics continue to highlight the combined impact of the lack of domestic media in many nations, the ubiquity

---

[14] https://www.pri.org/stories/2014-01-24/no-room-african-or-indian-languages-disney-s-multilingual-version-let-it-go. PRI reporter Patrick Cox. 24 January 2014·6:30 p.m. EST. (accessed on 14 October 2018).

Soc. Sci. **2019**, *8*, 105

of the western English-speaking media and the narrow understanding of being a girl perpetuated by Disney princesses become more evident. The role of educators, parents, and caretakers must be considered in providing alternative activities that allow for realistic and culture-specific portrayals in empowering young girls.

Funding: The first part of this study conducted in 2009 was funded by Internationales Zentralinstitut Fur Das (IZI) Jugend-Und Bildungsfernserhen, Munchen, Germany.

Acknowledgments: The author would like to thank all those who assisted in research, transcription and interpretation for this project. Thanks are due to Ratan Chauddhary (India), Renuka Prasad and Ana Kitolelei (Fiji), and Jenny Jansdotter and Charlotta Fox (Sweden) for assistance with interpretation and transcription. I would also like to thank Diana Nastasia who was a collaborator on the 2009 part of the study and vital to the development, design and implementation of the study.

Conflicts of Interest: The author declares no conflict of interest.

References

Åse, Cecilia. 2013. Monarchical Manoeuvres: Gender, Nation and the Boundary Problem in Post-War Swedish Constitutional Development. *NORA—Nordic Journal of Feminist and Gender Research* 21: 172–86. [CrossRef]

Balmer, John M. T. 2011. Corporate Heritage Identities, Corporate Heritage Brands and the Multiple Heritage Identities of the British Monarchy. *European Journal of Marketing* 45: 1380–98. [CrossRef]

Blowers, Lucy C., Natalie J. Loxton, Megan Grady-Flesser, Stefano Occhipinti, and Sharon Dawe. 2003. The Relationship between Sociocultural Pressure to Be Thin and Body Dissatisfaction in Preadolescent Girls. *Eating Behaviors* 4: 229–44. [CrossRef]

Clarke, Alison. 2007. Coming of Age in Suburbia: Gifting the Consumer Child. In *Designing Modern Childhoods: History, Space and the Material Culture of Child*. Edited by Maria Gutman and Ning De Coninck-Smith. The Rutgers Series in Childhood Studies; New Jersey: Rutgers University Press, pp. 253–68.

Dorfman, Ariel, and Armand Mattelart. 1975. *How to Read Donald Duck*. New York: International General.

Dundes, Lauren, and Madeline Streiff. 2016. Reel Royal Diversity? The Glass Ceiling in Disney's Mulan and Princess and the Frog. *Societies* 6: 35. [CrossRef]

England, Dawn Elizabeth, Lara Descartes, and Melissa A. Collier-Meek. 2011. Gender Role Portrayal and the Disney Princesses. *Sex Roles* 64: 555–67. [CrossRef]

Forman-Brunell, Miriam, and Rebecca C. Hains, eds. 2014. *Princess Cultures: Mediating Girls, Imaginations and Identities. (Mediated Youth)*. New York: Peter Lang, vol. 18.

Garabedian, Juliana. 2015. Animating Gender Roles: How Disney Is Redefining the Modern Princess. *James Madison Undergraduate Research Journal* 2: 22–25.

Glenn, Evelyn Nakano. 2008. Yearning for Lightness: Transnational Circuits in the Marketing and Consumption of Skin Lighteners. *Gender & Society* 22: 281–302. [CrossRef]

Golden, Julia C., and Jennifer Wallace Jacoby. 2018. Playing Princess: Preschool Girls' Interpretations of Gender Stereotypes in Disney Princess Media. *Sex Roles* 79: 299–313. [CrossRef]

Götz, Maya, and Dafna Lemish, eds. 2012. *Sexy Girls, Heroes and Funny Losers: Gender Representations in Children's TV around the World. Frankfurt am Main*. New York: Peter Lang.

Guillemin, Marilyn, and Sarah Drew. 2010. Questions of Process in Participant-Generated Visual Methodologies. *Visual Studies* 25: 175–88. [CrossRef]

Hains, Rebecca C. 2007. Inventing the Teenage Girl: The Construction of Female Identity in Nickelodeon's My Life as a Teenage Robot. *Popular Communication* 5: 191–213. [CrossRef]

International Data on Youth and Media. 2017. BR Current Surveys and Research Compiled by Heike vom Orde (IZI) and Dr. Alexandra Durner. Available online: http://www.br-online.de/jugend/izi/english/International%20Data%20on%20Youth%20and%20Media.pdf (accessed on 30 September 2018).

James, Allison, Chris Jenks, and Alan Prout. 1998. *Theorizing Childhood*. Repr. Cambridge: Polity Press.

Jiang, Jingjing. 2018. *How Teens and Parents Navigate Screen Time and Device Distract*. Washington: Pew Research Center, Available online: http://www.pewinternet.org/2018/08/22/how-teens-and-parents-navigate-screen-time-and-device-distractions/ (accessed on 20 September 2018).

Jönsson, Mats, and Patrik Lundell, eds. 2009. *Media and Monarchy in Sweden*. Göteborg: Nordicom.

Lawrence, Elizabeth A. 1986. In the Mick of Time Reflections on Disney's Ageless Mouse. *The Journal of Popular Culture* 20: 65–72. [CrossRef]

Lemish, Dafna. 2010. *Screening Gender on Children's Television: The Views of Producers around the World*, 1st ed. London and New York: Routledge.

Limbach, Gwendolyn. 2013. You the Man, Well, Sorta: Gender Binaries and Liminality in Mulan. In *Diversity in Disney Films: Critical Essays on Race, Ethnicity, Gender, Sexuality and Disability*. Edited by Johnson Cheu. Jefferson: McFarland & Company, pp. 115–28.

Literat, Ioana. 2013. 'A Pencil for Your Thoughts': Participatory Drawing as a Visual Research Method with Children and Youth. *International Journal of Qualitative Methods* 12: 84–98. [CrossRef]

Lövheim, Mia. 2011. Young Women's Blogs AS ETHICAL SPACES. *Information, Communication & Society* 14: 338–54. [CrossRef]

Nastasia, Diana, and Charu Uppal. 2010. *Learning About Being a Girl, From Disney Princesses*. Munich: TELEVIZION, pp. 34–37.

Nastasia, Diana, and Charu Uppal. 2014. Mono- or Multi-Culturalism: Girls Around the World Interpret Disney Princesses with Nonwestern Heritage. In *Princess Cultures: Mediating Girls' Imaginations and Identities*. Edited by M Forman-Brunell and Rebecca C. Hains. New York: Peter Lang, pp. 115–38.

Otnes, Cele, and Pauline Maclaran. 2015. *Royal Fever: The British Monarchy in Consumer Culture*. Oakland: University of California.

Pollen, Annebella. 2011. Performing Spectacular Girlhood: Mass-Produced Dressing-Up Costumes and the Commodification of Imagination. *Textile History* 42: 162–80. [CrossRef]

Projansky, Sarah. 2014. *Spectacular Girls: Media Fascination and Celebrity Culture*. New York: New York University Press.

Ralson, Helen. 1997. Arranged, 'semi-Arranged and 'Love' Marriages among South Asian Immigrant Women in the Diaspora and Their Non-Immigrant Sisters in India and Fiji: A Comparative Study. *International Journal of Sociology of the Family* 27: 43–68.

Rehmann, Bettina. 2010. *The Swedish Media System*. München: GRIN Verlag, Available online: http://nbn-resolving.de/urn:nbn:de:101:1-2010091613271 (accessed on 21 September 2018).

Schickel, Richard. 1997. *The Disney Version: The Life, Times, Art, and Commerce of Walt Disney*, 3rd ed. Chicago: Ivan R. Dee.

Statistics Sweden. 2018. Access to the Internet by Type of Device, Sex and Study Domain. Available online: https://www.scb.se/en/ (accessed on 31 March 2019).

Stehn, Molly. 2018. A Brilliant but Frosty Solution: Frozen® as an Allegory for the Central Relational Paradox. *Journal of Creativity in Mental Health* 13: 254–61. [CrossRef]

Turkle, Sherry. 2011. *Alone Together: Why We Expect More from Technology and Less from Each Other*. New York: Basic Books.

Verma, Suman, and Deepali Sharma. 2003. Cultural Continuity Amid Social Change: Adolescents' Use of Free Time in India. *New Directions for Child and Adolescent Development* 2003: 37–52. [CrossRef] [PubMed]

Wasko, Janet. 2001. *Understanding Disney: The Manufacture of Fantasy*. Cambridge: Polity, Malden: Blackwell.

Widestedt, Kristina. 2009. Pressing the Centre of Attention: Three Royal Weddings and a Media Myth. In *Media and Monarchy in Sweden*. Edited by Mats Jönsson and Patrik Lundell. Göteborg: Nordicom.

Wohlwend, Karen E. 2009. Damsels in Discourse: Girls Consuming and Producing Identity Texts Through Disney Princess Play. *Reading Research Quarterly* 44: 57–83. [CrossRef]

social sciences

MDPI

Article

From the Sleeping Princess to the World-Saving Daughter of the Chief: Examining Young Children's Perceptions of 'Old' versus 'New' Disney Princess Characters

Benjamin Hine [1,*], Katarina Ivanovic [1] and Dawn England [2]

[1] Department of Psychology, University of West London, St Mary's Road, London W5 5RF, UK; kativanovic7@gmail.com
[2] Middlesex University Dubai, Knowledge Park, Block 16, Dubai, UAE; D.england@mdx.ac.ae
*   Correspondence: Ben.Hine@uwl.ac.uk; Tel.: +44-0208-209-4571

Received: 28 August 2018; Accepted: 11 September 2018; Published: 14 September 2018

Abstract: Both popular and academic discourse has noted progressive change in the gender role portrayals of much-loved Disney princess characters. However, at present, little is known about children's recognition of such changes, or of their interpretation of princesses' gendered behavior. This study therefore asked 131 8–9-year-old UK children to attribute various feminine and masculine characteristics to 'princesses' both before and after watching an 'old' (*Sleeping Beauty*) versus 'new' (*Moana*) Disney princess movie. Post-movie they were also asked to attribute these characteristics to the princess characters (Aurora and Moana respectively) and were assessed on their labelling of thirteen popular female characters as 'princesses'. Results showed that whilst children recognized the largely feminine versus androgynous gendered profiles of Aurora versus Moana respectively, viewing a 'newer' Disney movie did not change their perception of 'princesses' more broadly. Moreover, a large proportion of children did not identify Moana as a princess at all. Results therefore simultaneously complicate and enhance the current discussion regarding the influence of gender role models, particularly those within the Disney franchise, on the development of gender knowledge and identity in young children.

Keywords: Disney; princess; gender roles; stereotyping; children's media

1. Introduction

Previous studies have highlighted numerous issues concerning gender representation in Disney animated movies (England et al. 2011). Utilizing both quantitative and qualitative approaches such studies have largely criticized the negative representations of women (principally princess characters), especially those in movies released before 2003 (Lacroix 2004; Dundes 2001; Do-Rozario 2004; Béres 1999). Such research posits that women are broadly feminine in their characteristics and behaviors (England et al. 2011), are shown in limited, usually traditional domestic roles (Towbin et al. 2004), and are largely passive in plot progression (Davis 2006; Towbin et al. 2004). Moreover, female characters lack participation in key rescue behaviors and are highly limited in their romantic outcomes (England et al. 2011; Davis 2006). Such findings support the notion that representations of women within pre-2003 animated Disney movies are not in line with societal developments regarding the role of women (Wiersma 2001).

Encouragingly however, the central observations of studies on more recent movies have identified the change in representations of women over time. For example, both Davis (2006) and England et al. (2011) highlight that princess characters from the 1990s were more empowered than their 1930s and 1950s counterparts. This is both in terms of their gendered characteristics, as well as their active participation in plot progression, and more developed romantic interests. Analyses of movies from 2009 onwards present even more positive messages, showing that princess characters are more androgynous (i.e., they demonstrate equal exhibition of masculine and feminine characteristics), participate in more rescue behavior, and show greater variation in romantic outcome (with some princesses rejecting romantic interests altogether, England et al. 2011; Hine et al. 2018). The overwhelming message from such studies is that newer princesses, whilst are by no means perfect (Streiff and Dundes 2017b, 2017a; Dundes and Streiff 2016; Dundes et al. 2018), present female characters that are much more fitting for the modern age (Hine et al. 2018).

No two Disney movies exemplify the dichotomy between outdated and more modern gender role representations than *Sleeping Beauty* (1959), featuring princess Aurora, and *Moana* (2016), featuring a central female character of the same name. Aurora falls under Davis (2006) 'Classic Years Women' categorization, with female characters of this era predominantly typified by passivity. This is exemplified through a plot which places Aurora at the whim of actions taken beyond her control, including by Prince Philip, who rescues Aurora with a kiss after she falls into a deathly sleep. Aurora's inaction and nonparticipation forms part of a wider behavioral profile which is overwhelming feminine in nature (88% of behavior coded as feminine, England et al. 2011). In direct contrast, Moana represents an empowered female character, whose behavioral profile is more balanced, and whose behaviors are actually more masculine than feminine (60% to 40% respectively, Hine et al. 2018). Moreover, Moana is central to plot progression, is physically assertive and athletic, challenges other (notably, male) characters, and rejects not only traditional romantic outcomes, but interest in romance altogether (Hine et al. 2018). This is supported by numerous articles in the popular media, which espouse that Moana is a brave heroine with a sense of humor and a commitment to saving the world without romantic distractions (Dunsmore 2017; Duralde 2016; Machado 2016; Ngata 2016; To 2016).

Such observations have been welcomed, considering the importance that many developmental theories place on the impact of models in the environment on the gender socialization of young children (e.g., Bussey and Bandura 1999). However, at present, few studies have investigated children's interpretations of Disney's changing representations of women. Specifically, whilst content coding analyses affirm the social progression reflected in 'newer' movies (Hine et al. 2018; England et al. 2011), it is not yet known if children interpret the progressive gender representations evidenced by princess characters in these films, particularly in comparison to the 'older' films and their associated restrictive gender role norms and stereotypes. Such exploration is important considering the influence of Disney princess movies specifically on children's understanding of gender norms and stereotypes (Coyne et al. 2016). The present study, therefore, examined children's attribution of gendered traits and characteristics in a 'new' and 'old' Disney princess movie, as well as their gendered conceptualizations of princesses before and after viewing these movies.

1.1. The Media and Gender Socialization

The influence of gender role models within the environment is highlighted by a number of developmental theories of gender. For example, both the Social Cognitive Theory of gender development (Bussey and Bandura 1999) and Identity Theory (Hogg et al. 1995) suggest that models within the environment help produce, perpetuate and teach gender norms and stereotypes to young children. The importance of the environment is also emphasized by constructivist approaches, for example, in Gender Schema Theory (Bem 1981; Martin and Halverson 1981), which proposes that children develop beliefs about the world based on their interpretations of observations and experiences (Martin et al. 2002; Graves 1999), which they then internalize into their own cognitive frameworks (or schemas).

Several approaches specifically identify the media as a key socializing agent for gender role development (Signorielli 2001). Cultivation theory proposes that visual media, such as television and film, may provide a particularly powerful vehicle to help develop concepts regarding social behavior and norms (Gerbner et al. 1994, 1980), and several studies directly highlight the impact of media consumption on subscription to traditional gender role representations (Frueh and McGhee 1975; Williams 1981; Signorielli 1990; Herrett-Skjellum and Allen 1996; Hust and Brown 2008; Coyne et al. 2014). Importantly, as media forms both shape and reflect the current state of society, the models presented in such media change both as part of, and in response to, changing societal norms (Eagly 2013). This in turn suggests that, against the backdrop of significant transformation in the role of women within society (UN Women 2017), media forms would operate to both help construct and mirror such developments. In addition, as outlined above, the Walt Disney Company appears to be no exception to this pattern, as princesses become more progressive in their gender role representations.

1.2. The Influence of Disney on Gender Development

The gendered content presented by Disney, and the impact this may have on the gender development of young children, is of particular interest when considering the organization's significant commercial reach. This is characterized by both financial success, with approx. $55.1 billion global revenue in 2016 (The Walt Disney Company 2017) and $5 billion box office sales for animated feature films released since 2008 (Box Office Mojo 2011, 2013, 2014, 2017, 2010), as well as substantial popularity with young children worldwide (Koonikova 2014; Gomez 2014; Rivas 2016).

As such, a number of qualitative studies have highlighted the presence and utilization of popular gendered narratives in children's play and other interactions, fueled by the ubiquity of Disney content in children's lives (Giroux and Pollock 2010). For example, Wohlwend (2009), demonstrated in her 3-year ethnographic study of literacy that young kindergarten girls that were identified as avid fans of Disney media enthusiastically took up familiar gendered narratives in their writing and pretend play. Baker-Sperry (2007) produced similar findings for first grade girls and boys after reading the story of Cinderella, as children gave well accounted gender representations and narratives. Possibly the most interesting finding from this study was the extensive 'gender work' (West and Zimmerman 1987) engaged in by children to correct divergent interpretations. Such results suggest that children therefore digest Disney princess storylines through a highly gendered lens, strictly reproducing the narratives observed within their own and others' play.

A more recent study conducted by Golden and Jacoby (2017) specifically investigated children's interpretations of Disney princess gender role stereotypes by analyzing the pretend play and discussions of 3- to 5-year-old girls. Four themes were identified: Beauty, a focus on clothing and accessories, princess body movements, and exclusion of boys. The first three themes speak specifically to the traditionally limited gender representations offered in princess characters (Towbin et al. 2004; Davis 2006), and the emphatic adoption of such information into young girl's gender schemas and scripts. Such findings are further supported by the limited quantitative research available, which demonstrates that engagement with Disney princess media/products is predictive of gender stereotypic behavior one year later (Coyne et al. 2016).

Current research therefore suggests that female characters in animated Disney movies, specifically princess characters, provide important and much revered, but ultimately severely limited, gender role models for young girls (England et al. 2011). As such, girls enthusiastically adopt numerous elements of typically feminine and gendered behavior into their day-to-day lives, reproduce such norms both within their own gendered play, and in the retelling of those familiar narratives (Wohlwend 2009; Baker-Sperry 2007; Golden and Jacoby 2017). However, Wohlwend (2009) also found that young girls were sometimes adapting familiar narratives when they identified limitations in character's behavior. Specifically, the kindergarten girls in this study changed some character elements where they deemed the existing narrative to be too restrictive. For example, one of the pairs in this study revised a kiss scene between the prince and the princess in *Sleeping Beauty* (which places the prince as active originator, and the princess as inactive recipient of this action) to a hug, which placed both parties as active within the interaction (Wohlwend 2009). Such examples demonstrate that, whilst character portrayals themselves may be limited, children may recognize such limitations, particularly within tales created as a representation of different socio-political landscapes.

1.3. The Present Study

As argued above, more positive gender-role representations now exist within the Disney franchise, with princesses in recent films providing more balanced behavioral profiles (Hine et al. 2018). However, whilst studies have demonstrated the influence of Disney's gendered content on the lives of young girls, children's interpretations of gendered behavior within more recent movies is yet to be explored. Such research is vital for two reasons. First, scholars have been united in their damnation of Disney's limited gender-role portrayal for women. However, such criticisms are largely levied at films released before 2003, and, if more positive portrayals exist, and children recognize these changes, such criticisms may require revision. Second, it is argued that continued examination of Disney princess characters is both important and necessary, considering the prolific and ubiquitous presence of such characters in the lives of young girls, and that this examination should involve the perceptions and interpretations of children themselves.

The present study therefore examined children's identification and attribution of gendered behavior to 'old' versus 'new' Disney princess characters. The study had three research questions.

RQ1: Do children notice the progression in gender role portrayals between the traditional and modern Disney princesses? Specifically, do children note that Moana displays both masculine and feminine characteristics, whereas Aurora displays mostly feminine behaviors?

RQ2: Do these findings affect children's broader conceptualization of princesses? Specifically, does viewing *Sleeping Beauty* or *Moana* influence how masculine or feminine children perceive "princesses" to be, in general?

RQ3: Are children recognizing these modern Disney princesses, with their more balanced gender role portrayals, as "princesses"?

2. Results

2.1. RQ 1—Attribution of Gendered Characteristics to Aurora and Moana

Two paired-sample *t*-tests assessed differences in participants' attribution of feminine versus masculine characteristics for Aurora or Moana; that is, if the princess they viewed was more masculine than feminine, or more feminine than masculine, or displayed equal rates of both traits. Mean attribution scores are shown in Table 1. Results showed that children who viewed Aurora attributed feminine characteristics to her character at a significantly higher level (M = 2.40, SD = 0.41) than masculine characteristics (M = 1.79, SD = 0.41), t (63) = 8.44, $p < 0.001$. Among the children who viewed *Moana*, results showed that participants did not attribute feminine (M = 2.32, SD = 0.39) and masculine characteristics (M = 2.45, SD = 0.41) to her character at significantly different levels.

In addition, two independent-sample *t*-tests were computed to compare masculine and feminine trait attribution across conditions; that is, if children in condition 1 attributed masculine and feminine characteristics to Aurora significantly differently to the attribution of masculine and feminine characteristics to Moana made by children in condition 2. Results indicated that, whilst feminine characteristics were attributed to Aurora and Moana at similar levels, Moana (M = 2.44, SD = 0.41) was attributed significantly more masculine characteristics than Aurora (M = 1.79, SD = 0.41).

Overall, these results suggest that children identify a much more androgynous and balanced gender profile for Moana, and a more feminine profile for Aurora.

Table 1. Means (standard deviations) for the attribution of masculine and feminine characteristics to specific princesses viewed, and princesses in general.

	Masculine	Feminine
Princesses—Specific		
Condition 1—Aurora	1.79 (0.41)	2.40 (0.41)
Condition 2—Moana	2.44 (0.42)	2.32 (0.39)
Princesses—General		
Pre-test		
Condition 1—Aurora	1.91 (0.45)	2.29 (0.42)
Condition 2—Moana	1.76 (0.44)	2.27 (0.52)
Post-test		
Condition 1—Aurora	1.86 (0.43)	2.44 (0.40)
Condition 2—Moana	1.86 (0.49)	2.34 (0.45)

2.2. RQ 2—Attribution of Characteristics to Princesses

Four mixed-design ANOVAs were computed to assess differences in participant's attribution of feminine and masculine characteristics to princesses in general across conditions (i.e., target movie viewed: *Sleeping Beauty* or *Moana*; and the time of measurement: Pre- and post-viewing). No significant differences were found for participants' attributions (see Table 1), suggesting that participants conceptualization of princesses, (i.e., their ratings of the masculinity and femininity of princesses as a group) did not change across conditions.

2.3. RQ 3—Princess Manipulation Check

Descriptive statistics were also calculated for the manipulation check measure to determine whether children viewed the female characters within the target movies, among others, as princesses. Response percentages for each princess are shown in Table 2. Interestingly, Aurora received the highest 'Yes' percentage (89.8%), whilst Moana received the highest 'No' percentage (47.4%). Moreover, percentages were similar for Aurora and Moana across both conditions. Other princesses who scored highly were Snow White, Cinderella, Belle, Rapunzel and Elsa/Anna, all of whom wear traditionally princess-like dresses. Princesses in less obviously princess-like garments, such as Mulan, Pocahontas, and the Little Mermaid, scored much lower. This suggests two things: First, that children may use specific visual cues in determining whether someone is a princess. Second, that children in this study did not identify Moana as a princess, possibly as she does not fulfil these visual cues.

Table 2. Response percentages for princesses presented during study manipulation check.

Disney Character	Yes	No	Don't Know
Snow White	75.4	8.5	16.1
Aurora	89.8	4.2	5.9
Cinderella	85.7	7.6	6.7
Little Mermaid	41.5	35.6	22.9
Belle	77.8	12.8	9.4
Jasmine	67.5	15.4	17.1
Pocahontas	31.0	25.0	44.0
Mulan	20.7	31.9	47.4
Tiana	62.9	12.1	25.0
Rapunzel	82.1	6.8	11.1
Merida	55.6	21.4	23.1
Elsa and Anna	82.9	9.4	7.7
Moana	39.7	47.4	12.9

3. Discussion

In response to findings highlighting the changing gender role representations of Disney princesses (Hine et al. 2018), this study provides an important contribution in assessing whether children themselves identify such changes. Specifically, this study addresses a key gap in the literature by quantitatively exploring children's interpretation of gendered behavior in princesses from different Disney 'eras', and by examining their attributions of masculine and feminine characteristics to central female characters representative of 'traditional' versus 'modern' gender role expectations portrayed in children's media. Findings from this study principally suggest that, whilst children correctly identified increased androgyny in the more modern princess (Moana), this did not influence their conceptualization of princesses more broadly. This presents interesting questions regarding the Disney princess brand and its ongoing influence on children's gendered perceptions and beliefs, despite its trend towards producing androgynous content.

3.1. What Makes a Princess?

Children in this study were aware of differences in the gendered behavior of Aurora and Moana. Specifically, whilst they attributed feminine characteristics to Aurora to a significantly greater extent than masculine characteristics, they noticed that Moana displayed relatively equal feminine and masculine characteristics. This supports studies utilizing content coding analysis (England et al. 2011; Hine et al. 2018) which suggest that princesses from older movies are more feminine in their behavioral profiles, and that modern princesses are more androgynous. Importantly, as children attributed feminine characteristics to Aurora and Moana to a similar extent, they recognized that, whilst more modern princesses are indeed becoming more masculine, this is not at the sacrifice of traditionally feminine attributes. In this sense, children acknowledged that modern princesses are demonstrating true context-dependent androgyny, as described by Bem (1975).

Children's identification of more positive gender role representations (i.e., the modern androgynous princess) is particularly important when considering the prevalence and significance of Disney role models within the lives of young children. Indeed, numerous studies have demonstrated that children utilize specific narratives and character profiles from older Disney titles within their pretend play and peer interactions (Baker-Sperry 2007; Golden and Jacoby 2017; Wohlwend 2009). It is therefore assumed, at least by those praising the recent trend by Disney and others towards producing more androgynous media, that children would do so with newer princess characters, and that the resulting behavior would be a reflection of the more positive character profiles outlined above. Indeed, it seems the general assumption of parents, teachers, and society more broadly, is that with models more representative of the current socio-political landscape, children will no longer have to adapt the outdated narratives of passive, hapless, helpless princesses (Wohlwend 2009), but rather, utilize ready-made storylines representative of increasing female empowerment.

The brand of 'princess' may be harder to kick however, as results from this study showed that children attributed feminine characteristics to 'princesses' to a significantly greater extent than masculine characteristics, regardless of whether they had viewed an 'older' or 'newer' movie. This suggests that viewing a more modern princess character is not enough to influence the conceptualizations of 'princess' that many young girls aspire to and hold dear, at least as evidenced in their play and conceptions of princesses (Coyne et al. 2016). This is complemented when looking at children's ratings of who is and is not a princess. They appeared to agree with Moana's iconic line from the movie "OK, first, I am not a princess", as they awarded her the highest percentage of 'No' classifications in response to the question 'Is she a princess?'. It is interesting that, in examining responses given for other princess characters, results seem to suggest that children may use predominantly visual cues (i.e., the presence of long flowing hair, a crown, and a long elegant dress). This is supported by the observation that princesses in traditional cultural garments (such as Mulan and Pocahontas) and those who are unable to wear garments at all (i.e., Ariel) also received lower 'Yes' and higher 'No' responses (although to a lesser extent than Moana). Indeed, other studies have noted the importance of physical appearance and dress in creating the context of a Disney princess (Wohlwend 2012; Do-Rozario 2004). This could explain why children appeared unaffected in their attributions of characteristics to princesses after watching *Moana*, as they conceptualize the character herself apart from the genre of character to which she supposedly belongs.

Such results undoubtedly complicate the discourse surrounding princess characters in the Disney franchise, as it is hard to draw comparisons between characters that may be conceptualized differently in the minds of young children, and there are several important considerations in interpreting this data. First, as children still have access to, and report watching, older Disney titles, their ideas of princesses may be shaped by the greater array of traditional princess characters still available to them. Further to this argument, it may be that, whilst newer representations may indeed be enough to change children's perceptions of princesses, one viewing of a 'newer' Disney princess, as provided in this study, is insufficient to stimulate change. Alternatively, children's ideas about princesses may be uninfluenced by representations such as Moana, as they may not see her as a princess at all.

3.2. "There Comes a Day When I Don't Have to Be a Princess. No Rules, No Expectations"—Merida, Brave

Numerous developmental theories of gender posit that role models within the environment inform children's understanding of gender norms and stereotypes (e.g., the Social Cognitive Theory of gender development, Bussey and Bandura 1999). Results from this study suggest that children identify that principal characters in newer Disney movies exhibit more positive and androgynous behavioral profiles, and it can be reasonably argued, therefore, that children exposed to such models may adopt more positive interpretations of the expected and permissible behavior and roles of women. It is therefore important to recognize children as critical viewers, and as agents in the construction of their own gendered knowledge (Martin and Halverson 1981), and that they recognize, particularly in comparison to characters in older movies, these more positive portrayals. Whether it is a new princess performing these behaviors, or simply an empowered female character whose royal status is either unknown or refuted, is of little importance to children, whose principle concern is identifying with, living through, and emulating their fantastical role models. That being said, considering the gendered baggage attached to so many of the traditional princesses represented within this franchise, it is perhaps encouraging that young viewers may be starting to detach new characters from such a toxic label.

The principal message therefore to production studios worldwide, including The Walt Disney Company, is that, despite the positive portrayals of more modern characters, children still invest both time and money in characters that do not conform to traditional gender archetypes. The financial success of more recent titles which feature female characters who are both strong and fragile, independent and loving, demonstrates that children do enjoy viewing, and ultimately identify with, role models who represent the pace and nature of change occurring in the world around them. Not only this, a number of media articles recognize the popularity of more recent princess movies with young boys (Koonikova 2014; Gomez 2014), possibly due to the increased presence of masculine behavior within these characters. In this sense, for Disney, and others, to continue to provide such role models not only has important implications for the positive psychosocial adjustment related to gender identity, but it also makes good business sense.

3.3. Limitations and Future Research Directions

Whilst this study attempted to control for previous exposure to Disney material, questions were limited to relatively simplistic self-report measures and it is incredibly challenging to map a child's environmental exposure of a media as prolific as the Disney princess line. A further methodological limitation is that children were not split randomly into conditions; rather they were split by class. Specific classroom dynamics and previous syllabus content could therefore have influenced children's interpretations. A final limitation is that children were not asked about whether they saw the differential portrayals of Aurora and Moana as negative or positive; all that is clear is that difference was indeed noted. However, as previous research suggests that the ability to express both typical and atypical gendered behaviors is positively related to psychosocial adjustment (Egan and Perry 2001), the authors feel confident in the assumption that children most likely had a more positive view of Moana. Indeed, given the results of this study, future research should incorporate longitudinal methods to measure the effects of long-term exposure to the modern princess movies, along with external environmental influences of gender roles (e.g., influences from parents, teachers, and other media), and more expansive assessment of children's views of characters. In addition, future research would benefit from analyzing the effect of viewing the modern Disney princess movies on children's beliefs about gender roles and norms for behavior.

3.4. Conclusions

Motion pictures produced by the Walt Disney Company have been ubiquitous in children's lives for over 80 years. Due to their pervasive presence, it is important that their content, and its relationship with children's understanding of gender roles and beliefs is examined. Results from this study encouragingly suggest that children themselves are able to astutely identify and interpret the gendered representations to which they are exposed, particularly regarding displays of masculine and feminine characteristics and behaviors, and that they recognize the change that has occurred in such representations over time. However, it appears that this has not yet influenced their conceptualization of princesses and the associated gender role portrayals. Importantly, the popularity that Disney princess films continue to enjoy has not waned in the face of young children recognizing more androgynous gender role portrayals. Thus, whilst further research is needed to examine the specific influence of these newer, more positive representations on the gendered knowledge and behavior of young children, it can be argued that by continuing to present more progressive and balanced gender role portrayals to young children, the Walt Disney Company has the opportunity to contribute to the gender empowerment of children worldwide.

4. Materials and Methods

4.1. Sample

Participants were 131 children (Mage = 8.48 years, SD = 0.50, 70 boys) attending two primary schools in West (*n* = 48) and South West London (*n* = 82). Children aged between 8- to 9-years-old were chosen for two reasons; first, children at this age are sufficiently adept at identifying and interpreting gendered information, without operating inflexibly within learned gender stereotypes (as they do at younger ages, Martin and Ruble 2010). Second, one of the films shown (*Moana*) is classified as a PG by the British Board of Film Classification (BBFC), and therefore should not unsettle children aged 8 years and older.

4.2. Materials

4.2.1. Target Films

Participants allocated to Condition 1 were shown *Sleeping Beauty* (1 h 16 min), and those in Condition 2 were shown *Moana* (1 h 47 min). *Sleeping Beauty* was identified in this study as an 'old' Disney animation (released in 1959), and depicts a young princess (Aurora), being hidden with her fairy godmothers from Maleficient, an evil witch who vows to kill Aurora on her 16th birthday. When Aurora falls victim to Malificient's curse, falling into a deathly sleep, it is Prince Philip who fights the witch and breaks the curse, then marrying Aurora. *Moana* was utilized as a 'new' Disney movie (released in 2016), depicting a young girl destined to repair the damage caused by demigod Maui in stealing the heart of Te Fiti—source of all creation. Moana, facing many obstacles and challenges, defies her father's wishes to restore the heart, thus saving the world as well as discovering who she truly is.

These films were chosen as they provide arguably stereotypical and limited versus androgynous and progressive gender role representations respectively.

4.2.2. Pre-Movie Measures

Control Measure—Engagement with Disney. Participants were administered five questions to measure their exposure and engagement with the Disney franchise prior to the study. Participants were asked whether they like Disney movies, had watched a lot of Disney movies, had watched [the movie allocated in their condition] more than 5 times, had been to/wanted to go to Disneyland, and had a lot of Disney toys. They could answer 'yes' or 'no' to these questions, with scores calculated by summing the total number of yes responses.

Attribution of Gendered Characteristics to Princesses. A 10-item scale was created for this study to examine participants' attribution of various masculine and feminine characteristics to princesses. Characteristics were taken from England et al. (2011), and all items are shown in Appendix A. Participants rated whether these masculine and feminine traits were 'really like princesses' (coded as 3), 'sometimes like princesses' (coded as 2), or 'never like princesses' (coded as 1). Separate masculine and feminine attribution scores were calculated by taking the mean across appropriate items.

4.2.3. Post-Movie Measures

All children completed the questionnaire measuring their Attribution of Gendered Characteristics to Princesses as a re-test. Two additional measures were added for the second wave of the data collection.

Attribution of Gendered Characteristics to [Target Movie Princess]. An additional version of the attribution scale outlined above was administered in the post-movie questionnaire pack, to examine participants' attribution of various masculine and feminine characteristics to the specific princesses they had observed (Aurora or Moana). Participants rated whether masculine and feminine traits were 'really like', 'sometimes like' or 'never like' the princess they had seen. As above, separate masculine and feminine attribution scores were calculated by taking the mean across appropriate items.

Manipulation Check. The final measure included in this study was a manipulation check, designed to assess whether children classified the characters within the target movies as princesses. Participants were presented with a small color picture of 14 Disney princesses (from Snow White through to Moana; see Appendix B) and were asked to indicate 'yes', 'no' or 'don't know' in response to the question 'is she a princess?'.

4.3. Procedure

This study utilized a quasi-experimental design. A group of children were shown either an older or more modern Disney princess movie and were assessed on their attribution of gendered characteristics to their target princess as well as to princesses more generally, both before and after the movie. Four primary schools in West/South West London were contacted and invited to take part in the study. Two schools responded and once participation was agreed, dates for testing were confirmed and parental opt-out consent forms were provided to parents of all children in Year 4.

The study was introduced using a short introductory script and the pre-movie questionnaire was administered to all children one week before children were shown their target movie. Once all children had finished, a holding debrief was given, explaining that the children would complete the same questionnaire the following week. For children whose parents had requested they be excluded from the study ($n = 7$), separate activities were provided in a different location.

One week later, participants were split into two conditions, and shown their target movie. Immediately after, children were asked to fill out the post-movie questionnaire. Once all participants had completed their questionnaires, a full debrief was given, explaining the purpose of the study, as well as thanking the children for their participation. Parental debrief sheets were also disseminated.

Author Contributions: Conceptualization, B.H. and K.I.; Methodology, B.H., K.I. and D.E.; Formal Analysis, B.H. and K.I.; Investigation, B.H. and K.I.; Data Curation, K.I.; Writing—Original Draft Preparation, B.H.; Writing—Review and Editing, B.H. and D.E.; Project Administration, B.H. and K.I.

Funding: This research received no external funding.

Conflicts of Interest: The authors declare no conflict of interest.

Appendix A. Attribution of Gendered Characteristics to Princesses Questionnaire

These questions are about princesses!

For each question, you need to read the characteristic shown on the left-hand side, and then fill in the circle that shows whether princesses are really like this, sometimes like this, or not at all like this.

Princesses Are ... ?	Really Like Princesses	Sometimes Like Princesses	Not at All Like Princesses
1. Physically Strong (e.g., They can lift heavy things)	O	O	O
2. Emotional (e.g., They cry when they are upset)	O	O	O
3. Independent (e.g., They can do things on their own)	O	O	O
4. Sensitive (e.g., They can tell when someone is upset)	O	O	O
5. Athletic (e.g., They are good at sports)	O	O	O
6. Helpful (e.g., They help other people when they need it)	O	O	O
7. Brave (e.g., They do things even if they are scary)	O	O	O
8. Fearful (e.g., They get frightened when something scary happens)	O	O	O
9. Leader (e.g., They are in charge of other people)	O	O	O
10. Needs help (e.g., They need other people to help them do things)	O	O	O

Appendix B. Manipulation Check

These questions are about who you think are princesses

For each question, you just need to answer yes or no or don't know!

Is She a Princess?	Yes	No	Don't Know
Snow White	O	O	O
Aurora	O	O	O

Is She a Princess?		Yes	No	Don't Know
	Cinderella	O	O	O
	Little Mermaid	O	O	O
	Belle	O	O	O
	Jasmine	O	O	O
	Pocahontas	O	O	O

Is She a Princess?		Yes	No	Don't Know
	Mulan	O	O	O
	Tiana	O	O	O
	Rapunzel	O	O	O
	Merida	O	O	O
	Elsa and Anna	O	O	O

Is She a Princess?		Yes	No	Don't Know
	Moana	O	O	O

References

Baker-Sperry, Lori. 2007. The production of meaning through peer interaction: Children and Walt Disney's Cinderella. *Sex Roles* 56: 717–27. [CrossRef]

Bem, Sandra. 1975. Sex role adaptability: One consequence of psychology androgyny. *Journal of Personality and Social Psychology* 31: 634–43. [CrossRef]

Bem, Sandra. 1981. Gender schema theory: A cognitive account of sex typing. *Psychological Review* 88: 354–64. [CrossRef]

Béres, Laura. 1999. Beauty and the Beast: The romanticization of abuse in popular culture. *European Journal of Cultural Studies* 2: 191–207. [CrossRef]

Box Office Mojo. 2010. The Princess and the Frog (2009). Available online: https://www.boxofficemojo.com/movies/?id=princessandthefrog.htm (accessed on 4 May 2017).

Box Office Mojo. 2011. Tangled (2010). Available online: http://www.boxofficemojo.com/movies/?id=rapunzel.htm (accessed on 4 May 2017).

Box Office Mojo. 2013. Brave (2012). Available online: http://www.boxofficemojo.com/movies/?id=bearandthebow.htm (accessed on 4 May 2017).

Box Office Mojo. 2014. Frozen (2013) International Box Office Results. Available online: http://www.boxofficemojo.com/movies/?id=frozen2013.htm (accessed on 4 May 2017).

Box Office Mojo. 2017. Moana (2016). Available online: http://www.boxofficemojo.com/movies/?id=disney1116.htm (accessed on 4 May 2017).

Bussey, Kay, and Albert Bandura. 1999. Social cognitive theory of gender development and differentiation. *Psychological Review* 106: 676–713. [CrossRef] [PubMed]

Coyne, Sarah, Jennifer Ruh Linder, Eric E. Rasmussen, David A. Nelson, and Kevin M. Collier. 2014. It's a bird! It's a plane! It's a gender stereotype!: Longitudinal associations between superhero viewing and gender stereotyped play. *Sex Roles* 70: 416–30. [CrossRef]

Coyne, Sarah, Jennifer Ruh Linder, Eric E. Rasmussen, David A. Nelson, and Victoria Birkbeck. 2016. Pretty as a princess: Longitudinal effects of engagement with Disney princesses on gender stereotypes, body esteem, and prosocial behavior in children. *Child Development* 87: 1909–25. [CrossRef] [PubMed]

Davis, Amy M. 2006. *Good Girls & Wicked Witches: Women in Disney's Feature Animation*. Hertfordshire: John Libbey Publishing Ltd.

Do-Rozario, Rebecca-Anne C. 2004. The princess and the magic kingdom: Beyond nostalgia, the function of the Disney princess. *Women's Studies in Communication* 27: 34–59. [CrossRef]

Dundes, Lauren. 2001. Disney's modern heroine Pocahontas: Revealing age-old gender stereotypes and role discontinuity under a façade of liberation. *The Social Science Journal* 38: 353–65. [CrossRef]

Dundes, Lauren, and Madeline Streiff. 2016. Reel Royal Diversity? The Glass Ceiling in Disney's Mulan and Princess and the Frog. *Societies* 6: 35. [CrossRef]

Dundes, Lauren, Madeline Streiff, and Zachary Streiff. 2018. Storm Power, an Icy Tower and Elsa's Bower: The Winds of Change in Disney's Frozen. *Social Sciences* 7: 86. [CrossRef]

Dunsmore, Carrie. 2017. Disney's Moana Is a Princess Head and Shoulders (and Feet) above the Rest. Available online: https://www.washingtonpost.com/news/parenting/wp/2017/02/09/disneys-moana-is-a-princess-head-and-shoulders-and-feet-above-the-rest/?noredirect=on&utm_term=.9de019963533 (accessed on 19 April 2018).

Duralde, Alonso. 2016. Dwayne Johnson Invigorates Disney's South Seas Saga. Available online: https://www.thewrap.com/moana-review-dwayne-johnson-invigorates-disneys-south-seas-saga/ (accessed on 19 April 2018).

Eagly, Alice H. 2013. *Sex Differences in Social Behavior: A Social-Role Interpretation*. Hillsdale: Lawrence Erlbaum.

Egan, Susan K., and David G. Perry. 2001. Gender Identity: A Multidimensional Analysis With Implications for Psychosocial Adjustment. *Developmental Psychology* 37: 451–63. [CrossRef] [PubMed]

England, Dawn E., Lara Descartes, and Melissa A. Collier-Meek. 2011. Gender role portrayal and the Disney princesses. *Sex Roles* 64: 555–67. [CrossRef]

Frueh, Terry, and Paul E. McGhee. 1975. Traditional sex role development and amount of time spent watching television. *Developmental Psychology* 11: 109. [CrossRef]

Gerbner, George, Larry Gross, Michael Morgan, and Nancy Signorielli. 1980. The "mainstreaming" of America. Violence Profile No. 11. *Journal of Communication* 30: 10–29. [CrossRef]

Gerbner, George, Larry Gross, Michael Morgan, and Nancy Signorielli. 1994. Growing up with television: The cultivation perspective. In *Media Effects: Advances in Theory and Research*. Edited by Jennings Bryant and Dolf Zillmann. Hillsdale: Lawrence Erlbaum Associates, Inc., pp. 17–41.

Giroux, Henry A., and Grace Pollock. 2010. *The Mouse That Roared: Disney and the End of Innocence*. Lanham: Rowman & Littlefield.

Golden, Julia C., and Jennifer Wallace Jacoby. 2017. Playing Princess: Preschool Girls' Interpretations of Gender Stereotypes in Disney Princess Media. *Sex Roles* 79: 1–15. [CrossRef]

Gomez, Jeff. 2014. Why 'Frozen' Became the Biggest Animated Movie of All Time. Available online: http://www.businessinsider.com/why-frozen-is-a-huge-success-2014-4?IR=T (accessed on 5 May 2017).

Graves, Sherryl Browne. 1999. Television and prejudice reduction: When does television as a vicarious experience make a difference? *Journal of Social Issues* 55: 707–27. [CrossRef]

Herrett-Skjellum, Jannifer, and Mike Allen. 1996. Television programming and sex stereotyping: A meta-analysis. *Annals of the International Communication Association* 19: 157–86. [CrossRef]

Hine, Benjamin, Dawn England, Katie Lopreore, Elizabeth Skora Horgan, and Lisa Hartwell. 2018. The Rise of the Androgynous Princess: Examining Representations of Gender in Prince and Princess Characters of Disney Movies Released 2009–2016. *Social Sciences* 7: 245.

Hogg, Michael A., Deborah J. Terry, and Katherine M. White. 1995. A tale of two theories: A critical comparison of identity theory with social identity theory. *Social Psychology Quarterly* 58: 355–69. [CrossRef]

Hust, Stacey J. T., and Jane D. Brown. 2008. Gender, media use, and effects. In *The Handbook of Children, Media, and Development*. Edited by Sandra L. Calvert and Barbara J. Wilson. Oxford: Blackwell, pp. 98–120.

Koonikova, Maria. 2014. How "Frozen" Took over the World. Available online: http://www.newyorker.com/science/maria-konnikova/how-frozen-took-over-the-world (accessed on 25 February 2017).

Lacroix, Celeste. 2004. Images of animated others: The orientalization of Disney's cartoon heroines from the Little Mermaid to the Hunchback of Notre Dame. *Popular Communication* 2: 213–29. [CrossRef]

Machado, Yolanda. 2016. Directors Reveal How They Made Disney's Next Hit. Available online: https://www.moviefone.com/2016/11/23/moana-directors-reveal-how-they-made-disneys-next-hit/ (accessed on 19 April 2018).

Martin, Carol L., and Charles F. Halverson. 1981. A Schematic Processing Model of Sex Typing and Stereotyping in Children. *Child Development* 52: 1119–34. [CrossRef]

Martin, Carol Lynn, and Diane N. Ruble. 2010. Patterns of Gender Development. *Annual Review of Psychology* 61: 353–81. [CrossRef] [PubMed]

Martin, Carol L., Diane N. Ruble, and Joel Szkrybalo. 2002. Cognitive Theories of Early Gender Development. *Psychological Bulletin* 128: 903–33. [CrossRef] [PubMed]

Ngata, Tina. 2016. Despite Claims of Authenticity, Disney's Moana Still Offensive. Available online: http://www.risingupwithsonali.com/despite-claims-of-authenticity-disneys-moana-still-offensive (accessed on 19 April 2018).

Rivas, Emily. 2016. Why Your Kid Might Love Disney's Moana Even More Than Frozen. Available online: https://www.todaysparent.com/blogs/why-your-kid-might-love-disneys-moana-even-more-than-frozen/ (accessed on 4 May 2017).

Signorielli, Nancy. 1990. Children, television, and gender roles: Messages and impact. *Journal of Adolescent Health Care* 11: 50–58. [CrossRef]

Signorielli, Nancy. 2001. Television's gender-role images and contribution to stereotyping: Past, present, and future. In *Handbook of Children and the Media*. Edited by Dorothy G. Singer and Jerome L. Singer. Thousand Oaks: Sage, pp. 341–58.

Streiff, Madeline, and Lauren Dundes. 2017a. From shapeshifter to lava monster: Gender stereotypes in Disney's Moana. *Social Sciences* 6: 91. [CrossRef]

Streiff, Madeline, and Lauren Dundes. 2017b. Frozen in Time: How Disney Gender-Stereotypes Its Most Powerful Princess. *Social Sciences* 6: 38. [CrossRef]

The Walt Disney Company. 2017. The Walt Disney Company Reports Fourth Quarter and Full Year Earnings for Fiscal. Available online: https://www.thewaltdisneycompany.com/walt-disney-company-reports-fourth-quarter-full-year-earnings-fiscal-2017/ (accessed on 15 February 2017).

To, Benjamin. 2016. Dance, Storytelling and the Art of Wayfinding: Behind the Scenes of Disney's Moana. Available online: http://www.nbcnews.com/news/asian-america/dance-storytelling-art-wayfinding-behind-scenes-disney-s-moana-n672141 (accessed on 19 April 2018).

Towbin, Mia Adessa, Shelley A. Haddock, Toni S. Zimmerman, Lori K. Lund, and Litsa R. Tanner. 2004. Images of gender, race, age, and sexual orientation in Disney feature-length animated films. *Journal of Feminist Family Therapy* 15: 19–44. [CrossRef]

UN Women. 2017. Commission on the Status of Women. Available online: http://www.unwomen.org/en/csw (accessed on 10 May 2017).

West, Candace, and Don H. Zimmerman. 1987. Doing gender. *Gender & Society* 1: 125–51.

Wiersma, Beth A. 2001. The gendered world of Disney: A content analysis of gender themes in full-length animated Disney feature films [Abstract]. *Dissertation Abstracts International* 61: 4973.

Williams, Tannis M. 1981. How and what do children learn from television? *Human Communication Research* 7: 180–92. [CrossRef]

Wohlwend, Karen E. 2009. Damsels in discourse: Girls consuming and producing identity texts through Disney princess play. *Reading Research Quarterly* 44: 57–83. [CrossRef]

Wohlwend, Karen E. 2012. 'Are you guys girls?': Boys, identity texts, and Disney princess play. *Journal of Early Childhood Literacy* 12: 3–23. [CrossRef]

social sciences

MDPI

Article

Mulan and Moana: Embedded Coloniality and the Search for Authenticity in Disney Animated Film

Michelle Anya Anjirbag

Centre for Research in Children's Literature at Cambridge, Faculty of Education, University of Cambridge, 184 Hills Road, Cambridge CB2 8PQ, UK; maa93@cam.ac.uk

Received: 1 October 2018; Accepted: 6 November 2018; Published: 11 November 2018

Abstract: As the consciousness of coloniality, diversity, and the necessity of not only token depictions of otherness but accurate representations of diversity in literature and film has grown, there has been a shift in the processes of adaptation and appropriation used by major film production companies and how they approach representing the other. One clear example of this is the comparison of the depiction of diverse, cross-cultural womanhood between Walt Disney Animation Studio's *Mulan* (1998) and *Moana* (2016). This paper will use a cross-period approach to explore the ways in which a global media conglomerate has and has not shifted its approach to appropriation of the multicultural as other and the implications for representational diversity in the context of globalization and a projected global culture. In one case, a cultural historical tale was decontextualized and reframed, while in the other, cultural actors had a degree of input in the film representation. By examining culturally specific criticisms and scenes from each film, I will explore how the legacy of coloniality can still be seen embedded in the framing of each film, despite the studio's stated intentions towards diversity and multiculturalism.

Keywords: diversity; hegemony; Disney; coloniality; adaptation

1. Introduction

Since the release of *Snow White and the Seven Dwarfs* in 1937, Disney has grown from a film studio to a multinational-media conglomerate—a cultural force that has made itself almost synonymous with contemporary understandings and experiences of childhood. As culture and society evolved from the 1930s through the present, Disney ostensibly responded to concerns regarding diversity and multiculturalism, a response seen particularly in efforts to relate narratives from other cultures during the Disney Renaissance (1989–1999). As Eleanor Byrne and Martin McQuillan write regarding this period, specifically, the transition in the company's depiction of the racial other leading up to *The Lion King* (1994):

> " ... some of the most recent Disney films have appeared to be actively engaging with questions of race, racism, ethnic cleansing and tolerance of cultural differences, marked by the climate of liberal social politics ushered in by the Clinton era, In the period immediately following his inauguration as President in 1993, from 1994 to 1996 Disney produced three films which signaled that bad old Disney would be purged and a new agenda for approaching race and national identity might emerge ... ". (Byrne and McQuillan 1999, pp. 100–1)

That social consciousness has (also ostensibly) continued through the corporation's contemporary films. However, when considering the legacy of depictions of racial and ethnic diversity in Disney animated film, a retrospective view makes clear that in many ways the multiculturalism represented in the corporation's films is indicative of and reinforces the hegemonic culture within which Disney as a corporation is firmly positioned: American, Caucasian, cis-gendered, straight, Anglo, Christian, able-bodied, etc. This is especially seen in how coloniality becomes embedded in animated depictions of other cultures despite Disney's reported efforts to tell more authentic stories from other cultures. When considering changes to Disney's methods of representing otherness, *Mulan* and *Moana* set up an interesting juxtaposition of telling stories from other cultures through the Disney lens almost two decades apart. This paper will explore the contexts of the criticisms levied at each film from the cultures from which the narratives are appropriated, centering these critiques as a necessary step to decolonizing the image of the reception of these films, despite their respective financial success at the box office and general positive reception from within Disney's own cultural sphere. Focalized through said criticisms, this paper will then use close reading to explore how narrative structure and the surrounding narrative elements can embed coloniality within the films despite stated intentions of the corporation. By examining, specifically, parallels in the opening sequences, artistic stylization, and how music and animation are layered together in each film, I hope to complicate Disney's representation of its stated more ethical intentions in representing non-Western cultures, demonstrating the gap between intentions and effect when a corporation rooted in the hegemonic status quo appropriates narratives from outside of its cultural space.

In 1998, Disney Feature Animation released *Mulan*, which was meant to mark a departure from the studio's previous princesses and modes of storytelling. Eighteen years later, Walt Disney Animation Studios' *Moana* (2016a) was meant to display again how the studio, and corporation at large, could evolve in its effort to tell more diverse stories—a trend that continues as Disney wraps production on a live-action remake of *Mulan* meant to attract the lucrative Chinese box office, which became the first foreign (not North American) market to cross \$4 billion in 2014 (Pomerantz 2015). When considering these two films as parallel transcultural adaptations, it is possible to view these two films as adaptation where, in one case, a cultural story was decontextualized and reframed deliberately to make it "universal," where universality means appealing to a Western audience (Yin 2014, p. 286), while in the other, the studio went to great lengths to prove there had been an evolution of the production process to promote a greater sense of sensitivity towards the adapted material and its original context, namely, the creation of the Oceanic Story Trust (Robinson 2016). Both films aim to retell stories with distinct cultural roots for a global audience. The production teams respectively claimed to have produced their adaptations with an eye to telling culturally authentic and authoritative stories, and to have partaken in cultural and historical research to inform the adaptation process (Bruckner 2018; Ward 2002, p. 96; Gilio-Whitaker 2016). Both films have also had a complex reception. *Mulan* and *Moana* were box-office successes with the former raking in \$304 million in the global box office in 1998 (Pomerantz 2015) and the latter grossing \$643 million worldwide (Moana 2016b), but simultaneously have surrounding them respective epitexts of criticism from their source cultures—which this paper will focus on. The claims made by Disney to authenticity and the manufacture of an authoritative version of culturally-specific stories, then projected to the rest of the world, have come under culturally-specific scrutiny. Additionally, both films also have provoked concerns that they promote a narrative capable of supplanting other more culturally-authoritative narratives as well as the global perception of that culture, via their reach and status as Disney films. Though, in listing these parallels, another eponymous, diverse, Disney princess/heroine might come to mind, I am deliberately excluding *Pocahontas* from this paper. *Moana* and *Mulan* both draw from legend or myth; *Pocahontas*, instead, is a misappropriated historical figure and the film has drawn criticism from indigenous communities for whitewashing and erasing a genocidal history. Thus, I am choosing to not conflate a narrative based in history with two narratives based on legend and folklore, and so hope to avoid contributing to that erasure and mischaracterization of both Pocahontas as a historical figure and that period of history.

Not only are both *Mulan* and *Moana* framed as and defined as being Disney films, both works are also encapsulated by being understood as "Disney fairy tales." Though the films are respectively adapted from legend and folklore of their originating culture, and are not originally fairy tales as understood within a Western literary context, wider understandings of who both titular characters are and what their stories are become transformed once incorporated under the Disney umbrella. Jessica Tiffin's post-structural approach to the definition of fairy tales considers the defining characteristic of this type of narrative to be the "element of recognition" (Tiffin 2009, p. 3), where their cultural currency depends in part on "the ability of fairy-tale narratives to retain their characteristic shape and function despite a changing social context and their cross-pollination with a diverse range of narratives" (Tiffin 2009, p. 2). She asserts that fairy tales signal their nature and function through "highly encoded structures, a complex interaction of characteristics and content which nonetheless operates with a simple and holistic effect to create a sense of nostalgic familiarity" (Tiffin 2009, p. 2). Essentially, the cultural currency of fairy tales in Western culture depends on the element of recognition, and such recognition of a fairy tale as a fairy tale by the audience or reader is part of how contemporary fairy tales are defined. The same principle of recognition can be applied to narratives appropriated by Disney to be adapted into feature films, where no matter what the cultural history and legacy of a particular narrative might be, audiences expect a certain kind of story to be told following a particular narrative arc, by virtue of the fact that this adaptation is now a Disney adaptation. Thus, the adaptations become defined as Disney stories, with the corporation leaving its distinct footprint on the narrative's legacy, even as the new adaptation and the choice to adapt certain narratives in certain ways redefines what comprises a Disney narrative in turn.

As a corporation, Disney has successfully branded itself as a creator of and site for global narratives, however, it is important to note that Disney also wields its global positionality (how the corporation is situated in relation to other cultures, industries, and actors) and power (its ability to exert influence) through narrative transmission rather than exchange. An example of the conceptualization of this can be seen in Jack Zipes' construction of the global capitalist culture machine (Zipes 2009, Relentless Progress), though Zipes focuses more on the power dynamics of capitalist economic structures, where I am more concerned with the socio-cultural power exchanges inherited as a byproduct of global colonization and imperialism, and Orientalism as conceptualized by Edward Said. Orientalism, in this case, becomes a lens through which East and West are constructed in opposition to each other, and where, specifically, "the West" then defines and creates "the East" as other to it, and such construction becomes the identifiable representation of people who would embody the cultures enveloped by that constructed definition. In essence, it can be a construction of diversity tailored to suit a certain culture's worldview, that then silences or impedes the Other that is being represented from asserting agency (Said 2003). While I would hesitate to go as far as Zipes, and others, and suggest that the Disney corporation is currently attempting to impose American value systems upon the rest of the world in a deliberately political, colonizing, or imperialist way, it remains important to talk about the power dynamics involved when a company such as Disney decides to tell stories from outside its own sphere, rooted in Western, Anglo-American, conservative-leaning hegemonic culture. The attraction to telling such diverse narratives, specifically, of commodifying diversity, is related to the success such efforts garner. In the words of bell hooks, "the commodification of Otherness has been so successful because it is offered as a new delight, more intense, more satisfying than normal ways of doing and feeling ... ethnicity becomes spice, seasoning that can liven up the dull dish that is mainstream white culture" (Hooks 1992, p. 21). Thus, through this understanding, both *Mulan* and *Moana* are part of that 'seasoning' on the hegemonic status quo. As such, by examining two expressions of how "desire for the Other is expressed, manipulated, and transformed by encounters with difference and the different" (Hooks 1992, p. 22) it becomes more possible to understand where even outwardly good intentions can still cause harm and potential exploitation of marginalized communities.

The language of diversity, appropriation, and Otherness is nebulous, in part because while Western hegemonic culture relies on binaries as a mode of communication, the conversations surrounding positionality of people of different ethnic or cultural backgrounds cannot simply be glossed over as "White" and "not-White." To express diversity only in this binary is to assume that all members of a particular group will hold the same opinions—an assumption that is dehumanizing yet relied upon to sanction depictions of diversity across mainstream Western media. While, as the criticisms I explore will demonstrate, some members of a community may object and problematize contemporary colonialization of culturally-specific narratives, others may see such appropriation and commodification as "a promise of recognition and reconciliation" or a sign that the hegemonic culture "can indeed be inclusive of difference" (Hooks 1992, p. 26). If diversity is understood as the incorporation of difference into hegemonic cultural institutions and norms, however, then the concept of diversity itself, too, must be problematized. Sara Ahmed writes about how the appearance of the word "diversity" within institutions has become, in some ways, a convention of speech, and that the effect of such designation to conventionality is to cause "what is being named as diverse [to become] less significant than the name "diversity"" (Ahmed 2012, p. 58). As such, it is the designation of diversity itself that holds value or political economy, not necessarily how such incorporation of difference is being functionally expressed nor the effect upon the people incorporated to bolster such claims of diversity. Through both hooks and Ahmed, however, we see that there is both an aesthetic and cultural value conferred through something being labeled as diverse; for Disney, specifically, there is the ability to fit different aesthetics into their formula and thereby sell the narrative as something 'new' to its target audience, simply by playing to Western predispositions to fascination with the 'exotic'—which I will demonstrate are catered to explicitly in my close reading of scenes from both films.

Intentionally or not, Disney's power and position when adapting narratives from other cultures perpetuate a pattern of "the West" constructing an Orientalized image of the other in its depictions of other cultures and ethnicities. The one-directionality of this transaction can be understood through coloniality—the conceptual and ideological matrix of power that came to be in the Atlantic world in the sixteenth century, and unified imperialism and capitalism, that remains the legacy of colonialism embedded in global social-cultural and economic institutions and practices (Bacchilega 2013, p. 22). For example, when Disney centers a Western, Orientalizing view of a constructed image of "China" or "Polynesia" and then projects that depiction outwards to a globalized entertainment market, it participates in and perpetuates that coloniality while setting up its version of the narrative as authoritative and authentic—usually through a nod in the credits to ambiguous, often unnamed cultural experts and consultants. Authenticity is generally understood as the quality of being "traditionally produced or presented" (Authenticity 2018), and cultural authenticity, more specifically, can be represented, simply, as work having the quality of reflecting "culturally specific realities experienced by ethnic groups" (Cai 2002, p. 38). This becomes more complicated with Disney's aforementioned 'ambiguous nods.' As noted by Prajna Parasher, "acknowledging real ownership is here transformed into self-created authority" (Parasher 2013, p. 44). While Parasher's work focused on depictions of Native Americans in Disney properties, similar criticisms have been raised concerning *Mulan* and *Moana* from both academic and public sources (Ward 2002; Dong 2011, pp. 159–87; Gilio-Whitaker 2016; Diaz 2016).

In this fashion, regardless of their respective cultural sources, positioning, and legacy, the narratives adapted by Disney to become *Mulan* and *Moana* become understood through the greater umbrella of the "Disney fairy tale" disconnected from their original context and, likewise, the titular characters become incorporated under and understood as part of the cultural umbrella of "Disney Princesses." And yet, both of these films are meant to have addressed, in some ways, what it means to be a "princess"—and part of the Disney story world—within the larger Disney canon and thus reflect a change in philosophy in storytelling by the corporation in different ways. Intertextuality and paratexts are present on several levels here. The adaptations are read as in dialogue with both the Disney canon and to their source material, and the context of the reception of the film within the cultures the narratives were derived from adds dimensions to the paratext surrounding the films as texts, specifically, the epitext. These are far from the only two instances where Disney has attempted to represent different kinds of diversity or tell stories from different parts of the world; while there are certainly discussions to be had about the connections between folklore and adaptations, and the projections of national identities, I would like to discuss instead the power dynamics involved when Disney, or similar corporations, tells stories from outside its own cultural space.

2. Criticisms and Contexts

With a profit $120.6 million domestically and $176.5 million overseas, *Mulan* is considered not only a financial success for Disney, but as Jing Yin notes, has embodied a popularity in popular culture that "confers [the corporation's] authority to tell the story of *Mulan* globally" (Yin 2014, p. 286). However, Yin, among others, notes that *Mulan* also embodies a process of appropriation of non-Western cultural materials by the U.S. culture industry, that ends with the reformulation of the perception of the non-Western—in this case Chinese—culture in the minds of a world audience. Yin's study of Disney's *Mulan* against its source material, *The Ballad of Mulan*, demonstrates how such a cultural artifact can be abstracted, westernized, and then supplant the original, culturally authoritative narrative. For context, briefly, the ballad itself depicts a well-known story of which there are multiple iterations, with the earliest recording dating from approximately 568 A.D., and the oldest currently available iteration of the text dating from the Song dynasty (12th century). In this narrative, a young woman disguises herself to take her father's place in the army out of a sense of filial duty—and this is the key part—with her parents' blessing. The secret of her sex is kept for twelve years after which she retires, refusing any reward (Yin 2014, p. 295).

In comparison, the Disney adaptation emphasizes a sense of individuality in the character of Mulan, adds a romantic interest, adds a magical talking animal sidekick, and uses the revelation of her sex as a plot device leading her to disgrace and dismissal from the army (Yin 2014; Dundes and Streiff 2016). Additionally, the film's depictions of China are stripped of context and embed historical inaccuracies such as the episode with the matchmaker, the presence of the Huns, the presence of the shrine to the ancestors, the clothing, and presenting villains as darker-skinned. Perhaps most importantly, Disney's iteration perpetuates Orientalized stereotypes by conflating racial and gender perceptions, where the Oriental other is both effeminate and irrational, and this depiction serves to motivate the conflict (Yin 2014; Dundes and Streiff 2016, p. 5; Dong 2011, pp. 172–73). The changes between the ballad and the film reveal a process where "Chinese cultural values were selectively disposed and replaced with Western ideologies that simultaneously pacify feminist criticism and reinforce the racial/cultural hierarchy" (Yin 2014, p. 286), and done specifically to "transform ethnic materials into a timeless or universal classic" (Yin 2014, p. 289). The underlying assumption embedded in this process is that only the dominant (Western) culture can be universally understood, and that the values of that culture are the default standard to be imposed on the rest of the world. Such domination under the guise of universalization also "imposes the perspectives or values of the dominant on the dominated, and does not allow the dominated to use their own perspectives or values," reinforcing the construct of the dominated group as "other" and the dominant group as the natural, standard Self (Yin 2014, p. 289). These changes altered the social and cultural values of the ballad in such a way that it altered the cultural currency of the narrative while reinforcing negative stereotypes and Orientalizing of Chinese people.

Though financially successful, reception of *Mulan* by critics in the USA at the time of release was mixed. Roger Ebert might have called it "an impressive achievement, with a story and treatment ranking with *Beauty and the Beast (IMAX)* and *The Lion King*"(Ebert 1998), but other critics felt less warmly towards the film, calling it a "rich dramatic tapestry lightly stained by some strained comedy, rigorous political correctness and perhaps more adherence to Disney formula than should have been the case in one of the studio's most adventurous and serious animated features" (McCarthy 1998), and "the most inert and formulaic of recent Disney animated films" (Maslin 1998). After being shown in the Hunan province in China, the titular character of *Mulan* was reported as being "'foreign-looking' in her Disney incarnation" and with mannerisms "too different from the Mulan of Chinese folklore for viewers to recognise (sic)" (BBC News 1999). In an article in the *South China Morning Post*, one viewer remarked, too, that they found the film strange, saying, "only foreigners could make this kind of film. It wasn't like watching the Chinese story of Mulan, it looked like any foreign cartoon" (Becker 1999). In fact, many of the criticisms center on the extent to which the very texture of the film made it seem more foreign, or more like a Western imagining of Chinese-ness than culturally authentic to the people who already had a baseline of knowledge about the original legend, and for "violating the main theme of the Chinese folk "Ballad"" (Dong 2011, p. 172).

Criticism of *Mulan* at the time of its release may not have permeated the Western mediasphere to the same extent as the praise, however, criticisms levied at the production of and presentation of *Moana* have been wide-ranging in the public sphere and easily accessible online. Arguably, this indicates that, despite its best efforts, Disney cannot control the altruistic narrative about cultural authenticity that was the main focus of the marketing campaign leading up to the film's release, which centered the formation of the Oceanic Story Trust in order to validate the authenticity of the film. Criticism centers around the ways in which Disney created and utilized the Trust, and then also crafted its "authentic" elements within the film, which can be seen through a close reading of the film. On the topic of criticism of the films, it should be noted that culturally-specific criticisms regarding how authentic indigenous voices are used in such productions need to come from, and are strongest and most valid from within, that wider community itself. Especially worth noting is a growing body of responses specifically from the Pacific reacting through op-eds, public and academic presentations, and engagement through the Mana Moana Facebook page, which addresses not only representation in *Moana* but depictions of indigenous people from across the Pacific in Hollywood and Western media culture and the reality and impact of such misrepresentations. Such criticism includes interrogating the colonial positioning of relationships between various indigenous groups across the Pacific arena and the Western mediasphere, and how often "admiration" of other cultures or indigeneity is almost synonymous with entitlement to said culture by a corporation such as Disney (Ngata and Kelly 2016). Pacific Island scholar Vicente M. Diaz, who is from Guam, writes:

> "Who gets to authenticate so diverse a set of cultures and so vast a region as Polynesia and the even more diverse and larger Pacific Island region that is also represented in this film? And what, exactly does it mean that henceforth it is Disney that now administrates how the rest of the world will get to see and understand Pacific realness, including substantive cultural material that approaches the spiritual and the sacred." (Diaz 2016)

Additionally, New Zealand educator Tina Ngata goes on to assert that this is not an indigenous story, as "having brown advisers doesn't make it a brown story. It is still very much a white person's story" (Herman 2016). Ngata in an open letter to Taika Waititi, who did early work on the first version of the screenplay, further outlined the ways in which the Walt Disney Corporation continues to profit from problematic depictions of otherness from the 1990s onwards, and her fears for her own culture in that light, writing:

> "We already have our own rich storytelling culture, Taika. It doesn't reposition itself to appeal to the racist humour and privileged wallets of our colonizer (as your chosen colleague has). It doesn't perpetuate imposed stereotypical norms of gender, culture, or sexual orientation (as your chosen colleague has), or minimalise our kaitieki, or mock our ways (as your chosen colleague has). The story of our voyaging tipuna is not just yours to place into the hands of Disney—it belongs to all our whanaunga across Te Moananui a Kiwa. It is rich, it is complex, and it is ongoing. The placing of this narrative in the hands of Disney is, at best, cavalier—and at worst a complete sellout. While we continue to promote and demand culturally appropriate platforms and relevant contexts for telling our own stories—the mass-consumptive power of machines such as Disney has the absolute ability to eclipse our voice and position." (Ngata 2014)

Though both the creation of the Oceanic Story Trust and Waititi's early involvement were meant to ratify Disney's cultural authority to tell this particular story in the public eye, the concerns of Ngata and others prove that this is far more complicated than having a relative handful of people sign off on the film. Especially when considering the prolific use of coconuts to either emphasize idyllic island pastorals about to be lost, or ridiculous coconut-armor-wearing pirate opponents, the coloniality embedded in the narrative despite the alleged attempt at being culturally accurate this time around becomes that much more noticeable and in need of being widely problematized. Two of the major critiques include the romanticization of the primitive set against the larger, often violent colonial history of the region and the current neocolonial relationships of many Pacific Islands, and the depictions of Maui. Putting aside the infamous Maui skin-suit merchandise which was quickly pulled from shelves and problematic for many reasons (Diaz 2016; Sonoda-Pale 2016)—Maui as drawn by Disney and brought to life by Dwayne "The Rock" Johnson has also been criticized as unintelligent, a buffoon placed for comic relief, and as perpetuating negative and offensive stereotypes of Polynesians as overweight (Schilling 2016). The demigod is a heroic figure across Polynesia, and is depicted in story, comics, and other culturally-specific media as a teenager nearing manhood, a sort of trickster figure, well-dressed, charming, and intelligent. Additionally, Maui's female counterpart is entirely omitted from the story, even from the metanarrative provided by the dancing tattoo version of himself, unbalancing Polynesian spiritual lore and further reshapes how the rest of the world comes to understand this cultural and spiritual figure. Despite these and other criticisms, however, this reshaping becomes sanctioned because of the specter of the cultural authority board that was meant to have authenticated this film.

3. Coloniality and Framing in Disney Animated Films

Keeping such culturally-rooted criticisms in mind and drawing on the parallels between the two films, I will close read scenes to understand how animated and musical narrative techniques that draw on the intention of "authentic" representation may instead become colonizing instruments based on the "Western" framing of "Othered" narrative elements. What I hope to reveal is how the contextualization of such narrative elements within the larger production frame of the film adds to the paratext that accompanies the viewer's experience of the film, and thus impacts how the viewer might not only construct but contextualize meaning about the represented culture's place in the larger world. In effect, othering messages might still be embedded in such films despite stated intentions of the directors, producers, and animators. It is my intent to complicate how we think of depictions of ethnic diversity by a multinational, multimedia corporation such as Disney. Thus, it is necessary to examine the potential impacts of embedded coloniality and globalizing impetuses of a corporation such as Disney, and how the effect of production decisions, use of different techniques, and overall framing can undermine the best of stated intentions.

Something that I find interesting in both films is how Disney animators use different animated and narrative techniques within films to layer depictions of otherness with a sense of communicating something authentic and pertinent to the culture from which the studio is appropriating a narrative. The changes are a part of deliberately crafting an element of otherness in introducing the viewer to the world encompassed by the film. Specifically, in both *Mulan* and *Moana*, this is seen in the following areas: in both films' opening sequences; in how the animation style itself is utilized to convey a sense of otherness connected specifically to a cultural aesthetic meant to add to the interpretation of that culture by the viewer; how music shapes the depiction of and reception of otherness; and, where all of these elements come together to communicate otherness while simultaneously communicating culturally specific information in the form of narratives embedded in songs and accompanied by different animation styles. By examining how these elements impact the perception of other cultures separately, it becomes possible to understand the fine line Disney walks between representing another culture with integrity, and Othering another culture, when these elements are understood as part of a greater whole.

4. Openings

Mulan's framing as a film depicting something "other"—other than the "normal" European-centric pattern of adaptation of fairy tales and cultural stories—begins from the moment the iconic castle and signature production logo appear on-screen with distinct auditory cues courtesy of Jerry Goldsmith's score. The castle fades to black and then opens to a background reminiscent of rice paper or parchment, and the opening credits unfold as a scrolling, animated stylized calligraphic depiction of mountains, trees, and clouds culminating in a depiction of the Great Wall of China, an easily recognized monument from and symbol of "the East" and "China" in Western culture (Dong 2011, p. 170). While the clouds scroll across the screen, in red typeface the words "Walt Disney Pictures Presents" appear and disappear before we see the title of the film itself, "Mulan," projected above the same clouds in a larger, black typeface with a heavily stylized Chinese dragon underscoring the name. It is only as this contextualizing text fades out that we see the beginning of the calligraphic-style Great Wall, onto which the title descends before it fades. The calligraphic depiction then fades itself, to be replaced by the Great Wall depicted in Disney's more traditional, realism-based animation style—what Paul Wells refers to as "visual orthodoxies of its own making" (Wells 2002, p. 120)—that its viewers have been conditioned to expect from previous Disney animated features. This opening framing is important because it subtly—or maybe not so subtly—frames exactly what the viewer is about to see. This is Disney's presentation of a (traditional) Chinese cultural story, and its presentation of (traditional, historical, Ancient) China. The film's otherness is framed by the music and the distinct animation style, but it is made acceptable, Western and relatable through the use of the Disney name and Western typesetting to communicate the necessary, concrete information. Even with the nod to difference, the narrative does not begin properly until we move away from the "old," "ethnic" drawing-style, and exchange it instead for the contemporary, Western drawing-style. Traditional here is used to convey a sense of simultaneous separation from and connection to a specific culture—the idea that this story is being told with permission and research in a way that does not "violate the integrity of a culture" (Cai 2002, p. 38). This pull between authenticity and otherness is continually reiterated throughout the films in terms of the visual and musical effects.

Likewise, *Moana*'s opening is meant to signal the entrance to another culture, time, and place to the audience. As the Disney castle appears, the opening notes of the first song of the soundtrack, "Tulou Tagaloa" are heard and the narrative moves forward from that musical framing. Instead of "once upon a time," we are offered "in the beginning there was only ocean" as the creation story of the world the narrative would be building out of unfolds on brightly colored tapestries, composed of repeating motifs and textures that recall woven fabrics and fibers that signify a very particular kind of idyllic island life (Herman 2016)—much as the Great Wall's existence in ancient China is meant to ensure a very particular idyllic existence. Eventually, the digitally generated tapestries give way to Disney's trademarked Computer-Generated Animation aesthetic as Moana's grandmother terrifies a group of children—all but Moana—with the impending fall of darkness and destruction of their home. So again, just as in *Mulan*, we have an auditory cue of otherness, a "zoomed-out" view of the culture we're being introduced to, and then, once the scene is set, we settle in on the "zoomed-in" view of our titular character. As young Moana claps at her grandmother's story, the viewer is firmly rooted in a sense of place as the textures of the tapestries depicting the story are echoed in the textures of the wood and fibers Moana herself is surrounded by. We as viewers accept the location and its validity through the visual signaling of culture, and are thus prepared to accept the validity of the narrative.

5. Musical Elements

As mentioned briefly above, *Mulan* was scored by Jerry Goldsmith and included original songs written by Mathew Wilder and David Zippel—themes of which were then incorporated into the score by Goldsmith. It should be noted that Goldsmith's own website proclaims him a master of 'ethnic scoring' and identifies "ethnic instruments" as part of how he constructs the signature sound of the film score (Jerry Goldsmith Online), feeding into the Orientalizing and coloniality embedded directly into the soundscape of the film itself. Close listening to the themes of the soundtrack that are meant to signal "Oriental" or "ethnic", specifically the rising and falling seven-note structure often heard when transitioning to scenes featuring the titular character, reveals that these musical riffs are voiced primarily on various woodwinds such as saxophones, oboes, and flutes, mid-voiced brass instruments such as trumpets and French horns, and on harps. In essence, the "Oriental" sound is created by utilizing not culturally specific instruments—instruments that would reflect the musical culture and tradition of China—but by using a Western symphony—instruments that are more prominently featured in Western symphonic and other popular musical productions, such as heavy percussion, sweeping use of string sections, mid-voiced brass such as trumpets and French horns, and woodwinds, including saxophones—for its voicing. This problematizes the depiction of the music as "ethnic" on several fronts. First, we must question what "ethnic" means in this context: Is it that it is simply signaling a non-Anglo-American/European sound, and, in context, viewers are meant to infer that, here, "ethnic" means not just "not white" but "from a specific not white part of the world"? Or is this scoring considered "ethnic" because it was utilizing melodic voicing that an American public had already been trained to recognize as "Asian" or "other" through a longer Orientalizing tradition? Furthermore, does "ethnic" then becomes synonymous with "Asian" or a homogeneous and all-encompassing construction of otherness that is not actually culturally specific, but defined simply by not containing the signifiers of the hegemonic culture? Though the DVD special features include a reel of clips of artists sketching in what is presumably China, and interviews with the directors describing research trips to discover how to represent this culture with integrity, the same purported research did not go into crafting the soundscape for this film.

In comparison, the music for *Moana* is by Lin-Manuel Miranda (Hamilton, In the Heights), Mark Mancina (the composer behind the *Tarzan* score), and Opetaia Foa'i, the founder of Oceanic music group Te Vaka. The collaboration on the songs, attested to in multiple interviews by Miranda and Foa'i (Chapman, Newman 2017; Binelli 2016; Burlingame 2016) is in some ways indicative of the step towards responsible cultural integration. From the use of Samoan and Tokelauan lyrics, to the sustained percussive rhythms driving both the score and the songbook, the soundtrack seems indicative of a new approach by Disney to really take on board community members with cultural authority in the production process and then let them truly drive the nature of the representation. However, as Robin Armstrong argues, the framing of the music within the context of the score and film points to, despite the intentions of the creators, a subjugation of the "authentic," culturally specific musical elements, and even control over production, exerted to some extent by Foa'i (Armstrong 2018). Armstrong writes: "Before, after, and during the Polynesian music in the film, Western sounds wrap around the 'other' sounds like a frame wraps around a picture, safely containing the 'other' sounds with those that are normative." Armstrong goes on to delineate the colonizing effects of music in this kind of framing; the argument is persuasive in terms of the net effect of framing and othering the Polynesian music embedded within a traditional American film score. It is not hard, then, to parallel this colonizing effect with the creation of the score for *Mulan* two decades prior. The auditory framing of otherness within Disney animated films has changed in that people with distinct cultural authority are becoming involved in the creation process at Disney's behest. However, the framing devices—consciously or unconsciously—nevertheless remain, and the signifying of the soundscape then combines with the various textures of animation to enhance and mediate the othering effect to different purposes at different points in the narrative.

6. Animation Texture

Whether considering the influence of traditional calligraphic forms and watercolor painting in the *Mulan* introduction or of the woven, fibrous tapestry opening from *Moana*, it is important to note that those elements boldly set the scene before being superseded by a more traditionally-Disney sense of animation, but they do not disappear completely from the visual texture of the film, either. For example, when we meet Mulan's father for the first time, as he stands in front of the family shrine and she rides off to town, we can see echoes of the same visual signifiers from the movie's introduction. The outline of his body, the strokes denoting his features, and the outline of the building itself behind him are very strongly foregrounded. They stand out like ink on a rice screen, while, in comparison, the trees in the background take on a very soft, blended texture, such as that of a dispersed watercolor ink on a fibrous paper. This effect is repeated with Mulan's mother in front of the building where the potential brides are meant to be prepared to meet the matchmaker. The strokes denoting her figure and features are so sharp in contrast to the softer textures of the background, that she almost appears to be standing in front of a scenery backdrop, rather than a part of the scenery she is meant to be a part of. The stylization is seen again, notably, in the swirling snow of the avalanche that buries the Huns, in effect, softening and blurring the violence of the scene. This stylization and use of visual texture—referred to as "poetic simplicity" by producer Pam Coats (Dong 2011, p. 168)—is apparent throughout the film to subtly remind the audience where the narrative is situated and to keep the visual construction of the animated world intact. While this seems to be a testament to the research efforts of the production team, as I will discuss further on, it is also a technique used to highlight where a distinction is being made between the audiences' cultural values and those of the embedded culture.

The visual effect of using different animated textures to simultaneously enhance worldbuilding and signal difference is used slightly differently in *Moana*, presumably because the medium is computer-generated rather than hand-drawn animation, but to no less an othering effect. The fibrous textures of the tapestries that depict the creation myth from the opening sequence fade to something that looks much more realistic. But, at the same time, just as the creation myth emphasizes a connection with the natural world, and affirms a mythical idyll, the visual textures of the film itself, especially those that depict interaction with natural elements, are highly stylized. There is a sense of a heightened realism to the sand and the ocean, especially when characters are seen interacting with them directly. The coconut fronds and the grain of the timber are also emphasized, as is the movement of Moana's hair. Essentially, the idyllic nature of Montunui is made so real that the spiritual elements are secondary to how much the visual signifiers convince the viewer of the validity of the world they are witnessing. And because those visual elements track with the ideal of island life—sand, ocean, coconuts—that a Western audience has been conditioned to expect from an "island narrative," it adds to the expectation and the idea that the story being communicated is culturally authentic through that hyperrealism via visual texture. Thus, we accept Montunui, and Disney's presentation of "Polynesia" as plausible.

7. Layered Animation within the Song Sequences

The above effects come together in two song sequences to signal otherness to different effects, specifically, in "A Girl Worth Fighting For" in *Mulan* and in "You're Welcome" in *Moana*. Looking at the animated musical numbers, in both scenes we find parallel elements that contextualize culture and otherness, and the viewer's relationship to the cultural material presented within the film. Both songs embody a male voice of identity and desire in a female-driven and named film. Additionally, both scenes use a change in animation style that signals difference as specifically related to cultural knowledge, identity, or information within the film. Whether modelled on Chinese calligraphic brushstrokes or traditional Marquesan tattoos (Flores 2016), the othering effect simultaneously attempts to communicate a sense of authenticity embedded in the information imparted through the particular scene, such as cultural definitions of gender roles or imparting historical socio-cultural information that motivates the plot further, but also heavily slants the reception of the information so that it is identified clearly and visually as different and separate from the rest of the Westernized adaptation of the cultural narrative.

"A Girl Worth Fighting For" is situated directly after Mushu, the dragon sidekick, engineers having Mulan's unit moved to the front to further his own goals. As the army laments needing to march long distances, Ling suggests in song that instead of thinking about their discomfort, they "think of instead/A girl worth fighting for" (Moana 1998, 48:01). When Mulan as Ping looks askance at the suggestion, he repeats the assertion: "that's what I said/a girl worth fighting for," pulling out a scroll from his armor and unfolding it (Moana 1998, 48:09). The scroll unrolls to reveal an Orientalized depiction of a woman, reminiscent of the ideal women off to see the matchmaker at the beginning of the film, hiding her face behind a fan, with writing in presumably Chinese characters vertically to the left of her. The camera then zooms in on this parchment, and, as it takes over the screen, this background is presented as having the same color and texture as the only other time we've seen this kind of

stylized drawing in the film. The written characters unravel themselves into stylized depictions of Ling, Chien-Po, and Yao as they all describe their ideal woman: pale, quiet, meek, willing to admire them, good at cooking—essentially subservient to them and there to improve their quality of life. Though as the song continues the visual narrative leaves the scroll and stylized animation to return to the "normal" animation style of the film, the momentary shift achieves a particular effect. In the film opening, the calligraphic style was used to solidify a localized connection between the (Orientalized and constructed) culture and the adapted narrative, thus bringing the viewer into Disney's version of Ancient China. What we see here is a continuation of that connection, but with an added element. The song contains a message that reiterates an alleged cultural message encoded previously in the film in the song "Honor to Us All"—a woman's worth is dependent on her ability to win a husband vis-à-vis her physical appearance, and knowing her duties and keeping to her place in society. This message is one that is meant to jar with the expectations of a Western, feminist audience—an audience being deliberately targeted by co-directors Tony Bancroft and Barry Cook, who are on the record as being motivated in part by wanting to disrupt Disney's pattern of heroines relying on a man to save them, in order to create a role model for their daughters (Bruckner 2018). The audience is meant to relate, again as in other preceding parts of the film, to Mulan's sense of isolation and not quite fitting in with where she is meant to "belong" based on her outward appearance within this culture, with the part in the song where Mulan as Ping asks "How 'bout a girl who's got a brain/Who always speaks her mind?" and is promptly rebuffed.

This is not the only time where Mulan becomes the outsider; however, it is one in which the culture represented in the film is most clearly othered in comparison to "Western" values. The audience separates the "Chinese-ness" of the film from the appealing, hybridized heroine. The "Chinese-ness" becomes identifiable when the lyrics of the song are compounded by and associated with the stylized, albeit Orientalized imagery. In comparison, Mulan, who is confused and made an outsider by the messages in the lyrics, simultaneously embodies the ideals of the independent teenage heroine searching from her place and the ideal of an "authentic" yet palatable hybridization of Western ideal dressed up in a projection of what the dominant power-holder in this iteration of globalized storytelling thinks the othered culture should look like. This is an example of Orientalizing and embedded coloniality: the patriarchal values of the song are partnered visually with images that cause the viewer to connect antiquated gender roles with a particular culture, which is then in turn identified as not contemporary, especially as compared with their values as embodied in the character of Mulan. By deliberately using a different style of animation to separate this mode of thinking about a woman's place in society as described by men, who are in this depiction conferred a higher status and more autonomy, the animators separate the message from the rest of the film, and assign it to the originating culture. In essence, through animation style, this shift communicates to the audience that 'this is not something that belongs to US (Disney/Western hegemonic cultural norms), this belongs to THEM (the culture that is being borrowed from and othered).' I argue that Disney uses its assumed, "self-created authority" (Parasher 2013, p. 44) to indicate that patriarchal thinking is inherent in Chinese culture, which thus is antiquated and not compatible with the sensibilities of a progressive and contemporary young woman (or audience). In this way, a seemingly innocuous or possibly comical song actually undermines any sense of incorporating Ancient China and Chinese culture into a sense of a contemporary norm through its rather blatant othering and Orientalizing. A culture that it alleged to try to represent with integrity instead is actively depicted as less progressive than "Western" culture.

Mulan directors Tony Bancroft and Barry Cook have in multiple interviews referred to the culturally specific research that went into the production of *Mulan* (Bruckner 2018; Dong 2011, p. 173). However, the relative lack of success of the film within its origin culture pointed to an area for improvement in terms of how Disney approached cross-cultural storytelling where the end product would remain accepted by the culture the original narrative came from (Dundes and Streiff 2016, p. 2). That is where the Oceanic Story Trust created for the production of *Moana* was meant to come in to fill the gaps between corporate, globalized storytelling practices and more local, culturally-specific storytelling, to create in the end a more glocalized, more hybridized mode of adapting a narrative from outside Disney's cultural sphere. Hence, I find it notable that, with such alleged attention to detail, a similar situation occurs in *Moana* where a different, supposedly culturally authentic art style is embedded within the larger scope of the animation in order to separate the "authentic" cultural information from the "authoritative" encompassing Disney narrative.

The song "You're Welcome" serves as the audience's introduction to the character of Maui, where, after his and Moana's first encounter, he breaks into a song meant to contextualize for Moana (and the audience) his identity within the cosmology of the film. The stories of Maui's adventures play out across his body through his tattoos, which, according to production designer Ian Gooding, were modelled on Marquesan tattoos, as part of an effort to base the islands and other components on "real areas at real times" (Flores 2016, p. 121). Technically speaking, these tattoos were the result of a combination of traditional 2D animation and the 3D, Computer Generated animation that comprises the rest of the film's aesthetic (Robertson 2016). The stylization is meant to convey that the stories and events retold by Maui in the song are actually part of a larger cultural sense—essentially, that Disney has not invented this cultural history, and its inclusion stands testament to the research they had done and their utilization of the Oceanic Story Trust. This goes a step farther than, say, the sequence surrounding the song "We Know the Way" which contains musical elements that are distinctly Polynesian, that retains a sense of authenticity supported by the fact that Foa'i, who primarily wrote the lyrics, has built a career on representing his people, traditions, and ancestors with knowledge and integrity as the founder of Te Vaka (Chapman). In comparison, "You're Welcome" retains an aural aesthetic much more in line with an American Broadway Musical songbook, and the instrumentation is largely Western. Outside of the lyrics, the denotation that this information is culturally specific and "real" comes from the 2D animated dancing tattoo embedded in the 3D dancing Disney-version of Maui.

However, Maui is an actual heroic figure who appears across various Polynesian and Pacific Island cultures, with contexts and histories outside of the Disney frame, which the audience may or may not know. Tongan cultural anthropologist Tēvita O. Ka'ili noted in an op-ed for the *Huffington Post* that the delineation of Maui's feats omits Hina, the companion goddess who helps him to achieve many of his wonders, who is also present in different forms across the vast Polynesian pantheon of goddesses. He also notes that because this removes symmetry and harmony, motifs in Polynesian cultural life and lore, it amounts to a kind of colonial erasure where the integrity of the culture is diminished in the retelling (Ka'ili 2016). Stuart Ching and Jann Pataraya-Ching's analysis of *Moana* in the context of the appropriation of Hawai'ian lore notes that:

> "the film's mythological, cultural and historical references from Samoa, Hawai'i and Maori New Zealand suggest that Moana is set in a generic version of Polynesia; just as Disney constructed a version of Ancient China that would appeal to the assumptions and presumptions of a Western audience's expectations, so too have they constructed a pastiche of symbols that signify "Polynesia" to outsiders, but removes the internal, culturally-specific nuances that are experienced by those with culturally-specific knowledge. The film opens with a Disney-invented legend that frames the ancient Polynesian legend of Māui as well as Polynesian creation myths within a Western framework". (Ching and Pataray-Ching 2017, p. 183)

The overall reframing of Polynesian mythology at large, and Maui as a figure within that mythology reflects institutionalized coloniality, or, "the film's potential to reflect, enact and sustain longstanding histories of global imperialism that exploit Polynesian culture and negatively impact the lives of Polynesia's indigenous peoples" (Ching and Pataray-Ching 2017, p. 183). There is an intertextual dialogue created between the film's iterations of the Maui stories, and the legends as they exist and are continually propagated within various Polynesian cultures' own retellings of the legends of Maui as a trickster rather than a buffoon. Additionally, the volume of not just criticism but overall intercultural, glocalized dialogues about the impact versus the intent of the adaptation creates a paratextual context through which viewers can potentially further understand the positionality of the film in a larger post-colonial context as well as Disney's manufactured globalized context.

8. Conclusions: Positioning the Films within the Paratexts of Culturally-Specific Criticism

Disney might be firmly positioned as a powerful stakeholder within the Western hegemonic mediasphere, but that does not mean that the films it produces are easily positioned or interpreted within a wider, global cultural context. *Mulan* and *Moana* each changed the perception of what a Disney narrative could be in terms of how they position the independence and agency of their titular female characters of ethnic minority (as defined within the culture scope Disney primarily operates within and addresses), and, have each come under culturally-specific scrutiny. Evaluating what might be positive or negative in each film varies based on the positionality of who is doing the evaluation. Extra-diegetic materials—such as original contexts of the stories, the other iterations of the narratives, the positionality of the producers and artists who create the filmic adaptations, and the various reactions and criticisms of the films by other viewers—adds to a paratext that in turn adds to how audiences can position and understand the films in different contexts and construct meaning. What we can learn from juxtaposing parallel elements of the films as well as various academic and cultural criticisms of the films, is that Disney's relationship with authentic cross-cultural storytelling, is, at best, complicated.

However, what has changed, clearly, is that criticisms of Disney are now far more accessible publicly, which arguably marks a transition in the balance of power between Disney as the monolithic media producer, and various socio-cultural groups that would levy criticism against the company's productions. It is also arguable that in the past two decades, the shift from sending a production team on a research trip and engaging consultants as needed, to deliberately involving people who are of and invested in a particular culture to be part of the adaptation and storytelling process, marks a significant change in how Disney has approached telling stories from other cultures. This latter move is, at face value, a positive step, as the studio begins a necessary process of potentially moving away from appropriating and transforming cultural property in decontextualized ways and perpetuating harmful, often colonializing, stereotypes.

That being said, this transition in production processes is only the first step in moving away from stereotypical, flat representations of diversity to authentic multicultural or transcultural storytelling, and needs to be viewed as such. While more authentic, ethical depictions of otherness may well begin to speak back to institutionally and culturally embedded biases and inequalities, these cannot function as such if the ethics and contexts of the production processes are not thoroughly examined. For example, it would be worth probing, in the future, how and why Disney insists on representing their so-called "diverse" characters as being of diverse only outside of the context of the US, and from distinct historical or semi-mythical periods of time. By problematizing, further, how the divide between cultures is maintained through various elements of film production, a better picture of how difference—not necessarily diversity—becomes encoded socially through such representations is possible. In essence, it is necessary for future research to probe how the separation between 'normal' and 'Other' is maintained through casting, construction of setting, use or disregard of historical contexts of various ethnic and cultural diaspora, and many other facets of cultural erasure and inequality within even just the socio-historical-cultural context of the United States. There will always be tension between the corporation's mandate to not only protect but increase its profit margins, and the assertions of the marginalized to their right to accurate and ethical representation. Coloniality is a system of economic and cultural exchange that reinforces current hegemonic power structures, and Disney's depictions of otherness simultaneously support that structure while also claiming to disrupt it through diversifying the kinds of stories they are adapting. The ways in which coloniality remains embedded in Disney's particular narrative structure needs further examination, to better understand how, beyond the intentions of any production team, the films can still encode negative representations of other ethnicities, or contribute to harmful stereotypes. Encoding that sense of otherness while also incorporating transcultural narratives under the Disney umbrella limits the opportunity for authentic representations of diversity within Disney animated films, as the viewers are invited into a narrative but constantly reminded of all the ways in which there are potential barriers between them and the source material, and thereby the source culture. A better understanding of coloniality as embedded within both the production of and presentation of Disney animated films as the company's oeuvre continues to deal in adaptations of its own multicultural material may lead to a better understanding of how to tell more authentic stories without compromising the integrity of the culture being borrowed from.

Funding: This research received no external funding

Conflicts of Interest: The author declares no conflicts of interest.

References

Ahmed, Sara. 2012. *On Being Included: Racism and Diversity in Institutional Life*. London: Duke UP.

Armstrong, Robin. 2018. Time to Face the Music: Musical Colonization and Appropriation in Disney's Moana. *Social Sciences* 7: 113. [CrossRef]

Authenticity, n. 2018. OED Online. Oxford University Press, July. Available online: www.oed.com/view/Entry/13325 (accessed on 9 August 2018).

Bacchilega, Cristina. 2013. *Fairy Tales Transformed?: Twenty-First Century Adaptations and the Politics of Wonder*. Detroit: Wayne State University Press.

Becker, Jasper. 1999. Disney's Mulan on Charm Offensive. *South China Morning Post*, February 27. Available online: https://www.scmp.com/article/273540/disneys-mulan-charm-offensive (accessed on 3 November 2018).

Binelli, Mark. 2016. 'Hamilton' Creator Lin-Manuel Miranda: The Rolling Stone Interview. *Rolling Stone*, June 1. Available online: https://www.rollingstone.com/culture/culture-news/hamilton-creator-lin-manuel-miranda-the-rolling-stone-interview-42607/ (accessed on 19 September 2018).

Bruckner, Rebekah. 2018. *Tony Bancroft Brings APU Animation Program to Life*. Azusa: Azusa Pacific University.

Burlingame, Jon. 2016. 'Moana' Offers Lin-Manuel Miranda a Break From 'Hamilton'. *Variety.com*, November 4. Available online: https://variety.com/2016/film/spotlight/lin-manuel-miranda-disney-moana-1201909204/ (accessed on 19 September 2018).

Byrne, Eleanor, and Marin McQuillan. 1999. *Deconstructing Disney*. London: Pluto Press.

Cai, Mingshui. 2002. *Multicultural Literature for Children and Young Adults: Reflections on Critical Issues*. London: Greenwood Press.

Chapman, Madelene. Moana composer Opetaia Foa'i on the story behind the best Soundtrack since The Lion King. *The Spinoff*, January 7.

BBC News. 1999. Chinese Unimpressed with Disney's Mulan. *BBC News*, March 19. Available online: http://news.bbc.co.uk/1/hi/entertainment/299618.stm (accessed on 2 November 2018).

Ching, Stuart, and Jann Pataray-Ching. 2017. Transforming Hawai'i and its Children through Technologies of Adaptation. *International Research in Children's Literature* 10: 178–93. [CrossRef]

Diaz, Vicente M. 2016. Don't Swallow (or be Swallowed by) Disney's 'Culturally Authenticated Moana'. In *Indian Country Today*. Washington: Indian Country Media Network.

Dundes, Lauren, and Madeline Streiff. 2016. Reel Royal Diversity? The Glass Ceiling in Disney's Mulan and Princess and the Frog. *Societies—Open Access Journal of Sociology* 6: 35. [CrossRef]

Dong, Lan. 2011. *Mulan's Legend and Legacy in China and the United States*. Philadelphia: Temple UP.

Ebert, Roger. 1998. Mulan. *RogerEbert.com*. June 19, Available online: https://www.rogerebert.com/reviews/mulan-1998 (accessed on 2 November 2018).

Flores, Terry. 2016. (Sort of) True Tales of the South Pacific. *Variety Magazine*, November 22, 121–22.

Gilio-Whitaker, Dina. 2016. Disney Refines Its Cultural Competence in Moana, But Bigger Questions Remain. In *Indian Country Today*. Washington: Indian Country Media Network.

Herman, Doug. 2016. *How the Story of "Moana" and Maui Holds Up Against Cultural Truths*. Smithsonian.com. Washington: Smithsonian Institution.

hooks, Bell. 1992. Eating the Other: Desire and Resistance. In *Black Looks: Race and Representation*. Boston: South End Press, pp. 21–39.

Ka'ili, Tēvita O. 2016. Goddess Hina: The Missing Heroine from Disney's Moana. *The Huffington Post*, December 6.

Maslin, Janet. 1998. Film Review; A Warrior, She Takes on Huns and Stereotypes. *The New York Times*, June 19. Available online: https://www.nytimes.com/1998/06/19/movies/film-review-a-warrior-she-takes-on-huns-and-stereotypes.html (accessed on 2 November 2018).

McCarthy, Todd. 1998. "Film Review: Mulan". *Variety*; Variety Media, LLC., June 8. Available online: https://variety.com/1998/film/reviews/mulan-2-1117477600/ (accessed on 2 November 2018).

Moana. 2016a. Directed by Ron Clements, and John Musker. *Performances by Auli'i Cravalho, Dwayne Johnson, Rachel House, Opetaia Foa'i and Lin-Manuel Miranda*. Burbank: Walt Disney Animation Studios.

Moana. 2016b. Box Office Mojo. Available online: www.boxofficemojo.com/movies/?page=main&id=disney1116.htm (accessed on 19 October 2018).

Moana. 1998. Directed by Tony Bancroft, and Barry Cook. *Performances by Ming-Na Wen, Eddie Murphy, and B. D. Wong*. Burbank: Walt Disney Feature Animation.

Newman, Melinda. 2017. Lin-Manuel Mirana on 'Moana' Music, Potential EGOT Status, and Staying Positive Under Trump. *The Hollywood Reporter*, November 1. Available online: https://www.hollywoodreporter.com/news/lin-manuel-miranda-moana-music-potential-egot-status-staying-positive-under-trump-963551 (accessed on 19 September 2018).

Ngata, Tina. 2014. For Whom the Taika Roars (An Open Letter to Taika Waititi). *The Non-Plastic Maori*, October 24. Available online: https://thenonplasticmaori.wordpress.com/2014/10/24/for-whom-the-taika-roars-an-open-letter-to-taika-waititi/ (accessed on 21 October 2018).

Ngata, Tina, and Anne Keala Kelly. 2016. Reclaiming Mana Moana. *Dialogue. Tangata Whenua*, October 9. Available online: http://news.tangatawhenua.com/2016/10/reclaimingmanamoana/?doing_wp_cron=1476010489.4788870811462402343750 (accessed on 21 October 2018).

Parasher, Prajna. 2013. Mapping the Imaginary: The Neverland of Disney Indians. In *Diversity in Disney Films: Critical Essays on Race, Ethnicity, Gender, Sexuality, and Disability*. Edited by Johnson Cheu. London: McFarland & Company, Inc., pp. 38–49.

Pomerantz, Dorothy. 2015. Live Action 'Mulan' in the Works as Disney Follows the Money. *Forbes*, March 30.

Robertson, Barbara. 2016. Navigating Polynesia. *CGW Magazine* 39: 8–16.

Robinson, Joanna. 2016. How Pacific Islanders Helped Disney's Moana Find Its Way. *Vanity Fair*, November 16.

Said, Edward. 2003. *Orientalism*. London: Penguin.

Schilling, Vincent. 2016. The Rock's Husky Polynesian God From Disney's Moana Get's Mixed Reviews. In *Indian Country Today*. Washington: Indian Country Media Network.

Sonoda-Pale, M. Healani. 2016. Disney's Commodification of Hawaiians. *Civic Beat*, October 7. Available online: www.civilbeat.org/2016/10/disneys-commodification-of-hawaiians (accessed on 21 October 2018).

Tiffin, Jessica. 2009. *Marvelous Geometry: Narrative and Metafiction in Modern Fairy Tale*. Detroit: Wayne State University Press.

Ward, Annalee R. 2002. *Mouse Morality: The Rhetoric of Disney Animated Film*. Austin: University of Texas Press.

Wells, Paul. 2002. *Animation and America*. New Brunswick, New Jersey: Rutgers University Press.

Yin, Jing. 2014. Popular Culture and Public Imaginary: Disney vs. Chinese Stories of Mulan. In *The Global Intercultural Communication Reader*. Edited by Molefi Kete Asante, Yoshitaka Miike and Jing Yin. Oxon: Routledge, pp. 285–304.

Zipes, Jack. 2009. *Relentless Progress*. London: Routlege.

social sciences

MDPI

Article

Time to Face the Music: Musical Colonization and Appropriation in Disney's Moana

Robin Armstrong

Music Department, McDaniel College, Westminster, MD 21157, USA; rarmstrong@mcdaniel.edu;
Tel.: +410-857-2536

Received: 16 May 2018; Accepted: 10 July 2018; Published: 13 July 2018

Abstract: Despite Disney's presentation of *Moana* as a culturally accurate portrayal of Polynesian culture, the film suffers from Western ethnocentrism, specifically in its music. This assertion is at odds with marketing of *Moana* that emphasized respect for and consultation with Polynesians whose expertise was heralded to validate the film's music as culturally authentic. While the composers do, in fact, use Polynesian musical traits, they frame the sounds that are unfamiliar within those that are familiar by wrapping them with Western musical characteristics. When the audience does hear Polynesian music throughout the film, the first and last sounds they hear are Western music, not Polynesian. As such, the audience hears Polynesian sounds meld into and then become the music that defines a typical American film. Thus, regardless of Disney's employment of Polynesian musicians, the music of *Moana* remains in the rigid control of non-Polynesian American composers. Rather than break new ground, *Moana* illustrates a musical recapitulation of white men's control and marketing of the representations of marginalized people. *Moana*'s music is subject to appropriation, an echo of how colonial resources were exploited in ways that prioritize benefits to cultural outsiders.

Keywords: *Moana*; Disney; music; colonialism; imperialism; appropriation; Polynesia

1. Introduction

Disney has a long history of telling other people's stories in feature-length cartoons. Despite the historical and cultural diversity of these stories, their agenda is uniform, proselytizing a conservative, white, middle-class set of "old-fashioned American" values (Wasko 2001). Disney's works promote "cultural privilege, social inequality and human alienation" (Artz 2004, p. 125). At the end of the twentieth century, to adjust to a market in need of more diverse stories (Artz 2004, p. 122), the company began plundering tales from more exotic locations. In response to criticisms of insensitive cultural appropriations, Disney began to hire traditional culture bearers to market themselves as culturally sensitive and authentic (Clark et al. 2017).[1]

Music has always been an important part of Disney films, and, just as the visual traits of the animation can be used to push a cultural agenda (Artz 2004), the musical traits in the sound track can also be used as a tool to make a statement that might even contradict the superficially egalitarian message of the direct narrative (Nooshin 2004). The purpose of this article is to explore Disney's use of music in *Moana* (2016) as a tool that pushes a colonial agenda under a patina of cultural authenticity. While Disney films all include scores that situate their stories within their narrative context, *Moana* presents an especially clear distinction between what Disney markets as its respect for

---

[1] Disney's portrayals of non-European cultures began early in their animated features such as *Song of the South* (1946) and *The Jungle Book* (1967), but until the 1990s the stories chosen were European/American stories about other cultures. Beginning in the 1990s the narrative point of view changes and the Disney corporation began adapting non-western stories, and thus began marketing their works as multi-cultural.

cultural authenticity, and the way in which it uses music to establish imperialistic authority over an appropriated culture.[2]

In the past, when Disney featured a culture deemed exotic to many Westerners, it catered to fascination with the "other," an Orientalism that dehumanizes and objectifies its subjects (Said 1978). While *Moana* has avoided the Orientalist portrayal of women in other cultures as "the exotic, the foreign and the sexual" (Lacroix 2004, p. 218), it nevertheless still presents a "Disneyfied" (Giroux and Pollock 2010) version of a non-Western part of the globe, using music as an important tool to closely control that "other."

2. Background on *Moana*'s Polynesian Content

The music of *Moana* (2016) received much attention for contrasting and contradictory reasons. Much pre-release news focused on the Polynesian contributors to the film (Bernardin 2016; Moore 2016). All of the main singing actors of the film are Polynesian, and one of the three composers, Opetaia Foa'i, is an award-winning Polynesian musician who is steeped in his culture's traditional sounds. At the same time, much attention has focused on the contributions of Broadway's golden boy, Lin-Manuel Miranda, best known for the blockbuster musical *Hamilton*. Detailed analysis of the sounds that comprise the music in *Moana* suggest that the score is much more Miranda than Moana: more Disney than Polynesia. Despite the hype about authenticity, Western musical traits open and close each song, framing and containing the Polynesian sounds. This musical containment of unfamiliar sounds by familiar ones limits the audience's access to the unfamiliar, controlling the representation of the otherness of Polynesian music. Disney, then, carefully controls the musical image of Polynesia that it markets to the world. Through this control, it appropriates and colonizes the music of Polynesia.[3]

From the earliest long-form animated films, Disney has taken fairy tales from Europe and simplified their stories to promote of a narrow set of conservative, small-town 'American' values (Sayers and Weisenberg 1965; Hunt and Frankenberg 1990; Wasko 2001). In the last several decades, they have turned to the stories of other places and cultures, but still focus on the same set of 'all-American' values in a true imperialistic fashion that exerts complete control over all parts of the narrative and its presentation (Kadi 1995; Cypher and Higgs 1997; Wasko 2001; Nooshin 2004; Clark et al. 2017). In all their endeavors, from films to parks, music has played a large role in both storytelling and in fashioning this imperialistic control (Carson 2004; Nooshin 2004). To combat the reputation of exploitation and appropriation, the Disney Corporation has begun to hire native experts in the cultures of the stories they tell to be able to claim authenticity rather than appropriation, to much less success than fanfare (Fleeger 2014; Clark et al. 2017).

On a superficial level, the music in *Moana*, like all Disney soundtracks, mixes a range of musical styles into a coherent score. Because Polynesian music has long been subject to stylistic synthesis (Thomas 1981; Moulin 1996) and because much of this musical mixing is a normal process for Polynesian musicians themselves (Colson 2014), this process is, in itself, not always colonial in nature. Moreover, Disney's employment of Opetaia Foa'i might seem to address issues of appropriation. This paper argues, however, that Disney went beyond synthesis and into imperialism and appropriation in the way in which they used Polynesian musical traits, where they put them, and who got to sing them.

---

[2] Issues of representation and authenticity with respect to music are unique for each film, and this essay will consider the music of *Moana* to examine the case that it presents. For discussions about music in other Disney films and products, see (Carson 2004; Clague 2004; Nooshin 2004; Tulk 2010; Fleeger 2014; Hess 2017; Rodoshtenous 2017).
[3] The term 'polynesian' refers to a subset of Pacific Island cultures of the region of Oceania. While *Moana*'s creators claim full Pacific Island and Oceania representation in this work (Julius and Malone 2016), the story relies most heavily on Polynesian cultures, since the character Maui is a Polynesian demi-god and the name Moana means ocean in several Polynesian languages (Tamaira et al. 2018). Outside of the "Oceanic Trust", media discussions of the Pacific Islanders and Americans of Pacific Island heritage that are involved in the movie, use the term Polynesian to identify their cultural heritage.

3. Purpose of Paper

The arguments presented in this paper provide an avenue for widening the discussion of the potential impact of Disney films by focusing on their musical facets as interpreted by an academic with expertise both in music and sociology. The music in *Moana* plays an important role in perceptions of Polynesia, a large group of different Pacific cultures that are not well known outside of their region. Disney's decision to appoint itself as able to distill elements of a culture, in the case of this analysis, in the form of music, raises concerns about exploitation of marginalized cultures that enter the world's stage via a "Disneyfied" version that the company misrepresents as authentic.

4. The Use of Cultural Natives in Disney Productions

Moana is not the first production for which Disney hired cultural 'natives' to grant cultural authority to offset criticism of imperialism. For the 2013 production of *Jungle Book*, which takes place in Rudyard Kipling's India, the creators traveled in India for two and a half weeks (Clark et al. 2017), and "infused Indian influences into the show's design, choreography and casting" (Weinert-Kendt 2013) by hiring an Indian dancer as a consultant and Indian musicians as performers (Clark et al. 2017). What the White American creators did not do in *Jungle Book*, and what they still fail to do in Moana, is allow non-westerners to fashion representations of themselves and their own cultures; control always stays in the hand of the colonizers.

Westerners have long fantasized and exoticized the Pacific Islands. In 2011, film directors John Musker and Ron Clements suggested Polynesia to Disney as the next big Disney adventure inspired by the books of Melville and Conrad, as well as the paintings of Gaugin (Berman 2016). They conducted research for their creation through visiting museums, reading original myths and stories, and traveling to Polynesian locations (Julius and Malone 2016; Mottram 2016). Disney even created an 'Oceanic Trust' of culture bearers to ensure that *Moana* would be Disney's most culturally authentic animated film yet (Robinson 2016). It published a book about this supposed authenticity to ensure the public's appreciation of their efforts (Julius and Malone 2016).

While the research inspired the film makers, the Oceanic Trust advised them, and Polynesian writers and musicians helped them, the film was conceived, created, and controlled by Disney's American white men. They took a Polynesian deity, Maui, as their starting point, but rather than dramatize a Polynesian story, they created a new one that suited their own commercial goals more than it reflected any Polynesian reality. Like physical, political colonizers, Disney is merely using Polynesian resources for their own profit (Diaz 2016; Herman 2016; Ngata 2016). The creation of the music followed much the same process with similar results.

Mark Mancina, a classically trained composer with many movie and television credits, wrote the score. Lin-Manuel Miranda, the creator of *Hamilton*, who is perhaps most known for bringing rap music into mainstream Broadway, added songs to the movie. Disney also hired Opetaia Foa'i, the founder of the contemporary Polynesian musical group Te Vaka. He advised on the score and wrote "We Know the Way" (Newman 2016). While the score does make use of Polynesian musical sounds, it also contains Broadway sounds, and both are embedded into a traditional American film score. Polynesian singers produce an authentic Polynesian choral style, but it is accompanied by a Western Symphony orchestra. As the film uses a Polynesian deity and island location to tell a Disney story, the music uses Polynesian sounds that combine with Broadway and symphonic sounds to produce a Disney sound track.

5. Key Plot Elements of *Moana* and Their Corresponding Musical Coding

The story of *Moana* revolves around definitions of Moana's peoples' traditions. Seeing her people in need, Moana is at first torn between following her father's definition of their tradition (staying "Where you Are") and leaving her home to seek a solution (in "How Far I'll go"). Once she learns that sea voyaging and exploration represent an older, and presumably more authentic tradition ("We Know the Way") than what her father claims, she leaves on her hero's journey. Her quest is to restore an important cultural totem to its traditional owner, and thus this voyage is about discovering, repairing, and restoring older authentic traditions.

While there is no single Polynesian musical style, there are nonetheless common musical traits; traditional Polynesian music is dominated by singing and drumming. Singing both with and without drumming was heard in solos, small groups, and big groups, and the styles of singing ran the gamut from chanting only a few notes repeatedly to wider, more tuneful melodies. Choirs sang the same notes (unison singing) more often than they sang in harmony before European missionaries arrived and taught them Western hymn singing (Smith et al. 2001). Percussion instruments are by far the most common instruments used. Polynesians make percussion instruments from many different materials and thus the instruments have many different sound qualities. These instruments were played alone as well as to accompany singers. Many places in Polynesia have flute-like instruments, and the conch shell played as a trumpet can also be found. Almost no string instruments existed in Polynesia before Europeans brought the guitar, and none were played, or sounded, like violins and cellos (Love et al. 1998). The sounds that are the most distinctly Polynesian throughout the score of *Moana* are the drum beats, male chorus chanting, and some solo and choral singing in a Polynesian language. Audiences do hear the influence of the Polynesian composer Opetaia Foa'i, but these sounds never stand on their own but are framed and/or accompanied by the music of American Broadway and film.

6. Musical Framing

Musical "framing" is a structure in which a familiar set of 'normal' musical sounds precede, follows, and accompanies a different set of unfamiliar or 'other' sounds. In the case of *Moana*, the familiar 'normal' sounds are the musical traits common to all Western musicals; the unfamiliar 'other' sounds are Polynesian musical traits like heavy drumming and male chorus chanting. When the audience does hear Polynesian music throughout the film, the first and last sound they hear is Western music, not Polynesian. Before, after, and during the Polynesian music in the film, Western sounds wrap around the 'other' sounds like a frame wraps around a picture, safely containing the 'other' sounds with those that are normative (McClary 1991).

Moana begins like any other Disney movie: the audience first sees a sky, and as the scene moves on—a western countryside, a river, a train going over the river, the Disney Castle, and then on to Mickey Mouse as Steamboat Willie. The music we hear during this Disney opening is the first song on the *Moana* soundtrack, "Tulou Tagaloa." This song begins with a long, low note played by cellos and basses seconds before a bright, female voice calls out "Tulou, toulo tagaloa." In between the second and third word of this call we hear a strong, low drum beat. A full choir of men's and women's voices join in, always tuning their notes to the cellos and basses that continue to hold the same long notes. While the voices, language, and drums are traditional Polynesian sounds, the music that accompanies them is Western, especially the long note in the bottom held by the cellos and basses. Uniform, consistent pitches and melodic string instruments like cellos are essential in American symphonic film scores, but not important in pre-colonial Polynesian music (Smith et al. 2001). The cellos continue to play the same low note throughout this short song. Towards the end, their note dips down briefly and returns to the original note, in a standard musical formula that is actually the most common progression in all European and American classical and commercial music. The song ends with all voices on the same pitch that the cellos have been holding throughout.

As the pictures of Disney's castle and Mickey Mouse at the beginning of this movie frame Moana's story as a Disney creation, the consistent, persistent pitch in the low notes played by instruments found in Western film/symphony orchestras frames the music as an American creation as well, regardless of how many Polynesian musical traits the audience may hear. At the end of the opening song, when all voices sing the same pitch with which the cellos and basses opened the scene, the audience is literally hearing Polynesian voices becoming westernized as they join the long-held, uniform pitch played by the cellos and bases.

The framing of Polynesian musical traits can also be seen as a colonial 'civilizing process.' Heavy percussion and rhythmic emphasis in commercial music received much criticism in the United States throughout the twentieth century. Because African music focuses on rhythm, and the musical traits that slaves brought into the Americas included more rhythmic energy than their European counterparts, conservative critics have long lamented the 'barbaric' and 'savage' sounds of any musical styles in the United States that sported heavy rhythm and percussion. Rock and Roll, which flourished during the civil rights movement of the 1950s and 1960s, received especially loud outcries (Maddock 1966; Haines 2011). Concurrent with conservative outrage at such 'barbaric' and 'savage' music, the Disney Corporation worked long and hard to create a "Disney Universe" based on conservative social 'family values' of their own imagined small-town America (Wasko 2001). As loud, strong (Black) drumming did not fit into the (White) 'American' value set that Disney has historically transmitted in their works, neither do the equally strong, equally rhythmic drums of Polynesian music. To include these highly percussive sounds in a family-oriented film soundtrack, then, they need to be 'civilized' through the containment of the symphonic frame. Thus, the framing process is in this instance a colonial process, since "[t]he idea of 'the civilizing mission', as we all know very well, is firmly rooted in the history of colonization and imperialism" (Van Krieken 2011).

7. The Dominance of Western Musical Elements

Throughout the film, Western music continues to dominate Polynesian sounds, even in songs that are purportedly about Polynesian traditions, where one might—because of the topic of the songs—expect to hear Polynesian music predominate. Moana's father sings "Where We Are" shortly after the opening scenes. As the film shows her people going about their daily lives engrossed in their traditional arts and other activities, he and the chorus of men accompanying him are teaching their values. Dancers only dance ancient dances, not new ones. People eat traditional coconut, fish, and taro. Baskets and paintings are created in the traditional manners. In fact, he lectures, "This tradition is our mission" (Miranda 2016).

The music of this song is an appealing synthesis of Polynesian and American traits. The introduction begins with a high, light male chanting 'ooh' backed by drums; an acoustic guitar joins in, and then Moana's father begins to sing a tune that would fit into any movie musical. He is joined by others who support his rules. To highlight the words, "The dancers are practicing/They dance to an ancient song," a low-voiced male chorus chants a rhythmic accompaniment and then join in with their own lyrics "Who needs a new song? This old one's all we need" (Miranda 2016). In the next segment of text, Moana's father is joined by a chorus of men and women singing in harmony, who accompany him off and on for the rest of the song. The instrumental accompaniment includes guitars and a bass as well as a variety of types of percussion.

In the middle of the song, Moana's grandmother sings two verses with a different message, telling Moana to listen to her heart. In the first of these verses, the guitar and light percussion accompanies the grandmother's singing. Then the percussion drops out, and the guitar accompaniment is joined by very soft violins and flutes. The percussion comes back in as we hear music from the beginning introduction leading us to the final verse sung by her father and the full chorus. At this point, different singers take different lines of text with independent melodies but singing them simultaneously. The resulting short segment is more complex than when they all sing the same melodies together. Moana sings the melody at the very end of the song, backed up in full harmony by the large chorus, and the symphonic strings join in the final few notes.

This song depicting island traditions is Disney's representation of a tropical island. The center of the song describes the role of the coconut, and the accompanying action illustrates the text.

Consider the coconut (the what?)
Consider its tree

We use each part of the coconut
That's all we need
We make our nets from the fibers (we make our nets from the fibers)
The water is sweet inside (the water is sweet inside)
We use the leaves to build fires (we use the leaves to build fires)
We cook up the meat inside (we cook up the meat inside)
Consider the coconuts (consider the coconuts)
The trunks and the leaves (ha!)
The island gives us what we need

(Miranda 2016)

In reality, this simply is Disney's version of the "tiresome ... cliché [of] the 'happy natives with coconuts' trope. Coconuts ... are part of the shtick of caricatures about Pacific peoples." (Herman 2016).

The music works in the same manner as the coconut "shtick." Polynesian music and commercial music share enough musical traits that this pop song can represent Polynesian music in Disney's lexicon. Most sounds that are Polynesian in this song are also common in contemporary commercial music: the high male "oooh" and the light, high percussion could easily be mistaken for any Latin-influenced pop song, many of which have similar types of percussion instruments playing as we hear in this song. Because this song discusses life on an island, and most 'latin' musical sounds originate in the Caribbean islands, one way of understanding this song is as generic 'island' music that conflates cultures in Pacific and the Caribbean into one essentialized 'island' culture, i.e., the 'island schtick' in music.

We do not hear the low drums we heard earlier, and we only hear the low male chanting to punctuate the line about dancing at the beginning of the song. Many of the sounds heard here are not sounds heard in traditional Polynesian music, especially the way that the chorus sings towards the end, where each singer has a different melody but they all sing them at the same time. That is standard fare for Broadway and movies, but not for Polynesia. While we do not have continual orchestral presence, we hear the orchestra play at very strategic points: when Moana's grandmother tells her to ignore her father in favor of her own inner voice, and at the very end, like a frame. The song "Who We Are" claims to present a Polynesian representation of life on their island but instead tells an American version of a rather generic island story. Similarly, Disney implies that the lead singer is the Polynesian actor Temeru Morrison who voices the role of Chief Tui, when in fact the song is dubbed by the American actor Christopher Jackson. As the story told in the song "Where We Are" is more Disney than Polynesian (Chinen 2016), the music is more American than Polynesian.

The most important song in which we might expect to hear traditional Polynesian sounds is the one that teaches Moana about the older, voyaging traditions of her people, "We Know the Way." This song served as one of the early promotional trailers, to great fanfare, and was called a "Love letter to the culture of the Pacific Islanders" (Garis 2016). It was the first song that Polynesian composer Opetaia Foa'i wrote when he landed the contract to contribute music to the film (Te 2018). Of course, Disney did not leave his finished product alone, but rather gave it a few "tweaks here and there" (Te 2018).

"We Know the Way" does contain the traditional Polynesian musical sounds of low-pitched male chanting, solo singing in a Polynesian language, and varied percussion. Like the first song of the movie, "Tulou Tagaloa" (discussed above), these Polynesian sounds are framed by a low, bass pitch played by strings both at the beginning and end, and much of the song is lightly accompanied throughout by a typical film/symphony orchestra. The Westernization goes further than this, however, for while Opetaia Foa'i sang the Polynesian lyrics, American Broadway composer and performer Lin-Manuel Miranda sang the English.

Who sings this song is especially important when considering questions of authenticity and appropriation in the music of *Moana*. All of the important roles in the film are voiced by actors of Polynesian ancestry. The composer of this song was hired to ensure musical traditional accuracy.

This composer is also a professional singer in his own right, and sings some of this song. In live performances of this song, such as the one at the New Zealand Music Awards in November of 2017, he sings all lyrics in both languages. Lin-Manuel Miranda, on the other hand, is famous in the United States and is selling many tickets on Broadway, but is not of Polynesian ancestry. The song "We know the Way" is a first-person narrative of the most ancient and authentic wayfaring traditions of Polynesian people, yet is sung by a non-Polynesian actor. Having a non-Polynesian sing this song seems counter to everything Disney has claimed about their respect for authenticity and authentic voices. It is consistent with a desire to appropriate Polynesian culture.

8. Conclusions

Colonialism is based on who sets the rules and who defines representation. While the narrative of *Moana* contains authentic Polynesian elements, Disney still controls what and who is depicted, and how they are portrayed. Despite Polynesian input, these representations are still more Disney formula than Polynesian (Wasko 2001). The music contains Polynesian musical traits but follows Western rules: the musical structure and symphonic context are Disney, not Polynesia. The framing of the Polynesian traits ensures that the Polynesian musical sounds literally follow Western music. The combination and synthesis of musical traits is firmly controlled by Disney. Even in the song written by a Polynesian musician whose lyrics describe the oldest of traditions, the majority of those lyrics are sung by a Broadway actor rather than a Polynesian singer. Despite Polynesian contributions, Disney firmly controls the film's musical representations.

Because of the marketing claims of respect for, consultation with, and employment of authentic culture bearers, audiences might believe that musical representations in *Moana* are in fact authentic. Instead, the Disney version stifles the voices of marginalized people while making money from the production, complete with campy coconut stereotypes. As in the *Jungle Book*, the creators can disavow colonialism so that Disney and its audiences can enjoy the "guilt-free" pleasures and profits of Island exoticism (Clark et al. 2017). Nevertheless, despite marketing claims of respect, Disney colonizes Polynesian music, counting on audience acceptance of their version of authenticity.

Funding: This research received no external funding.

Conflicts of Interest: The author declares no conflict of interest.

References

Artz, Lee. 2004. The righteousness of self-centred royals: The world according to Disney animation. *Critical Arts* 18: 116–46. [CrossRef]

Berman, Eliza. 2016. Why Disney Decided to Make Moana the Ultimate Anti-Princess. *Time*, September 1. Available online: http://time.com/4473277/moana-disney-princess-directors-interview/ (accessed on 3 March 2018).

Bernardin, Marc. 2016. Lin-Manuel Miranda Navigates the Pacific to Help Send 'Moana' on a Daring Adventure. *Los Angeles Times*, December 8. Available online: http://www.latimes.com/entertainment/movies/la-en-mn-1208-lin-manuel-miranda-envelope-20161120-story.html (accessed on 3 May 2018).

Carson, Charles. 2004. 'Whole New Worlds': Music and the Disney Theme Park Experience. *Ethnomusicology Forum* 13: 228–35. [CrossRef]

Chinen, Nate. 2016. Consider the Coconut: How *Moana* Uses Polynesian Culture to Create a Prototypical Disney Story. *Slate*, November 22. Available online: http://www.slate.com/articles/arts/culturebox/2016/11/how_moana_uses_polynesian_myths_to_create_a_disney_story.html (accessed on 5 March 2018).

Clague, Mark. 2004. Playing in 'Toon: Walt Disney's "Fantasia" (1940) and the Imagineering of Classical Music. *American Music* 22: 91–109. [CrossRef]

Clark, Emily, Galella Donatella, Stefanie A. Jones, and Catherine Young. 2017. 'I Wanna Be Like You': Negotiating Race, Racism and Orientalism in *The Jungle Book* on Stage. In *The Disney Musical on Stage and Screen: Critical Approaches from 'Snow White' to 'Frozen'*. Edited by George Rodoshtenous. New York: Bloomsbury Publishing, pp. 185–201.

Colson, Geoffroy. 2014. A Fresh Approach to Transculturation in Contemporary Music in Tahiti. *Eras* 16: 1–22.

Cypher, Jennifer, and Eric Higgs. 1997. Colonizing the Imagination: Disney's Wilderness Lodge. *Capitalism Nature Socialism* 8: 107–30. [CrossRef]

Diaz, Vicente M. 2016. Don't Swallow (or be Swallowed by) Disney's 'Culturally Authenticated Moana'. *Indian Country Today*, November 13. Available online: https://indiancountrymedianetwork.com/news/opinions/dont-swallow-or-be-swallowed-by-disneys-culturally-authenticated-moana/ (accessed on 1 March 2018).

Fleeger, Jennifer. 2014. *Mismatched Women: The Siren's Song through the Machine*. New York: Oxford University Press.

Garis, Mary Grace. 2016. Lin-Manuel Miranda Releases 'We Know The Way' & It Perfectly Sums Up The Adventurous Spirit of Moana. *Bustle*, November 7. Available online: https://www.bustle.com/articles/193693-lin-manuel-miranda-releases-we-know-the-way-it-perfectly-sums-up-the-adventurous-spirit-of (accessed on 22 February 2016).

Giroux, Henry A., and Grace Pollock. 2010. *The Mouse that Roared: Disney and the End of Innocence*. Lanham: Rowman & Littlefield Publishers.

Haines, John. 2011. The Emergence of Jesus Rock: On Taming the 'African Beat'. *Black Music Research Journal* 31: 229–60. [CrossRef]

Herman, Doug. 2016. How the Story of 'Moana' and Maui Holds Up Against Cultural Truths. *Smithsonian*, December 2. Available online: https://www.smithsonianmag.com/smithsonian-institution/how-story-moana-and-maui-holds-against-cultural-truths-180961258/#0frUoRyRIqQCiCIF.99 (accessed on 6 February 2018).

Hess, Carol A. 2017. Walt Disney's *Saludos Amigos*: Hollywood and the Propaganda of Authenticity. In *Tide Was Always High: The Music of Latin America in Los Angeles*. Edited by Josh Kun. Berkeley: University of California, pp. 105–23.

Hunt, Pauline, and Ronald Frankenberg. 1990. It's a Small World: Disneyland, the Family and Multiple Re-representations of American Childhood. In *Constructing and Reconstructing Childhood: Contemporary Issues in the Sociological Study of Childhood*. Edited by Allison James and Alan Prout. London: Palmer Press, pp. 99–117.

Julius, Jessica, and Maggie Malone. 2016. *The Art of Moana*. San Francisco: Chronicle Books.

Kadi, Joanna. 1995. Disney's Dominion: How Popular Culture Advances Imperialism. *Colors* 4: 44–48.

Lacroix, Celeste. 2004. Images of animated others: The orientalization of Disney's cartoon heroines from The Little Mermaid to The Hunchback of Notre Dame. *Popular Communication* 2: 213–29. [CrossRef]

Love, Jacob W., Neville H. Fletcher, Don Niles, Douglas L. Oliver, Allan Thomas, Gerald Florian Messner, Adrienne L. Kaeppler, Michael Webb, Amy Ku'uleialoha Stillman, Jay W. Junker, and et al. 1998. Musical Instruments. In *Australia and the Pacific Islands*. Garrland Encyclopedia of World Music. Edited by Adrienne L. Kaeppler. New York: Garland Publishing, vol. 9, pp. 371–403.

Maddock, Shane. 1966. 'Whole lotta shakin' goin' on': Racism and Early Opposition to Rock Music. *Mid-America* 78: 181–202.

McClary, Susan. 1991. *Feminine Endings: Music, Gender, and Sexuality*. Minneapolis: University of Minnesota Press.

Miranda, Lin-Manuel. 2016. *'We know the Way' Moana (Original Motion Picture Soundtrack)*. Burbank: Walt Disney Records.

Moore, Caitlin. 2016. Disney's 'Moana' is a Breath of Fresh Island Air. *The Washington Post*, November 22. Available online: https://www.washingtonpost.com/goingoutguide/movies/disneys-moana-is-a-breath-of-fresh-island-air/2016/11/22/96bd1f90-a50f-11e6-8fc0-7be8f848c492_story.html?noredirect=on&utm_term=.3bd74464ff37 (accessed on 6 February 2018).

Mottram, James. 2016. Directors of Disney's Moana on the great lengths to portray Tahitian culture as accurately as possible. *The National*, November 27. Available online: https://www.thenational.ae/arts-culture/directors-of-disney-s-moana-on-the-great-lengths-to-portray-tahitian-culture-as-accurately-as-possible-1.213500 (accessed on 5 March 2018).

Moulin, Jane Freeman. 1996. What's Mine Is Yours? Cultural Borrowing in a Pacific Context. *The Contemporary Pacific* 8: 127–53.

Newman, Melinda. 2016. Lin-Manuel Miranda, Mark Mancina & Opetaia Foa'i on Creating Disney's 'Moana' Music as 'Hamilton' Exploded. *Billboard*, November 23. Available online: https://www.billboard.com/articles/news/7588008/lin-manuel-miranda-mark-mancina-opetaia-foai-disney-moana-music (accessed on 3 March 2018).

Ngata, Tina. 2016. Maui 'Skin Suit' Isn't the End of 'Moana' Trouble.". *Honolulu Civil Beat*, September 27. Available online: http://www.civilbeat.org/2016/09/maui-skin-suit-isnt-the-end-of-moana-trouble/ (accessed on 1 March 2018).

Nooshin, Laudan. 2004. Circumnavigation with a Difference? Music, Representation and the Disney Experience: 'It's a Small, Small World.'. *Ethnomusicology Forum* 13: 236–51.

Robinson, Joanna. 2016. How Pacific Islanders Helped Disney's *Moana* Find Its Way. *Vanity Fair*, November 16. Available online: https://www.vanityfair.com/hollywood/2016/11/moana-oceanic-trust-disney-controversy-pacific-islanders-polynesia (accessed on 1 March 2018).

Rodoshtenous, George, ed. 2017. *The Disney Musical on Stage and Screen: Critical Approaches from 'Snow White' to 'Frozen'*. New York: Bloomsbury Publishing.

Said, Edward. 1978. *Orientalism: Western Representations of the Orient*. New York: Pantheon.

Sayers, Frances Clarke, and Charles M. Weisenberg. 1965. Walt Disney Accused. *The Horn Book Magazine*, December 7, 602–11.

Smith, Barbara B., Adrienne L. Kaeppler, Kevin Salisbury, Mervyn McLean, Amy K. Stillman, Jane F. Moulin, Richard M. Moyle, Thomas Allan, and Dieter Christensen. 2001. *"Polynesia." Grove Music Online*. New York: Oxford University Press, Available online: https://doi.org/10.1093/gmo/9781561592630.article.41191 (accessed on 21 January 2018).

Tamaira, Marata Ketekiri, Vilsoni Hereniko, Tagi Qolouvaki, J. Uluwehi Hopkins, and Candice Elanna Steiner. 2018. *Moana* by Jared Bush (review). *The Contemporary Pacific* 30: 216–34. [CrossRef]

Te, Vaka. 2018. When You Wish Upon a Star. Available online: http://www.tevaka.com/moana (accessed on 21 May 2018).

Thomas, Allan. 1981. The Study of Acculturated Music in Oceania: 'Cheap and Tawdry Borrowed Tunes'? *The Journal of the Polynesian Society* 90: 183–91.

Tulk, Janice Esther. 2010. An Aesthetic of Ambiguity: Musical Representation of Indigenous Peoples in Disney's Brother Bear. In *Drawn to Sound: Animation Film Music and Sonicity*. Edited by Rebecca Coyle. London: Equinox, pp. 120–40.

Van Krieken, Robert. 2011. Three faces of civilization: 'In the beginning all the world was Ireland'. *Sociological Review* 59: 24–47. [CrossRef]

Wasko, Janet. 2001. *Understanding Disney; the Manufacture of Fantasy*. Malden: Blackwell Publishers, Inc.

Weinert-Kendt, Rob. 2013. Cutting Through a Cultural Thicket: 'The Jungle Book' Comes to the Stage. *New York Times*, June 20. Available online: https://www.nytimes.com/2013/06/23/theater/the-jungle-book-comes-to-the-stage.html (accessed on 1 May 2018).

social sciences

MDPI

Article

Disney 'World': The Westernization of World Music in EPCOT's "IllumiNations: Reflections of Earth"

Matthew Hodge

Musical Theatre Department, William Peace University, Raleigh, NC 27604, USA; rmhodge@peace.edu

Received: 24 July 2018; Accepted: 11 August 2018; Published: 13 August 2018

Abstract: Although Disney's EPCOT theme park markets itself as a place to experience other cultures and reflect on Earth's history, the dominance of a Western perspective omits true authenticity, specifically in the music of its nighttime show IllumiNations: Reflections of Earth. This 13-minute long presentation offers a visual retelling of humanity's existence accompanied by an original musical score that guides the narrative. The consecutive music section titles provide insight into critical points within Disney's story arc: Prologue: Acceleration, Chaos, Space, Life, Adventure, Home, Celebration, and Meaning. While sounds of music from other cultures do present themselves—albeit in stereotypical and clichéd fashions— they are arbitrarily highlighted within a framework of Western musical components. This framing allows Disney composers to control the perception of 'others' through music. Furthermore, the final Meaning section is entirely built of Euro-American musical conventions, insinuating that cultures arrive at their most enlightened, evolved selves when they become Westernized. Despite its impressive technological advances and complex musical composition, IllumiNations: Reflections of Earth is guilty of implementing Western musical frameworks that Disney utilizes in the majority of its films and theme parks.

Keywords: Disney; EPCOT; music; appropriation; world; park; entertainment; sounds; cultures

1. Introduction

For the majority of Americans, "Disney" is synonymous with high-quality entertainment and comforting family values (Anderson and Tavin 2003). By the end of the twentieth century, hundreds of millions of people were annually watching a Disney film in theaters or on home video, watching weekly Disney television shows, listening to Disney music on home audio players, and visiting Disney theme parks (Eisner 1995). To this day, Walt Disney theme parks consistently rank highest globally in amusement park attendance (Rubin 2018), firmly cementing their place in immersive entertainment. One popular—albeit sometimes controversial—cornerstone of the Disney immersion experience is the role of thematic music in transporting audiences to other 'worlds.' One staple attraction exemplifying this use of thematic 'worldy' music is IllumiNations: Reflections of Earth, the current nightly entertainment event at Disney's EPCOT[1] theme park in Orlando, Florida. This nighttime show presents itself as a retelling of humanity's story from Earth's creation to modern day life, all through visuals and music. As the story evolves from the beginning of time to the modern-day world (a finale section entitled "Meaning"), the music evolves from sounds of other cultures, often stereotypical, to a completely Western Euro-American music soundscape, thus insinuating that the evolution of humanity's 'progress' throughout time finally reaches 'meaning' once cultures become Westernized.

Disney has an established history of heavily utilizing music in films and theme parks in attempts to create aural soundscapes of exotic locales, foreign cultures, and globally vast civilizations. The very concept of so-called 'world' music is a broad notion based on musical exoticism and musical folklore

---

[1] An acronym for Experimental Prototype Community of Tomorrow.

where "easily recognized musical characteristics from an alien culture are assimilated into a more familiar style, giving it an exotic color and suggestiveness" (Bellman 1998, p. ix). Though extremely popular and commercially successful, Disney music warrants frequent criticism for combining Western (Euro-American) musical elements with folk world music stereotypes often related to appropriation to present a "Disneyfied" version that is interpreted by American audiences as 'authentic' (Armstrong 2018). Furthermore, millions of international tourists visit Walt Disney World theme parks in Florida every year, comprising approximately 18–20% of total attendance (Garcia 2013). Consequently, people from nonWestern countries may view this Americanized perspective of their music and cultures as a problematic, false representation of themselves. Thus, the purpose of this article is to explore Disney's use of an insinuated 'world music' narrative within a Westernized framework in EPCOT's IllumiNations: Reflections of Earth.

2. The EPCOT Experience

Contextual deconstruction of the musical effects within IllumiNations: Reflections of Earth warrants an introductory analysis of the broader EPCOT experience from which the nighttime show is one fabric piece. Since its opening in 1982, EPCOT has flourished under the reputation of inviting guests to come "travel around the world" (EPCOT 2018). This enticing marketing stays true to the vision that Walt Disney himself stated should be the foundation of his visitors' immersive experiences: "I don't want the public to see the world they live in while they're in the park ... I want them to feel they're in another world" (Wilson 1991, p. 161). EPCOT's attendees achieve this 'world traveling' experience through three massive, immersive encounters: its World Showcase section, its Future World section, and its IllumiNations: Reflections of Earth nighttime show (which debuted in 1999).

EPCOT's unique World Showcase section stands as a circular display of eleven "countries" surrounding a large lagoon (the nighttime show resides in the center of this body of water). Each country is exhibited in a world's-fair-style pavilion (Carson 2004) with promises of offering visitors 'authentic'—yet often clichéd—interactions with clothing, architecture, food, art, dance, and music from its represented nation. Park guests are invited to spend the day 'sampling' countries as they 'travel' from one nation to the other in a symbolic cultural buffet-like carousel.

Disney's fondness for world-fair-style attractions is understandable due to its history with these infamous fairs. Per example, Walt Disney debuted his now iconic attraction "It's A Small World" for the Pepsi/UNICEF pavilion at the 1964 World's Fair (Baber and Spickard 2013). The attraction consisted of visitors boarding guided passenger boats and riding through several "countries" from around the world; each "country" represented through animatronic doll-like figures wearing native folk costumes and singing the same catchy "It's A Small World" tune (but with varying languages and musical accompaniment). Composed by Robert and Richard Sherman,[2] the uplifting music, singable melody, and heartwarming lyrics of the song "It's A Small World" reinforced the visual core message of the ride: we are all united living together on one planet under "just one moon and one golden sun" (Sherman and Sherman 2017). An instant hit with audiences, Disney advertised "It's A Small World" as an "enchanting tribute to the popular American fantasies of life overseas" (Baber and Spickard 2013)—a validation of Disney's self-proclaimed vision of transporting people to other 'worlds.'

EPCOT's World Showcase acts as a grander dramatic expansion of the single-ride experience of "It's A Small World", but encourages the same spectatorship and passivity through stereotypical appropriated nostalgia (Giroux 1999, p. 43). The immersive 'global' experience within the World Showcase (as with many Disney theme park attractions) largely stems from marketing the spectacle of the "other", often in live form, with a heavy Euro-American perspective (Nooshin 2004). EPCOT, much like American world's fairs, has one principal aim: "the packaging of world cultures and

---

[2]   A successful songwriting duo who composed for several Disney projects including *The Sword in the Stone* (1963), *Mary Poppins* (1964), *The Jungle Book* (1967), *The Aristocats* (1970), and *The Many Adventures of Winnie the Pooh* (1977) (Price 2018).

new technologies as entertainment for consumption by a mass American audience" (Nelson 1986). One not-so-subtle reminder of this Western perspective is the location of the American Pavilion in the direct center of the World Showcase, granting it the strongest geographic visibility from any angled position within the park. Its metaphorical "head of the table" seat in the World Showcase, and its accompanying lagoon seems to reinforce a mythologized notion of America's status as a beacon for all to see while (literally) being the center of the world.

In the same vein as World Showcase, EPCOT's front half of the park, named Future World, boasts several rides and attractions dedicated to the pursuit of knowledge and awareness of 'other' places and people. Soarin' Around the World invites guests to take a virtual flight adventure hang gliding above natural and man-made wonders spanning the globe; Spaceship Earth welcomes riders on a slow-moving 'time-travel' odyssey exploring the historical evolution of human communication across the planet; Mission Space gives participants a motion simulation experience of orbiting the Earth and literally traveling around the world; Living with the Land offers boat tours through greenhouses giving insight into diverse ecosystems, global produce, agricultural history, and the "future of food production" (EPCOT 2018). These staple Future World attractions within the front half of the park partner with the World Showcase pavilions in the back half of the park to create a symbiotic relationship—together they claim a completed realized immersive exploration through the past, present, and future of Earth and its diverse inhabitants.

In the evening, once visitors have experienced touring the world, they are encouraged to gather around the World Showcase Lagoon and witness IllumiNations: Reflections of Earth, an award-winning nighttime entertainment show that invites park attendees to "behold the past, present, and future of Earth at this stunning fireworks show that celebrates the spirit of humanity" (EPCOT 2018). This 13 minute-long senses spectacular utilizes fireworks, lasers, pyrotechnics, water jets, and visual projections, all accompanied by an original musical score composed by British film composer Gavin Greenaway (Greenaway 1999). The visual anchor of the show is a massive revolving globe floating in the center of the lagoon: cut away oceans give an "airy and elegant feel to the structure" (Mirarchi 2011) while continents illuminate with colors, lights, images, and videos. The globe is an impressive technological feat: it is the world's first spherical video display system (Mirarchi 2011). The aural anchor of the show is a cinematic musical experience meant to evoke the symbolic soundscape of a historically evolving world. Witnessing IllumiNations: Reflections of Earth live means literally 'seeing the world' (a spinning globe framed in a rainbow-shaped backdrop of foreign country pavilions) while 'hearing the world' (a carefully-timed and themed orchestration with insinuated sounds of world music)—all from the beauty and safety of American soil. The EPCOT experience concludes visitors' day-long globe-trotting journeys with the comforting tried-and-true Disney tenet: we can all be united, overcome our differences, and find peace around the world (Baber and Spickard 2013).

EPCOT has proven itself to be a staple tourist destination for people (especially Americans) wanting to experience exoticized "others" (Carson 2004). In 2017, Epcot ranked as the seventh most attended theme park worldwide and the fourth most attended theme park in the United States (ranked only behind three other Disney parks), totaling an average of nearly twelve million annual visitors in recent years (Rubin 2018). Although the park does offer some rides and attractions beyond the 'travel around the world' theme, there is no denying a tremendous amount of visitors' attention is centered on this appealing idea of an immersive 'passport' (since the overwhelming majority of attractions, rides, and entertainment within the park follow this collective theme). It is quite evident that millions of Americans every year visit EPCOT with expectations of experiencing the 'rest' of the world.

3. The Organization of IllumiNations: Reflections of Earth

As previously stated, IllumiNations: Reflections of Earth presents itself as a boisterous visual and musical anthem celebrating globalness and progress. In contrast to the often live-performed music found among the World Showcase Pavilions, the IllumiNations: Reflections of Earth soundtrack is a prerecorded score which is amplified through massive speakers strategically placed around the park.

This is not a rare or 'lesser' approach to the execution of music. Recorded music is often used in Disney theme parks to condition an audience response (Camp 2017), especially if the desired sound source is a massive symphonic orchestra able to produce dramatic cinematic-style music (as is the case for Gavin Greenaway's densely orchestrated instrumental score for EPCOT's nighttime spectacular).

Both the IllumiNations: Reflections of Earth live show, and Greenaway's specific score divide into sections which chronologically convey the narrative 'story' of humanity. The nighttime show begins with an Introduction consisting of narration that serves to gather the attention of park guests and welcome them to the evening event; background 'mood' music accompanies the narration. Famous Disney voice actor Jim Cummings speaks this prerecorded narration.[3] Once the Introduction section concludes and the narration ceases, the main show moves forward with a narrative 'story' sectioned into three "parts": PART ONE: The Earth is Born, PART TWO: The Triumph of Life, and PART THREE: Hope for the Future (EPCOT 2018). Within these three broader "parts" Greenaway's score is divided into nine continuous miniature musical sections (eight instrumental and one vocal): Prologue: Acceleration, Chaos, Space, Life, Adventure, Home, Celebration, Meaning, and the vocal song "We Go On" (Greenaway 1999). Although none of these show "parts" or musical sections are announced for the audience, nor are there any continuity breaks within the show to elicit an awareness of purposeful distinct sections, the divided headings are listed and described on EPCOT's official website and the CD album jacket for the official IllumiNations: Reflections of Earth soundtrack.

This article acknowledges that Greenaway's listed musical sections lack assignment to the three broader "parts" of the show in any written validation. The soundtrack's album jacket listing of the nine music sections omits recognition of the three broader "parts" of the show, so one must use a combination of logical listening of the score and interpretation of the written "parts" descriptions on EPCOT's website to estimate how Greenaway's musical sections group under the three larger umbrella headings. For analysis purposes, this article assumes the following logical estimation:

INTRODUCTION: Narration (background 'mood' music)[4]

"PART ONE: The Earth is Born" (Prologue: Acceleration, Chaos)

"PART TWO: The Triumph of Life" (Space, Life, Adventure, Home Celebration, Meaning)

"PART THREE: Hope for the Future" ("We Go On")

4. Musical Westernization of the World's 'Story'

Greenaway's music for IllumiNations: Reflections of Earth is meant to emotionally take us through humanity's progression from "chaos" to "meaning." However, the musical devices woven within the complex score seems to structure an alternative subliminal 'progression': nonWestern to Western. Although the sounds of other cultures embed in appropriate sections of the music's 'timeline', Western musical elements dominate the score. Additionally, as the timeline continues, the prevalence of 'world' sounds decrease while foundational components of Western music prevail in the foreground, concluding in an entirely Euro-American finale.

Some might argue that the 'progression' represented in Greenaway's score actually symbolizes humans' advancement of music organization and construction (as a product of evolving organized societies), which would coincidentally put Euro-American music as the symbol of the progression's ultimate arrival of 'success', the concluding celebration of Euro-American music is inevitable, not pompous. However, this would still be a false narrative. While it is true that organizational components of Western music are prevalent in countries all throughout the world, this does not negate the existence of a plethora of other organized systems of music. The modern world contains hundreds of different native instruments, tones, and notation systems not used in conventional Western music

---

[3] Jim Cummings has voiced several legendary Disney characters including Winnie the Pooh and Tigger (EPCOT 2018).
[4] Narration and accompanying music is not on the soundtrack album; it can only be heard live or in video recordings.

(Gaare 1997). Therefore, Greenaway's arrival at a purely Westernized musical finale for the insinuated enlightenment of "meaning" perpetuates an assumption that Western music is the music of humanity: humans' global journeys have all led to the doorstep of a bright, beautiful Euro-American world.

5. Musical Framing and its Purpose for Disney

To accurately analyze the musical "framing" used in EPCOT's nighttime show, it is essential to define musical "framing" first and evaluate Disney's pattern of employing it in their endeavors.

The structure of "framing" refers to the concept of the 'different' being surrounded by the familiar 'normal' (McClary 1991). Thus, in musical "framing", foreign 'other' musical sounds are preceded, followed, and accompanied by contrasting recognizable 'normal' sounds (Armstrong 2018). This structure allows the composer to control the depiction, portrayal, and perception of the 'other' (Armstrong 2018). Musical "framing" has been a staple in Disney music, especially since the surge of Broadway-style animated musical films during the 1990s and the construction of several theme parks in recent decades.

Disney composers invest in music's ability to navigate an inventory of complicated and conflicting objectives. These objectives include framing songs in the traditional Western musical sounds that American consumers desire, inserting enough native folk-often stereotypical-musical elements to establish 'authenticity' of the represented culture in the story, and promoting Disney's emphasis on moralism and suburban 'American' values of family, patriotism, and progressiveness (Wills 2017, p. 6). The combination of these objectives is Disney's solution in creating catchy and memorable music for Western audiences that still sound 'authentic' within story settings frequently deemed 'exotic' or 'far away' (basically not in America). Critics highlight several famous examples: 'Caribbean' music in The Little Mermaid; 'French' music in Beauty and the Beast; 'Middle Eastern' music in Aladdin; 'African' music in The Lion King; 'Native American' music in Pocahontas; 'Chinese' music in Mulan; 'Polynesian' music in Moana; 'Mexican' music in Coco.

Initially, Disney did not put effort into hiring music professionals from the cultures represented to participate in the music. 'Caribbean'-sounding songs in The Little Mermaid, 'French'-sounding songs in Beauty and the Beast, 'Middle Eastern'-sounding songs in Aladdin, 'Native American'-sounding songs in Pocahontas, and 'Chinese'-sounding songs in Mulan were all written by American or British songwriters and sung by American voice actors (with the exception of Filipina singer Lea Salonga in Aladdin and Mulan).

Eventually, Disney did attempt to provide more authenticity through the inclusion of music professionals representative of the desired culture; however, Euro-American influences still control the music. Although South African producer Lebohang Morake sang and conducted an African choir for selected songs in The Lion King, all of the songs were written by British composers Elton John and Tim Rice, and mostly performed by American and British actors. Despite Polynesian musician Opetaia Foa'i writing and performing certain songs in Moana, American Broadway composer Lin-Manuel Miranda (who is not of Polynesian ancestry) composed most of the central songs. While a variety of Mexican actors and musicians performed the majority of the songs in Coco, the central theme, that is repeated throughout the film as the musical anchor, was written by American Broadway writing team Robert Lopez and Kristen Anderson-Lopez (who are not of Mexican ancestry). Ironically, Disney even missed opportunities to have complete authenticity within films centered on American-styled music. The music of Hercules and The Princess and the Frog centers on African-American-influenced styles of gospel, jazz, blues, and R&B; however, none of the composers involved in these films were African-American (except for singer-songwriter Ne-Yo who contributed a song for the ending credits in The Princess and the Frog).

While the standalone merits of Disney music are undeniable (most Disney musical films earn several wins or nominations for prestigious music awards), their use of exoticism, orientalism, and Western music "framing" cannot go unacknowledged (Roca 2012). The desired effect of these music tactics is to ensure a "facade of otherness" (Wang and Yeh 2005).

6. A Musical Breakdown of Greenaway's *IllumiNations: Reflections of Earth*

6.1. Introduction

The evening show begins with an Introduction consisting of a prerecorded voiceover against a visual backdrop of blazing torches surrounding the World Showcase Lagoon. The narrator's words encourage an inner reflection of Earth's ancestry and heritage; his tone evokes a comforting, familiar quality exuding the wisdom of an elder, ancestor, tribal chief, or spiritual leader (Mirarchi 2011):

> "Good evening. On behalf of Walt Disney World, the place where dreams come true, we welcome all of you to EPCOT and World Showcase. We've gathered here tonight, around the fire, as people of all lands have gathered for thousands and thousands of years before us; to share the light and to share a story. An amazing story, as old as time itself, but still being written. And though each of us has our own individual stories to tell, a true adventure emerges when we bring them all together as one. We hope you enjoy our story tonight: Reflections of Earth."

> (Mirarchi 2011)

Once the narration starts, slowly crescendoing music, consisting of several sound layers, work in tandem to evoke feelings of mysticism, exoticism, and drama. These layers include both low and high long notes played by synthesizers (electric keyboards), choral voices with pitch-bends, a rainstick-sounding rattle, and dissonant harmonies most likely created from tone clusters (three or more adjacent notes in a scale) or polychords (two or more chords stacked on top of each other). Additionally, harp glissandos (an 18th Century European finger strumming style) enter in the vein of stereotypical "flashback" or "dream" sequence conventions (Day-O'Connell 2007, p. 147).

The combination of these layers creates an initial soundscape that debuts the grander notions the entire score's framework will represent. The first notion is Earth's 'story' told through the perspective of a modern-day platform. The instrumentation symbolizes the dichotomy of the 'new' telling about the 'old': synthesizers (a very modern and technologically advanced instrument in music's history) serve as the consistent drone foundation for sporadic historical older 'native' sounds such as a rainstick, harp, and singing voices. Secondly, the notion of a Western musical "frame" becomes established. Although hand percussion instruments, such as rainsticks and vocal pitch-bends are natively nonWestern, cliché harp glissandos, electronic keyboards, and droning synthesizer harmonies are all derivatives of Western music. Thus, the majority of the Introduction's music forges a consistent Western foundation that serves to anchor the randomly heard nonWestern sounds. As a result, two different Westernized musical "frames" have been architected: the completion of a miniature "frame" within the specific Introduction section and the setup of a broader "frame" for the entire upcoming score. The establishment of these framed perspectives (new defines old, Western defines nonWestern) creates a symbolic, yet conflicted connection to the narrator's words: "And though each of us has our own individual stories to tell, a true adventure emerges when we bring them all together as one" (Mirarchi 2011). Although the narration's sentiment of equality is recognized within the music, the representation of all of the Earth's 'individual' music coming together as 'one' is heavily one-sided.

Once the narrator finishes his final sentence, the music ceases and he 'blows' out the torches in a dramatic simultaneous fashion, leaving the audience in darkness and silence.

6.2. "Part One: The Earth is Born"

EPCOT's official description of PART ONE is as follows:

> "Earth's fiery birth begins with flames and fireworks erupting from the lagoon. Beneath a swarm of heavenly explosions, red and golden lights blaze on the shimmering waters. As the volcanic effects subside, a glowing globe glides peacefully across the waters."

> (EPCOT 2018)

6.2.1. Prologue: Acceleration

During the darkness, a large low sounding drum begins beating. The drumming starts slow, each hit's reverb dramatically ringing through the open air. After a few slow beats, the drumming begins to pound faster, accelerating to an intense, rapid pounding. The acceleration leads up to a climax where a haunting 'screech' sound abruptly cuts off the drum. During the 'screech' effect, a single firework cannons upwards and arcs across the sky until another firework (unseen up to this point) explodes above the middle of the lagoon; this is a clear representation of the 'big bang' (or any alternative theory to the sparking of Earth's creation).

This musical section is an example of an appropriate 'world' music choice. Drums are historically the oldest, most primitive ways in which humankind began interpreting sound. Built of animal bones and hide, drums became a crucial part in various aspects of human life; some historians even hypothesize that humans may have communicated through "drumming language" (as observed in African wild chimpanzees) before the creation of spoken language (Dean 2012, p. 4). Greenaway's acceleration of the drum pounding is also a wise choice because it erases the perception of an organized rhythm or beat; humans were drumming before conscious notions of structured rhythm and beat were ever conceived. Thus, choosing the sound of a single out-of-rhythm drum as representation of the beginning of our planet is defendable.

6.2.2. Chaos

At the exact moment of the first firework's explosion, a symphony orchestra bursts with a lively and complex musical tapestry, thus commencing Chaos. Fireworks synchronize with powerful music 'hits' while massive fire flames continuously erupt from ground areas. The musical score is itself fiery. Violins and violas speed through a reoccurring melody (called a motif) outlining the notes heard in a medieval European music scale known as the 'Dorian mode.' Cellos (and perhaps basses) lay an underneath foundation of a technique called 'ostinato', referring to a repeated pattern of notes and rhythms. Various pitched and nonpitched percussion instruments mimic the rhythm of the melodic motifs and provide dramatic moments of percussive 'hits' (these include cymbals, tambourine, gong, and drums). Woodwind and mallet instruments provide secondary melodies and harmonies that both complement and contrast the string parts. Low brass instruments (especially french horns) create theatrical cinema-style musical passages while high brass instruments, such as trumpets, join certain woodwind and mallet 'hit' moments in climatic fashion. The organized beats of the music (called 'meter') are consistently odd and purposefully scattered. The music alternates between 7-5-11-9 beats per measure, thus creating an unstable, off-balanced feel for the listener due to the uneven number of beats (Mirarchi 2011).

It is in this Chaos section that we return to the Western music framework. The music anchors itself in an entirely Western symphonic orchestra structure. This 'chaotic' music assembles in very structured concepts of rhythm, harmony, tonality, and instrumentation that is specifically Euro-American. This section of the score is in the exact vein of American symphonic film scores, referred to by music theorist Frank Lehman as the "Hollywood-style" tonality and elements (Lehman 2018). Bowed string instruments, dramatic brass instruments, woodwind sections, European music modes, melodic motifs, and ostinatos are all a part of the "Hollywood-style" symphonic orchestra. Thus, we have another piece to the Western framework of the world's 'story': before we arrive at the upcoming Life section where humans begin existing (historically in Africa), Western music has already claimed its dominance.

6.3. "Part Two: The Triumph of Life"

EPCOT's official description of PART TWO is as follows:

"Our individual stories culminate in one adventurous tale. The illuminated surface of the globe reveals the history of humanity and the achievements of our time."

(EPCOT 2018)

6.3.1. Space

The fiery Chaos music quickly ceases and lands on a low drone note played by basses. The basses decrescendo as synthesized long notes present themselves, first hovering and then pitch bending downwards towards a new tonal center. Once arrived at this new tonality, string instruments enter playing a fluid melodic passage. Accompanying the strings is a harp playing gentle arpeggios (17th Century European technique of playing the notes of a chord one at a time). Soon after, an oboe enters with a new melody, in the same flowing convention as the strings previously established. As the music swells, strings in higher octaves join the oboe, marrying its melodic contours.

This music accompanies the first visual appearance of the spinning globe. Fireworks cease so the illumination of the globe's surfaces can pierce through the darkness; the only other light sources are green lasers in the sky and a cluster of lit torches on the ground. Color schemes project across the globe in order of blue, white, green, then red. The perceived intent of these four particular colors can be subjective. On the surface, these colors could be apparent representations of water, sky, land, and man. However, from a Western perspective, they also broadcast the three colors of the American flag and American iconography.

The score for this section wholly balances three frequently used Western music techniques. First, synthesizers and digital keyboards (Western-born instruments) often appear in scored 'space' settings; electronic instruments give listeners technologically-driven soundscapes which can aurally suggest 'unknown' or 'alien' atmospheres. Secondly, symphonic orchestral instruments such as harp, strings, and oboe are regular pillars of European and American film scores. Thirdly, the majority of the music in this section contains melodies, harmonies, and techniques rooted in Western music.

6.3.2. Life

This section begins with new instruments entering with rhythmic and percussive qualities, while long, low notes played by cellos, basses, and synthesizer drone underneath. A marimba comes to the foreground, playing repeated melodic patterns that evoke a sense of energy, curiosity, and youthfulness. A flute sounding of Native American origins interjects ornamented phrases. Violins and violas play staccato (sharp detached) pitches that mirror the marimba. Drums enter and beat out steady pulses while the music swells with melodic violins and violas in high octaves. The oboe and harp enter towards the end of this section similarly to the previous Space section, accompanied by a picked acoustic guitar.

Effort is given here to portray the 'exoticness' of older civilizations. Both the marimba and drums originated in Africa and spread to Asia and Latin America. The Native American flute is credited to the indigenous peoples of pre-Columbian North America and is a descended of bone whistles, which are considered one of the oldest instruments in the world. The picked six-string guitar has Spanish roots. However, these instruments are still only given moments of independence and spotlight against a backdrop of dominating Western symphonic orchestral strings and contemporary synthesizers, all still existing in Western tonality.

6.3.3. Adventure

This music section is entirely Euro-American. Strings and woodwinds play lively melodies built on traditional European scales; brass roar dramatic American Hollywood-style fanfare themes; auxiliary percussion play energetic rhythms organized in Western beat structures. The only continuous 'world' sound is the pulsating beat of 'tribal' drums. All other music heard is composed in traditional European music structures and performed by a Western symphonic orchestra in the style of conventional American film scores.

6.3.4. Celebration

The liveliness of the Adventure music remains, but this Celebration music lowers to softer dynamic levels to elicit the sounds of 'dances' done by an individual or a group of people. Clear intentions are made to represent sounds of 'others' dancing. The pulsating marimba and drums conjure sounds of African tribal rituals. A syncopated tambourine and a spirited recorder evoke Renaissance court dances and Irish jigs. A solo melodic bass guitar conjures the stylings of popularized Reggae and Calypso music.

Although these effective—albeit clichéd—sounds do produce the effect of multiple world cultures 'celebrating' together, the symphonic orchestra still centers the entire section. Each 'other' gets their spotlighted moments, but the general consistency and transitions lie deeply rooted in Western foundation.

6.3.5. Meaning

The score's final instrumental section is entirely Westernized, like the previous Adventure section. The music swells to a triumphant, powerful dramatic theme. All of the 'world' sounds have disappeared, and only the traditional symphonic orchestra remains. The melody of the upcoming "We Go On" song soars loudly with an 'inspirational' and almost 'patriotic' flair while fireworks explode rapidly.

6.4. *"Part Three: Hope for the Future"*

EPCOT's official description of PART THREE is as follows:

"Comets of light race into the sky, before the globe blossoms like a lotus flower, revealing a torch ablaze with our dreams. A chorus of voices rises as the entire lagoon dances with bursts of joyous white light."

(EPCOT 2018)

Don Dorsey (the director of IllumiNations: Reflections of Earth) wrote lyrics to Greenaway's music, which eventually became the song "We Go On" (Mirarchi 2011). American artist Kellie Coffey sings the prerecorded vocals. The lyrics reestablish the intended message of the show: people all over the world can unite and find 'meaning' by become 'one':

With the stillness of the night there comes a time to understand

To reach out and touch tomorrow, take the future in our hands

We can see a new horizon built on all that we have done

And our dreams begin another thousands circles 'round the sun

We go on to the joy and through the tears; we go on to discover new frontiers

Moving on with the current of the years; we go on moving forward, now as one

Moving on with a spirit born to run ever on with each rising sun

To a new day, we go on.

(Greenaway 1999)

As the song plays, the spinning globe displays video projections of people of various ethnicities and cultures lighting candles. Once again, the accompaniment music is a Westernized symphonic orchestra; all of the 'world' instruments portraying the 'exotic' sounds of 'others' have ceased. The song is written in traditional American pop structure: verse-chorus form, even-number beats, and conventional Euro-American melodies and harmonies. English is the only sung language. A background choir joins in on the chorus singing harmonies reminiscent of American gospel music. This thoroughly Westernized finale completes the broader musical "frame" that began with the Westernized Introduction music.

7. Conclusions

The scope of IllumiNations: Reflections of Earth is a conflicting musical journey. Although specific sections contain clear intentions of giving representation to music of various global cultures, there is never a lack of Western musical dominance. As the score moves forward to its triumphant climax, the 'world' music fades away as the Euro-American music prevails. The show's message of humanity finding meaning in 'oneness' infers a subliminal insinuation of finding meaning in 'Westerness.'

While IllumiNations: Reflections of Earth boasts an impressively composed score by Greenaway, it still serves as another representation of Disney's instinct to construct Western musical frameworks within its projects. Disney invites people to visit EPCOT and experience the 'other' parts of the world, but through a controlled perspective of familiarity, tropes, and narrow scopes. Disney's consistent use of this framework in films and theme parks potentially gives people (particularly Americans) a false sense of awareness of both themselves and 'others': the Western world is the world. Connecting concepts of primitiveness with 'world' music and meaning with Western music perpetuates a false narrative of an evolved Euro-American world and unevolved 'others.'

Funding: This research received no external funding.

Conflicts of Interest: The author declares no conflicts of interest.

References

Anderson, David, and Kevin M. Tavin. 2003. Teaching (Popular) Visual Culture: Deconstructing Disney in the Elementary Classroom. *National Art Education Association* 56: 21–35.

Armstrong, Robin. 2018. Time to Face the Music: Musical Colonization and Appropriation in Disney's Moana. *Social Sciences* 7: 113. [CrossRef]

Baber, Katherine, and James V. Spickard. 2013. Crafting Culture: 'Tradition', Art, and Music in Disney's 'A Small World'. *Journal of Popular Culture* 48: 225–39. [CrossRef]

Bellman, Johnathan. 1998. *The Exotic in Western Music*. Boston: Northeastern University Press, p. xi.

Camp, Gregory. 2017. Mickey Mouse Muzak: Shaping Experience Musically at Walt Disney World. *Journal of the Society for American Music* 11: 53–69. [CrossRef]

Carson, Charles. 2004. 'Whole New Worlds': Music and the Disney Theme Park Experience. *Ethnomusicology Forum* 13: 228–35. [CrossRef]

Day-O'Connell, Jeremy. 2007. *Pentatonicism from the Eighteenth Century to Debussy*. Rochester: University of Rochester Press, p. 147.

Dean, Matt. 2012. *The Drum: A History*. Lanham: The Scarecrow Press, p. 4.

Eisner, Michael. 1995. Planetized Entertainment. *New Perspectives Quarterly* 12: 8.

EPCOT. Official Website. Available online: https://disneyworld.disney.go.com/destinations/epcot (accessed on 20 July 2018).

Gaare, Mark. 1997. Alternatives to Traditional Notation. *Music Educators Journal* 83: 17–23. [CrossRef]

Garcia, Jason. 2013. International Tourists Drive Disney Attendance Growth. *Orlando Sentinel*. August 9. Available online: http://articles.orlandosentinel.com/2013-08-09/business/os-disney-international-attendance-grows-20130809_1_walt-disney-world-attendance-records-disney-dining (accessed on 2 August 2018).

Giroux, Henry A. 1999. *The Mouse that Roared: Disney and the End of Innocence*. Oxford: Roman & Littlefield, p. 43.

Greenaway, Gavin. 1999. *'Reflections of Earth' Epcot IllumiNations (Soundtrack)*. Burbank: Walt Disney Records.

Lehman, Frank. 2018. *Hollywood Harmony: Musical Wonder and the Sound of Cinema*. New York: Oxford University Press, pp. 10–11.

McClary, Susan. 1991. *Feminine Endings: Music, Gender, and Sexuality*. Minneapolis: University of Minnesota Press, pp. 89–104.

Mirarchi, Chuck. 2011. Back to the Future-Illuminations: Reflections of Earth. *Disney Information Station (DIS)*. May 1. Available online: http://www.wdwinfo.com/columns/back-to-the-future-illuminations-reflections-of-earth.cfm (accessed on 22 July 2018).

Nelson, Steve. 1986. Walt Disney's EPCOT and the World's Fair Performance Tradition. *The Drama Review* 30: 106–46. [CrossRef]

Nooshin, Laudan. 2004. Circumnavigation with a Difference? Music, Representation and the Disney Experience: It's A Small, Small World. *Ethnomusicology Forum* 13: 236–51. [CrossRef]

Price, Kathryn M. 2018. *Walt Disney's Melody Makers: A Biography of the Sherman Brothers*. n.p.: Theme Park Press.

Roca, Roxanne Elizabeth. 2012. Depictions of NonWestern Musical Cultures in Disney's Film Music of the 1990s. M.M. Thesis. Boston University Theses & Dissertations, Boston University, Boston, MA, USA.

Rubin, Judith. 2018. TEA/AECOM 2017 Theme Index and Museum Index. *Themed Entertainment Association* and *Economics at AECOM*, May 23. Available online: http://www.teaconnect.org/images/files/TEA_268_653730_180517.pdf (accessed on 21 July 2018).

Sherman, Richard, and Robert Sherman. 2017. *'It's A Small World (From It's A Small World)' Disney Theme Park Classics*. Burbank: Walt Disney Records.

Wang, Georgette, and Emillie Yueh-yu Yeh. 2005. Globalization and hybridization in cultural productions: The cases of Ulan and Crouching Tiger, Hidden Dragon. *International Journal of Cultural Studies* 8: 175–93. [CrossRef]

Wills, John. 2017. *Disney Culture*. New Brunswick: Rutgers University Press, p. 6.

Wilson, Alexander. 1991. *The Culture of Nature: North American Landscape from Disney to the Exxon Valdez*. Toronto: Between The Lines, p. 161.

social sciences

MDPI

Article

Star Wars: The Last Jedi, Beauty and the Beast, and Disney's Commodification of Feminism: A Political Economic Analysis

Kailash Koushik and Abigail Reed *

School of Communication, Florida State University, 3100 University Center, Building C, Tallahassee, FL 32306, USA; kk15h@my.fsu.edu
* Correspondence: a.reed@fsu.edu

Received: 1 October 2018; Accepted: 28 October 2018; Published: 15 November 2018

Abstract: This paper seeks to explore the strategies Hollywood utilizes to capitalize on feminist social movements through replacing hegemonic male characters with female ones or updating traditional stories through a more "feminist" retelling. By analyzing both 2017's *Star Wars: The Last Jedi* and *Beauty and the Beast* as representative of this corporate trend, we critique the ways in which these pseudo-feminist texts contribute little to the social conversation surrounding the evolving roles of women and their representations in media through the lenses of critical political economy, feminist political economy, and feminist film criticism. We conclude that creating "feminist" reimaginings of classic narratives ultimately serves to uphold the existing economic structures that maintain social and financial capital within the largest Hollywood studios. Thus, little to no social progress is made through the creation of these retellings.

Keywords: Disney; gender; feminism; political economy of film; feminist film criticism; feminist political economy of media

1. Introduction and Literature Review

In 2017, Hollywood saw two contradicting trends. On one hand, it was rocked by sexual harassment and abuse scandals, with women coming forward and revealing not only the names of their abusers, but also the rampant prevalence of such harassment. Along with unequal pay/remuneration in Hollywood between men and women, this scandal brought to light the dismal working conditions of women in Hollywood. On the other hand, the top three box office hits in America—*Star Wars: The Last Jedi, Beauty and the Beast,* and *Wonder Woman*—were all movies with women in lead roles. Following the trend of movies such as *Hidden Figures* and *Ghostbusters*, and paving the way for movies such as *Ocean's 8*, which has an all-woman cast, along with movements such as #meToo and Time's Up, Hollywood is positioning itself to be championing the causes of women by producing films with women as protagonists. Instead of simply celebrating this trend, there needs to be a critical evaluation of it, lifting the curtains and looking behind the screen to analyze the political economy of these movies and whether or not they truly empower oppressed groups.

Disney's unique claim on the cultural marketplace both in the U.S. and worldwide makes studying this trend important as it has vast ramifications for smaller cultural producers and the public discourse at large. A 2006 study of the worldwide cultural reach of Disney's intellectual property highlights how widespread and integrated Disney characters and narratives are in global culture (Wasko et al. 2006). Thus, detailed examinations of contemporary media produced by Disney have great significance as they are disseminated into our shared global media culture. Furthermore, *Star Wars: The Last Jedi* and *Beauty and the Beast* are significant not only because of their status as two of the top three highest grossing films worldwide in 2017, but because they are emblematic of Disney's growing tendency to commodify the core tenants of social movements and repackage them in a fashion better suited to their global market interests. In the interest of exploring the specific ways in which this is done, this analysis is positioned at the intersection of feminist film criticism, political economy of film, and feminist political economy of media. By utilizing these methodologies and approaching the films from a critical perspective, Disney's commodification of feminist movements are highlighted. Specific examples of this are analyzed in the narratives of both the films, as well as details from their production, to underscore that these texts are not made to empower the audience; rather, they are made to sell merchandise.

1.1. Methodologies

Political Economy of Film. The political economy of media is defined as "the study of social relations, power relations in particular, that mutually constitute the production, consumption, and distribution of resources, in particular communication resources" (Hardy 2014; McChesney 2008; Mosco 2009). The political economy of film focuses on production, consumption, and distribution of films and how the mode of production influences the content of specific movies (Wasko 2003). In most parts of the world, and certainly in the United States, films are produced and consumed within a capitalist mode of production, in which films are produced for sale, with the intent to earn profit (Mirrlees 2013). Within this system, it is important to understand films as commodities, which exist both as a material commodity and as a service, being exchanged in the capitalist economy (Pendakur 1990, p. 39).

In the current age of global transnational capitalism and a New International Division of Cultural Labour (NIDCL), the production, distribution, and consumption of Hollywood movies occur with inputs of resources from around the world, ranging from investments and shooting locations to cultural labor, changing the once existent flow of movies produced only in Western countries and exported to other parts of the world (Miller et al. 2005). This shift in production has decentralized the filmmaking process and spread it across the world, creating an illusion of Hollywood diluting its hold over film production.

The shift, however, has not reduced the domination of Hollywood. Nonetheless, the US movie industry is constantly trying to capture a larger global market with films worth US$ 16.3 billion exported during 2014 alone (Robb 2016). The current global capitalist landscape or the global distribution of production processes have not altered the concentrated ownership in Hollywood either. Hollywood still remains an oligopolistic monopoly, with a few transnational companies dominating the film industry: Disney, Time Warner, Viacom, Comcast, News Corporation, and Sony [GE sold NBC to Comcast] (Baker 2013; Hardy 2014). These corporations are not just involved in film production, but all aspects of distribution and exhibition. For example, The Walt Disney Company has operations in TV media networks, entertainment parks, studios, and consumer products (Walt Disney Company 2017). To illustrate further, out of the top 20 highest grossing movies in 2017, six were produced by Disney, while Time Warner, Comcast and Viacom produced the rest (Box Office Mojo 2017).

Synergy, integration, and intellectual property rights allow these companies to dominate the market. These companies are integrated horizontally and vertically, allowing them complete control over the production process, from the conception of a movie, the theaters at which it is shown, other distribution markets, to any merchandise sold based on the movie (Croteau and Hoynes 2006; Hardy 2014). The presence of this kind of control over all aspects of production makes these studios financially favorable to investors, as there will be opportunities for lending money in exchange for ownership of shares or copyrights (Bettig and Hall 2012). These companies are able to lure investors with incentives like partial ownership of copyrights, because they also own the rights for the movie produced (Bettig and Hall 2012). These transnational conglomerates control and own marketing firms and other media, allowing them to promote their films not just domestically, but also globally (Bettig and Hall 2012). To further the Disney illustration, Disney can produce a movie in its studios, promote it on its TV networks, produce merchandise, stream the same in its interactive media, and build rides based on the same in its entertainment parks. Transnational media conglomerates like Disney are in possession of the resources that enable them to distribute and promote their movies globally, ensuring its success due to its control of global movie distribution (Gomery 2004, p. 194).

Under these conditions of the production and distribution of films, political economy reveals structural inequalities in such flows, combining it with an analysis of larger influences on production and distribution, considering the polyvalency of texts such as film within ideological boundaries (Hardy 2014, p. 167). It peels off the layers of the celebration of the success of Hollywood to reveal how the conditions of the mode of production influence the film process and its implications on socio-political aspects of society (Wasko 2003).

One of the main motivations under the capitalist mode of production is the maximization of profit. Transnational media companies constantly engage in production activities that achieve the largest amount of profits and the lowest levels of risk. The creation of sequels is one of the ways this can be achieved. Creation of synergistic entertainment franchises ensure a steady stream of movies that depend upon a pre-constituted audience, who ensure not just the consumption of the media text, but also consumption of merchandise related to the franchise (Proffitt et al. 2007; Meehan 2005). Mirrlees (2014) provides a detailed explanation of how these sequels most often have a "globally popular design" ensured to attract not just a pre-constituted audience, but also general populations globally. Studios also cast famous actors, hire famous directors, and recycle older versions of a film motivated by the same logic of maximizing profits, resulting in a constant recycling, repackaging, revisioning, and recirculating of films (Meehan 2005). Consequently, studios also bring out merchandise, video games, and collaborate with other companies such as fast food companies and sport franchises to constantly engage the audience not only within the theater, but also in everyday activities, creating an audience guaranteed to consume prequels, sequels, live action animation and the like (Jess-Cooke 2009).

Political economy, then, deals with the question of who controls film and media, and how such a structure influences the production of content. Consequently, for political economy of media, power, and the analysis of power in society, becomes central to the theory's rationale (Hardy 2014). It examines the interrelations between power, wealth, and knowledge (Norris 1990). In such an attempt to understand power in society, issues of gender become significant.

Feminist Political Economy of Media. Analyzing the ways in which narratives and ideologies that are oppressive toward women function in the production and consumption of films requires adding a feminist theory perspective onto a political economic view of film and the culture industry at large. This article uses the ideology of socialist feminism, in conjunction with feminist political economy, as the most natural position from which the two frameworks coincide (Steeves and Wasko 2002). A feminist political economic methodology seeks to enhance analyses and criticisms of the power structures present within economies and financial structures with a theoretical lens that highlights how women are specifically marginalized within these structures according to their gender (Rai and Waylen 2013). Broadly speaking, feminist political economy, "presents ways to move away from conceptualizing political economy as only looking at labor or class relations in order to broaden our understanding of accumulation and the reproduction of capitalism" (Riordan 2002, p. 7). Meehan (2005) also provides a feminist perspective of political economy, wherein she views the same problems of the capitalist market with the lens of gender. The ideologies that naturalize the oppression of women also shape the corporate decisions taken at all points of production and consumption of a movie (Meehan 2005). When examining any piece of media from a critical lens, it is especially important to engage with its ideological assumptions and implications regarding marginalized populations. Because the two films being analyzed in this article are marketed toward women and girls and deliberately include "progressive" representations of women, it is essential to integrate a multidimensional critical perspective.

Feminist Film Criticism. Furthermore, the tradition of feminist film criticism is invoked in order to facilitate a nuanced understanding of the way in which female characters are presented in both

Beauty and the Beast and *The Last Jedi*. The aim of this essay is to problematize and to "look back" at the narratives of women that contemporary corporate Hollywood is presenting to a global audience. Laura Mulvey began doing this when she theorized that men exercised their scopophilia and the desire to objectify women by going to the cinema and, conversely, women experienced the sensation of "to-be-looked-at-ness" (Mulvey 1975). The cinema was thus a place for men and male fantasy and women were constructed to be the object of this cinematic fantasy. Linda Williams takes this idea further in a detailed examination of films within the horror genre and the construction of the female horror victim as a figure of pleasure for the male spectator (Williams 1984). She challenges the reader (specifically the female reader) to examine the films critically and trouble their representation of "free sexuality" at the cost of violence against the female body. In other words, Williams challenges the female audience to gaze back at the very film that is objectifying them.

Contemporary feminist film criticism has expanded from this core mission to integrate a more interdisciplinary approach. Queer theory, critical race studies, disability studies, and political economy have all been coalesced into the larger body of literature to address issues of marginalization within cinema. This article aligns itself with a feminist political economic approach that harkens back to the philosophical assumptions that feminist film criticism was built upon in the 70s and 80s. Bringing a political economic perspective into film criticism serves to question the structural existence of Hollywood and problematize the way in which films are created and how audiences are meant to enjoy them. Specifically, the political economy of film, feminist political economy, and feminist film criticism will be used to peel the layers off the success and celebration of *Star Wars: The Last Jedi* and *Beauty and the Beast* as "triumphantly feminist films" and interrogate their position in relation to contemporary feminism.

1.2. The Gendered Commodity Market

Meehan (2002) outlines how media companies have progressively changed their content creation and advertising strategy from targeting the "universal" market of white men aged 18–34 to pinpointing certain niche markets that were not being catered to (such as women who stayed home during the day and watched television) (Meehan 2002, p. 217). What is occurring in the current media landscape, and specifically with the *Star Wars* franchise, is that texts created for the "universal" white male 18–34 audience are being recreated with specific attention paid to niche markets (particularly women) and specific elements of the narratives and the marketing strategy are catered to the niche market, while the media product as a whole is still created for the "universal" audience. An example of this is the HerUniverse clothing line that was created for female fans of the *Star Wars* franchise in order to capitalize on that commodity market, whereas before *Star Wars* themed clothing was marketed toward male consumers. However, instead of using this space created for female fans to destabilize gender norms, the goods sold rely on classic princess tropes that reify traditional gendered stereotypes (Johnson 2014).

The princess line of dolls released by Disney includes Belle from *The Beauty and the Beast*, which was described by *Variety*, as "a global marketing machine shrewdly designed to accessorize young girls with all the sparkly merchandise their little hearts desire" (quoted in Bettig and Hall 2012, p. 213). *Beauty and the Beast* had 60% female audience members in its opening weekend with industry reporters attributing it to the "feminist DNA" of the movie (Lang 2017). But since 2009, Belle was marketed exclusive to young girls through the princess merchandise line.

As Meehan observes, in this economic environment that focuses on niche audiences, media content is not truly what is being created. Referencing Smythe (1977), she states: "the media manufactured only one commodity—audiences. By this, Smythe meant that all media assembled, packaged, and sold audiences to advertisers. Content was secondary—a free lunch at best" (Meehan 2002, p. 211). Because content is secondary to the commodity markets being built (specifically the gendered commodity market), it is all the more important to examine how gender is being deployed both within the world of the film and in our own world (specifically in the content of the contemporary discourses of neoliberalism, postfeminism, and commodity feminism; which will be addressed in the discussion section), as both serve the primary purpose of selling goods to audiences.

1.3. Merchandise Market

Merchandising, and Disney princesses in particular, remains a strong source of revenue for Disney, with annual sales of Disney princess merchandise averaging at around US$4 billion in 2016–2017 (Barnes 2017). *Star Wars* in particular has long been in the news for the sale of its merchandise. Toys R Us sold 1.25 million units of *The Phantom Menace* merchandise in 1999, with sales averaging US$150,000 in the first three and a half hours in their New York City flagship store. The prediction about the "biggest event in the history of toy history," was between US$500 million to a billion by the end of 1999. Apart from this, the movie also had tie ins with fast food joints and fantasy novels (Jensen 1999). The trend remained similar for *The Force Awakens* and *Rogue One*, but slightly weakened for *The Last Jedi*. In 1999, merchandising was not available until the day before the movie was released (Jensen 1999). However, Disney opened merchandising three months before *The Force Awakens* in 2015, and for *The Last Jedi* in 2017 (Townsend 2018). Although sales of merchandising was successful in 2015, this backfired in 2017. According to the CEO of Hasbro Inc, this was due to the three-month time period, which was difficult to maintain interest in the customers (Townsend 2018). *Star Wars* toys were still top selling during the holiday season of 2017, even though sales fell in comparison to the previous film in 2016 (Palmeri and Townsend 2017).

Disney has stumbled in its offerings of merchandise featuring major female characters in the *Star Wars* universe. Upon the release of 2015's *The Force Awakens*, consumers quickly noticed the widespread lack of Daisy Ridley's Rey in the new merchandise. Even in packages of action figures of the main characters in the new film, Rey, the primary main character, was not featured. This led to the #WheresRey movement on social media platforms. Customers asked Disney why Rey was excluded from the new wave of toys if she was the main character of the new trilogy, particularly since *Star Wars* has historically had such a robust presence in the toy aisle (Scott 2017).

Although sales numbers are not available for *Beauty and the Beast* merchandise, analysts believe the movie to be a merchandising powerhouse, capable of targeting consumers from two different generations: the young adults who grew up with the animated 1991 film, and the next generation watching the live action movie for the first time (Davis 2017). Hasbro Inc. reported that Disney princesses as a whole were strong in 2017, but the top seller was Belle from *Beauty and the Beast*, and the company expected her to remain on top due to the success of the movie (La Monica 2017).

1.4. Gender and the Remaking of Old Narratives

Hegemonic gender stereotypes can be found throughout the *Star Wars* universe, including the toys, films, video games, novels, and beyond. George Lucas, original creator of the franchise, often cites Joseph Campbell's 1949 text, *The Hero with a Thousand Faces*, as being of prime importance when he was formulating the *Star Wars* mythos (Mythic Discovery 2015). Campbell sought to establish a universal human monomyth that explained the classical "hero's quest" narrative that is commonly found in disparate cultures throughout time by establishing certain archetypes that are typically adhered to in these myths. When setting out to create *Star Wars*, Lucas sought to create a hero's story largely devoid of culturally specific marks. However, Campbell's conception of the universal hero's journey is one that is decidedly male (Larabee 2016). This mythic template works when dealing with male protagonists such as Luke or Anakin Skywalker (the main characters of the Original and Prequel trilogies, respectively, who are responsible for both the ruin and the restoration of the galaxy) who nicely fit into hegemonic male gender confines. However, things become far more complex when you introduce a female character as the hero, as is the case with Rey in the Disney films. How does Rey fit into this classical "universal" mythos that Campbell theorized, one that has been made for men and maintained by men (both within the fictional and the real world) (Larabee 2016)? This is further complicated upon analysis of the Skywalker Saga's central hero/villain: Anakin (also known as Darth

Vader). In fact, it has been argued that Anakin, by his alignment with Trujillo's (1991) six characteristics of hegemonic masculinity (which include physical force, control, occupational achievement, familial patriarchy, frontiersmanship, and heterosexuality), is freed from the responsibility of his actions; clearing the path for his redemption at the end of this life, which is shown at the end of 1983's *Return of the Jedi* (Atkinson and Calafell 2009, p. 2). It is debatable (and yet to be seen) whether or not a female protagonist will be afforded these same allowances within this mythos.

Just as Disney is attempting to update *Star Wars* with more female characters to capitalize on female consumers, it is diving into its old filmography and rethinking their old fairy tale classics. On 13 April 2017, Disney announced that its live action animation remake of *The Beauty and the Beast* grossed US$1.0024 billion worldwide, making it Disney's 14th film to cross the billion-dollar mark (Mendelson 2017). The movie has a star cast with Emma Watson playing Belle, Dan Stevens as the Beast, and Luke Evans playing Gaston (Barnes 2017). The movie followed in Disney's tradition of remaking old films with new technology and star casts, with live action filmmaking combined with digitally created characters and backdrops, pushed to such an extent that the character of the Beast himself was full digitized, using motion sensors placed on Dan Stevens' face (Barnes 2017). This retelling of the same story, using new technology, provides an illusion that Disney is producing something revolutionary, but is really old wine in a new bottle.

Disney's strategy of swapping the gender of the primary protagonist in the new *Star Wars* films in order to connect with a young female consumer base is not completely dissimilar from the strategy it used to update *Beauty and the Beast*. Both narratives have very old roots in traditional mythology. Additionally, *Beauty and the Beast* already benefited from having a main female protagonist. Thus, Disney was able to change key characteristics about Belle in order to make her appear more "feminist" according to contemporary standards.

2. Analysis

2.1. Making Star Wars Great Again

When *The Force Awakens* was being promoted, some fans were in an uproar about the gender and race of two of the new protagonists. *Star Wars*, in the popular imagination, has always been a boy's story (more specifically, a white boy's story) and changing this hallowed tradition is sacrilegious according to some fans of the franchise. This combined with the betrayal and distrust that many *Star Wars* fans have of those in charge of the franchise (a topic that will be returned to) created a toxic environment within which Rey was debuted to the world. This is the stage for the premiere of 2017's *The Last Jedi*, which has a critical score of 91% and an audience score of 47% on Rotten Tomatoes (Star Wars: The Last Jedi 2017). Why is there such a vast discrepancy between these two groups of people? This depends on who is asked. Some credit the "alt-right" for hijacking both the Rotten Tomatoes audience score and the online discourse surrounding the film because of their self-professed dislike of the incorporation of female protagonists (Sharf 2017). There are countless think pieces revolving around the issue of gender in the film (Barsanti 2018; Florio 2017; Gertrude 2018; Gonzalez 2018; Moore 2017; Robinson 2017; Smith 2017; Weekes 2017; Why the Last Jedi Isn't just Bad: It's Toxic 2017), highlighting the stark divide in the audience between some who think the text offers a positive, progressive representation of women and those who think that women are best left out of meaningful roles in the franchise.

An Old Plot Made New? In *The Last Jedi*, Rey's journey as a fledgling Jedi Knight leads her on an expedition to find Jedi Master Luke Skywalker who is in hiding after the failure of his new Jedi Order. Luke reluctantly agrees to train Rey, but only in the interest of demonstrating to her why the Jedi need to be extinct. Simultaneously, fighter pilot Poe Dameron and General Leia Organa are continuing the Resistance's struggle with the fascist First Order, culminating in a battle that positions their small armada (all that remains of the fight against totalitarianism in the galaxy) against the First Order. Leia is injured in the battle and unable to continue acting as a general. Thus, Vice Admiral Holdo takes over and clashes with Poe over military strategies, leading him to enact a coup against her. As this occurs, Rey's training with Luke leads her to confront Kylo Ren, second-in-command of the First Order, himself a former student of Luke, and his nephew. Together, Kylo and Rey defeat Snoke, Supreme Leader of the First Order, leading Kylo to offer Rey a position next to him as rulers of the galaxy. Rey rejects his offer, solidifying the conflict between them. The film's third act ends with the separate narrative threads colliding in a final battle on the planet Crait wherein Kylo attempts to kill Luke but is unable to, and Rey rescues the remaining Resistance members. At the end of the film, Luke disappears (presumably becoming one with the Force) due to the effort of telekinetically projecting himself onto Crait from his remote hiding location on the planet Ahch-To.

Rey, General Leia, and Vice Admiral Holdo all hold positions of power within the narrative. Rey is positioning herself to become a Jedi as well as a leader in the Resistance. Leia is a well-established leader in both the military and political spheres. Holdo has an impressive record as a military commander. As more public pressure is put on Hollywood to both make the men who act in damaging ways accountable and to produce more progressive narratives, the female characters in *The Last Jedi* do seem to be a reaction to this culture change. Furthermore, one can see that the filmmakers are purposefully crafting a message that is friendly to a broader market so that the commodity market of young female consumers can also be targeted alongside the young males who make up the traditional audience for *Star Wars*. This aligns with Meehan's conception that media-makers attempt to acknowledge the market power of female consumers by establishing the "niche" gendered commodity audience, while keeping them separate from "the" audience of white males ages 18–34 (2002). Hence, the narrative of *The Last Jedi* attempts to craft female characters that are conducive to marketing campaigns aimed at female consumers while keeping the film relevant to their primary audience of young male consumers.

Above all, Disney is a company interested in building branded, family-friendly entertainment that has widespread appeal. It is (mostly) not in the business of pushing boundaries or creating ground-breaking characters who stray far from the established norms of traditional gender representation, as is made apparent by a cursory glance through its classic film library (*Cinderella, Sleeping Beauty, The Little Mermaid*, etc.). This is also true in Disney's *Star Wars* films. While it has recognized that there is a large female fan base ready to spend money on the franchise and has begun to create content (both textually and extra-textually) to cater to that audience (Johnson 2014; Scott 2017), it has not fundamentally changed the structure of *Star Wars* from Lucas' vision modeled after the Joseph Campbell monomyth thesis. This would not be problematic if the series were not created to mimic a narrative structure created specifically for the male hero (Larabee 2016).

In *The Last Jedi*, the narrative focuses on Rey and her journey to become a Jedi and a member of the resistance against the First Order. Rey's story is not only functioning within the traditional male hero quest structure, but also directly mirrors Luke's narrative journey in the middle chapter of the original trilogy (episodes IV–XI). This is not to say that a female character cannot function in a heroic role that has traditionally male, but that one cannot expect the character to function well when she has been copied and pasted into a story that was made for a man and has centuries of historical baggage associated with it regarding traditional gender roles. In other words, it would be much easier to "flip the script" of *Star Wars* with Rey's character and make her a heroic female if the story were not rooted in the conception that there is a universal human monomyth that has existed for thousands of years and the hero of that story is male. Recently there have been Disney films that appear to break some traditional gender models, such as the animated film *Frozen*. However, upon closer reflection, many authors have ultimately concluded that the film does rely on the very gender stereotypes (such as the power-hungry female villain, or feminine compassion) that the film appears to be breaking (Azmi et al. 2016; Streiff and Dundes 2017).

Keeping this in mind, the narrative of the film does allow for the three primary female characters to have memorable moments, but this is often in lieu of real character development. The audience is given little information regarding Holdo, we spend little time with Leia, and most of Rey's arc is focused on her relationships with Luke Skywalker and Kylo Ren. While the women are clearly taking the lead in this film (as is apparent with the leadership roles that both Holdo and Leia inhabit and Rey's ongoing journey to embody the light or "good" side of the Force) the male characters still enjoy the most development and richest scenes. Luke and Kylo are both allowed to display more emotion as they develop throughout the film, whereas the women are more even-keeled. Kylo oscillates between intense anger, a desire to connect with other characters, and stoicism. Luke is seen progressing from deep resignation, frustration, anger, to peace. Contrast this with Leia and Holdo who are both shown consistently as stoic in the face of surmounting odds, without much added emotional depth. Rey is allowed a bit more complexity, but even her emotional expression is fairly limited to stone-faced tears. In the official trailer for *The Last Jedi*, Rey is repeatedly shown pleading to both Luke and Kylo to either teach her or to "show me my place in all this," implying that she is more dependent on the male characters in the story than she actually is. This highlights the way in which the female characters are being positioned as leaders and important figures in the story, but are still subordinated to male wisdom, emotions, and experience regardless.

Alternatively, these three characters can be interpreted through a more positive and progressive lens. At the end of the second act, Holdo sacrifices herself by destroying the lead ship of the First Order, giving the surviving members of the Resistance the ability to flee to safety. Rey refuses Kylo's offer to rule alongside him and appears resolute in her quest to ride the galaxy of the evil of the First Order. Leia acts as a guardian of wisdom, passing down her knowledge to the next generation of leaders, whereas Luke refuses to do so for most of the narrative. Although there is no doubt that these characters present many good qualities and their narratives contain progressive elements, it is important to also acknowledge the classic sexist tropes that exist in this film that serve the interests of the gendered commodity market and the capitalist economy by which it is dictated. Can films made within this economic system truly be feminist or exhibit feminist themes? This is a question that will be returned to later in this article.

Kennedy vs. the Fans. It is important to note that, while the Disney *Star Wars* films have more recognizable and significant female characters, behind the scenes, the *Star Wars* franchise is overwhelmingly male. When *The Last Jedi* was released in December of 2017, and in the proceeding months, there was a great deal of vitriolic discourse amongst the fan community regarding the quality of the film. Many fans have chosen to blame Lucasfilm president Kathleen Kennedy (who took over when George Lucas sold the company to Disney) for whatever they do not like about the films or for any perceived failures that may occur. In the wake of disappointing box office returns for *Solo: A Star Wars Story*, "The Daily Caller" writer Jordan Whitley penned an op-ed blaming Kennedy for injecting feminism into the new *Star Wars* films, ignoring the core male customer base, openly mocking them, and showing preferential treatment to the female fans of the franchise (Whitley 2018). Notably, Kennedy is currently the only visible woman involved in the creation of the *Star Wars* films. Kennedy also has not been shy about making statements that have upset the core male fan base. She has explicitly stated that she does not owe anything to the male fans of *Star Wars* (Lucasfilm President Kathleen Kennedy Says She Doesn't Need to Cater to Male Star Wars Fans 2016), and she has proposed an industry commission to make Hollywood a safer place for women in the wake of the Weinstein scandal (Kathleen Kennedy Proposes Industry Commission and 'Zero Tolerance' in Wake of Weinstein Claims 2017). Kennedy's statements and actions as president, in conjunction with the increased presence of female characters in *Star Wars* films, has only increased the level of vitriol that many fans feel in a context that is already rife with racism and misogyny (Katz 2018).

While the narrative that, under the leadership of Kennedy, Lucasfilm gives preferential treatment to female audiences at the expense of the male fan base is popular, it is easy to see that the primary goal of Lucasfilm (and Disney) is to reach the largest possible audience. The official trailer for *The Last Jedi* was released during a Monday Night Football segment (notably, ESPN and ABC who broadcast Monday Night Football are both owned by Disney) (Thilk 2017). The cut of this trailer is also of note because it overemphasizes Kylo Ren's narrative in comparison to its significance in the film. Holdo is also absent from this preview of the film, and Leia does not speak. Thus, while the trailer is not representative of the actual narrative of the film, it is clear that Lucasfilm is trying to appeal to a male audience (although the Monday Night Football audience is most likely not the same audience as its most vocal fan base) by downplaying the significant female characters in the film within the trailer.

These small examples are an illustration of how Disney treats the female characters in *the Star Wars* franchise. While it is eager to incorporate women into the narrative so that they can access new markets, they are not interested in telling women's unique stories. The narratives of Rey, Holdo, and Leia, while promising at first glance, reveal that Disney is using the narrative language of feminism and women's movements in lieu of crafting female characters that are more than simply female versions of male character archetypes. This should not be framed as a successful feminist narrative. In order for a narrative or a character to be successfully feminist, that character or story should be conceived in such a way that her gender is a part of who she is, not simply a consequence of a marketing strategy constructed to broaden the audience of a film in the interest of selling merchandise. The works of author Angela Carter are an excellent example of how characters that are drawn from a traditional mythos can be reconceived with a feminist perspective (see *The Bloody Chamber* (Carter 1979) as an example). Thus, while the incorporation of major female characters seems to be positive, ultimately it amounts to little more than tokenism done in the interest of serving marketplace interests.

2.2. Beauty and the Beast for a New Audience

In an article in "The Huffington Post," Disney's latest rendition of *Beauty and the Beast* is praised as a film that "goes to great lengths to demonstrate Belle's agency in every part of the story," further appreciating the way Disney produced (retold) a movie providing more voice and agency to the female character (Gray 2017). Similar articles about the movie circulated during its release, creating a popular discourse that celebrated *Beauty and the Beast* as a feminist retelling of the fairy tale. However, a deeper analysis reveals that the movie perpetuates many tropes that reinforce the prevalent position of men and women in society.

To understand the origin of *Beauty and the Beast* as a contemporary fairy tale, it is important to look at the original story and its evolution thereon. The original story was written by Marie De Beaumont in the 18th century (Jeffords 1995, p. 165). In the original, a daughter of a merchant is held captive by a beast after she is asked to take the place of her father, who has stolen a rose from the Beast's garden. However, the daughter is pleasantly surprised that all her wishes are fulfilled in the magical castle. Slowly she begins to appreciate the Beast's intelligence and generosity, although she rejects his proposals for marriage. When the daughter realizes her father is ill, the Beast lets her go under the condition that she returns on her own within a specified time. The daughter fails to return to the castle, but realizes through a dream that the Beast is dying. She returns to the castle and expresses her love to the Beast, and, as a result, transforms the Beast into a handsome prince. The prince tells her about the curse he was under and with his power and wealth restored, marries the daughter, and they live happily ever after (Cummins 1995; Jeffords 1995).

This story was retold by Disney in 1991 in its animated version of *The Beauty and the Beast*, with some significant modifications to the story and the characters. Disney tried to bring the fairy tale to the big screen on two different occasions during the 1930s and 1950s, before it finally made it in 1991. In the past two attempts, the writers of Disney had found it hard to adapt the story to the big screen film format ('Beauty and the Beast 2017). Over five decades after the first Disney fairy tale film *Snow White and Seven Dwarfs, The Beauty and the Beast*, directed by Gary Toursdale and Kirk Wise, took over three and a half years to create (Ames 1991). The creators were able to overcome the constraints writers faced in the previous two attempts, by converting the long dinner conversations between the Beast and Belle in the original tale, into musical performances, along with the reimagination and introduction of various supporting characters (Ames 1991). The first draft, written by screenwriter Linda Woolverton, was not a musical, and did not have any of the talking household objects. However, everything changed with the release of *The Little Mermaid*. Disney had experienced a slump and needed something unique to recover. This pushed the producers to include music and the talking objects (Thomas and Hoad 2017). The writers were also aware of the criticism Disney had received for *The Little Mermaid*, for being sexist. This lead Woolverton to create Belle to be a strong, independent character. The movie was presented as a work-in-progress at the New York Film Festival in September 1991, with more than 35 percent of its animation still in black and white, yet it received a standing ovation for more than 10 minutes. The film was popular even before its official release (Ames 1991).

The Disney version has now become the canonical and definitive version of the fairy tale (Cummins 1995). This version privileges the romance plot, resulting in the sidelining of feminist elements of the original story (ibid). This change to favor the romance plot, emphasizes the relationship between Belle and the Beast, wherein Belle is objectified not just as the Beast's desire, but also an object that relieves the Beast of the curse. This objectification is revealed when Belle first enters the Beast's castle and the Beast's servants (cursed to take the form of household objects) comment that she is the girl who can undo the curse and that she is beautiful. Belle becomes the necessary object in the heterosexual relationship needed by the Beast. Her beauty supersedes her interests in books, as even her interests are used as a bait to woo her (Bryant 1989). Furthermore, Lieberman (1986) argues that fairy tales that end with marriage convey the message that marriage is the most important part of a woman's life. She points out that an ending with marriage automatically focuses the action of the film on courtship. This phase of courtship provides the woman with agency, but it all ends with the marriage. On the other hand, Rowe (1986) points out that marriages act as bridges between the realm of fantasy and reality, and thus construct the expectations of women viewers. The "Long, long ago in a place far, far away" leads the viewer into the world of fantasy; the marriage and courtship rituals connect them back to reality. Disney's retelling of the fairy tale, whether the 1991 animation or the more recent live-action rendition, emphasize the romantic relationship between Belle and the Beast, and conclude with them together. Both focus on the courtship period between Belle and the Beast, with the curing of the curse, and subsequently their marriage being the resolution. The resolution in both these retellings by Disney connect viewers back to reality; a reality that reinforces the prevalent hegemonic views of men and women, providing only a mask of agency to the female protagonist. What is interesting is that, when the animated movie was released in 1991, critics and reviewers appreciated the character of Belle as different compared to other Disney princesses, as she broke the prevalent sexist tropes and was a strong, independent female character (Cummins 1995). The same appreciation and celebration is seen in 2017, 26 years after the release of the animated movie.

The story in 2017 remained the same as Disney's 1991 animated rendition of *The Beauty and the Beast*. Belle, a bibliophile woman from a small French village is taken captive by a beast. The Beast (who is a prince) and other household items of the castle who are alive (and live as the prince's servants) are under a spell that can only be broken if the beast can make someone fall in love with him, which will bring them all back to their human form. The Beast falls in love with Belle, but lets her go when it becomes clear that her father is in danger. A soldier named Gaston wants to marry Belle, so he rallies the village to kill the Beast. Gaston is successful in mortally wounding the Beast, but Belle returns and confesses her love for the Beast, immediately breaking the spell and bringing the prince back to life (Barnes 2017). This plot, which was loosely adopted from the 18th century fairytale by Marie de Beaumontt (Jeffords 1995), remain intact with both renditions by Disney. However, certain significant changes in the film storylines shift the narrative voice from that of Belle to the Beast, a clear shift in favor of the male character.

Focus on the Beast. Disney's version also shifts the focus of the story from Belle to the Beast. Unlike the original story, where the readers come to know about the curse only at the end of the story, once the curse has been lifted, in the Disney versions (both the 1991 and 2017 versions) the viewers are introduced to the story with the prince being cursed by an enchantress, and thereby making it the story of the Beast (Jeffords 1995, p. 166). Instead of the curse appearing as the resolution part of narrative, in the Disney movies, it sets up the narrative. This reordering of the original narrative shifts the focus from Belle to the Beast. Cummins summarizes the story as "Beast gets girl, Beast loses girl, Beast gets girl back" (Cummins 1995, p. 23). The 2017 remake follows the same narrative and plot, making the movie the Beast's story. This also shifts the focus from Belle, to the victimization of the Beast, as viewers see that the Beast is also a prisoner in the castle like Belle, a trope that is absent in the original story in which the Beast controls all the magic in the castle (Jeffords 1995, p. 168). The focus of the story becomes how the Beast evolved to become better, and in that evolution, Belle is just an object. This makes the Beast the protagonist of the story, while Belle becomes a plot device needed for romance and as a solution to the Beast's problems, revealing the influence of the oedipal myth in Western narratives, in which the woman's story is nothing but the man's story, a narrative in which if the woman is successful, the man will get her/marry her (Bryant 1989).

Belle: Reading Woman to Inventor. Disney also brought in a lot of changes to the character of Belle. Belle has always been heralded by Disney as someone unlike other Disney princesses due to her interest in reading and adventure (Cummins 1995; Jeffords 1995, p. 167). "We spent a lot of time on Belle, trying to make her as modern as possible. She knows how to ride a horse, she knows how to shoot, she knows how to invent something, she knows how to fight, she knows how to read and teach. We wanted to give her modern qualities that are aspirational to young girls today. Everybody, including Emma, made a contribution to that" states the producer of the movie, Todd Lieberman (Rifkin 2017). According to director Bill Condon, the remake of the 1991 classic was needed to reinvent the protagonist Belle as a "21st-century heroine" and present the story in a new format that was photoreal and live action in format. The major changes to the character of Belle was that she was an inventor, and apart from that, Disney added details of Belle's childhood and what happened to her mother (Holmes 2017). The movie illustrates that Belle wants to know about her childhood, but her father repeatedly avoids telling her. The Beast uses magic to reveal all the details of her childhood and provides closure to her questions. Here, the male characters adopt tropes such as a protective father, or benevolent beast, while the agency of Belle, her constant attempts to discover her history and her inquisitiveness, are overshadowed by the actions of the male characters. They protect Belle, they enable Belle to discover her past, while her own agency remains in the shadows.

Although Disney celebrates her as a princess who reads books, in the 1991 version, it is not clear what she reads about. In comparison, in the original tale by Beaumont, the author makes it clear that Beauty (and her readers subsequently) reads books about history, politics, philosophy, and religion. The 2017 version of the story shows Belle reading romantic tales about prince charming, her favorite Shakespearean drama being *Romeo and Juliet*, and she appreciates the Beast for reading a romantic novel. Here, Disney, as stated earlier, is not only emphasizing the romantic plot in the story as whole, but also emphasizing it in the interests of Belle, the kind of books she reads, and consequently her view of the world: her adventures will lead her to prince charming. This worldview of Belle (and ultimately the viewers) is reinforced in the song that she sings about a character meeting prince charming. Originally, Beaumont, writing in the context of 18th-century France, wanted to bring out a heroine who was a reading woman, who was not in pursuit of frivolous pleasures but in pursuit of knowledge, shown through the emphasis she put on the Beauty's love for music and specific kinds of books (Cummins 1995). In the 1991 and 2017 Disney versions, although reading is emphasized visually and in the narrative, it does not emerge as a significant trait except for in the beginning and a few scenes in the castle. Instead, Belle's ability to nurture takes over, be it the nurturing of the Beast or of her father.

The 2017 version of *Beauty and the Beast* was heralded as feminist because Belle was shown as an inventor. The movie portrays Belle working with her father in his workshop, displaying her knowledge in technology, by providing the tools her father needs even before her father realizes he needs them. Apart from this, Belle is also show working on an invention, testing a prototype, and the invention is finally revealed to the audiences to be a washing machine run by the power of a mule. While her invention is at work, Belle sits next to it reading a book, and then teaches a little girl how to read. The imagery of women and machines has transformed drastically in the last century. The images of women working in factories during the world wars, to Rosie the Riveter, influenced a change in how people perceived women and machines (Wosk 2001). However, after the Second World War, the agenda was for women to return to domestic life, and images of women with modern home appliances started to fill the postwar period of increased production. Refrigerators, washing machines, and stoves, which were technologically advanced and handled by women, created an image of technically adept women making use of their wartime knowledge of technology for domestic chores (Wosk 2001). This turn returned the woman back to domestic chores from the factory floor. The image of Belle inventing a machine to help in her household chores, putting it to use and nurturing a child, furthers this postwar image of the woman, who can do her daily chores while she nurtures her children thanks to technology. The tech innovator Belle of 2017 might be an inventor, but is limited to household chores similar to how women were expected to return to domestic chores after the war (Wosk 2001). The transformation of Belle from a reading woman in the original tale, to an adventure loving and educated one in 1991, to a tech innovator in 2017, is a significant one, but confines her within the gendered roles prevalent in society, especially women holding the responsibility of housework.

The reversal of roles in celebrated in this movie; it does not challenge the dominant patriarchy, but instead remains within the comfort of reinstating what it means to be masculine and feminine in a patriarchal society. To understand this reinstatement, one needs to look at the changes in society during the 80s. Although, there was a radical change in the kind of work taken up by women in the 80s, there was no change in the gender perspectives associated with domestic labor: in addition to any new responsibility women took up, they still had to undertake domestic labor (Lupri 1983). This shift in roles of gender was reflected in Hollywood too, with movies such as *Kindergarten Cop* and *Three Men and a Baby*, which reiterated the need for women to be in domestic spaces by representing the awkwardness of men in female/domestic roles (Traube 1992). The concept of the "cult of the home" by Benston (1971) argues that the domestic role of women and their presence in that particular labor is essential to, but inferior to, the wage-earning labor of men, and acts as a constant reserve of surplus labor. Movies portraying such gender role reversals consequently represent women being required to give-up their new responsibilities and return to the domestic realm to sustain the dominant hegemonic gender roles (Carrier 2015). Gender role reversals also provide mixed messages, in which the female character always displays domesticated femininity, during her role as a strong, independent character (Ross and Carolyn 2006). In most cases, movies with strong, independent female characters, display opposing traits such as, "acts of rebellion combined with gestures of respect, beauty and brains, power and submission, sexuality and timidity"- so all viewers can relate to and enjoy something (Dutt 2014, p. 9). This is explicitly seen in *Beauty and the Beast*, in which Belle rebels against Beast and enters the restricted west-wing, portraying rebellion and power, immediately juxtaposed by timidity (fear of retribution, the act of running away, fear of the wolves), and the heroic rescue by the Beast. Following the rescue, Belle automatically assumes a submissive role to a domestic caretaker by helping and treating the injured Beast and thanking the Beast for saving her. The display of opposing traits is also portrayed when Belle is made the object of beauty in Gaston's eyes (consequently in the viewer's eyes as well), but is immediately shown as the "brainy" kind of woman with her reading of books and inventing of gadgets. However, this image of "inventor, brainy Belle" is short-lived, when she invents a washing machine, bringing her back to the submissive realm of domesticity.

Beauty and the Beast in the Age of Watson and Weinstein. Although the latest rendition of *Beauty and the Beast* has aspects that can be read as feminist, a deeper analysis reveals that painting the movie as feminist is problematic. In an age when Hollywood is rocked by the sexual assault scandals of Harvey Weinstein, Susan Jeffords analysis of the 1991 *The Beauty and the Beast* as a "tale helps to forward the image of unloved and unhappy white men who need kindness and affection, rather than criticism and reform, in order to become their 'true selves' again" (1995, p. 165) rings relevant to *Beauty and the Beast*. The rendition of the same tale with a few changes, most importantly having the ambassador of United Nations' HeForShe campaign, Emma Watson, play Belle, and her becoming a plot device to transform men (the Beast), cannot be a feminist retelling. The story still focuses on the Beast, the construction of masculinity/femininity is still hegemonic, the Beast's wrongdoing is not his fault but he needs a woman to make himself into a complete man, and in the end, the desire of Belle for adventure and travels end with her being with the prince. As a cherry on the cake of constructing hegemonic masculinity, Belle even asks the prince if he can grow a beard in the final shot of the 2017 movie.

The movie *Beauty and the Beast* might not be a feminist retelling, but when one looks at the content in relation to the political economy, the rationale for the production of the movie at this particular moment becomes clear. Disney revamped their plans for movie production, focusing on sequels and remakes, of which *Beauty and a Beast* was one.

Disney CEO Bob Iger informed his shareholders about the enthusiasm behind *Beauty and the Beast* by pointing out the number of views the movie's trailer had on YouTube. The movie had to bring in money as it had to cover Disney's massive US$300 million budget for production and global marketing (Rainey 2017). The movie was produced by David Hoberman and Todd Lieberman, both veteran movie producers (Rainey 2017). The producers had approached Disney in 2008 to produce a remake of *The Beauty and the Beast* from the perspective of the Beast and create a darker version of the original. Disney was skeptical about producing a dark version of one of the favorite movies of its renaissance period. With the tremendous success of *Frozen* in 2013, Disney knew the advantage of presenting strong female protagonists, and therefore asked the producers to remake *Beauty and the Beast* accordingly (Rainey 2017; Rysdall and Bodnar 2017). Disney and the producers of the movie state that they are in the business of providing upbeat happy endings, and business in the past few years has been good (Hayes 2017).

Iger noted in his annual report that Disney was having great success in re-imagining all the classics in live action format, beginning with *Maleficent*, *Cinderella*, and *The Jungle Book*. He said that reimagining *Beauty and the Beast* for the new generation was part of the plan to release *The Lion King*, *Aladdin*, *Dumbo*, and *Mulan* in the next few years in live action format (Iger 2017). Commenting on the same, Christine McCarthy, senior executive director and CFO, Walt Disney Company, commented that the strategy was to have movies that would cross a certain threshold in the box office. Disney's strategy is to create brands and franchises that support the studio financially (tent poles). Based on this strategy, she noted, "In general you will see one to two *Star Wars*, two to three animated movies and they could be both from Pixar and Feature animation, two to four Marvel movies, we do have four next year that are being released. And the balance will be Disney live action" (McCarthy 2017, p. 9). Furthermore, she noted that the strategy for Disney live action was to reimagine Disney intellectual properties in live action format, which began with *Maleficent*, and each of these reimaginations, including *Beauty and the Beast*, has averaged US$650 million at the box office, which shows the success of the strategy (McCarthy 2017). Commenting on the reboot culture of Disney, Desta (2017) pointed out, "Disney's rebooting strategy is also working to reel in new viewers (who will hopefully then take their children to the reboot of the reboot in 2037, and so on and so forth, forever and ever, amen)."

At a time when a majority of audiences of Hollywood movies are women, 60% of the audience for *Beauty and the Beast* were women, while 72% were women during the opening weekend in North America (Desta 2017). Their marketing was also aimed at millennial mothers. Disney marketed *Beauty and the Beast* on *The Bachelor* (season 21), with Luke Evans and Josh Gad hosting the show on 30 January, which included a release of one of the trailers (Freeman 2017). *The Bachelor* is a telecast on ABC, which is also owned by Disney. Advertisers are interested in *The Bachelor*, as almost 75% of its audience are women. Moreover, its biggest audience is the 18–49 demographic and rates high in households with an average annual income of US$100,000 or more (Berg 2016). Disney even bought ads in the newly released Google Home assistant, in which Google Home provided the weather and news and ended it with, "By the way, *Beauty and the Beast* opens in theaters today. In this version, Belle is the inventor. Sounds more like it to me" as reported by several users (Roberts 2017). Disney's cross promotions and tie ins were aimed at products and services that would suit and attract millennial mothers (Palmeri and Townsend 2017).

It is evident from these examples that the motive driving Disney to release *Beauty and the Beast* was not a feminist one, but profit and market logic, targeted at specific audiences. The profit arising from sales is supplemented by the fact that *Beauty and the Beast* is a Disney property, thereby allowing the company to extract more revenue exploiting its ownership of the rights, a phenomenon which, according to the CEO, will continue for the next few years.

3. Discussion

The reality of the gendered commodity market and the ways in which it functions within the contemporary film industry brings up many complex theoretical issues from both a feminist political economy perspective and a socialist feminist theory perspective. Questions about the role of neoliberalism within the marketplace, the politics of postfeminism, commodity feminism, and the possibility of creating feminist media texts within this economic and cultural space all rise to the surface when addressing these films. The rise of neoliberal politics appears to be at the root of these inquiries.

In David Harvey's *A Brief History of Neoliberalism*, he defines the term as, "a theory of political economic practices that propose that human well-being can best be advanced by liberating individual entrepreneurial freedoms and skills within an institutional framework characterized by strong private property rights, free markets, and free trade" (Harvey 2005, p. 2). While Meehan does not bring up this particular ideology in her work on the gendered commodity market (2002), it seems as though neoliberalism has particular relevance in the context of these two media texts and the cultural landscape of this decade in general. As Harvey states: "It [neoliberalism] has pervasive effects on ways of thought to the point where it has become incorporated into the common-sense way many of us interpret, live in, and understand the world" (Harvey 2005, p. 3). A focus on individual determination and rising above circumstance in the service of rejecting critiques of systemic oppression characterizes a neoliberal social position.

This social position fuels the postfeminist perspective of female "empowerment." Rosalind Gill calls this a "sensibility" as opposed to a concretely definable philosophy and characterizes it as: "the notion that femininity is a bodily property; the shift from objectification to subjectification; the emphasis upon self-surveillance; monitoring and discipline; a focus upon individualism; choice and empowerment; the dominance of a makeover paradigm; a resurgence in ideas of natural sexual difference; a marked sexualization of culture; and an emphasis upon consumerism and the commodification of difference" (Gill 2007, p. 149). This sensibility clearly builds off of the rhetoric of neoliberalism and works to benefit the goal of the gendered commodity market: commodifying difference.

This leads to a discussion of what has been termed "commodity feminism." Goldman, Heath, and Smith describe this phenomenon as a restructuring of feminist ideology to work within a western patriarchal society (Goldman et al. 1991). They say, "When framed by ideologies of possessive individualism and free choice, feminism in its 'new' commodity form forgets its origins in a critique of unequal social, economic and political relations" (Goldman et al. 1991, p. 336). In other words, feminism (specifically the postfeminist sensibility) becomes focused on "girl power" and a women's ability to "vote with her wallet" as opposed to seeking ways to deconstruct harmful social structures. Commodity feminism allows women to identify with their femininity and their "empowerment" through consumerism; it allows them to adopt a set of heavily-sterilized feminist "attitudes which they can then wear" (Goldman et al. 1991, p. 336).

At the narrative level, *The Last Jedi* appears to offer a rather bland message of collective action in the face of a fascist threat (a threat that is all too real in the "real world"). Rey, Holdo, and Leia act as female leaders of that collective action. However, there is no examination of the social structures that may have led to the resurgence of fascism in the galaxy after its defeat by the rebellion (e.g., ineffective chains of individualistic command and respect for military authority, a lack of a concerted effort to educate "regular" people in the use of the Force and democratize traditional Jedi knowledge, etc.). Instead, the film offers the type of role-reversal that is characteristic of liberal feminist politics which seeks to preserve traditional social structures, but with more women and other oppressed individuals gaining power. Under a socialist feminist agenda, however, oppressive social structures would be dismantled that would create a more equitable society for all. This alliance with the sensibility of liberal feminism allows for the narrative to be easily crafted into a marketing campaign that targets both the audience of males 18–34 as well as the gendered commodity market of women, who have been exposed to postfeminist rhetoric and bombarded with an ethics of commodity feminist consumerism on a daily basis. A similar narrative can be found in *Beauty and the Beast*, in which the radical transformation which Belle brings about in the Beast (leading to lifting of the curse), makes the Beast as an individual a "better person." Once the curse is lifted, the audience witnesses a transformation of the Beast, the castle, the talking objects and the castle garden. However, the position of Beast/Prince as the owner of the castle, and the transformed talking objects as the "loyal" servants, remain unchanged. Belle also takes up a position parallel to the Beast/Prince, with the servants subordinate to her. This reflects, as stated before, the characteristic of liberal feminist politics.

Apart from the neoliberal feminist narratives in these films, the design elements of both characterize what Mirrlees (2014) terms globally popular entertainment media or, "Blockbuster Event films" in particular. These films are designed in a way to reach and relate to audiences across the whole world, suit their preferences and ensure profits for corporations (Mirrlees 2013). Design characteristics of such movies include global stars, pre-sold properties, genre hybridity, classical narrative structures, universal themes and visual spectacles (Mirrlees 2013). *The Last Jedi* and *Beauty and the Beast* are Blockbuster Event Films.

The casting of stars in a Hollywood movie are important because the presence of this "image-commodity" attracts some viewers to consume the movie (Mirrlees 2013). While *Beauty and Beast* cast the globally popular Emma Watson, *The Last Jedi* roped in an international cast including the British actors Daisy Ridley and John Boyega, as well as Kelly-Marie Tran, the Vietnamese-American (Lopez 2017). Both movies are also pre-sold properties which have an existing audience who has either seen previous movies, or read comic books and fairy tales. While *Beauty and the Beast* can be classified within the fantasy genre of film, *The Last Jedi* contains elements of both fantasy and science fiction. A characteristic of Blockbuster event films is that they do not represent reality, but instead create a completely new "fantastical reality" (Mirrlees 2013, p. 187). Both movies perform this act of constructing a new fantastical realm, be it the French village and the castle in *Beauty and the Beast*, or the continuation of the *Star Wars* galaxy in *The Last Jedi*. This construction of new realms allows Disney to target a wider audience, create merchandise, and allow for the creation of 'esoteric knowledge,' resulting in fan groups and communities (Mirrlees 2013). As observed in the analysis of the two movies, although the films create a whole new reality, they still conform to hegemonic norms of patriarchy. This conformation is also observed in the conservative narrative form of the two movies. The absence of complex experimental camera shots, radical use of lighting, and unrelatable scenarios are avoided in blockbuster event films (Mirrlees 2013). The discontinuation of *Beauty and the Beast* in 2008, which was supposed to have a darker version points to this phenomenon; as an experimental narrative such as that would not be relatable to a large audience.

Finally, both movies offer a visual spectacle displaying "spectacular imagery, often utilizing the latest in special effects and other technologies" (King 2002, p. 178). The use of live-animation action in *Beauty and the Beast* and complex CGI and visual effects in *The Last Jedi*, provide audiences a visually rich experience, devoid of heavy dialogues, with constant presentations of, what Jenkins (2006) calls, "Wow Climax" (e.g., the ballroom dance in *Beauty and the Beast*; the sacrifice of vice-admiral Holdo in *The Last Jedi*).

Furthermore, both films exhibit the economic characteristics of a blockbuster event film: big budget [*The Last Jedi* had a net production cost of $200 million (D'Allesandro 2018b)]; big marketing [Disney spent $175 million on worldwide ads of *Beauty and the Beast* (D'Allesandro 2018a). For *The Last Jedi*, Disney spent $185 million (D'Allesandro 2018b)]; big release [*The Last Jedi* had a global box office collection of $1332 million (D'Allesandro 2018b). *Beauty and the Beast* had $1263 million (D'Allesandro 2018a)]; big synergy and global audience (Mirrlees 2014). The categorization of both these films as blockbuster event films points to the fact that for Disney, these two are commodities designed to ensure profits, through creating a specific design of films which can be consumed by the masses, but also to capitalize on commodity feminism.

Disney, at the end of the day, is a corporation and aims to create profits for its shareholders. Disney also owns the copyrights for both *Beauty and the Beast* and *The Last Jedi*, and therefore capitalizes on revenue from these copyrights. It owns these two commodities perceived to be pro-feminist movies. Bob Iger has also presented Disney's plan for the next few years as one involving re-imagining Disney properties, reducing the possibility of Disney producing films with new narratives and original female characters created from scratch. Moreover, Disney as a corporate entity has not been a champion of achieving gender rights within the company. The top management team and the Board of Directors consists of 23 executives, of which only seven are women (About 2018). Apart from the underrepresentation of female characters in its movies (Robehmed 2016), Disney has also reported that in its wing located in England, a male employee is paid 22% more than a female employees, while there exists a 41.9% gap in bonuses paid (Clarke 2018). No information about wage or salary gaps were found for Disney's United States wing. Alan Horn, Chairman of Walt Disney Studio, noted, "Audiences have proven that there's an appetite and a market for dynamic female leads and female-driven stories, and as an industry, we have a responsibility to create those roles for women and compensate them accordingly" (Berg 2015). What this quote conveys is the motive and rationale behind Disney creating "feminist" films is not concern for women in society, but the market which they want to capture, to ensure constant profits.

Thus, this raises the question: can a feminist film be made? The answer, predictably, is complicated. Because of the inherently oppressive nature of capitalism, it is hard to envision a film that can truly be feminist from both a critical theoretical standpoint and a political economic standpoint. Capitalist systems will inevitably encourage the exploitation of workers and, even more so, women in the film industry (as the Weinstein scandal has revealed to the masses). On this premise alone, a truly feminist film cannot be made within a capitalist system. However, this is not to suggest that some films cannot contain feminist themes or achieve greater degrees of feminism than others. It is certainly not ideal to measure films or compare them according to their degrees of feminism, but under the current global economic system, capitalism is the status quo and it is very hard to work outside of that system. Even "independent" cinema as is traditionally conceived is no longer truly independent, as indie film companies are consistently purchased by media conglomerates. Hence, for a film to function more actively as a (socialist) feminist text within the contemporary capitalist structure, it might exhibit some of the following characteristics: including characters from oppressed populations who are neither defined by their oppressed status nor are simply code-switched with originally privileged characters; ensuring that individuals from oppressed communities are involved in all levels of the production of the film and are fairly compensated; avoiding marketing strategies that target commodity audiences; avoid neoliberal and postfeminist rhetoric and sensibilities that overemphasize individual ability to overcome structural marginalization; ensuring that any feminist themes in either the narrative of the film or extratextual materials do not embody an ethics of commodity feminism, and instead one of active, participatory feminism.

4. Conclusions

In 2017 alone, Disney has shown that, while it is happy to present itself as a company that holds the interests of girls and women at heart, it is truly only concerned with profiting from them. The narratives of both *Beauty and the Beast* and *The Last Jedi* exemplify that there is not a willingness within the company to search for new narratives outside of what it has tried and succeeded with before. Not only are both of these films either reboots or sequels, but they both reimagine traditional characters in a way that the audience is supposed to read as "feminist" when they are not truly more progressive than originally conceived.

Disney saw that there was a growing social movement fueled by grassroots activism and internet connectivity that brought women and other marginalized groups together more than ever, encouraging each other to speak up on behalf of each other's rights. This presented an economic opportunity to sell much of its repurposed film library as "feminist" retellings of classic stories and produce merchandise

Soc. Sci. **2018**, *7*, 237

that focused on "girl-power" and catered to women specifically. However, this is no substitute for telling the story of women in the real world, in the fantasy world, or in the world far, far away. More must be demanded of our media makers who create narratives and they should be held to a higher standard when they imply that they are telling these narratives for the greater good of the world.

Author Contributions: K.K. conceived of the analysis. He wrote the political economy section of the literature review, as well as the analysis of *Beauty and the Beast*. A.R. contributed material regarding feminist political economy and feminist film theory and criticism to the literature review. She wrote the analysis *of Star Wars: The Last Jedi*. Each author revised sections of the paper.

Funding: This research received no external funding.

Acknowledgments: The authors wish to thank Jennifer Proffitt and the anonymous reviewers for their many helpful suggestions during the revision process.

Conflicts of Interest: The authors declare no conflict of interest.

References

About. 2018. The Walt Disney Company. Available online: https://www.thewaltdisneycompany.com/about/ (accessed on 18 October 2018).

Ames, Katrine. 1991. Just the Way Walt Made Em. *Newsweek*, November 17. Available online: https://www.newsweek.com/just-way-walt-made-em-202018 (accessed on 10 May 2018).

Atkinson, Joshua, and Bernadette Calafell. 2009. Darth Vader made me do it! *Anakin Skywalker's avoidance of responsibility and the gray areas of hegemonic masculinity in the Star Wars Universe. Communication, Culture & Critique* 2: 1–20. [CrossRef]

Azmi, N.J., Radzuwan Ab Rashid, Mairas Abd. Rahman, and Safawati Basirah Zaid. 2016. Gender and speech in a Disney princess movie. *International Journal of Applied Linguistics and English Literature* 5: 235–39. [CrossRef]

Baker, Liana. 2013. GE to sell rest of NBC stake to Comcast for $16.7 billion. *Reuters*, February 13. Available online: https://www.reuters.com/article/us-ge-nbc-idUSBRE91B1IM20130212 (accessed on 10 May 2018).

Barnes, Brooks. 2017. 'Beauty and the Beast': Disney's $300 Million Gamble. *New York Times*, March 8. Available online: https://www.nytimes.com/2017/03/08/movies/beauty-and-the-beast-disneys-300-million-Gamble.html (accessed on 10 May 2018).

Barsanti, Sam. 2018. Some creep made an overtly sexist edit of The Last Jedi, and even they think it's awful. *AV Club*, March 7. Available online: https://www.avclub.com/some-creep-made-an-overtly-sexist-edit-of-the-last-jedi-1822104868 (accessed on 7 March 2018).

'Beauty and the Beast': Revisiting the Animated Classic. 2017. *Biography*, March 15. Available online: https://www.biography.com/news/beauty-and-the-beast-facts-animated-movie (accessed on 10 May 2018).

Benston, Margaret. 1971. The Political Economy of Women's Liberation. In *Roles Women Play: Readings toward Women's Liberation*. Edited by Michele Hoffnung. Belmont: Brooks/Cole Publishing Company.

Berg, Madeline. 2015. Everything You Need To Know About The Hollywood Pay Gap. *Forbes*, November 12. Available online: https://www.forbes.com/sites/maddieberg/2015/11/12/everything-you-need-to-know-about-the-hollywood-pay-gap/#47b417955cf1movie (accessed on 18 October 2018).

Berg, Madeline. 2016. For ABC And 'The Bachelorette,' The Honeymoon Period Is Everlasting. *Forbes*, August 2. Available online: https://www.forbes.com/sites/maddieberg/2016/08/02/for-abc-and-the-bachelor-the-honeymoon-period-is-everlasting/#52ff8f606ac8movie (accessed on 10 May 2018).

Bettig, Ronald, and Jeanne Hall. 2012. *Big Media, Big Money: Cultural Texts and Political Economics*. Boulder: Rowman & Littlefield Publishers, Inc.

Box Office Mojo. 2017. Available online: http://www.boxofficemojo.com/yearly/chart/?view2=worldwide&yr=2017&p=.htm (accessed on 30 March 2018).

Bryant, Slyvia. 1989. Reconstructing Oedipus through Beauty and the Beast. *Criticism: A Quarterly for Literature and Arts* 31: 439–53.

Carrier, Micheal. 2015. Men and the Movies: Labor, Masculinity, and Shifting Gender Relations in Contemporary Hollywood Cinema. *Ohio University*. Available online: https://etd.ohiolink.edu/!etd.send_file?accession=ohiou1430322393&disposition=inlinemovie (accessed on 18 October 2018).

Carter, Angela. 1979. *The Bloody Chamber*. New York: Penguin.

Clarke, Stewart. 2018. Disney Reports 22% Pay Gap in Favor of Men in Britain, NBCU a Gap of 3.2%. *Variety*, March 30. Available online: https://variety.com/2018/biz/news/disney-nbc-gender-pay-gap-uktv-all3media-1202740354/ (accessed on 18 October 2018).

Croteau, David, and William Hoynes. 2006. *The Business of the Media: Corporate Media and the Public Interest*. Thousand Oaks: Pine Forge Press.

Cummins, June. 1995. Romancing the Plot: The Real Beast of Disney's Beauty and the Beast. *Children's Literature Association Quarterly* 20: 22–28. [CrossRef]

D'Allesandro, Anthony. 2018a. No. 2 'Beauty and the Beast' Box Office Profits—2017 Most Valuable Blockbuster Tournament. *Deadline*, March 27. Available online: https://deadline.com/2018/03/beauty-and-the-beast-box-office-profits-1202351594/ (accessed on 18 October 2018).

D'Allesandro, Anthony. 2018b. No. 1 'Star Wars: The Last Jedi' Box Office Profits—2017 Most Valuable Blockbuster Tournament. *Deadline*, March 28. Available online: https://deadline.com/2018/03/star-wars-the-last-jedi-box-office-movie-profits-1202351603/ (accessed on 18 October 2018).

Davis, Scott. 2017. Disney as Master Marketer: A Tale as Old as Time. *Forbes*, March 22. Available online: https://www.forbes.com/sites/scottdavis/2017/03/22/beautyandthebeast/#18766e8a44cc (accessed on 18 October 2018).

Desta, Yohana. 2017. How Beauty and the Beast Became One of Disney's Most Profitable Gambles. *Vanity Fair*, March 23. Available online: https://www.vanityfair.com/hollywood/2017/03/beauty-and-the-beast-animated-box-office (accessed on 10 May 2018).

Dutt, Reema. 2014. Behind the curtain: women's representations in contemporary Hollywood. LSE. Available online: http://www.lse.ac.uk/media@lse/research/mediaWorkingPapers/MScDissertationSeries/2013/msc/112-Dutt.pdf (accessed on 18 October 2018).

Florio, Angelica. 2017. Why Laura Dern's Holdo Is the Most Badass Character in the Last Jedi. *Bustle*, December 18. Available online: https://www.bustle.com/p/laura-derns-holdo-in-the-last-jedi-defies-a-sexist-trope-to-become-a-badass-hero-7611685 (accessed on 2 April 2018).

Freeman, Molly. 2017. Beauty and the Beast Stars to Host Episode of the Bachelor. *ScreenRant*, January 18. Available online: https://screenrant.com/disney-beauty-beast-bachelor-luke-evans-josh-gad/ (accessed on 10 May 2018).

Gertrude, Bitter. 2018. Why so Many Men Hate the Last Jedi but can't Agree on Why. *BitterGertude*, April 2. Available online: https://bittergertrude.com/2018/01/04/why-so-many-men-hate-the-last-jedi-but-cant-agree-on-why/ (accessed on 2 April 2018).

Gill, Rosalind. 2007. Postfeminist media culture: Elements of a sensibility. *European Journal of Cultural Studies* 10: 147–66. [CrossRef]

Goldman, Robert, Deborah Heath, and Sharon L. Smith. 1991. Commodity Feminism. *Critical Studies in Mass Communication* 8: 333–51. [CrossRef]

Gomery, Douglas. 2004. The economics of Hollywood: Money and Media. In *Media Economics: Theory and Practice*. Edited by Alison Alexander, James Owers, Rod Carveth, Ann Hollifield and Albert Greco. Mahwa: LEA Publishers, pp. 193–206.

Gonzalez, Umberto. 2018. JJ Abrams Slams Star Wars Fans Who Didn't Like Last Jedi as 'Threatened' by Women. *The Warp*, February 16. Available online: https://www.thewrap.com/jj-abrams-star-wars-fans-last-jedi/ (accessed on 2 April 2018).

Gray, Emma. 2017. How Disney Subtly Made 'Beauty and the Beast' More Feminist. *HuffPost*, March 21. Available online: https://www.huffingtonpost.in/entry/how-disney-subtly-made-beauty-and-the-beast-more-feminist_us_58cfd97ce4b0ec9d29dd676f (accessed on 10 May 2018).

Hardy, Jonathan. 2014. *Critical Political Economy of the Media: An Introduction*. New York: Routledge.

Harvey, David. 2005. *A Brief History of Neoliberalism*. New York: Oxford University Press.

Hayes, Dade. 2017. Beauty and the Beast' Producers Build Business on Happy Endings. *Forbes*, March 17. Available online: https://www.forbes.com/sites/dadehayes/2017/03/17/beauty-and-the-beast-producers-build-business-on-happy-endings/#45541fcb24f7 (accessed on 18 October 2018).

Holmes, Andy. 2017. Why Beauty and the Beast Needed to Be Remade, According to the Director. *CinemaBlend*, May 14. Available online: https://www.cinemablend.com/news/1625579/why-beauty-and-the-beast-needed-to-be-remade-according-to-the-director (accessed on 10 May 2018).

Iger, Bob. 2017. Q2 FY17 Earnings Conference Call. [REPORT]. Available online: https://www.thewaltdisneycompany.com/wp-content/uploads/q2_fy17_earnings_transcript.pdf (accessed on 10 May 2019).

Jeffords, Susan. 1995. The Curse of Masculinity: Disney's Beauty and the Beast. In *From Mouse to Mermaid the Politics of Film Gender and Culture*. Edited by Elizabeth Bell, Lynda Haas and Laura Sells. Bloomington: Indiana University Press, pp. 161–72.

Jenkins, Henry. 2006. *The Wow Climax: Tracing the Emotional Impact of Popular Culture*. New York: New York University Press.

Jensen, Jeff. 1999. 'Star Wars' Toys Create a Buying Frenzy. *Entertainment Weekly*, May 6. Available online: https://ew.com/article/1999/05/06/star-wars-toys-create-buying-frenzy/?fbclid=IwAR2V2bPxgZnm1YlcbSBLk8ADLqJ81M6xkrnRaI5eZezsNFh5cvyPJeUhHdQ (accessed on 18 October 2018).

Jess-Cooke, Carolyn. 2009. *Film Sequels: Theory and Practice from Hollywood to Bollywood*. Edinburgh: Edinburgh University Press.

Johnson, Derek. 2014. May the Force be with Katie: Pink media franchising and the postfeminist politics of HerUniverse. *Feminist Media Studies* 14: 895–911. [CrossRef]

Kathleen Kennedy Proposes Industry Commission and 'Zero Tolerance' in Wake of Weinstein Claims. 2017. *Hollywood Reporter*, October 16. Available online: https://www.hollywoodreporter.com/news/kathleen-kennedy-demands-zero-tolerance-policies-wake-weinstein-allegations-1049421 (accessed on 31 May 2018).

Katz, Brandon. 2018. Racism, Misogyny & Death Threats: How Star Wars Fans Turned to the Dark Side. *Observer*, May 16. Available online: http://observer.com/2018/05/star-wars-fandom-toxic-disney-lucasfilm/ (accessed on 31 May 2018).

King, Geoff. 2002. *New Hollywood Cinema: An Introduction*. New York: I.B. Tauris.

La Monica, Paul. 2017. Hasbro has 'Monopoly' with toy fans as Mattel struggles. *CNN Business*, June 22. Available online: https://money.cnn.com/2017/06/22/investing/hasbro-mattel-toys/index.html (accessed on 18 October 2018).

Lang, Brett. 2017. 'Beauty and the Beast': 5 Reasons the Disney Fantasy Scored at the Box Office. *Variety*, March 19. Available online: https://variety.com/2017/film/box-office/beauty-and-the-beast-emma-watson-box-office-1202011723/ (accessed on 18 October 2018).

Larabee, Ann. 2016. Editorial: Star Wars and the girl hero. *The Journal of Popular Culture* 49: 7–9. [CrossRef]

Lieberman, Marcia. 1986. Someday my prince will come. In *Don't bet on the Prince: Contemporary Feminist Fairy Tales in North America*. Edited by Jack Zipes. New York: Methuen.

Lopez, Ricardo. 2017. Women and Non-White Characters Are Speaking More in Recent Star Wars Movies. *Variety*, December 8. Available online: https://variety.com/2017/film/news/star-wars-diversity-dialogue-bechdel-test-rogue-one-1202633473/ (accessed on 18 October 2018).

Lucasfilm President Kathleen Kennedy Says She Doesn't Need to Cater to Male Star Wars Fans. 2016. *Comicbook*, November 29. Available online: https://comicbook.com/starwars/2016/11/29/lucasfilm-president-kathleen-kennedy-says-she-doesnt-need-to-cat/ (accessed on 31 May 2018).

Lupri, Eugen. 1983. The Changing Positions of Women and Men in Comparative Perspective. In *The Changing Position of Women in Family and Society*. Edited by Eugen Lupri. Leiden: Brill.

McCarthy, Christine. 2017. 4th Annual MoffettNathanson Conference [Speech Transcript]. Available online: https://www.thewaltdisneycompany.com/wp-content/uploads/cmm-moffnath-transcript-051717.pdf (accessed on 10 May 2018).

McChesney, Robert. 2008. *Political Economy of Media: Enduring Issues, Emerging Dilemmas*. New York: Monthly Review Press.

Meehan, Eileen. 2002. Gendering the Commodity Audience: Critical Media Research, Feminism, and Political Economy. In *Media and Cultural Studies: Key Works*. Oxford: Blackwell, pp. 311–21.

Meehan, Eileen. 2005. *Why TV Is Not Our Fault: Television Programming, Viewers, and Who Is Really in Control*. Boulder: Rowman and Littlefield Publishers, Inc.

Mendelson, Scott. 2017. Beauty And The Beast' Passes $1 Billion As Disney And Universal Rule The Box Office. *Forbes*, April 13. Available online: https://www.forbes.com/sites/scottmendelson/2017/04/13/beauty-and-the-beast-passes-1-billion-as-disney-and-universal-dominate-top-tier-box-office/#1351344522f4 (accessed on 10 May 2018).

Miller, Toby, Nitin Govil, John McMurria, Richard Maxwell, and Ting Wang. 2005. *Global Hollywood 2*. London: British Film Institute.

Mirrlees, Tanner. 2013. *Global Entertainment Media*. New York: Routledge.

Mirrlees, Tanner. 2014. xXx: Global imperial pop. *American Communication Journal* 16: 29–42.

Moore, James. 2017. Star Wars: The Last Jedi Has Been Killed off by PC Culture. No Really, People Actually Think That. *Independent*, December 21. Available online: http://www.independent.co.uk/voices/star-wars-last-jedi-john-boyega-daisy-ridley-pc-culture-backlash-rotten-tomatoes-a8122146.html (accessed on 7 March 2018).

Mosco, Vincent. 2009. *The Political Economy of Communication*. Thousand Oaks: Sage.

Mulvey, Laura. 1975. Visual pleasure and narrative cinema. *Screen* 16: 6–18. [CrossRef]

Mythic Discovery: Revisiting the Meeting between George Lucas and Joseph Campbell. 2015. *StarWars*, October 22. Available online: https://www.starwars.com/news/mythic-discovery-within-the-inner-reaches-of-outer-space-joseph-campbell-meets-george-lucas-part-i (accessed on 21 April 2018).

Norris, Vincent. 1990. The political economy of communications: An exploration of fundamental concepts. In *Circulation: Working Papers*. State College: School of Communications, Pennsylvania State University.

Palmeri, Chirstopher, and Matthew Townsend. 2017. Beauty and the Beast's Biggest Target? *Nostalgic Millennials. Bloomberg*, March 16. Available online: https://www.bloomberg.com/news/articles/2017-03-16/beauty-and-the-beast-s-biggest-target-nostalgic-millennials (accessed on 10 May 2018).

Pendakur, Manjunath. 1990. *Canadian Dreams and American Control: The Political Economy of the Canadian Film Industry*. Detroit: Wayne State University Press.

Proffitt, Jennifer, Djung Yune Tchoi, and Matthew P. McAllister. 2007. Plugging back into The Matrix: The intertextual flow of corporate media commodities. *Journal of Communication Inquiry* 31: 239–54. [CrossRef]

Rai, Shirin M., and Georgina Waylen. 2013. Feminist Political Economy. In *New Frontiers in Feminist Political Economy*. Edited by Shirin Rai and Georgina Waylen. New York: Routledge, pp. 1–18.

Rainey, James. 2017. Meet the Producers Who Breathed New Life into 'Beauty and the Beast'. *Variety*, March 15. Available online: http://variety.com/2017/film/features/disney-live-action-beauty-and-the-beast-1202007900/ (accessed on 10 May 2018).

Rifkin, Jesse. 2017. A Tale as Old as Time: 'Beauty and the Beast' Producers Todd Lieberman and David Hoberman on Disney's Latest Live-Action Fairy Tale. *BoxOffice Pro*, March 14. Available online: https://pro.boxoffice.com/tale-old-time-beauty-beast-producers-todd-lieberman-david-hoberman-disneys-latest-live-action-fairy-tale/ (accessed on 10 May 2018).

Riordan, Ellen. 2002. Intersections and New Directions: On Feminism and Political Economy. In *Sex and Money: Feminism and Political Economy in the Media*. Edited by Eileen R. Meehan and Ellen Riordan. Minneapolis: University of Minnesota Press, pp. 3–15.

Robb, David. 2016. MPAA: US Film and TV Industry Generates $121 Billion in Wages. *Deadline*, September 2. Available online: http://deadline.com/2016/09/mpaa-u-s-film-tvindustry-generates-121-billion-in-wages-1201812945/ (accessed on 18 October 2018).

Robehmed, Natalie. 2016. Men Have More Lines Than Women In Disney Movies, Rom-Coms And Every Other Genre. *Forbes*, April 8. Available online: https://www.forbes.com/sites/natalierobehmed/2016/04/08/men-have-more-lines-than-women-in-disney-movies-rom-coms-and-every-other-genre/#d7a64a221ee4 (accessed on 18 October 2018).

Roberts, Al. 2017. Is Google's 'Beauty and the Beast' ad the future of paid voice search? *Search Engine Watch*, March 23. Available online: https://searchenginewatch.com/2017/03/23/is-googles-beauty-and-the-beast-ad-the-future-of-paid-voice-search/ (accessed on 21 April 2018).

Robinson, Joanna. 2017. Star Wars: The Last Jedi offers the harsh condemnation of mansplaining we need in 2017. *Vanity Fair*. December 18. Available online: https://www.vanityfair.com/hollywood/2017/12/star-wars-last-jedi-laura-dern-admiral-holdo-listen-to-women (accessed on 7 March 2018).

Ross, Karen, and Byerly Carolyn. 2006. *Women and Media: A Critical Introduction*. Malden: Blackwell.

Rowe, Karen. 1986. Feminism and Fairy Tales. In *Don't Bet on the Prince: Contemporary Feminist Fairy Tales in North America*. Edited by Jack Zipes. New York: Methuen, pp. 209–26.

Rysdall, Kai, and Bridget Bodnar. 2017. 'Frozen' got the new 'Beauty and the Beast' made. *Marketplace*, March 24. Available online: https://www.marketplace.org/2017/03/24/life/what-frozen-had-do-beauty-beast-reboot (accessed on 30 April 2018).

Scott, Suzanne. 2017. #Wheresrey?: Toys, spoilers, and the gender politics of franchise paratexts. *Critical Studies in Media Communication* 34: 138–47.

Sharf, Zack. 2017. The Alt-Right claims credit for 'Star Wars: The Last Jedi' backlash. *IndieWire*. December 21. Available online: http://www.indiewire.com/2017/12/star-wars-last-jedi-backlash-alt-right-female-characters-1201910095/ (accessed on 7 March 2018).

Smith, Anna. 2017. A Force for Good: Why the Last Jedi Is the Most Triumphantly Feminist Star Wars Movie yet. *The Guardian*, December 18. Available online: http://www.theguardian.com/film/2017/dec/18/star-wars-the-last-jedi-women-bechdel-test (accessed on 2 April 2018).

Smythe, Dallas W. 1977. Communications: Blindspot of western Marxism. *Canadian Journal of Political and Social Theory* 1: 1–27.

Star Wars: The Last Jedi. 2017. Rotten Tomatoes. Available online: https://www.rottentomatoes.com/m/star_wars_the_last_jedi/ (accessed on 22 April 2018).

Steeves, Leslie H., and Janet Wasko. 2002. *Sex and Money: Feminism and Political Economy in the Media*. Edited by Eileen R. Meehan and Ellen Riordan. Minneapolis: University of Minnesota Press, pp. 16–29.

Streiff, Madeline, and Lauren Dundes. 2017. Frozen in Time: How Disney Gender-Stereotypes Its Most Powerful Princess. *Social Sciences* 6: 38. [CrossRef]

Thilk, Chris. 2017. Star Wars: The Last Jedi—Marketing Recap. *Cinematic Slant*, December 13. Available online: https://cinematicslant.com/2017/12/13/star-wars-the-last-jedi-marketing-recap/ (accessed on 31 May 2018).

Thomas, Ben-Beaunmont, and Phil Hoad. 2017. How We Made Beauty and the Beast. *The Guardian*, March 13. Available online: https://www.theguardian.com/culture/2017/mar/13/how-we-made-beauty-and-the-beast (accessed on 18 October 2018).

Townsend, Matthew. 2018. Hasbro CEO Admits Making Mistake with 'Last Jedi' Toys. *Bloomberg*, March 29. Available online: https://www.bloomberg.com/news/articles/2018-03-28/hasbro-ceo-admits-making-strategic-mistake-with-last-jedi-toys?fbclid=IwAR2FiHH14f_FD9aaQm6waOrKhBUU8yYTp60kHw4bCifqLZlqUDxu0QfZ4SQ (accessed on 18 October 2018).

Traube, Elizabeth G. 1992. *Dreaming Identities: Class, Gender, and Generation in 1980s Hollywood Movies*. Boulder: Westview Press.

Trujillo, Nick. 1991. Hegemonic masculinity on the mound: Media representations of Nolan Ryan and American sports culture. *Critical Studies in Mass Communication* 8: 290–308. [CrossRef]

Walt Disney Company. 2017. Available online: https://www.thewaltdisneycompany.com/walt-disney-company-acquire-twenty-first-century-fox-inc-spinoff-certain-businesses-52-4-billion-stock-2/ (accessed on 5 May 2018).

Wasko, Janet. 2003. The Political Economy of Film. In *A Companion to Film Theory*. Edited by Toby Miller. Oxford: Blackwell Publishing, pp. 221–33.

Wasko, Janet, Eileen Meehan, and Mark Phillips. 2006. *Dazzled by Disney? The Global Disney Audiences Project*. New York: Bloomsbury.

Weekes, Princess. 2017. Treatment of POC & women in Star Wars: The Last Jedi. *The Mary Sue*, December 22. Available online: https://www.themarysue.com/poc-women-in-the-last-jedi/ (accessed on 2 April 2018).

Whitley, Jared. 2018. SJW Politics Have Handed Star Wars Its First Bomb in Solo. *Daily Caller*, May 29. Available online: http://dailycaller.com/2018/05/29/sjw-politics-solo-star-wars/ (accessed on 30 May 2018).

Why the Last Jedi Isn't just Bad: It's Toxic. 2017. *Scavenger's Holocron*, December 22. Available online: http://scavengersholocron.com/category/home/why-the-last-jedi-isnt-just-bad-its-toxic/ (accessed on 2 April 2018).

Williams, Linda. 1984. When the woman looks. In *Re-Vision: Essays in Feminist Film Criticism*. Edited by Mary Ann Doane, Patricia Mellencamp and Linda Williams. Los Angeles: University Publications of America, pp. 83–99.

Wosk, Julie. 2001. *Women and the Machine: Representations from the Spinning Wheel to the Electronic Age*. London: John Hopkins University Press.

social sciences

MDPI

Article

Balancing Gender and Power: How Disney's Hercules Fails to Go the Distance

Cassandra Primo

Departments of Business and Sociology, McDaniel College, Westminster, MD 21157, USA; crp002@mcdaniel.edu

Received: 26 September 2018; Accepted: 14 November 2018; Published: 16 November 2018

Abstract: Disney's *Hercules* (1997) includes multiple examples of gender tropes throughout the film that provide a hodgepodge of portrayals of traditional conceptions of masculinity and femininity. Hercules' phenomenal strength and idealized masculine body, coupled with his decision to relinquish power at the end of the film, may have resulted in a character lacking resonance because of a hybridization of stereotypically male and female traits. The film pivots from hypermasculinity to a noncohesive male identity that valorizes the traditionally-feminine trait of selflessness. This incongruous mixture of traits that comprise masculinity and femininity conflicts with stereotypical gender traits that characterize most Disney princes and princesses. As a result of the mixed messages pertaining to gender, *Hercules* does not appear to have spurred more progressive portrayals of masculinity in subsequent Disney movies, showing the complexity underlying gender stereotypes.

Keywords: gender stereotypes; sexuality; heroism; hypermasculinity; selflessness; Hercules; Zeus; Megara

1. Introduction

Disney's influence in children's entertainment has resulted in the scrutiny of gender stereotypes in its films (Do Rozario 2004; Dundes et al. 2018; England et al. 2011; Giroux and Pollock 2010). Disney's *Hercules* (1997), however, has been largely overlooked in academic literature exploring the evolution of gender portrayals by the media giant. The animated film is a modernization of the classic myth in which the eponymous hero is a physically intimidating protagonist that epitomizes manhood. Yet Disney's updated mythical hero had only moderate success at the box office. To date, *Hercules* has had a lifetime domestic gross total of just under $100 million—only slightly exceeding its budget of $85 million. While *Hercules* is comparable to *Tarzan* (1999)—another non-princess film released in a similar time period—*Tarzan's* gross proceeds have topped $170 million. Both of these films, however, pale in comparison to the monetary success of the most recent Disney princess movie, *Moana*, with a lifetime gross of almost $250 million after just two years (Box Office Mojo 2018a, 2018b, 2018c), one barometer of the films' success.

The fact that *Hercules* was "clearly a disappointment for Disney, whose aggressive marketing of the film included a traffic-choking Saturday night parade through Manhattan" (Fabrikant 1997, para 6) raises unanswered questions about the causes of its lackluster appeal, at least in comparative terms. Part of the answer to this question may relate to Disney's portrayal of a variety of gender tropes. In the reimagined age-old mythical character, Hercules, stereotypes were paired with an anomalous twist on conventional masculinity that may have been too avant-garde at the time of the film's release in 1997—and perhaps too progressive even more than 20 years later in 2018, judging from the subsequent and recent portrayals of Disney's male heroes.

In this analysis of *Hercules*, the title superhero exemplifies what seems to be a relatively early attempt by Disney to reconceive masculinity. However, coupled with manifold examples of gender stereotypes that pervade the film, the result is a hodgepodge of gender portrayals in which Disney fails to construct an appealing version of masculinity. As a result of these flaws, Disney neither challenges gender tropes nor presents a revised version of masculinity (see Macaluso 2018) that is likely to resonate with viewers, who must transcend a surfeit of cultural cues that valorize unambiguous hypermasculinity, such as the type embodied by Maui in *Moana* (2016).

1.1. Plot Summary

Baby Hercules is taken from Mount Olympus by Hades. As a result, he ends up living his life on Earth as a half-mortal until his teenage years. As he comes of age, Hercules begins to realize he is different and embarks on a journey of self-discovery to the Temple of Zeus. In the song "Go the Distance," Hercules avows his determination to overcome his insecurities and find his place, as well as a sense of belonging. Zeus reveals that he is Hercules' father and directs him to the satyr Philoctetes (Phil) to learn to become a "true hero" and return home.

On his mission to become a "true hero," Hercules travels to Thebes. On the way, Hercules meets Megara, a slave of Hades, with whom he falls in love. No matter how many monsters Hercules defeats, no act of strength and valor is enough to get him home to Mount Olympus. It is not until Hercules is willing to sacrifice his own life to save Megara that he is deemed a true hero, although he declines the power and position associated with such an honor, choosing instead the love of a woman, Megara.

1.2. How Disney Modified the Original Story

Disney's version strays significantly from the original myth, appropriating and altering major characters, such as Hera and Zeus, as well as Hercules. In the original myth, Hercules was born of adulterous relations between Zeus and Alcmene: a god and a mortal. Hercules was thus a living representation of betrayal that consumed Hera (the wife of Zeus), causing him to become the subject of her wrath; Hera attempted to kill him as a baby, but was unsuccessful. She brooded about this slight until she saw another opportunity to ruin Hercules. When he marries Megara, Hera compels Hercules into a temporary insanity, causing him to murder his wife, his own children, and several nephews.

Hercules also was scrubbed of violent traits in the Disney version, including the omission of killing his music teacher (Linus) and taking women at will. There is near erasure of these barbarous attributes in the Disney rendition, as the animated version built on a *tabula rasa* of sorts to create a portrayal designed to resonate with contemporary audiences in order to translate into marketable merchandise to build the Disney franchise.

Hera is also reconfigured from stepmother to mother of Hercules, and from frightening to gentle. Zeus is no longer a lustful adulterer, but instead is jocular and loyal to his wife (Burchfield 2013). In ancient myths, Hercules kills everyone he loves and falls into a suicidal depression, but in the Disney version, he is the champion of the tale, portrayed as a true hero that saves the girl (Burchfield 2013), diverging from the tragic ending that must be avoided in marketable Disney animated films (Pomeroy 2017).

1.3. The Range of Gender Stereotypical Behavior Examined

This paper suggests the film's weaknesses stem not only from its portrayal of Hercules, but also other depictions of gendered behavior. The film includes the representation of traditional femininity in Hera along with the Fates that are antithetical to idealized femininity, tropes that are common in Disney films (England et al. 2011). Phil and Pegasus reinforce gendered norms and further promote masculine superiority in their speech and actions. The tendency to emasculate male villains (Putnam 2013) is seen in Hades and his henchmen, Pain and Panic, which further encourages traditional masculinity, as well as hyper-heterosexuality.

This analysis explores how these characters overarchingly create mixed messages concerning the role of men and women in society. This paper relies on content analysis of the film, and findings from existing literature, both that includes coverage of *Hercules* and studies of gender in Disney films.

In the realm of female gender norms, Disney has become less rigid; in *Moana* (2016), there is evidence that a more androgynous portrayal of the title character is apparent to child viewers who do not, however, generally consider Moana to be a princess (Hine et al. 2018). Because of the $3 billion in retail sales in 2011 of the Disney Princess brand (Goudreau 2012), there are clearly financial obstacles to more progressive gender roles that deviate from stereotypical princess traits. While *Hercules* is not considered a Disney princess film due to the characterization and implications of the would-be prince and princess, the reasons for the film's exclusion from this category illustrate how certain gender norms are deeply entrenched and are only recently starting to depart from longstanding tropes, at least in the case of princesses (Hine et al. 2018), that arguably have more latitude in terms of acceptable behavior that is gendered (Coyle et al. 2016).

2. Zeus and Hera

2.1. Display of Traditional Gender Roles

Gender stereotypes manifest from the beginning of the film, with a scene that depicts a baby Hercules with his doting parents, Zeus and Hera. Hera's portrayal in the film does not go beyond this limited maternal role. In the 21st century, women are no longer expected to solely act as their child's caretaker during the child's formative years (Henderson et al. 2016). Yet in the 1980s and into the 1990s, mothers experienced social pressure to stay at home and, when possible, to avoid or minimize daycare or preschool programs, ostensibly for children's safety and well-being (Walker 2010). Disney's modernization of the story reflects this zeitgeist, changing Hera from a terrifying adversary to a completely docile character who is an appendage of Zeus and whose only purpose is to serve as Hercules' mother. Her role is reinforced in the mere nine lines she speaks, all of which relate to her maternity, with the outlier being a comment on the loveliness of flowers.

Hera is seen in only three scenes throughout the film; she serves her one-dimensional, stereotypical function as a mother during the celebration of Hercules' birth, again when he is kidnapped, and last when Hercules is being welcomed home (Zipes 1999). When Hera and Zeus discover that Hercules has disappeared, she can be seen hiding behind Zeus before dramatically falling to the ground and breaking down in tears. In direct contrast to what can be labeled as Hera's "womanly reaction" (Sharrock 2011), Zeus becomes exceedingly angry. The sky mirrors his rage, manifested in flashes of lightning and roars of thunder–storm power that is typically the domain of men (Dundes et al. 2018) and reflected in the thunderbolt gold medallion Hercules wears even as a baby. Thus, Hera is portrayed as helpless and as nothing more than a grieving mother, whereas Zeus can be seen demanding and instigating action in response to crises. These characters in Disney's version of *Hercules* exemplify both classic stereotypes and modern constructs of men and women: physical versus emotional, strong versus incapable, and tough versus beautiful (Smelik 2015). The implications of the portrayals of Zeus and Hera include those traditionally embedded in Disney films (Towbin et al. 2004); Zeus encourages physical response to emotion, strength, and heroism, while Hera personifies the anachronistic idealized woman: beautiful, domesticated, and helpless.

2.2. Supplanting Hera

The very first setting of the movie is Mount Olympus in the midst of a celebration of the birth of Hercules, where Hera can be seen cradling her baby and showing stereotypical motherly affections: cooing, kissing, adoring, and protective actions. When Hera asks Zeus what gift to bestow on Hercules, in keeping with a baby shower (Afflerback et al. 2014), Zeus ponders the question and then, without consulting his wife, uses his power to create and give life to Pegasus, who emerges from his hand, an example of male parthenogenesis in which procreativity is achieved manually (Dundes et al. 2018). Thus, Zeus effectively usurps even the biological female ability to give birth—further promoting his superiority. This paints Hera in a powerless light, where she is not only incapable, but also essentially superfluous in providing for Hercules.

3. The Fates

3.1. Women in Power

In *Hercules*, a trio of cadaverous and ghoulish crones, the Fates, are purportedly omniscient, eternal beings, who relish having the life of every single mortal at their mercy. Their severe physical deformities coexist with their power over life and death, suggesting that powerful women pay a price for their dominance over mortal men. The Fates are also blind, gaining sight through a singular eye that they pass around to see the present unfold, a handicap limiting their power. Beyond this unbecoming disfigurement, the Fates are not depicted as neutral beings, but in fact serve Hades in his attempt to overthrow Zeus. As a result, they arguably are subordinate to the primary power dynamic, which is male against male. Furthermore, these powerful, immortal beings are adversarial to the hero's quest, essentially making them villains (Coville 2010).

It is no mistake that Hera, the maternal figure in the film, embodies the definition of beautiful, while the Fates have an unmatched level of power, but are physically repulsive. They echo the modern trend in which women who choose a demanding career in which they struggle to accommodate a husband and co-parenting risk accusations of selfishness and thoughtlessness (Griffin et al. 2017).

3.2. Other Powerful Disney Women

Powerful women in animated Disney movies are typically portrayed by evil, old, disfigured, or altogether villainous characters (Coville 2010), e.g., Ursula in *The Little Mermaid*, the queen in *Snow White*, the stepmother in *Cinderella*, Maleficent in *Sleeping Beauty*, or Te Kā as the lava monster in *Moana* (Streiff and Dundes 2017a). While Elsa in *Frozen* is an exception as a conventionally attractive character, her power (that she struggles to control when beset by emotion) seems to preclude male romantic interest (Streiff and Dundes 2017b). These powerful Disney women are often juxtaposed against purity and attractiveness, and their own morality and appearance distinctly oppose the ultra-feminine title princess. This pattern—in accordance with the Fates and in contradistinction to Hera—suggest a reality where women cannot have it all; they are either beautiful and powerless or powerful and ugly.

4. Phil and Pegasus

4.1. Comments on Female Intelligence

Phil (Hercules' personal trainer and coach) implies an association between femininity and incompetence when he attempts to promote his own masculine abilities by derogating women with his quip, "Who do you think taught Jason to sail? Cleopatra?" [26:12–21]. The subtext of this statement is that Cleopatra, with her legendary beauty, did not also have nautical skills, which presumably would have humiliated Jason (leader of the Argonauts). This statement is encompassed by Phil's boasts of his superior abilities in training infamous male heroes; the only mention of a woman is a disparaging comment projecting the impossibility of female excellence in a profession traditionally portrayed as contingent on male determination.

4.2. Feminization of Pegasus

There are also gender implications in the ostensibly comedic feminization of Pegasus. In one instance, when Zeus says that Pegasus has "the brain of a bird," [22:23–26] Hercules' equine companion transforms dramatically from the strong, "magnificent horse" Zeus describes just seconds before. Similarly, after Hercules completes his training, one of his first aspirations is to go "rescue some damsels" [31:21–23]. In this scene, Pegasus attempts to resemble a damsel, which changes his physical appearance and mannerisms. In both of these instances, there is some incorporation of the following: Pegasus' eyelashes extend, his wings and feathers appear flashier and more bouffant, and he adopts a stance or struts in poses associated with feminine beauty ideals (Baker-Sperry and Grauerholz 2003). These scenes portray male feminization as comedic (Patterson and Spencer 2017) and support the implications of Phil's commentary. The personification of a "bird brain" with female sensibility and the belief that women need rescue from a valorous, male hero are both overarching themes concerning women in Disney films (Towbin et al. 2004). Both Phil and Pegasus insinuate that women do not have and cannot match the intelligence of their male counterparts, which arguably indoctrinates children to assume female inferiority.

5. Pain, Panic, and Hades

5.1. Male Dominance and Sexuality

To compensate for his feminine actions, Pegasus affirms his masculinity at the end, when one of Hades' henchmen, Pain, says to Pegasus: "My intentions were pure! I really was attracted to you" and is then pummeled by Pegasus. Pain's avowal of attraction to Pegasus refers to when he and Panic transform themselves into a highly sexualized and feminine horse that causes Pegasus to extend his tongue, as if panting in lust [1:05:50–1:06:10]. The mare has a heart on its back flank in a position similar to the so-called "tramp-stamp" (found on the small of a woman's back), which is seen as indicating openness to sexual relations (Leader 2016). Having assumed the form of a seductive female horse, the pair lead Pegasus to a candlelit room with a bed and proceed to discard the previously worn lace saddle (presumably pseudo lingerie). Soon after, they unwittingly reveal their actual identity. Pegasus then beats them in an attempt to reassert his masculinity after inadvertently showing sexual interest in characters who displayed transgendered qualities, a pattern previously noted (see Putnam 2013). This homophobic act of Pegasus clobbering Pain arguably serves to bolster Pegasus' masculinity at the expense of Pain (whose sexuality is unclear) [1:17:56–1:18:01]. Pegasus' distress caused by his accidental attraction to men makes him like a female—the ones who are supposed to be attracted to males. This is insulting because in being feminized, the implication is that he loses status, a problem exacerbated by the stigma associated with gay males.

Pain's sexuality is suggested during his character's introduction, when he is sexually impaled twice when tumbling down stairs [7:04–17]. The first instance is of Pain landing on a three-pronged decoration. The second occurs at the end of the tumble, where Panic's phallic head-forks penetrate Pain long enough for them to be seen by Hades in a vulnerable, homoerotic state. Shortly thereafter, Pain and Panic grovel before Hades in an unequivocally humiliating manner; this repentance alongside the transformation of both men into worms (a term of contempt) could evince that deviation from heterosexual norms, and thus traditional maleness, is undesirable and necessitates forgiveness or even remediation.

5.2. The Association of Male Villainy with Queerness

Characterized as Hades' henchmen, Pain and Panic are designed to be unattractive, detestable creatures who relish the opportunity to harm and deceive. This is evident first when the pair smiles over baby Hercules during their attempt to murder him, and again when they fail, but decide to delude Hades. Pain and Panic embrace these classically villainous traits, and evoke an association between evil and the deviation from masculinity and heterosexuality (Patterson and Spencer 2017; Putnam 2013).

Hades also conveys uncertain sexuality, especially in comparison to his adversary, Zeus. In the original myth, Hades ruled the underworld alongside his queen, Phosphorene. In the Disney revival, though, Zeus retains his queen, while Hades rules the underworld alone. This lack of a partner—and no apparent interest in females—coupled with a head that is literally "flaming," could connote that a "flaming gay male" (which Hades personifies) is most challenging to heteronormativity (Clarkson 2008). In fact, effeminate Disney villains are a consistent pattern (Towbin et al. 2004; Patterson and Spencer 2017; Putnam 2013).

The absolute villainization of Hades is historically incorrect per mythology, which raises the question of why he was characterized this way in the Disney film. Ancient adversaries, such as

Zeus and Hades, classified each other as rivals, not as demonic and inhuman (Burchfield 2013); yet Hades is depicted as just that: a hellish ghoul with razor sharp teeth and unsightly stature—very different from his classic normative appearance. This illustration arguably works to further mark his subordination to his hypermasculine, hyper-heterosexual brother, Zeus, who dominates Hades in every battle. The comedic vilification of Hades reflects a societal marginalization of the "flaming gay man" and invites audiences to laugh at the character. Pain and Panic's fear of Hades may also mirror debate among gay males about how to reconcile the "heteronormative sex and gender regime" with gay identity (Clarkson 2008, p. 379).

Despite a successfully cultivated connection to the gay community (Griffin 2000), Disney continues to demonize characters who are overtly queer. Pain and Panic impersonate a highly sexualized female to achieve their goal of distracting Pegasus, supporting the claim that male villains are often subjected to feminization to prove their inferiority to the hypermasculine hero (Li-Vollmer and LaPointe 2003). Their actions also argue that female usefulness comes from their power of seduction, which is further perpetuated by Hades via his interactions with Megara.

6. Megara

6.1. Oversexualization

Megara, a princess character from mythology (the daughter of King Creon of Thebes), exemplifies gender stereotypes by the emphasis on her looks and sexuality. Megara is Hades' slave because she sold her soul to him, and as such, Hades expects her to help to win his war using the sway of her hips; within the context of the film, Megara chose to "sell herself", and it is worth noting that this is played out in terms of her sexuality. Primarily, Hades identifies her as having "the right curves" to throw at Hercules and wants her to bring him down by "handling him as a man." When Meg finally complies, won over by Hades' promises of freedom, the portrayal of Meg with Hercules depicts her speaking in a sultry voice while seductively cavorting and touching Hercules provocatively [56:40–58:58] (Rabison 2016). As a *femme fatale*, blatantly exploiting her sexuality, her actions are patently treacherous, designed to invite contempt (Valenti 2009). Not only is she reduced to what society views as a disgraceful woman, she is also unsuccessful in her ploy, as Hercules is revealed to be a superior, respectful man, turning down her repeated sexual advances.

Her role as a seductress is further established by Hades through his use of derogatory "pet" names that show dominance (rather than sexual interest). Notably, after declaring she will no longer honor his demands, she is physically bound and held hostage to ensure Hercules' compliance. After the execution of the final step in Hades' plan, despite Megara's disobedience, Hades refers to her as "sugar, sweetheart, babe," terms of endearment that in this context reinforce both Megara's subservient role and her sexuality.

6.2. Megara and the Muses

Megara's role as a *femme fatale* is made more prominent by her lead singing role in "I Won't Say I'm In Love," with the Muses as accompanists. In this song, the baring of her inner struggles not only signals her importance to the plot, but also makes use of songs as a tool to enhance audience connection with the characters (McGill 2018). By exposing the audience to Megara's emotional turmoil when she develops feelings for someone she is also betraying (Hercules), the song reinvents her character and promotes a powerful connection between her and the audience (a phenomenon explored by McGill (2018)). The song solidifies Megara's tribulations as a woman in love—facilitating the audience's ability to feel a rapport with her as they recognize the complications surrounding love and see the centrality of sex and love in Megara's life.

In this musical scene, the Muses fulfill a prominent supporting role, not only musically, but also as characters who encourage Megara to let herself fall in love with Hercules. However, these Black women who belt out gospel music only serve a subsidiary role as sexualized women who voice appreciation for Hercules' manly attributes; as women of color, they are not taken seriously as romantic prospects for Hercules, a facet of the film that has been condemned (see Foote 2010). Instead, they serve as the chorus, both in the plot and musically, working to promote Megara's—but not their own—interests. This portrayal reinforces long-term patterns of women of color in helping roles (Dundes and Streiff 2016; Gregory 2010), part of a matrix of oppression that demands not just improvement, but wholesale redress (Harris 2018).

What explains Megara's melodramatic mood when singing about her repressed affection for Hercules? She believes him to be entirely unlike her last love, who betrayed her, and she even openly admits that she thinks Hercules is perfect. So why does she fight falling in love with this ideal man? Megara's seductive prowess is as a tool to seduce Hercules and satisfy the man who supervises the use of her sexual allure (Hades), and thus she feels emotionally constrained (in line with common perceptions of expectations for paid sex workers). Megara is perfectly aware of her position and the impracticality of falling for a man she has been assigned to seduce. She refers to love as "rotten judgment" and urges herself to "get a grip" over her emotions during the song. The Muses, however, as a useful instrument for Megara, propel her towards an epiphany: She realizes she does indeed love Hercules. Ultimately, this scene enhances her complexity as she grapples with her deceit, which is now a form of betrayal.

6.3. Selflessness

Megara not only acts in the role of deceitful seductress, but also embodies stereotypically female characteristics, such as sacrifice, selflessness, affection, and nurturing (England et al. 2011). When offered her freedom in return for information on how to defeat Hercules, Megara decides she would rather remain a slave than be responsible for the downfall of someone she loves. She later demonstrates the same kind of altruistic sacrifice when she pushes Hercules out of the way of a falling pillar, ultimately ending up underneath the structure herself—an intentionally lethal move. Megara performs this act without glorification; despite inconsistencies with traditional Disney princesses, that is, Megara's typology as "street-wise" paired with "sexual confidence" (see Davis 2006, p. 210), she nevertheless demonstrates that selflessness for women is expected, not extraordinary.

6.4. Not A Disney Princess

Megara is perhaps the most complex female protagonist Disney had designed to date at the release of *Hercules*. She is not inherently pure like the classic princesses—e.g., Snow White, Aurora, Cinderella—as she is the first to express being in a relationship prior to meeting her "prince." For this previous partner, she was willing to give her freedom for his life, yet he ran off with another woman in the end. This theme deviates from the stories of prior princesses and has yet to be explored again within the princess franchise. Her sexual innocence is lost due to this history with another man, and her character is then further compromised through extensive sexualization by Hades.

Megara, however, is also not a traditional Disney villainess, as she is attractive, young, and ultimately desired by the title hero. She works for the main villain, but against her will as a "slave." Unlike the Fates, who are also associated with Hades, Megara does not derive pleasure from the downfall of Hercules, but rather is seen encouraging his success throughout the film. Furthermore, her climax comes in the moment she is willing to sacrifice everything for the one she loves, which aligns with the classic princess theme of female sacrifice.

Nevertheless, the complexity of Megara's role as a beautiful villain that ultimately ends up with the hero sharply contradicts what children are socialized to believe about how princess characters behave. Thus, while Megara is a character representative of a woman in the real world, she is not an idealized princess, nor the epitome of evil. She performs both insidious and altruistic acts, but arguably all in the name of love. This behavior upends the usual gender norms portrayed in a Disney fairy tale story and is perhaps responsible for keeping her from joining the esteemed ranks of a Disney princess.

7. Hercules

7.1. As a Traditional Male Hero

Like Megara, Hercules models traits that defy gender norms associated with male heroes: intimidating physical dominance and strength, courage and bravery, a journey of growth, lack of sexual inhibition, and emotional apathy (Campbell 1949; England et al. 2011; Davis 2013; Gillam and Wooden 2008; Matyas 2010; Towbin et al. 2004). Hercules clearly has uncommon brawn, proven by his ability to slay monsters and titans in Thebes and Mount Olympus. Prior to his journey of growth (in which he discovers his purpose, endures trials in Thebes, and refuses to return to Mt. Olympus (Campbell 1949)), Hercules appears physically inferior, judging from his musculature; however, his strength is unmatched by any mortal man. After training with Phil, Hercules' developed muscles and toned figure align with his physical ability. The Muses in *Hercules* even emphasize his hypermasculine physique in their song "Zero to Hero," in which Hercules is described as a "hunk" and a "gladiator." For example, the Muses sing, "Folks lined up; Just to watch him flex; And his perfect package; In a pair of pretty pecs."

Hercules also executes grand displays of courage and bravery as he engages and slays each one of Hades' monsters. He performs so well against and without fear of these adversaries that the city of Thebes immortalizes him in statues, art, and everyday items (cups, toys, etc.). Hercules displays ample confidence in this regard, actively acknowledging his status and accomplishments. The Muses reinforce this behavior in the same way they rank his physical traits, singing, "Sweet and undefeated; And an awesome 10 for 10."

On his journey of growth, Hercules meets Megara, and falls for her based solely on her physical beauty. Both his first and second trials as a hero revolve around his newfound love interest—the first is an attempt to save her from Nessus (the river guardian) and the second trial is at her behest (to save Pain and Panic, disguised as children). Despite falling in love with her, however, Hercules does not succumb to sexual temptation. Instead he encourages decency and abstinence: He replaces her dress strap after it falls from her shoulder and discourages her advances by his refusals to take advantage of her sexual availability [57:43–58:58]. This reveals how Hercules differs from the traditional male hero, specifically his sexual restraint that is driven by either fear from inexperience or perhaps an emotional connection that replaces apathy, cited as a conventionally heroic trait (above).

7.2. As a Novel Male Hero

Hercules' juxtaposition against Zeus throughout the film includes a culminating scene in which Hercules prefers sacrificing his strength and glory for love, eschewing the traditional masculinity exuded by his father. The underlying plot of the film revolves around the power struggle between Zeus and Hades, neither of whom are particularly relatable to viewers. Thus, the climatic heroic act is the saving of Megara from the underworld. In this instance, Hercules faces with determination the ultimate challenge of his ability for the sake of one life, and he is victorious (as Zeus deems this act to be of true heroism, elevating him from demigod to god in power). What makes Hercules different from male protagonists, such as Eric of *The Little Mermaid*, or Prince Phillip of *Sleeping Beauty*, is that the heroic act of saving the woman results in the revocation of the hero's status, authority, and power.

These major sacrifices support conflicting implications of what determines a male hero. Hercules' journey of growth includes the development of physical brawn, which bolsters his strength and overall power—supporting the general theme that masculine heroes should strive to be physically strong. When granted the ultimate strength of a god, though (literally shown theatrically through the glowing of his skin), Hercules willingly sacrifices his newfound power (and therefore his glow) to stay with Megara, potentially suggestive of the male preoccupation about shininess that is associated with sexual readiness (see Dundes et al. 2018). Thus, Hercules' climatic act of heroism involves his sacrifice of the masculine reward of power in lieu of love.

In this way, the ending of *Hercules* differs from other Disney films. In *Pocahontas* (1995), it is the title character who gives up adventure and love for duty and to meet the needs of others (Dundes 2001). In *The Little Mermaid* (1989), it is Ariel who gives up family and community and even her own voice for a time, for love (Hynes 2010). In *Hercules*, though, the male hero gives up greatness in a way that upstages the female protagonist and her willingness to sacrifice.

7.3. Not a Disney Prince

In his choice to remain with Megara, Hercules forgoes his long-sought, rightful place at Zeus' right hand and the accompanying power of the position. This is arguably the most pertinent point, suggesting Hercules is not a Disney prince. No prince prior was required to sacrifice their position to be with the princess (and Aladdin is even elevated in status and authority through his union with Jasmine (*Aladdin*, 1992)). Because it is impossible for Megara to become his princess should he choose to remain with his royal parents, he surrenders his princely title to stay with the woman of choice.

This is a novel dynamic in a Disney film for its time: A man engages in a sort of selflessness that creates a happier outcome for both himself and the woman he loves. Hercules does not want to be superior in status to Meg, but rather merely wishes to be an equal. This is radical compared to male characters in the Disney animated films prior to *Hercules*, as male protagonists have tended to be the heroic love interest, exuding masculinity, rather than characters that engage in self-sacrifice (England et al. 2011). The ending of *Hercules* arguably promotes gender equality in that a male was willing to sacrifice stature for the sake of woman, in fact, for a woman without power or position.

The implication of Hercules' decision is that love is more important than any power or authority, which is typically a sentiment reserved for the female protagonist in Disney films (Towbin et al. 2004). His selflessness occurs in the absence of compensatory acts that support traditional masculinity and contrast with his phallic thunderbolt-wielding father Zeus, whose power far exceeds that of Hercules. In theater, the hero is ultimately supposed to save the day, win the love of a woman, and retain their power and status; however, Hercules departs from the traditional male gender role in that he not only prioritizes love, but finds happiness in giving up power. This raises the question of whether Hercules may fail to resonate with viewers socialized to embrace characters that exemplify traditional masculinity.

In addition to the more blatant departure from gender norms, Hercules also agonizes about "Going the Distance" (in his only song that presents his plight to viewers), with lyrics that show his anxieties as he is coming of age. The song could be obliquely referencing sexual anxiety (given the argot about "going all the way"). He does not embrace his physical power, which makes him different, but is more concerned about how his superhuman strength means that he does not fit in. In contrast, Elsa (in *Frozen*, 2016), who like Hercules is powerful and does not fit in, nevertheless embraces this difference, making her a compelling and popular character. In lowering his status to become a mere mortal at the end, Disney has inadvertently feminized him, making him less appealing to viewers who expect to see males who aspire to gain stature at the same time as they pursue a worthy romance. While such a portrayal may be more in line with erasing gender roles, Hercules still possesses other elements of hypermasculinity—and ultimately has limited ability to serve as a role model if he is not relatable.

8. Impact on Subsequent Films

8.1. Movement Away from Princes and Princesses

Less than a year after the release of *Hercules*, *Mulan* premiered in theaters, and this debut was followed a year later by *Tarzan*; both films were likely already in production and were not influenced by the success or failure of *Hercules*. At the turn of the 21st century, however, there is a distinct shift in the content of Disney films—there is no princess/prince dynamic again until 2009 with *Princess and the Frog*. Disney/Pixar largely focused on stories of parental and platonic love, altering their focus from male/female love stories ending in matrimony; *Monsters Inc.*, *Finding Nemo*, and *The Incredibles* are some of the greatest successes of this decade. The larger point is the noticeable absence of a Disney princess title film. Even the live-action remake films did not begin producing princess renditions until 2014 with *Maleficent*. *Hercules* may have had an impact on this decision since the success Disney experiences as a company is based both on blockbuster films and their merchandise (Tracy 1999). Prior to the release of *Hercules*, the most lucrative Disney franchise was that of the Disney princess, and it continues to be most popular among young girls (Coyne et al. 2016). Hercules is perhaps too great a departure from the gender patterns of the princess genre.

8.2. *Tangled* (2010)

The resurgence of princess movies arguably began with *Tangled* (2010), which achieved greater success than *Princess and the Frog* (2009). Reactions to the lack of conformity to gender stereotypes in *Hercules* were possibly considered in the characterization of the protagonists, Rapunzel and Eugene, in *Tangled*. Rapunzel is absolute in her purity, naivety, and beauty. Her purity is due to a total lack of romantic experience, unlike Megara who engaged in a romantic entanglement prior to Hercules. Rapunzel is also impossibly naïve, having no concept of the "outside world" or the reality of the world she lives in (a theme recapitulated in princess Anna of *Frozen*); this is distinctly opposite of Megara, who arguably has too much knowledge of the world. Perhaps most obvious, though, are Rapunzel's looks, specifically her eyes, which have returned to that of the classic princess. In complete contradistinction to Megara, Rapunzel's eyes are wide with awe and wonder, not narrow in suspicion and deceit. The frying-pan-wielding princess may seem strong and independent, but just like Ariel, her adventurous soul is overcome by love and it is her prince that climatically saves the day with a heroic deed (Elnahla 2015).

Eugene, however, is not a prince in the same way Megara is not a princess. His self-interested thieving makes him a borderline villain at the start of the film. Regarding male gender roles, however, and in comparison to Hercules, Eugene's character has qualities of the traditional male hero: strength, courage, a journey of growth, and physical masculinity (Campbell 1949; Davis 2013; England et al. 2011; Gillam and Wooden 2008; Towbin et al. 2004). In the "Snuggly Duckling" pub scene, Eugene's hypermasculinity is emphasized through the foil of the physically intimidating 'thugs' who all aspire to do domestic work (like bake cupcakes and knit) versus Eugene's proclamation that he does not share their tendencies toward the so-called "touchy-feely."

Eugene's character is even taken a step further than prior Disney princes, designed with facial hair to bolster his masculinity. Perhaps most importantly though, Eugene never has to sacrifice power, authority, or status, differentiating him from Hercules. In fact, through his heroic deeds, he gains these things in his relationship with Rapunzel. The greatest sacrifice Eugene makes is that of his life for Rapunzel's—which has been deemed the act of a true hero when performed by men, and therefore only again serves to fortify Eugene's masculinity and his ability to win the heart of the virginal Rapunzel. The extent to which Rapunzel and Eugene reflect traditional gender roles is arguably partially a result of the failings of *Hercules* in navigating appealing gender roles.

8.3. *Moana* (2016)

While recent research (Hine et al. 2018) shows Disney moving towards androgenic portrayals of female leads in films like *Moana*, there has yet to be such latitude permitted to male heroes. Disney's character Maui, for example, in *Moana* (2016), who like Hercules is a demigod, gains status through hypermasculinity, which is exaggerated to the point of his violating the goddess Te Fiti with his beloved phallic fishhook (Streiff and Dundes 2017a). The presumed likeability of Maui's character further illustrates that audiences may be more likely to embrace traditional male heroes. While Herculean is an adjective denoting strength, Hercules' willingness to sacrifice power for love of a woman could be seen as too empowering for women and thus too threatening to male hegemony—and the failure of his character to resonate with viewers arguably influenced the hypermasculinity of the subsequent demigod Maui.

9. Conclusions

Disney is historically one of the most prominent creators of animated children's movies and has achieved an almost unmatched level of influence via expansive media coverage of its productions (Giroux and Pollock 2011). However, its films generally reflect, but do not necessarily change societal values of an era—leading to the socialization of children to imitate the gender-specific roles performed by their favorite princes and princesses (Garabedian 2014). In *Hercules*, these roles are confusing and do not align with prior learned behaviors. Lackluster engagement with the film, both while in theaters and with post-release merchandise, may therefore have slowed Disney's promotion of a new prince and princess paradigm.

Disney has the power to help teach young boys and girls to both respect themselves and others as they are. It has the ability to show girls they can be both loveable and powerful, and to show boys they can be both powerful and kind. Critics that bemoan the influence that Disney wields often fail to acknowledge the role of audience predilections. This perhaps includes audiences' limited embrace of characters like Megara, who is morally ambiguous, and Hercules, who does not capitalize on masculine traits like physical strength (and relies on Zeus for the dramatic dispatch of adversaries). While Hercules does not display the characteristics normally expected in order to establish the hero's dominance (when he relinquishes power and authority), his behaviors also exist within a context replete with other gender stereotypical behavior, which show that in expanding conceptions of male heroism, Disney may have created a character that was not sufficiently relatable. In addition, Hercules' preference for the more mundane rewards of a relationship in lieu of the exhibition of hypermasculinity may have been too avant-garde in 1997. Another possibility may be that the complexities of gender traits and their implications could have been too confusing for young viewers to grasp. Time will tell if the film or others with similar themes will appeal to new generations of viewers as normative gender roles evolve.

Funding: This research received no external funding.

Conflicts of Interest: The author declares no conflict of interest.

References

Afflerback, Sara, Amanda Koontz Anthony, Shannon K. Carter, and Liz Grauerholz. 2014. Consumption Rituals in the Transition to Motherhood. *Gender Issues* 31: 1–20. [CrossRef]

Baker-Sperry, Lori, and Liz Grauerholz. 2003. The Pervasiveness and Persistence of the Feminine Beauty Ideal in Children's Fairy Tales. *Gender and Society* 17: 711–26. [CrossRef]

Box Office Mojo. 2018a. Hercules (1997). Available online: https://www.boxofficemojo.com/movies/?page=main&id=hercules.htm (accessed on 24 September 2018).

Box Office Mojo. 2018b. *Moana* (2016). Available online: https://www.boxofficemojo.com/movies/?page=main&id=disney1116.htm (accessed on 24 September 2018).

Box Office Mojo. 2018c. *Tarzan* (1999). Available online: https://www.boxofficemojo.com/movies/?id=tarzan.htm (accessed on 24 September 2018).

Burchfield, Amy. 2013. Going the Distance: Themes of the Hero in Disney's Hercules. *Brigham Young University Scholars Archive. All Theses and Dissertations.* 4291. Available online: https://scholarsarchive.byu.edu/cgi/viewcontent.cgi?article=5290&context=etd (accessed on 25 July 2018).

Campbell, Joseph. 1949. *The Hero with a Thousand Faces.* Novato: New World Library, vol. 13.

Clarkson, Jay. 2008. The Limitations of the Discourse of Norms. *Journal of Communication Inquiry* 32: 368–82. [CrossRef]

Coville, Stephanie J. 2010. Representations of Women in Films Aimed at Young Girls: An Extended Literature Review. *Faculty of Education Graduate Projects.* Available online: https://qspace.library.queensu.ca/handle/1974/5578 (accessed on 2 September 2018).

Coyle, Emily F., Megan Fulcher, and Darinka Trübutschek. 2016. Sissies, Mama's Boys, and Tomboys: Is Children's Gender Nonconformity More Acceptable When Nonconforming Traits Are Positive? *Archives of Sexual Behavior* 45: 1827–38. [CrossRef] [PubMed]

Coyne, Sarah M., Jennifer Ruh Linder, Eric E. Rasmussen, David A. Nelson, and Victoria Birkbeck. 2016. Pretty as a Princess: Longitudinal Effects of Engagement with Disney Princesses on Gender Stereotypes, Body Esteem, and Prosocial Behavior in Children. *Child Development* 87: 1909–25. [CrossRef] [PubMed]

Davis, Amy. 2006. *Good Girls and Wicked Witches: Women in Disney's Feature Animation*. London: John Libbey Publishing.

Davis, Amy. 2013. *Handsome Heroes and Vile Villains: Masculinity in Disney's Features Films*. Bloomington: Indiana University Press.

Do Rozario, Rebecca-Anne C. 2004. The princess and the magic kingdom: Beyond nostalgia, the function of the Disney princess. *Women's Studies in Communication* 27: 34–59. [CrossRef]

Dundes, Lauren. 2001. Disney's modern heroine Pocahontas: Revealing age-old gender stereotypes and role discontinuity under a façade of liberation. *The Social Science Journal* 38: 353–65. [CrossRef]

Dundes, Lauren, and Madeline Streiff. 2016. Reel Royal Diversity? The Glass Ceiling in Disney's Mulan and Princess and the Frog. *Societies* 6: 35. [CrossRef]

Dundes, Lauren, Madeline Streiff, and Zachary Streiff. 2018. Storm Power, an Icy Tower and Elsa's Bower: The Winds of Change in Disney's Frozen. *Social Sciences* 7: 86. [CrossRef]

Elnahla, Nada Ramadan. 2015. Aging with Disney and the Gendering of Evil. *Journal of Literature and Art Studies* 5: 114–27.

England, Dawn Elizabeth, Lara Descartes, and Melissa A. Collier-Meek. 2011. Gender Role Portrayal and the Disney Princesses. *Sex Roles* 64: 555–67. [CrossRef]

Fabrikant, Geraldine. 1997. Hercules Is Too Weak to Lift Disney Stock. *New York Times*. Available online: https://www.nytimes.com/1997/07/10/business/hercules-is-too-weak-to-lift-disney-stock.html (accessed on 14 October 2018).

Foote, Lena. 2010. "I Want to be a Princess Too": Exploring the Blackout of Disney's Princess and the Frog and Its Effects on African American Girls. *Film Matters* 2: 13–22. [CrossRef]

Garabedian, Juliana. 2014. Animating Gender Roles: How Disney is Redefining the Modern Princess. *James Madison Undergraduate Research Journal* 2: 22–25.

Gillam, Ken, and Shannon R. Wooden. 2008. Post-Princess Models of Gender: The New Man in Disney/Pixar. *Journal of Popular Film and Television* 36: 2–8. [CrossRef]

Giroux, Henry A., and Grace Pollock. 2010. *The Mouse That Roared: Disney and the End of Innocence*. Lanham: Rowman & Littlefield.

Giroux, Henry A., and Grace Pollock. 2011. Is Disney Good for Your Kids? How Corporate Media Shape Youth Identity in the Digital Age. In *Kinderculture*, 3rd ed. Edited by Shirley R. Steinberg. New York: Taylor & Francis, pp. 73–92.

Goudreau, Jenna. 2012. Disney Princess Tops List of the 20 Best-Selling Entertainment Products. Forbes. Available online: https://www.forbes.com/sites/jennagoudreau/2012/09/17/disneyprincess-tops-list-of-the-20-best-selling-entertainment-products (accessed on 24 October 2018).

Gregory, S.M. 2010. Disney's second line: New Orleans, racial masquerade, and the reproduction of whiteness in The Princess and the Frog. *Journal of African American Studies* 14: 432–49. [CrossRef]

Griffin, Sean. 2000. *Tinker Belles and Evil Queens: The Walt Disney Company from the Inside Out*. New York City: New York University Press.

Griffin, Martyn, Nancy Harding, and Mark Learmonth. 2017. Whistle While You Work? Disney Animation, Organizational Readiness and Gendered Subjugation. *Organization Studies* 38: 869–94. [CrossRef]

Harris, Heather E. 2018. Queen Phiona and Princess Shuri—Alternative Africana "Royalty" in Disney's Royal Realm: An Intersectional Analysis. *Social Sciences* 7: 206. [CrossRef]

Henderson, Angie, Sandra Harmon, and Harmony Newman. 2016. The Price Mothers Pay, Even When They Are Not Buying It: Mental Health Consequences of Idealized Motherhood. *Sex Roles* 74: 512–26. [CrossRef]

Hercules [Motion Picture]. 1997. Directed by Ron Clements, and John Musker. Burbank: Walt Disney Pictures.

Hine, Benjamin, Katarina Ivanovic, and Dawn England. 2018. From the Sleeping Princess to the World-Saving Daughter of the Chief: Examining Young Children's Perceptions of 'Old' versus 'New' Disney Princess Characters. *Social Sciences* 7: 161. [CrossRef]

Hynes, Ashlee. 2010. Raising Princesses? Gender socialisation in early childhood and the Disney Princess franchise. *Critical Social Thinking: Policy and Practice* 2: 205–18.

Leader, Karen. 2016. "On the book of my body": Women, Power, and "Tattoo Culture". *Feminist Formations* 28: 174–95. [CrossRef]

Li-Vollmer, Meredith, and Mark E. LaPointe. 2003. Gender Transgression and Villainy in Animated Film. *Popular Communication* 1: 89–109. [CrossRef]

Macaluso, Michael. 2018. Postfeminist Masculinity: The New Disney Norm? *Social Sciences* 7: 221. [CrossRef]

Matyas, Vanessa. 2010. Tale as Old as Time: A Textual Analysis of Race and Gender in Disney Princess Films. *Graduate Major Research Papers and Multimedia Projects*. Available online: https://macsphere.mcmaster.ca/handle/11375/14406 (accessed on 2 September 2018).

McGill, Craig M. 2018. 'This Burning Desire is Turning Me to Sin': The intrapersonal sexual struggles of two Disney singing villains. *Queer Studies in Media & Popular Culture* 3: 27–49.

Patterson, G., and Leland G. Spencer. 2017. What's so funny about a snowman in a tiara? Exploring gender identity and gender nonconformity in children's animated films. *Queer Studies in Media & Popular Culture* 2: 73–93.

Pomeroy, Arthur J. 2017. *A Companion to Ancient Greece and Rome on Screen*. Malden: John Wiley & Sons, Inc., pp. 214–15.

Putnam, Amanda. 2013. Mean ladies: Transgendered villains in Disney films. In *Diversity in Disney Films: Critical Essays on Race, Ethnicity, Gender, Sexuality and Disability*. Edited by Johnson Cheu. Jefferson: McFarland & Company Inc., pp. 147–62.

Rabison, Rebecca. 2016. Deviance in Disney: Of Crime and the Magic Kingdom. In *Debating Disney: Pedagogical Perspectives on Commercial Cinema*. Edited by Douglas Brode and Shea T. Brode. Lanham: Rowman & Littlefield, pp. 199–210.

Sharrock, Alison. 2011. Womanly wailing? The mother of Euryalus and gendered reading. *Eugesta* 1: 55–77.

Smelik, Anneke. 2015. A close shave: The taboo on female body hair. *Critical Studies in Fashion & Beauty* 6: 233–51.

Streiff, Madeline, and Lauren Dundes. 2017a. From shapeshifter to lava monster: Gender stereotypes in Disney's Moana. *Social Sciences* 6: 91. [CrossRef]

Streiff, Madeline, and Lauren Dundes. 2017b. Frozen in Time: How Disney Gender-Stereotypes Its Most Powerful Princess. *Social Sciences* 6: 38. [CrossRef]

Tangled [Motion Picture]. 2010. Directed by Byron Howard, and Nathan Greno. Burbank: Walt Disney Pictures.

Towbin, Mia Adessa, Shelley A. Haddock, Toni Schindler Zimmerman, Lori K. Lund, and Litsa Renee Tanner. 2004. Images of Gender, Race, Age, and Sexual Orientation in Disney Feature-Length Animated Films. *Journal of Feminist Family Therapy* 15: 19–44. [CrossRef]

Tracy, James F. 1999. Whistle While You Work: The Disney Company and the Global Division of Labor. *Journal of Communication Inquiry* 23: 374–89. [CrossRef]

Valenti, Jessica. 2009. *The Purity Myth: How America's Obsession with Virginity is Hurting Young Women*. Berkeley: Seal Press.

Walker, Bela August. 2010. Deciphering Risk: Sex Offender Statutes and Moral Panic in a Risk Society. *University of Baltimore Law Review* 40: 184–213.

Zipes, Jack. 1999. Breaking the Disney Spell. In *The Classic Fairy Tales: A Norton Critical Edition*, 1st ed. Edited by Maria Tatar. New York: W. W. Norton & Company, pp. 333–52.

social sciences

MDPI

Article

The Rise of the Androgynous Princess: Examining Representations of Gender in Prince and Princess Characters of Disney Movies Released 2009–2016

Benjamin Hine [1,*], Dawn England [2], Katie Lopreore [3], Elizabeth Skora Horgan [4] and Lisa Hartwell [5]

[1] Department of Psychology, University of West London, St Mary's Road, London W5 5RF, UK
[2] School of Health and Education, Middlesex University Dubai, Knowledge Park, Block 16, Dubai, UAE; D.england@mdx.ac.ae
[3] Department of Nursing, Middle Tennessee University, 13-1 E Main Street, Murfreesboro, TN 37132, USA; kl3t@mtmail.mtsu.edu
[4] Department of Human Development and Family Studies, University of Wisconsin-Madison, Madison, WI 53706, USA; eskora@wisc.edu
[5] Master's Counseling Department, Messiah College, One College Avenue, Mechanicsburg, PA 17055, USA; lisahartwell13@gmail.com
* Correspondence: Ben.Hine@uwl.ac.uk; Tel.: +44-0208-209-4571

Received: 5 October 2018; Accepted: 16 November 2018; Published: 22 November 2018

Abstract: Previous quantitative research examining Disney movies has highlighted that whilst prince characters display largely balanced gender profiles, princesses exhibit biased gender role portrayals—performing mostly feminine characteristics, rarely participating in rescue behavior, and concluding movies in romantic relationships with the prince. However, such research, as well as public commentary, has also suggested that princess characters in movies released across the 2000s and 2010s may have more positive gender role portrayals. This study aimed to test these assertions by utilizing content coding analysis to examine the behavioral characteristics, rescue behavior, and romantic conclusions of prince and princess characters in five iconic Disney films released between 2009 and 2016 (*The Princess and the Frog*, *Tangled*, *Brave* (released under Pixar), *Frozen*, and *Moana*). Comparisons were also made with earlier titles to assess historical changes. Results showed that princesses in "2000s to 2010s" movies exhibited an almost equal number of masculine and feminine behaviors, thus demonstrating more egalitarian profiles over time. In contrast, princes appeared to adopt a more feminine behavioral profile in later movies. In addition, characters engaged in equal numbers of rescue behaviors, and princesses were more likely to remain single in "2000s to 2010s" movies. Results therefore suggest that Disney is indeed presenting more diverse, androgynous, balanced characters to viewers, and the theoretical and practical implications for the socialization of young child viewers are discussed.

Keywords: Disney; princess; prince; gender roles; content coding analysis; children's media

1. Introduction

1.1. Gender Role Portrayal in Children's Visual Media

Over the past 25 years, several studies have demonstrated that male characters in cartoons and other television programs are given much more prominence and appear more frequently (Aubrey and Harrison 2004; Calvert et al. 2003; Thompson and Zerbinos 1995), display more aggression (Luther and Legg 2010; Signorielli et al. 1995), display more planning (Browne 1998), engage in more of almost all the noted behaviors (Hentges and Case 2013) and talk significantly more (Hentges and Case 2013). Scholars have therefore suggested that representations of both male and female gender roles in children's programming are frequently too narrow and stereotypical (Leaper et al. 2002; Signorielli 2001; Steyer 2014). Negative representations of gender are also found in other forms of children's media, such as video games. For example, male gaming characters are much more likely to be aggressive, with female characters more likely to be sexualized, scantily clad, and to show a mix of sex and aggression (Dill and Thill 2007). Patterns such as these are reflected in media for adults, as demonstrated in a number of comprehensive reviews (Rudy et al. 2010a, 2010b). Women are still vastly under-represented across a range of settings (e.g., television, movie and printed media) and, when they are shown, tend to be given restricted and traditional portrayals. Women are also often sexualized or subordinated in various ways, and portrayed as fulfilling traditional roles such as homemaking, as non-professionals, as wives or parents, or as sexual gatekeepers (Collins 2011; Lemish 2010). Representations of men also remain largely unchanged, and centered around traditionally masculine traits (Signorielli 2001).

However, a number of studies suggest positive advances in gender role portrayal within children's media in recent decades, finding, for example, a great deal of gender neutrality across a number of first and second grade children's television programs (Aubrey and Harrison 2004; Baker and Raney 2007). Furthermore, when examining the most popular children's television networks in the U.S. (i.e., the Disney Channel, Cartoon Network and Nickelodeon) Hentges and Case (2013) found few differences in stereotyped behaviors when comparing male and female characters in post-1980, versus pre-1980, cartoons. Taken together, such research suggests that, whilst gender role portrayals in children's media continue to be problematic, a possible progression exists towards less narrow representations of gender, which, interestingly, were most exemplified on the Disney Channel, where the fewest differences in gendered behavior were found (Hentges and Case 2013).

1.2. The Relationship between Media and Gender Development

Several theories highlight the importance of such gendered information to the development of children's sense of gender identity (see Blakemore et al. 2009 for a review). For example, both Social Cognitive Theory (Bussey and Bandura 1999) and Identity Theory (Hogg et al. 1995) suggest that environmental models (such as parents, peers, or those in the media) help to transmit and teach gender norms and stereotypes to young children, particularly through modelling. Constructivist approaches also stress the importance of environmental stimuli, for example in Gender Schema Theory (Bem 1981; Martin and Halverson 1981), which proposes that children internalize their observations and experiences into cognitive frameworks or schemas, which subsequently guide their behavior (Graves 1999; Martin et al. 2002). Several approaches identify the media specifically as a key socializing agent for gender role development (Signorielli 2001). For example, cultivation theory proposes that visual media, such as television and film, may provide a particularly important mechanism for the development of concepts regarding social behavior and norms (Gerbner et al. 1994, 1980), and several studies directly highlight the impact of media consumption on subscription to traditional gender role representations (Coyne et al. 2014; Frueh and McGhee 1975; Herrett-Skjellum and Allen 1996; Hust and Brown 2008; Signorielli 1990; Williams 1981).

Social Role Theory (Eagly 2013; Eagly et al. 2000) provides a particularly important framework for assessing change in gender roles, and their representations, over time. Similar to many of the theories outlined above, it proposes that cultural expectations present in society influence an individual's roles and behaviors (Mead 1934), and that beliefs about gender are derived from observations of role performances exhibited in their environment. Importantly, this theory argues that culturally expected gendered roles and behaviors which children learn are dynamic and are influenced by changing cultural norms and environmental contexts (Eagly 2013). It therefore follows that any substantive shifts in societal constructions of gender roles (for example, increased flexibility afforded to women) would, and should, be reflected in changes to representations in the media. Such observations are particularly pertinent to prolific media forms, such as Disney movies, due to their contribution in shaping societal fabrics (Bryman 1999).

1.3. Representations of Women in Disney Movies

As such, several studies have investigated gender role portrayals by female characters in Disney feature movies released before 2010. For example, in 2011, England and colleagues produced a comprehensive quantitative analysis of Disney Princess movies released between 1937 and 2009, arguing prince and princess characters exhibited many traditionally gendered behaviors (England et al. 2011). This was found when examining the frequency of masculine and feminine characteristics, as well as rescue behavior (i.e., rarely performed by the princess) and romantic outcomes (i.e., the conclusion often resulted in heterosexual, heteronormative, 'love at first sight' marriage). These results are supported by studies using qualitative approaches which have criticized traditional or stereotypical portrayals of women (Matyas 2010), commenting on aspects such as their over sexualization and focus on the exotic (Lacroix 2004), sacrifice to higher or communal goals (Dundes 2001), and troubled relationships with male characters (Béres 1999; Do-Rozario 2004). Towbin and colleagues (2004) further highlighted that, in 26 Disney movies released between 1937 and 2000, female characters: have their appearance valued more than their intellect, were helpless and in need of protection, were domestic and likely to marry, and, if overweight, were ugly, unpleasant and unmarried.

Davis (2006) provides perhaps the most thorough qualitative appraisal of women in Disney movies up until 2003, largely from a film studies perspective. Several themes, similar to those in Towbin et al. (2004), were found for 'Classic Years' Disney women (1937–1967), including happiness found through marriage (e.g., Anita in *One Hundred and One Dalmatians*), and passivity, exemplified most strongly by the three princesses of this age, Snow White, Cinderella and Aurora (from *Snow White and the Seven Dwarfs*, *Cinderella*, and *Sleeping Beauty* respectively). In contrast, 'Eisner Era' Disney women (1989–2005) garner more favorable, captured most clearly by the evolution of Disney princesses (namely, Ariel, Jasmine, Pocahontas and Kida, from *The Little Mermaid*, *Aladdin*, *Pocahontas* and *Atlantis: The Lost Empire* respectively) into more well-rounded, independent, strong-willed, determined characters, insistent on being true to themselves. The introduction of 'tough gals', such as Megara in *Hercules*, is also presented as cause for celebration, whose strength, brashness and confidence are in stark contrast to their timid counterparts of old (Primo 2018). Nonetheless, the characters outlined above are still not entirely gender-progressive, and each still has their significant flaws (take, for example, Ariel's willingness to risk her life just for the possibility of finding love). Furthermore, the storylines of 'good daughter' characters (such as Belle, Mulan and Jane, from *Beauty and the Beast*, *Mulan*, and *Tarzan* respectively), whilst again containing some progressive elements, still present archetypal portrayals in which women are rewarded for acting selflessly for others, and where women engage in a lateral move between submission to a fatherly male authority figure, and a husbandly one. Taken together, such studies suggest that, whilst gender portrayals in pre-2003 Disney movies have improved over time, they are by no means in-keeping with societal developments in gender equity (Wiersma 2001). As summarized by Davis (2006), even the 'Eisner Era' women are 'devout care-takers of those around them, require the protection ... of a male authority figure ... and live out adventures which are at least sanctioned ... by the patriarchies in which all of the characters live' (p. 219).

Since these works, Disney has released a number of modern princess movies across the late 2000s and 2010s, including specific Disney Princess titles, such as *Tangled* (2010) and *Brave* (2012, released under Pixar), as well as those not officially associated but involving central, royal, female characters, including *Frozen* (2013) and *Moana* (2016), which have accumulated approximately $3 billion in gross global ticket revenue to date (Box Office Mojo 2011, 2013, 2014, 2017). These movies have also enjoyed staggering popularity amongst young girls and increasingly, in the case of *Frozen* and *Moana*, young boys worldwide (Gomez 2014; Koonikova 2014). The mainstream media has likewise responded favorably, and a number of articles have argued that these movies contain significantly more androgynous princess characters (Pulver 2016), portray a progressive rejection of typical romantic conclusions (Pulver 2016), and present increasingly self-sufficient princesses who take an active role in plot progression (Abersol 2014). The highest level of media praise is afforded to Moana, with many critics identifying a brave heroine with a sense of humor and a commitment to saving the world without romantic distractions (Dunsmore 2017; Duralde 2016; Machado 2016; Ngata 2016; To 2016). Importantly, these releases have taken place against a backdrop of unprecedented political, social and economic advancement for women worldwide, as well as increasing social discourse and acceptance surrounding gender-role flexibility and fluidity (Marsh 2016).

Yet work examining female portrayals in Disney movies released after 2003, particularly from a quantitative perspective, is still surprisingly sparse. England et al. (2011) provided some limited analysis, finding that, in their most recent movie analyzed, *The Princess and the Frog* (2009), the female character was more egalitarian than those in previous movies. Some qualitative appraisals also exist, which remain critical of newer female characters, for example arguing that women still cannot possess both love and power (e.g., Elsa in *Frozen*, Dundes et al. 2018; Streiff and Dundes 2017a), and that women are abusive of the power they gain (e.g., Te Kā in *Moana*, Streiff and Dundes 2017b). However, at present, no study has thoroughly examined gender representations in female characters in Disney movies released after 2003, particularly from a quantitative perspective. This is despite considerable appetite for more research on titles released since the turn of the millennium, as demonstrated by the existence of numerous undergraduate and postgraduate research projects (Garabedian 2014; Hartwell 2015; Lopreore 2016; Saladino 2014), as well as a number of media pieces (Abersol 2014; Pulver 2016) on the subject. Such research is also vital considering concerns expressed regarding the vulnerable nature of young girls absorbing gendered messages from Disney movies (Best and Lowney 2009; Orenstein 2006, 2011; Signorielli 2001), as well as the possible positive implications for gender role development resulting from exposure to more well-rounded characters.

1.4. Representations of Men

Even fewer studies have examined the behavior of men in Disney movies, however some appraisals do exist. The work by Towbin et al. (2004) outlined above provides some evidence, finding that male characters were more likely to: use physicality to express their emotions, lack control over their sexual impulses, be naturally strong and heroic, have non-domestic jobs, and, if overweight, have negative characteristics. This suggests that the men in these movies may suffer from similarly traditional and restrictive gender role portrayals as women. Again, whilst examinations on individual movies exist (e.g., of the characters in *Hercules*, Primo 2018), Davis (2013) provides possibly the most comprehensive qualitative assessment of Disney men up to, and including, those in *Wreck-It-Ralph* (released in 2012). Men are largely labelled as either 'Dashing Heroes' (e.g., Aladdin in *Aladdin*, or Flynn Rider/Eugene in *Tangled*) or 'Handsome Princes' (e.g., Prince Eric in *The Little Mermaid* or Prince Naveen in *The Princess and the Frog*), the former characterized by their sense of injustice and their motivation to be their best possible selves for the women they love, the latter characterized by the journeys they must take to earn manhood after a substantial 'fall from grace', and to become true, good men (/princes). Importantly, and in contrast to Towbin et al. (2004), Davis notes that whilst many stereotypically masculine traits are present in these characters, they are often accompanied by typically feminine traits, such as emotional sensitivity (exemplified most clearly in 'Action Men' John Smith and Li Shang from *Pocahontas* and *Mulan* respectively).

Other scholars support these more positive assessments of male characters, particularly in movies released in the 1990s and 2000s (such as Pixar titles *Toy Story*, *The Incredibles*, and *Cars*), where men grow to accept their feminine characteristics (Gillam and Wooden 2008). Indeed, quantitative appraisals provide further evidence for very balanced gender profiles in central male characters across Disney Princess movies up to 2009 (England et al. 2011). Thus, whilst some have been critical of male characters in more recent movies (e.g., the hyper-masculinized Maui in *Moana*, Streiff and Dundes 2017a), it is strongly argued that representations of men do appear to have evolved and matured over time, not only in relation to themselves as characters, but in their interactions with, and growing respect for, female protagonists (Davis 2013). Indeed, similar to her observations regarding female characters, Davis concludes that 'Disney's depictions of masculinity are not perfect. But ... they are improving' and that 'The sheer variety and diversity of types of male characters in Disney's animated feature films is continuing to improve, setting up good role models of masculinity for both boys and girls who are watching' (Davis 2013, p. 253). However, in-depth quantitative examination of gender role portrayals by male Disney characters since England et al.'s (2011) study has not yet occurred. This is desperately needed in order to investigate the messages regarding gender which young boys and men receive from such media (Coyne et al. 2016), often overlooked.

1.5. Rescue Behavior

Other important gendered messages for young children lie in the themes of heroism and love in Disney movies. Research examining heroism through rescue behavior suggests that, whilst princesses performed an equal amount of rescues to prince characters, they were also significantly more likely to require saving (England et al. 2011). Princesses were also rarely responsible for 'climactic' rescue scenes, in other words the final, most dramatic, and most significant scene of the movie, requiring a central, often male character to save another from a dangerous situation and provide significant plot resolution and the abating of peril (England et al. 2011). Such research agues therefore that princesses are mostly presented as characters who cannot act effectively or independently in important and often life-threatening situations. This may in turn present young children with the message that heroism, and associated concepts such as risk and strength, are inherently masculine, and that women are weak, passive, and in need of assistance.

Some researchers have provided interesting commentary on the heroic actions of specific 1990s princesses, such as *Pocahontas*, arguing that she presents a stronger type of princess who performs numerous brave behaviors throughout the movie and ultimately saves the lead male character (John Smith) from death by the hand of her father (Dundes 2001). Indeed, the 'Eisner Era' princesses and 'good daughters' described by Davis (2006) demonstrate numerous acts of bravery, including self-sacrifice and physical combat. Moreover, recent media commentary, focused on the releases of *Brave*, *Frozen*, and *Moana*, has further highlighted changes in the presentation of princesses' heroic behavior, specifically their progression from 'passive damsels' to 'active heroes' (Hugel 2013), suggesting that, when it comes to heroism, the reign of men may be over.

1.6. Romance & Living 'Happily Ever After'

The presentation of romantic narratives in Disney movies, and the messages given to children regarding the formation of romantic relationships, has also been subject to scrutiny. For example, Cokely has highlighted the unanimously heterosexual nature of romantic resolutions in Disney movies, as well as their magical, fantastical and unrealistic nature (Cokely 2005; Garlen and Sandlin 2017). Hefner and colleagues (Hefner et al. 2017) further emphasizes that such romantic ideals are consistently rewarded in Disney films, whereas challenges are punished. Other researchers have observed that children are routinely exposed to the social script that "one falls in love either very quickly, at first sight (Snow White, Sleeping Beauty), against all odds (Beauty and the Beast, Mulan, The Princess and the Frog), or both (Cinderella, The Little Mermaid, Aladdin, Pocahontas)" (Davis 2006; England et al. 2011, p. 565). Princesses also rarely remain single at the end of these movies (England et al. 2011), suggesting that finding love is a key goal for any princess (and by extension any young girl/woman).

However, in the two most recent films analyzed by England et al. (2011), *Mulan* and *The Princess and the Frog*, the two central characters fell in love over a longer period of time, whilst overcoming obstacles and achieving joint goals. Other scholars support these observations, noting a shift to more well-rounded princess characters with deeper romantic narratives (Davis 2006; Stover 2013). Therefore, whilst some are still critical of developments in the romantic storylines of princesses (such as Elsa's replacement of romance with power in *Frozen*, Streiff and Dundes 2017a), it would appear that most observations of later films are positive in this regard. Thus, examination of both rescue behavior and romantic outcomes in Disney movies released post-2000 is therefore much needed, both to inform and support current media discourse, as well as to explore how such behaviors constitute part of gender portrayal for these characters.

1.7. The Ubiquity of Disney in the Lives of Young Children

Such an endeavor is arguably worthwhile considering results from several studies which suggest that the gendered content presented by Disney is enthusiastically incorporated into the narratives and interactions of young girls, fueled by the pervasiveness of Disney content in children's lives (Giroux and Pollock 2010). For example, both Baker-Sperry (2007) and Wohlwend (2009) found that young girls in kindergarten and 1st grade who identified as avid fans of Disney took up familiar princess narratives in their writing and pretend play, fiercely correcting divergent interpretations by peers. Moreover, Golden and Jacoby (2017) identified four themes emergent during 3- to 5-year-old girls' Disney-themed pretend play and discussions: a focus on clothing and accessories, beauty, princess body movements, and exclusion of boys. Such topics demonstrate that traditionally limited gender representations offered in princess characters are emphatically adopted into a young girl's gender schemas and scripts. An observation further supported by the limited quantitative research available, which demonstrates that engagement with Disney Princess media/products is predictive of increased gender stereotypic behavior 1 year later (Coyne et al. 2016).

Such research supports the notion that media such as Disney movies may be specifically designed and produced to be consumed through a gendered lens, and that such media forms are constructed in a way to directly appeal to children in this way (Oliver and Green 2001). These observations have important implications, principally that young girls viewing visual media with restrictive and limiting female gender role portrayals, such as Disney movies, may adopt such representations for themselves. This is not to say that an increased performance of feminine behaviors in response to such media is problematic in its own right, as acknowledged by Coyne et al. (2016). Instead, the transmission of presentations of women that may serve to restrict their behavior and choices is cause for serious concern. Such issues exist regarding media consumption by young male viewers also, though they garner significantly less attention both academically and in the popular press (Streiff and Dundes 2017a).

This makes the identification of more positive gender role portrayals all the more pressing, as the existence of popular media forms which seek to remove and challenge restrictive stereotypes may, by direct contrast, have more positive and liberating effects on children's understandings of gender norms and stereotypes. Indeed, some studies already demonstrate that young girls adapt existing princess narratives in response to social limitations in princess identities and behavior, revising character qualities and storylines to form counter narratives of their own that are more representative of them as individuals and are less restrictive (Wohlwend 2009). Moreover, recent research has shown that young viewers are aware of the changing gender-role portrayals of princesses (in that they identify princesses such as Moana as more balanced in their portrayal of masculine and feminine characteristics than Aurora from *Sleeping Beauty*, Hine et al. 2018). However, a more comprehensive investigation of gender portrayals in movies released after the year 2000 remains absent.

1.8. The Present Study

As outlined above, a number of theories suggest that gender role representations within the media, including those within the world of Disney (Coyne et al. 2016; Wohlwend 2009), play an important and dynamic role in shaping young children's conceptualizations of gender (Graves 1999; Martin et al. 2002). Therefore, considering the Walt Disney Company's continued and considerable commercial success (The Walt Disney Company 2017); the widespread access to Disney films afforded to children of all ages; the popularity of Disney movies featuring princess characters in particular (Davis 2006, 2013); and the iconic nature of the characters presented therein (Orenstein 2006), it is reasoned that investigating gender role representations within this franchise is a worthwhile pursuit. Furthermore, to examine gender role portrayals in more recent Disney titles is argued to be particularly important when considering the significant role media forms play in both shaping and representing social change (Eagly 2013). This is emphasized, for example, by the Walt Disney Company's own acknowledgement of, and contribution towards, discourse surrounding female empowerment in the launching of its #DreamBigPrincess campaign to support the aspirations of young girls worldwide (The Walt Disney Company 2016).

The present study therefore examined the gendered behavior of prince and princess characters, as well as rescue behavior and romantic conclusions, in five "2000s to 2010s" Disney movies: *The Princess and the Frog* (2009), *Tangled* (2010), *Brave* (2012, released under Pixar), *Frozen* (2013), and *Moana* (2016), and compared these to the eight older titles previously analyzed in England et al. (2011). There were four hypotheses:

Hypotheses 1 (H1A). *Prince and Princess Characteristics: We predicted that both princes and princesses in movies released in the 2000s to 2010s would have androgynous behavioral profiles (i.e., they would display an equal number of masculine and feminine characteristics), both when examined for princes and princesses individually (e.g., the princess character shows masculine and feminine characteristics with equal frequency) and in comparing princes and princesses (e.g., the princess character portrays as many masculine characteristics as the prince counterpart).*

Hypotheses 1 (H1B). *Differences in Gender Expression over Time: We also predicted that the gendered behavior exhibited by princesses, but not princes, would have changed historically (i.e., from "1930s to 1950s" to "2000s to 2010s" movies). Namely, whilst princes would maintain an androgynous expression of behavior across time (e.g., show a similar number of masculine behaviors in "2000s to 2010s" compared to earlier movies), princesses would change from displaying mostly feminine behaviors in "1930s to 1950s" movies to more androgynous patterns in "2000s to 2010s" movies.*

Hypotheses 2. *Rescue Behavior: Our third hypothesis predicted that rescue behavior in "2000s to 2010s" movies would also be more egalitarian, both when examined for princes and princesses individually (e.g., the princess character performs rescues with similar frequency to being rescued) and in comparing princes and princesses (e.g., the princess character performs as many rescues as the prince counterpart).*

Hypotheses 3. *Romantic Outcomes: The final hypothesis predicted changes in romantic outcome across time, specifically that princesses in "2000s to 2010s" movies would be less likely to marry or 'live happily ever after' with the prince than those in earlier movies.*

2. Results

2.1. Hypothesis 1A—Prince and Princess Characteristics

Two same sample *t*-tests were conducted to assess whether the percentage of masculine behavior shown by all princes and princesses across "2000s to 2010s" movies were significantly different to a value of 50% (i.e., the percentage that would represent an exactly equal split between masculine and feminine behavior). Only masculine behaviors were assessed as values representing the percentage of feminine behaviors provide the corresponding values and would mirror results. The masculine behavior percentage for princesses was not significantly different to 50%, suggesting that both masculine (52.6%) and feminine behaviors (47.7%) accounted for close to half of overall princess behavior. Conversely, the masculine behavior percentage for princes was found to be significantly different to 50%, t (3) = 4.87, $p < 0.05$, suggesting that princes' masculine behavior constituted significantly less than half of their overall behavior (38.5%), with feminine behavior comprising significantly more (61.5%). Broadly, these results suggest that both masculine and feminine attributes are highly valued, and frequently exhibited by female central characters, thus capturing a clear representation of androgyny (Bem 1974, 1975). Central male characters, however, show a less balanced behavioral profile, exhibiting more feminine behaviors overall.

An independent sample t-test was conducted to compare the overall expression of masculine characteristics of princes versus princesses. Again, only masculine percentages were examined as feminine percentages comprise corresponding values, producing mirrored results. Results showed that princess characters exhibited significantly more masculine characteristics (M = 52.6, SD = 7.98) than princes (M = 38.5, SD = 4.73), t (7) = 3.09, $p < 0.05$. This also demonstrates that princes showed more feminine characteristics overall (61.5%) than princesses (47.4%). Examining the top five most frequently displayed behaviors by prince and princess characters in each movie provides further detail, as several shared characteristics are identified. In *The Princess and the Frog*, the prince and princess shared "affectionate", "athletic" and "assertive" in their top five characteristics; in *Tangled* and *Frozen* they shared "athletic", "fearful" and "assertive"; and in *Brave* they shared "athletic" and "assertive". "Athletic" and "assertive" were therefore in the top five characteristics for both princes and princesses in all "2000s to 2010s" movies with both characters, and characteristics relating to affection and fear were shared by both princes and princesses in three of the movies. This shows that, whilst princesses are shown to be more masculine, and less feminine, than princes overall, when examining the most frequent behaviors, similar masculine and feminine characteristics were valued and expressed by central characters of both genders (See Table 1).

Table 1. Most frequent traits in for princes and princesses in the five "2000s to 2010s" movies.

Prince Trait	Tallies	% Total Behavior	Princess Trait	Tallies	% Total Behavior
Shows emotion	268	24.36	Assertive	282	13.43
Athletic	137	12.45	Athletic	269	12.81
Assertive	102	9.27	Fearful	211	10.05
Fearful	97	8.82	Tentative	167	7.95
Victim	62	5.64	Physically strong	127	6.05
Affectionate	61	5.55	Affectionate	121	5.76
Physically strong	50	4.55	Wants to explore	82	3.90
Tentative	36	3.27	Submissive	71	3.38
Unemotional	36	3.27	Brave	68	3.24
Curious ab. Princess	36	3.27	Troublesome	68	3.24
Submissive	32	2.91	Intellectual activity	56	2.67
Troublesome	28	2.55	Independent	54	2.57
Helpful	26	2.36	Asks for advice/help	52	2.48
Physically weak	17	1.55	Inspires fear	46	2.19
Gives advice	17	1.55	Unemotional	46	2.19
Inspires fear	14	1.27	Victim	46	2.19
Asks for advice/help	10	0.91	Helpful	44	2.10
Leader	9	0.82	Leader	44	2.10
Gets rescued	9	0.82	Ashamed	43	2.05
Wants to explore	7	0.64	Nurturing	37	1.76
Brave	7	0.64	Physically weak	30	1.43
Sensitive	7	0.64	Gives advice	28	1.33
Intellectual activity	6	0.55	Performs rescue	23	1.10
Descr. as attractive	6	0.55	Sensitive	22	1.05
Performs rescue	6	0.55	Gets rescued	21	1.00
Nurturing	5	0.46	Tends to phys. app.	18	0.86
Tends to phys. app.	4	0.37	Descr. as attractive	15	0.71
Ashamed	3	0.27	Collapses crying	13	0.62
Independent	2	0.18			
Collapses crying	0	0.00			

2.2. Hypothesis 1B—Differences in Gender Expression over Time

One-way ANOVAs were conducted to test the effects of the chronological grouping of movies on the gendered characteristics observed, one using data for princes and another for princesses.

This involved comparing data newly generated in this study on "2000s to 2010s" movies with data generated by England et al. (2011) for older titles. Again, only the values for percentage of masculine behaviors were used. For prince characters, a borderline significance was found ($p = 0.09$), suggesting that the percentage of masculine characteristics exhibited by princes has changed modestly over time. Examining these patterns more closely, it appears that prince characters were lower on masculine characteristics in "1930s to 1950s" (M = 45.33, SD = 14.15) and "2000s to 2010s" movies (M = 38.5, SD = 4.73) than in "1980s to 1990s" movies (M = 59.2, SD = 15.55). In contrast, princess characters have experienced a clear and significant change in their performance of gendered behavior across time, with the proportion of masculine characteristics increasing significantly, F (2, 12) = 43.99, $p < 0.001$. Post hoc tests using Tukey's HSD revealed significant differences between "1930s to 1950s" and "1980s to 1990s", $p < 0.001$, and "1930s to 1950s" and "2000s to 2010s" movies, $p < 0.001$, as well as "1980s to 1990s" and "2000s to 2010s" movies, $p < 0.05$. These results therefore suggest that, whilst prince characters have once again become more feminine in their behavior, princesses have become progressively more androgynous over time, demonstrating the most balanced behavioral profiles in "2000s to 2010s" movies.

2.3. Hypothesis 2—Rescue Behavior

Paired sample *t*-tests were conducted to investigate the performance of rescue behaviors by prince and princess characters in "2000s to 2010s" movies respectively, with results demonstrating no significant differences in characters' performance of rescues and their instances of being rescued. In addition, independent-samples *t*-tests compared the total number of rescue behaviors by princes and princesses. No significant differences were found for either being rescued, or performing rescues, suggesting that prince and princess characters performed these behaviors with equal frequency. These results suggest that prince and princess characters are very similar in their demonstration of rescue behaviors in "2000s to 2010s" movies. Interestingly, princesses in these movies took a greater role in climactic rescue scenes, as well as engaging in more collaborative problem-solving with the prince, than in earlier films. A more detailed examination of rescue behavior by both prince and princess characters is included in the discussion.

2.4. Hypothesis 3—Romantic Outcomes

A chi-square test of independence was performed on the romantic outcomes codes for all movies to examine the relationship between movie era and romantic outcome. The relationship between these variables was significant, χ^2 (2, N = 13) = 6.24, $p < 0.05$, with results showing that princess characters in "2000s to 2010s" movies were less likely to end up married and/or living happily ever after than princesses in "1930s to 1950s" or "1980s to 1990s" movies who almost unanimously conformed to this outcome. "2000s to 2010s" Disney Princess movies therefore represent a significant sea change in the presentation of romantic narratives. Specifically, whilst the princesses in *The Princess and the Frog* and *Tangled* do indeed marry the prince, *Brave*, *Frozen* and *Moana* take a significant departure from this pattern. Neither Merida nor Elsa (*Brave* and *Frozen*, respectively), are shown to be significantly romantically involved, married to or as living happily ever after with a prince character at the conclusion of the movie. *Moana* contains no romantic narrative at all. These patterns suggest Disney is becoming less rigid in their presentation of romantic storylines, occasionally even foregoing this plot line completely.

3. Discussion

"I am Moana of Motunui. Aboard my boat *I* will sail across the sea and restore the heart of Te Fiti" —Moana, after 'I am Moana (Song of the Ancestors)'

As proposed, this study examined the expression of gendered characteristics by the central prince and princess characters in five "2000s to 2010s" Disney movies—*The Princess and the Frog*, *Tangled*,

Brave (released under Pixar), *Frozen*, and *Moana*. Changes in the frequency of masculine and feminine characteristics exhibited by prince and princess characters over time were also assessed, as was the frequency of rescue behavior and romantic outcomes. This is the first study to quantitatively document the behavior of prince and princess characters in Disney movies released post-2009, and to compare them to previous Disney titles featuring princess characters. Results showed that princess characters in "2000s to 2010s" movies exhibit an androgynous pattern of behavior, particularly in comparison to their historical counterparts. Interesting patterns also emerged for prince characters, as a traditionally androgynous profile became increasingly feminine. Results also suggest that prince and princess characters in "2000s to 2010s" movies participate equally in important rescue behaviors, and that traditional romantic trajectories have changed to include non-romantic outcomes.

3.1. The Rise of the Androgynous Princess

Hypothesis 1A was generally supported, as princess characters in "2000s to 2010s" movies exhibited a similar amount of masculine and feminine behaviors. This supports previous research (England et al. 2011), as well as articles from the popular press (Abersol 2014; Pulver 2016), suggesting that princesses in "2000s to 2010s" Disney movies exhibit more balanced, or androgynous behavioral profiles. This is further reflected in the behaviors most frequently exhibited by princess characters, where traits such as being "athletic" and "assertive" sat beside "fearful" and "tentative". Indeed, the behavioral makeup of princesses in "2000s to 2010s" movies is markedly different from the traditional, gender-typical profiles seen in earlier titles (Davis 2006; England et al. 2011; Towbin et al. 2004). Results therefore also supported hypothesis 1B, as princesses were found to be less feminine and more balanced in their behavioral profiles over time.

In other words, the largely passive behavior of older princesses such as Snow White and Cinderella (Davis 2006) have been replaced by the active, strong, and independent characters of Merida and Moana. These findings reflect children's own awareness of the changing behavioral profiles of princess characters (Hine et al. 2018), and support suggestions by the press that popular media sources, including Disney, may be starting to provide positive and behaviorally balanced role models, such as Moana, for young girls (Dunsmore 2017; Duralde 2016; Machado 2016; Ngata 2016; To 2016). Such results are consistent with patterns of social change proposed by Social Role Theory (Eagly 2013), as the new gender profiles seen in "2000s to 2010s" Disney movies both reflect and subsequently shape the changing role and increased freedom of women and girls in Western society (Marsh 2016). This change is particularly important considering the numerous theories which highlight the importance of such models within the environment for gender identity formation (for example, Gender Schema Theory, Martin and Halverson 1981), and the suggested positive implications for the socio-emotional wellbeing of young girls of observing such models (Hine et al. 2018).

3.2. The Changing Prince

In contrast, prince characters had largely unbalanced profiles in "2000s to 2010s" movies, exhibiting greater amounts of feminine than masculine behavior across all titles. This is unsurprising considering that feminine behaviors such as "Shows Emotion", "Fearful" and being a "Victim", were some of the most frequently exhibited characteristics (accounting for approximately 39% of their behavior). Princes were also shown to be significantly less masculine, and more feminine, than princess characters, and had intriguing patterns of change over time (with both "1930s to 1950s" and "2000s to 2010s" princes demonstrating more feminine profiles than "1980s to 1990s" princes, although these results were not significant). Such results therefore suggest that, whilst England et al.'s characterization of prince characters as largely androgynous is broadly supported in this study, clear trends towards a more feminine behavioral profile exist. In other words, the largely absent, passive princes of the 1930s and 1950s, and the muscular, brave heroes of the 1980s and 1990s appear to have been succeeded by a troop of sensitive, fearful, but dashing men in the 21st century, thus supporting the argument that the men of Disney are complicated, to say the least.

Previous work has argued that it is important and valuable to show both women and men as capable of expressing both masculine and feminine characteristics (Bem 1975), and the positive implications for children's gender identity development, and associated psychosocial outcomes, are clear (Martin et al. 2016). However, the higher proportion of feminine behavior by prince characters is certainly no reflection of any obvious role change for men and young boys in society, or greater acceptance of men's feminine interests, as numerous studies suggest they are still consistently and firmly guided away from such pursuits (e.g., playing with feminine toys, see Kollmayer et al. 2018). The reasons behind more feminine behavior in princes are therefore unclear. One explanation is that Disney seeks to discourage feminine behavior in young boys, and thus reinforce broader societal norms, by presenting these characteristics in a negative light. For example, whilst the valence of the behaviors was not directly assessed in this study, negative or overly-dramatic portrayals of "fearful" or "tentative" traits (for example, as demonstrated by Prince Naveen throughout *The Princess and the Frog*), or of being overly "affectionate" or "sensitive" (exemplified by characters like Kristoff in *Frozen*) may seek to discourage young boys from adopting such behaviors. This explanation would fit well with post-feminist interpretations of masculinity within popular media forms, including Disney movies (Macaluso 2018), which seek to present men "as somewhat hapless, bumbling 'victims' or 'losers' in the 'sex wars'" (Gill 2014), and with arguments centered around the reinforcement of hegemonic masculinity through the demonization of feminine traits and attributes, particularly when performed by men (Connell 2005).

Alternatively, rather than mocking gender atypicality in men, it is possible that Disney is instead acting as a catalyst for a dissection and re-evaluation of masculinity, and the strict gender norms imposed upon young boys and men. This is the explanation offered by both Davis (2013) and Coyne and colleagues (Coyne et al. 2016), who propose that Disney films may actually offer important models of feminine behavior for boys amongst a plethora of hyper-masculine messages present in child and adult media (Brown et al. 2009). For example, stoicism (emotional restraint) is traditionally regarded as an important and idealized masculine trait (Donaldson 1993), and yet "Shows emotion" accounted for almost a quarter of prince behavior in "2000s to 2010s" movies. Clearly such behaviors are therefore important to princes, as they form such a large proportion of their interactions. Further, one need only look to the 'I've got a dream' scene in *Tangled* (35:50–40:46) to see big, burly, aggressive vigilante men sing, openly and positively, about the largely feminine dreams and interests they hold. Perhaps Disney is simply reflecting that traditional constructions of masculinity are under increasing scrutiny, as the requirements of a traditional male gender role in the modern world are questioned (John 2002). Whatever the motivation behind such portrayals may indeed be, continued analysis of Disney masculinity is clearly warranted.

3.3. New Hero(ine)s

Hypothesis 2 was also supported, in that both prince and princess characters performed rescues, and were themselves rescued, with similar frequency. In addition, princesses performed as many rescues, and were also rescued as often as princes. This expands upon the work of England and colleagues (2011) which showed that later princesses performed rescues equally as often as princes, and challenges traditional observations that princesses are more likely to end up as 'damsels in distress'. Moreover, and in contrast to earlier movies, princesses played an increasingly key role in climactic rescue scenes. For example, instead of scenes exemplified by 1930s and 1950s princesses such as Snow White and Aurora, who require saving by the central male character from some precarious scenario, these situations have begun to involve either the prince and princesses working together (such as in *Tangled*, where, within the same scene, Flynn saves Rapunzel from a life of servitude by cutting her hair, and Rapunzel saves Flynn by using her tears to heal his fatal wound), or princesses performing the climactic rescue act solo (such as in *Brave*, when Merida sews together the ripped tapestry to save her mother from the witch's spell). "2000s to 2010s" princesses also increasingly shared responsibility with prince characters in other scenes of jeopardy, as a hero(ine) who can bring, or help bring about a resolution (such as in *Frozen*, where Anna and Kristoff work together to fend off an pursuing wolf pack), instead of simply being a passive recipient of help. Importantly, they perform this role both by suggesting ideas *and* by contributing physically. Princesses in these movies also frequently engaged in 'self-saving', rather than relying on the prince to perform the rescue. Results from this study therefore support observations in the popular media that princesses are increasingly portrayed as independent, self-reliant, competent, active and brave characters, who are fundamentally important to the resolution of situations containing misfortune, peril, and mortal danger (Abersol 2014).

3.4. Remaining Single and Saving the World

Hypothesis 3 was also supported, as princess characters in "2000s to 2010s" movies were significantly less likely to end up married or living happily ever after than in "1930s to 1950s" or "1980s to 1990s" movies. This study therefore furthers initial observations of "1980s to 1990s" movies that characters were starting to fall in love over longer periods of time (England et al. 2011), and suggests that, for some characters, love is no longer a priority. For example, whilst Tiana and Rapunzel (in *The Princess and the Frog* and *Tangled* respectively) *are* still presented as married at the end of their movies, this was neither of their initial goals. Instead, both end up realizing through interacting with those male counterparts that they may be interested in a romantic involvement and subsequently fall in love. This is significantly different from the already less extreme romantic narratives presented in "1980s to 1990s" movies where princes and princesses may spend more time together but are still willing to make great personal sacrifices to achieve true love (for example, in *The Little Mermaid*).

Brave, *Frozen* and *Moana* present a more significant departure from the traditional romantic narrative offered in Disney (and Pixar) movies, as these characters were coded as 'single' at the end of their movies. This suggests that finding love is no longer presented as a key endeavor or foregone conclusion (a phenomenon arguably started in some 1990s princesses, Davis 2006), and devices utilized in both *Brave* and *Frozen* serve to parody and even ridicule traditional romantic narratives (e.g., Merida fighting for her own hand in marriage, and the presentation of Anna's desire to marry a man she has just met as ridiculous). The greatest exemplification of this shift is found in *Moana*, where no romantic narrative is offered at all. This is a stark contrast to the love-at-first-sight narratives presented in "1930s to 1950s" movies, where princesses meet or awake to their prince charming and live happily ever after with them (Davis 2006). Indeed, the presentation of alternative romantic conclusions is particularly ground-breaking for a company that has presented traditional hetero-romantic messages for nearly a century. Such changes are especially important considering the impact that romantic scripts in media have on children's understanding of relationship formation and maintenance (Holmes 2007; Morr-Serewicz and Gale 2008), as well as the expression of sexual desire within relationships (Eggermont 2006).

3.5. Limitations and Future Research Directions

There are, however, a number of methodological limitations to this study. First, this study used a strictly quantitative approach for the coding and analysis of these movies. There is much to be gained from this methodology, particularly in understanding the frequency of behavior and how this changes over time, the categorical outcomes of these movies, and the balance of masculine versus feminine behavior by princes and princesses. However, further qualitative or novel mixed-methods approaches to analyzing "2000s to 2010s" Disney movies are still necessary to provide a richer understanding of the behavioral profiles of characters, particularly with regards to the negative versus positive valence of behaviors, as well as the circumstances in which behaviors are performed. Future studies should seek to employ a variety of methods in order to fully understand the gendered messages presented by central characters in these movies.

A second methodological limitation of this study is the coding system utilized. The codes employed in this study were consistent with the research upon which this study expands (England et al. 2011), and achieved high inter-rater reliability scores. However, some codes may not capture the richness of behavior exhibited. For example, the "Shows Emotion" code for princes was important in the original scheme, as, princes in "1930s to 1950s" and "1980s to 1990s" movies did not exhibit enough emotional behavior for this to be separated into distinct acts (as it is for princess characters). However, the high proportion of emotional behavior shown by princes in "2000s to 2010s" movies suggests that summing all emotional behaviors of male characters is no longer appropriate, and demonstrates that future studies should consider revision to the coding scheme. That being said, it was important to maintain for this study to highlight the change and allow for direct comparison.

It is also worth noting that the very notions of "femininity" and "masculinity" are subject to changing political, historical and cultural norms and discourse. Particularly relevant for this study is the emergence of a so-called 'Fourth Wave' of Feminism from around 2008 (Baumgardner 2011), after the original coding of England et al. (2011) but before the coding for the current study took place, and the subsequent gender discourse that this new, technology-enhanced feminism stimulated. It is quite possible, even probable, that some of the behaviors classified as "feminine" or "masculine" within this study no longer carry such distinct labels, or indeed neatly fit into one category or the other. For the purposes of this study, and in order to enable direct comparison with previous literature and the conclusions therein, an identical coding system was utilized. However, future research should seek to construct coding frameworks using the most up-to-date and appropriate definitions of behavior, possibly informed by how, or even if, young viewers categorize behaviors coded in such a way.

A third limitation is represented by the decision to focus exclusively on Disney movies involving prince and princess characters. Indeed, other popular Disney and Pixar movies exist across the time frame chosen for this study (e.g., *Toy Story* 3, released in 2010, *Wreck-It-Ralph*, released in 2012, and *Big Hero 6*, released in 2014) and beyond (e.g., *Coco*, released in 2017 and *The Incredibles* 2, released in 2018), and examining the behavioral profiles of male and female characters within these movies may prove worthwhile. It is also worth noting that even within these two production houses, differences in managerial style, company history and creative focus may influence representations of gender within work produced (Davis 2006). Moreover, analyzing the behaviors of secondary characters within such movies, both independently and in contrast to principles, may also provide rich material for furthering our understanding of gender representations. Examination of villainous characters, and the possible use of gender-atypicality to exemplify villainy (Li-Vollmer and LaPointe 2003; Ramadan 2015), is also worthy of future exploration.

A particularly important avenue for research is the assessment of the impact of these gendered messages on young children. Whilst preliminary evidence suggests that greater engagement with the Disney Princess franchise as a whole results in increased feminine behavior by both young girls and boys (Coyne et al. 2016), at present no research has examined the impact of movies from different Disney 'eras' on the gendered beliefs and identities of young children. The specific impact of modern, androgynous gender-representations in princess characters on the gender identity development of young girls is therefore yet to be fully assessed. In addition, considering the increased feminine behavior by male characters in "2000s to 2010s" movies, the investigation of young boys' engagement with both prince and princess characters in Disney movies, as well as the impact of such media on young boys' gender role development, is an important focus for future investigation.

3.6. Conclusions

Several popular press articles have suggested that princess characters in "2000s to 2010s" Disney Princess movies have become more androgynous and balanced in their expression of masculine and feminine behavior. This study aimed to empirically assess these observations, finding not only that princesses were largely androgynous in their behavioral profiles, but that they are increasingly instrumental in the resolution of dangerous situations, and are no longer restricted to traditional romantic resolutions. Interesting results regarding the increasingly feminine behavior of prince characters were also found, and both are worthy of further investigation. Importantly, the arguments presented in this paper strongly suggest that these "2000s to 2010s" movies could have a significant impact on the socialization of gender in young children, possibly promoting healthier and more inclusive attitudes regarding gender and gendered behavior.

However, these messages should be interpreted with caution, as a number of concerns with Disney movies still exist which are not specifically addressed in this study, such as negative presentations of body image (Baker-Sperry and Grauerholz 2003; Griffin 2000; Northup and Liebler 2010; Towbin et al. 2004) and race (Cheu 2013; Foote 2010; Gregory 2010) to name a few. Furthermore, Disney is yet to enter into the arena of non-heteronormative relationships, despite the increasingly open discourse surrounding sexuality in society. It is therefore still vitally important, despite the indication of more positive representations suggested by this study, for parents to both encourage and engage in critical consumption of Disney movies (particularly older titles) in order to challenge more traditional gender stereotypes and messages, and to promote a healthy dialogue with children around gender (Coyne et al. 2016). At present however, Disney does appear to have taken significant, important and much welcomed steps towards a more positive and balanced presentation of both male and female central characters in Disney movies, in line with cultural advances in gender role flexibility.

4. Materials and Methods

Content coding analysis was utilized to identify and record gendered characteristics in five Disney/Pixar movies released across the 2000s and 2010s featuring human, royal, female characters, typically princesses: *The Princess and the Frog, Tangled, Brave, Frozen* and *Moana*. These films were chosen using the following parameters, in that they: (a) were produced and distributed by Walt Disney Animation Studios or Pixar Animation Studios after the year 2000, (b) feature a princess specifically from the Disney Princess line (in the case of *The Princess and the Frog, Tangled,* and *Brave*), or a royal female character, typically a princess (in the case of *Frozen* and *Moana*), and (c) had achieved more than $200 million in box office takings worldwide. This provided movies that had both popular central characters for analysis and had enjoyed substantial international financial success. Table 2 provides an overview of the characters coded in each movie, along with their categorization as princes/princesses, and thus reason for selection. For the purposes of this study, due to the overwhelming majority of characters being clearly classified as princes or princess by either birth or marriage, and due to both the popular media and children's recognition of almost all of the central female characters below as princesses (Hine et al. 2018), these characters will be referred to as princes and princesses throughout.

Table 2. An Overview of Characters Selected for Coding in each Target Movie and their Justification for Inclusion.

Movie	Princess Characters	Categorization	Prince Characters	Categorization
The Princess and the Frog	Tiana	Princess by Marriage & Official Disney Princess	Naveen	Prince by Birth
Tangled	Rapunzel	Princess by Birth & Official Disney Princess	Eugene/Flynn Rider	Prince by Marriage
Brave	Merida	Princess by Birth & Official Disney Princess	Wee Dingwall Young Macintosh Young MacGuffin	Prince by Birth Prince by Birth Prince by Birth
Frozen	Anna Elsa	Princess by Birth Princess by Birth (then Queen)	Hans Christoph	Prince by Birth Strongly Romantically linked to Anna
Moana	Moana	Daughter of the Chief	None Chosen	N/A

This "2000s to 2010s" group of movies was also compared to eight previously coded Disney Princess films (England et al. 2011, see Table 3 for chronological groupings). Such an approach (i.e., applying a previously established coding system to new media, and conducting comparative statistical analysis on the 'old' and 'new' data) is substantially supported (Krippendorf 2004; Macnamara 2005; Neuendorf 2002; Riff et al. 2014). It is important to note that *The Princess and the Frog*, whilst originally coded in England et al. (2011), was recoded for this study. This decision was taken to provide clarity within the analysis (i.e., with a distinctly coded group of "2000s to 2010s" movies being compared to previously coded older titles), and because *The Princess and the Frog* formed an important part of the new conceptual grouping explored within this study.

The coding framework was identical to that used by England and colleagues (2011) in order to facilitate direct comparisons among all movies, and the items within this framework have been recognized as useful and valid in previous research (Thompson and Zerbinos 1995; Towbin et al. 2004). The full coding scheme utilized in this study is outlined in Table A1, and characteristics were determined as masculine or feminine based on prior content analysis research for gender portrayal (Thompson and Zerbinos 1995; see England et al. 2011 for full review). Prince and princess characters were assessed for both the masculine and feminine traits and a code was assigned for each characteristic or behavior based on the following criteria: (a) whenever the observed prince/princess exhibited the characteristic, (b) when another character described the prince/princess as possessing the characteristic, (c) when the characteristic occurred for more than 3 s (i.e., in rare instances when a characteristic was exhibited for longer than 3 s, it was tallied once per 3 s demonstration), (d) when the prince/princess performed a characteristic behavior (e.g., tending to his/her physical appearance) and the screen's image changed briefly but then returned to the character, who continued to perform that same act (i.e., this would receive two tallies for that code). The five "2000s to 2010s" movies were also coded for instances of rescuing conducted by the prince and princess characters, as well as the number of times they were rescued, with qualitative observations noted for climactic rescue(s) that occurred at the end of the movie. In addition, all movies, including those originally utilized in England et al. (2011), were coded categorically for the romantic resolution of the movie, namely whether the prince and princess had significant romantic involvement, marriage or the suggestion of 'happily ever after' (1), or whether the princess was single (0).

Table 3. Total Codes and Percentage of Total Behavior Coded as Masculine in Princes and Princesses across "1930s to 1950s", "1980s to 1990s" and "2000s to 2010s" Princess Movies.

Movie	Year	Prince			Princess		
		Total Codes	% Masculine Characteristics	M	Total Codes	% Masculine Characteristics	M
"1930s to 1950s"				45			13
Snow White	1937	22	54		150	9	
Cinderella	1950	7	29		229	18	
Sleeping Beauty	1959	111	53		86	12	
"1980s to 1990s"				59			42
The Little Mermaid	1989	130	60		262	39	
Beauty and the Beast	1991	85	64		164	47	
Aladdin	1992	172	37		127	39	
Pocahontas	1995	212	55		235	45	
Mulan	1998	61	80		208	42	
"2000s to 2010s"				39			53
The Princess and the Frog	2009	189	32		174	47	
Tangled	2010	447	42		474	44	
Brave	2012	14	36		309	62	
		16	44				
		12	33				
Frozen	2013	286	41		279	48	
		136	43		183	52	
Moana	2016				685	60	

Soc. Sci. **2018**, *7*, 245

Three undergraduate research assistants were intensively trained by the first and second authors of this study on how to use the coding system, using Disney movies that were not part of the current study. Disney movies were utilized to ensure that coders were familiar with the style of animation employed in such films, including how characters engage in particular behaviors. Lead and undergraduate coders then completed coding separately for the first ten minutes of the four target movies coded in this study. After the lead and undergraduate coder had completed coding this ten-minute segment for princess characteristics, inter-coder reliability analysis was conducted using Krippendorff's alpha (KALPHA, Krippendorf 2004) to compare the frequency of codes for each behavior (shown in Appendix A). Values ranged from 0.78 to 0.99 suggesting very high inter-coder reliability across all characteristics. In addition, KALPHA values for each movie (across all behaviors) were computed, with values of 0.97 (*The Princess and the Frog*), 0.94 (*Tangled*), 0.99 (*Brave*), 0.97 (*Frozen*), and 0.99 (*Moana*), demonstrating high inter-coder reliability. Any significant discrepancies that arose were examined and reviewed until agreement was reached on how to code future instances of said behaviors. Satisfied with high reliability values and resolution of inconsistencies, undergraduate coders then coded the remainder of each target movie.

Author Contributions: Conceptualization, B.H. and D.E.; methodology, D.E. and K.L.; formal analysis, B.H. and D.E.; investigation, B.H., D.E. and K.L.; resources, E.S. and L.H.; data curation, B.H. and K.L.; writing—original draft preparation, B.H.; writing—review and editing, B.H. and D.E.; project administration, B.H. and K.L.

Funding: This research received no external funding.

Conflicts of Interest: The authors declare no conflict of interest.

Appendix A. Full Coding Scheme

Table A1. Full Coding Scheme.

Characteristic	Description	Inter-Coder Reliability
Masculine		0.87
Curious about princess	Exhibiting a studious, concerned expression when looking at the princess. This behavior suggested that the female had a mystique that was captivating and romantically compelling. This was only coded for the prince characters.	1.00
Wants to explore	To search for, to investigate, to want to find out or explore the unknown.	0.99
Physically strong	Hitting or moving something, providing evidence that the character had a strong physical effect on the person or object. This was different from a simple athletic display. There was a separate code for athletic, defined below, and the codes were mutually exclusive, as it was understood that displays of physical strength often incorporated some athleticism.	0.96
Assertive	Insistence upon a right or claim, the action of declaring or positively stating. Assertiveness included polite assertiveness with a hint of aggression. Assertiveness was a strong, direct assertion of a position or idea.	0.99
Unemotional	Repression of emotion, indifference to pleasure or pain. A character was unemotional in response to something that might seem to warrant an emotional response, such as a death	1.00

Table A1. *Cont.*

Characteristic	Description	Inter-Coder Reliability
Independent	Not depending on the authority of another, autonomous, self-governing. A character was considered independent when performing an independent action against many, being alone when it was not the norm, or not participating in the expected culture.	1.00
Athletic	A specific jump or kick that was large enough to require some athleticism. Running was also coded as athletic.	1.00
Engaging in intellectual activity	Engaging the intellect, including reading or showing the use of thought.	0.97
Inspires fear	Causing someone to respond with fear, which is defined as uneasiness caused by the sense of impending danger. This includes portraying violence and aggression, intimidation, or unintentionally inspiring fear as well.	0.97
Brave	Courageous, daring, intrepid. Bravery often involved a rescue or leadership in the face of danger.	1.00
Described as physically attractive (masculine)	A character's expression about the handsomeness of the prince.	1.00
Gives advice	Providing suggestions, recommendations or consultation. This was coded regardless of whether advice was asked for or whether it was warranted, appreciated, or helpful.	1.00
Leader	One who leads, a commander. Leader was only coded if the character was leading a group of people, not animals and not just him- or herself. It also was only used to describe physical leadership in which a person is seen in front of and directing people and involved giving orders.	0.99
Feminine		
Tends to physical appearance	Adjusting physical appearance for the purpose of making it look better or to draw attention to it.	0.78
Physically weak	Not being able to succeed in something that takes physical strength. It was often accompanied by needing help or else failing.	1.00
Submissive	Yielding to power or authority, humble and ready obedience. This trait was usually in response to another character's assertiveness.	0.96
Shows emotion	The expression of both positive and negative representation of feeling. This was only coded for princes because initial piloting of the coding scheme indicated princesses consistently displayed emotion at each opportunity throughout and it was unreasonable to code.	1.00
Affectionate	Having warm regard or love for a person or animal, fond, loving. This required direct interaction and required a physical display of love such as a hug, a kiss, or an individual touch for the point of illustrating affection.	0.93
Nurturing	To care for and encourage the growth or development of, to foster. Being nurturing required direct interaction and was often shown as mothering. It involved prolonged touching and attention in a soothing manner (different than a brief instance of affection) or lending care and help in a loving way to either animals or people.	1.00

Table A1. *Cont.*

Characteristic	Description	Inter-Coder Reliability
Sensitive	Perception, knowledge, connected with. This code was distinguished as a form of empathy, as being sensitive required being aware of another person's or animal's issues from a distance without interacting directly with them at that time.	1.00
Tentative	In an experimental manner, uncertain, cautious, seen in behavior or speech.	0.99
Helpful	Rendering or affording help, useful when assistance is needed. This required a specific action performed that gave another person or animal direct assistance. It was not used in a broader way to describe a character's role in a scene.	0.99
Troublesome	Causing trouble, turmoil, disturbance. This was recorded when the character was being discussed by other characters in a way that made clear that the character had caused trouble that others were trying to solve.	1.00
Fearful	An instance of emotion, a particular apprehension of some future evil, a state of alarm or dread.	1.00
Ashamed	Affected with shame, the painful emotion arising from the consciousness of dishonoring and guilt. While both characters were eligible to be coded for ashamed, it was only portrayed by the princesses and thus is considered a female trait.	1.00
Collapses crying	The character puts his/her face down, such that it was no longer visible, and cries, usually in rocking shakes and sobs. Sitting and crying while showing the face did not count; the character must have thrown him/herself on or against something (e.g., a bed, the floor) in a statement of physical and mental helplessness.	1.00
Described as physically attractive (feminine)	Another character's expression about the beauty of the princess.	1.00
Asks for or accepts advice or help	The character asks directly for help, or needs assistance and is open to receiving assistance such that it is clear the character wants it and accepts it. Assistance could be physical, mental, or emotional.	1.00
Victim	Subjected to torture by another, one who suffers severely in body or property through cruel or oppressive treatment. Physical harm or abuse was used as a defining factor in this code. Victimization was coded even if it was voluntary.	1.00

References

Abersol, Kaitlin. 2014. How Fourth-Wave Feminism is Changing Disney's Princesses. Available online: http://www.highbrowmagazine.com/4388-how-fourth-wave-feminism-changing-disney-s-princesses (accessed on 1 April 2017).

Aubrey, Jennifer Stevens, and Kristen Harrison. 2004. The gender-role content of children's favorite television programs and its links to their gender-related perceptions. *Media Psychology* 6: 111–46. [CrossRef]

Baker, Kaysee, and Arthur Raney. 2007. Equally Super? Gender-role stereotyping of superheroes in children's animated programs. *Mass Communication and Society* 10: 25–41. [CrossRef]

Baker-Sperry, Lori. 2007. The production of meaning through peer interaction: Children and Walt Disney's Cinderella. *Sex Roles* 56: 717–27. [CrossRef]

Baker-Sperry, Lori, and Liz Grauerholz. 2003. The pervasiveness and persistence of the feminine beauty ideal in children's fairy tales. *Gender & Society* 17: 711–26. [CrossRef]

Baumgardner, Jennifer. 2011. *F'em! Goo Goo, Gaga, and Some Thoughts on Balls*. Berkeley: Seal Press.

Bem, Sandra. 1974. The measurement of psychological androgyny. *Journal of Consulting and Clinical Psychology* 42: 155–62. [CrossRef] [PubMed]

Bem, Sandra. 1975. Sex role adaptability: One consequence of psychology androgyny. *Journal of Personality and Social Psychology* 31: 634–43. [CrossRef]

Bem, Sandra. 1981. Gender schema theory: A cognitive account of sex typing. *Psychological Review* 88: 354–64. [CrossRef]

Béres, Laura. 1999. Beauty and the Beast: The romanticization of abuse in popular culture. *European Journal of Cultural Studies* 2: 191–207. [CrossRef]

Best, Joel, and Kathleen S. Lowney. 2009. The disadvantage of a good reputation: Disney as a target for social problems claims. *The Sociological Quarterly* 50: 431–49. [CrossRef]

Blakemore, Judith E. Owen, Sheri A. Berenbaum, and Lynn S. Liben. 2009. *Gender Development*. New York: Psychology Press.

Box Office Mojo. 2011. Tangled (2010). Available online: http://www.boxofficemojo.com/movies/?id=rapunzel.htm (accessed on 4 May 2017).

Box Office Mojo. 2013. Brave (2012). Available online: http://www.boxofficemojo.com/movies/?id=bearandthebow.htm (accessed on 4 May 2017).

Box Office Mojo. 2014. Frozen (2013) International Box Office Results. Available online: http://www.boxofficemojo.com/movies/?id=frozen2013.htm (accessed on 4 May 2017).

Box Office Mojo. 2017. Moana (2016). Available online: http://www.boxofficemojo.com/movies/?id=disney1116.htm (accessed on 4 May 2017).

Brave. 2012. Directed by Mark Andrews, and Brenda Chapman. Burbank: Walt Disney Studios Motion Pictures.

Brown, Lyn Mikel, Sharon Lamb, and Mark Tappan. 2009. *Packaging Boyhood: Saving Our Sons from Superheroes, Slackers and Other Media Stereotypes*. New York: St. Martin's Press.

Browne, Beverly A. 1998. Gender stereotypes in advertising on children's television in the 1990s: A cross-national analysis. *Journal of Advertising* 27: 83–96. [CrossRef]

Bryman, Alan. 1999. The Disneyization of Society. *The Sociological Review* 47: 25–47. [CrossRef]

Bussey, Kay, and Albert Bandura. 1999. Social cognitive theory of gender development and differentiation. *Psychological Review* 106: 676–713. [CrossRef] [PubMed]

Calvert, Sandra L., Jennifer A. Kotler, Sean M. Zehnder, and Erin M. Shockey. 2003. Gender stereotyping in children's reports about educational and informational television programs. *Media Psychology* 5: 139–62. [CrossRef]

Cheu, Johnson. 2013. *Diversity in Disney Films: Critical Essays on Race, Ethnicity, Gender, Sexuality and Disability*. London: McFarland.

Cokely, Carrie L. 2005. Someday my prince will come: Disney, the heterosexual Imaginary and animated film. In *Thinking Straight: The Power, the Promise, and the Paradox of Heterosexuality*. Edited by Chrys Ingraham. London: Routledge, pp. 167–82.

Collins, Rebecca L. 2011. Content analysis of gender roles in media: Where are we now and where should we go? *Sex Roles* 64: 290–98. [CrossRef]

Connell, Raewyn. 2005. *Masculinities*. Berkeley: University of California Press.

Coyne, Sarah, Jennifer Ruh Linder, Eric E. Rasmussen, David A. Nelson, and Kevin M. Collier. 2014. It's a bird! It's a plane! It's a gender stereotype!: Longitudinal associations between superhero viewing and gender stereotyped play. *Sex Roles* 70: 416–30. [CrossRef]

Coyne, Sarah, Jennifer Ruh Linder, Eric E. Rasmussen, David A. Nelson, and Victoria Birkbeck. 2016. Pretty as a princess: Longitudinal effects of engagement with Disney princesses on gender stereotypes, body esteem, and prosocial behavior in children. *Child Development* 87: 1909–25. [CrossRef] [PubMed]

Davis, Amy M. 2006. *Good Girls & Wicked Witches: Women in Disney's Feature Animation*. Hertfordshire: John Libbey Publishing Ltd.

Davis, Amy M. 2013. *Handsome Heroes & Vile Villains: Men in Disney's Feature Animation*. Hertfordshire: John Libbey Publishing Ltd.

Dill, Karen E., and Kathryn P. Thill. 2007. Video game characters and the socialisation of gender roles: Young people's perceptions mirror sexist media depictions. *Sex Roles* 57: 851–64. [CrossRef]

Donaldson, Mike. 1993. What is hegemonic masculinity? *Theory and Society* 22: 643–57. [CrossRef]

Do-Rozario, Rebecca-Anne C. 2004. The princess and the magic kingdom: Beyond nostalgia, the function of the Disney princess. *Women's Studies in Communication* 27: 34–59. [CrossRef]

Dundes, Lauren. 2001. Disney's modern heroine Pocahontas: Revealing age-old gender stereotypes and role discontinuity under a façade of liberation. *The Social Science Journal* 38: 353–65. [CrossRef]

Dundes, Lauren, Madeline Streiff, and Zachary Streiff. 2018. Storm Power, an Icy Tower and Elsa's Bower: The Winds of Change in Disney's Frozen. *Social Sciences* 7: 86. [CrossRef]

Dunsmore, Carrie. 2017. Disney's Moana is a Princess Head and Shoulders (and Feet) above the Rest. Available online: https://www.washingtonpost.com/news/parenting/wp/2017/02/09/disneys-moana-is-a-princess-head-and-shoulders-and-feet-above-the-rest/?noredirect=on&utm_term=.9de019963533 (accessed on 19 April 2018).

Duralde, Alonso. 2016. Dwayne Johnson Invigorates Disney's South Seas Saga. Available online: https://www.thewrap.com/moana-review-dwayne-johnson-invigorates-disneys-south-seas-saga/ (accessed on 19 April 2018).

Eagly, Alice H. 2013. *Sex Differences in Social Behavior: A Social-Role Interpretation*. Hillsdale: Lawrence Erlbaum.

Eagly, Alice H., Wendy Wood, and Amanda B. Diekman. 2000. Social role theory of sex differences and similarities: A current appraisal. In *The Developmental Social Psychology of Gender*. Edited by Thomas Eckes and Hanns M. Trautner. Mahwah: Lawrence Erlbaum Associates, pp. 123–74.

Eggermont, Steven. 2006. Television viewing and adolescents' judgment of sexual request scripts: A latent growth curve analysis in early and middle adolescence. *Sex Roles* 55: 457–68. [CrossRef]

England, Dawn E., Lara Descartes, and Melissa A. Collier-Meek. 2011. Gender role portrayal and the Disney princesses. *Sex Roles* 64: 555–67. [CrossRef]

Foote, Lena. 2010. "I Want to be a Princess Too": Exploring the Blackout of Disney's Princesses and Controversies Surrounding The Princess and the Frog and Its Effects on African American Girls. *Film Matters* 2: 13–22. [CrossRef]

Frozen. 2013. Directed by Chris Buck and Jennifer Lee. Burbank: Walt Disney Studios Motion Pictures.

Frueh, Terry, and Paul E. McGhee. 1975. Traditional sex role development and the amount of time spent watching television. *Developmental Psychology* 11: 109. [CrossRef]

Garabedian, Juliana. 2014. Animating gender roles: How Disney is redefining the modern princess. *James Madison Undergraduate Research Journal* 2: 22–25.

Garlen, Julie C., and Jennifer A. Sandlin. 2017. Happily (n)ever after: The cruel optimism of Disney's romantic ideal. *Feminist Media Studies* 17: 957–71. [CrossRef]

Gerbner, George, Larry Gross, Michael Morgan, and Nancy Signorielli. 1980. The mainstreaming" of America. Violence Profile No. 11. *Journal of Communication* 20: 10–27. [CrossRef]

Gerbner, George, Larry Gross, Michael Morgan, and Nancy Signorielli. 1994. Growing up with television: The cultivation perspective. In *Media Effects: Advances in Theory and Research*. Edited by Jennings Bryant and Doli Zillmann. Hillsdale: Lawrence Erlbaum Associates, Inc., pp. 17–41.

Gill, Rosalind. 2014. Powerful women, vulnerable men and post-feminist masculinity in men's popular fiction. *Gender and Language* 8: 185–204. [CrossRef]

Gillam, Ken, and Shannon R. Wooden. 2008. Post-princess models of gender: The new man in Disney/Pixar. *Journal of Popular Film and Television* 36: 2–8. [CrossRef]

Giroux, Henry A., and Grace Pollock. 2010. *The Mouse That Roared: Disney and the End of Innocence*. Lanham: Rowman & Littlefield.

Golden, Julia C., and Jennifer Wallace Jacoby. 2017. Playing Princess: Preschool Girls' Interpretations of Gender Stereotypes in Disney Princess Media. *Sex Roles*, 1–15. [CrossRef]

Gomez, Jeff. 2014. Why 'Frozen' Became the Biggest Animated Movie of All Time. Available online: http://www.businessinsider.com/why-frozen-is-a-huge-success-2014--4?IR=T (accessed on 5 May 2017).

Graves, Sherryl Browne. 1999. Television and prejudice reduction: When does television as a vicarious experience make a difference? *Journal of Social Issues* 55: 707–25. [CrossRef]

Gregory, Sarita. 2010. Disney's Second Line: New Orleans, Racial Masquerade, and the Reproduction of Whiteness in The Princess and the Frog. *Journal of African American Studies* 14: 432–49. [CrossRef]

Griffin, Sean. 2000. *Tinker Belles and Evil Queens: The Walt Disney Company from the Inside Out*. New York: NYU Press.

Hartwell, Lisa M. 2015. A Content Analysis of Gender Portrayals in Disney Films in Comparison to Miyazaki Films. Unpublished Bachelor's thesis, University of Pittsburgh, Pittsburgh, PA, USA.

Hefner, Veronica, Rachel-Jean Firchau, Katie Norton, and Gabriella Shevel. 2017. Happily Ever After? A Content Analysis of Romantic Ideals in Disney Princess Films. *Communication Studies* 68: 511–32. [CrossRef]

Hentges, Beth, and Kim Case. 2013. Gender representations on Disney Channel, Cartoon Network, and Nickelodeon broadcasts in the United States. *Journal of Children & Media* 7: 319–33. [CrossRef]

Herrett-Skjellum, Jannifer, and Mike Allen. 1996. Television programming and sex stereotyping: A meta-analysis. In *Communication Yearbook 19*. Edited by Brant R. Burleson. Thousand Oaks: SAGE, pp. 663–80.

Hine, Benjamin, Katarina Ivanovic, and Dawn England. 2018. From the sleeping princess to the world-saving daughter of the chief: Examining young children's perceptions of 'old' versus 'new' Disney princess characters. *Social Sciences* 7: 161. [CrossRef]

Hogg, Michael A., Deborah J. Terry, and Katherine M. White. 1995. A tale of two theories: A critical comparison of identity theory with social identity theory. *Social Psychology Quarterly* 58: 355–69. [CrossRef]

Holmes, Bjarne M. 2007. In search of my one-and-only": Romance-related media and beliefs in romantic relationship destiny. *The Electronic Journal of Communication* 17: 1–29.

Hugel, Melissa. 2013. How Disney Princesses Went from Passive Damsels to Active Heroes. Available online: https://mic.com/articles/73093/how-disney-princesses-went-from-passive-damsels-to-active-heroes#.lTo66Am78 (accessed on 25 March 2017).

Hust, Stacey J. T., and Jane D. Brown. 2008. Gender, media use, and effects. In *The Handbook of Children, Media, and Development*. Edited by Sandra L. Calvert and Barbara J. Wilson. Oxford and Malden: Blackwell, pp. 98–120.

John, Beynon. 2002. Masculinities and the notion of 'crisis'. In *Masculinities and Culture*. Edited by Beynon John. Philadelphia: Open University Press.

Kollmayer, Marlene, Marie-Therese Schultes, Barbara Schober, Tanja Hodosi, and Christiane Spiel. 2018. Parents' judgments about the desirability of toys for their children: Associations with gender role attitudes, gender-typing of toys, and demographics. *Sex Roles*, 1–13. [CrossRef] [PubMed]

Koonikova, Maria. 2014. "How Frozen" Took over the World. Available online: http://www.newyorker.com/science/maria-konnikova/how-frozen-took-over-the-world (accessed on 25 February 2017).

Krippendorf, Klaus. 2004. *Content Analysis: An Introduction to Its Methodology*. Thousand Oaks: SAGE.

Lacroix, Celeste. 2004. Images of animated others: The orientalization of Disney's cartoon heroines from the Little Mermaid to the Hunchback of Notre Dame. *Popular Communication* 2: 213–29. [CrossRef]

Leaper, Campbell, Lisa Breed, Laurie Hoffman, and Carly Ann Perlman. 2002. Variations in the gender-stereotyped content of children's television cartoons across genres. *Journal of Applied Social Psychology* 32: 1653–62. [CrossRef]

Lemish, Dafna. 2010. *Screening Gender on Children's Television: The Views of Producers around the World*. New York: Routledge.

Li-Vollmer, Meredith, and Mark LaPointe. 2003. Gender transgression and villainy in animated film. *Popular Communication* 1: 89–109. [CrossRef]

Lopreore, Katie M. 2016. Gender Role Portrayals of Modern Disney Royalty: Stereotypical or Androgynous? Unpublished Master's thesis, Middle Tennessee State University, Murfreesboro, TN, USA.

Luther, Catherine A., and Robert Legg, Jr. 2010. Gender differences in depictions of social and physical aggression in children's television cartoons in the US. *Journal of Children & Media* 4: 191–205. [CrossRef]

Macaluso, Michael. 2018. Postfeminist Masculinity: The New Disney Norm? *Social Sciences* 7: 221. [CrossRef]

Machado, Yolanda. 2016. Directors Reveal How They Made Disney's Next Hit. Available online: https://www.moviefone.com/2016/11/23/moana-directors-reveal-how-they-made-disneys-next-hit/ (accessed on 19 April 2018).

Macnamara, Jim R. 2005. Media content analysis: Its uses, benefits and best practice methdology. *Asia-Pacific Public Relations Journal* 6: 1–34.

Marsh, Sarah. 2016. The Gender-Fluid Generation: Young People on Being Male, Female or Non-Binary. Available online: https://www.theguardian.com/commentisfree/2016/mar/23/gender-fluid-generation-young-people-male-female-trans (accessed on 19 April 2018).

Martin, Carol L., and Charles F. Halverson. 1981. A Schematic Processing Model of Sex Typing and Stereotyping in Children. *Child Development* 52: 1119–34. [CrossRef]

Martin, Carol L., Diane N. Ruble, and Joel Szkrybalo. 2002. Cognitive Theories of Early Gender Development. *Psychological Bulletin* 128: 903–33. [CrossRef] [PubMed]

Martin, Carol L., Naomi C. Z. Andrews, Dawn E. England, Kristina Zosuls, and Diane N. Ruble. 2016. A dual identity approach for conceptualizing and measuring children's gender identity. *Child Development*. [CrossRef] [PubMed]

Matyas, Vanessa. 2010. A Textual Analysis of Race and Gender in Disney Princess Films. Unpublished Master's thesis, McMaster University, Hamilton, ON, Canada.

Mead, George H. 1934. *Mind, Self & Society*. Edited by Charles W. Morris. Chicago: University of Chicago Press, pp. 227–34.

Moana. 2016. Directed by Ron Clements and John Musker. Burbank: Walt Disney Studios Motion Pictures.

Morr-Serewicz, Mary C., and Elaine Gale. 2008. First-date scripts: Gender role, context, and relationship. *Sex Roles* 58: 149–64. [CrossRef]

Neuendorf, Kimberly A. 2002. *The Content Analysis Guidebook*. Thousand Oaks: SAGE.

Ngata, Tina. 2016. Despite Claims of Authenticity, Disney's Moana Still Offensive. Available online: http://www.risingupwithsonali.com/despite-claims-of-authenticity-disneys-moana-still-offensive (accessed on 19 April 2018).

Northup, Temple, and Carol M. Liebler. 2010. The good, the bad, and the beautiful: Beauty ideals on the Disney and Nickelodeon channels. *Journal of Children & Media* 4: 265–82. [CrossRef]

Oliver, Mary B., and Stephen Green. 2001. Development of gender differences in children's response to animated entertainment. *Sex Roles* 45: 67–88. [CrossRef]

Orenstein, Peggy. 2006. What's Wrong with Cinderella? Available online: http://www.nytimes.com/2006/12/24/magazine/24princess.t.html?_r=0 (accessed on 10 December 2018).

Orenstein, Peggy. 2011. *Cinderella Ate My Daughter*. New York: HarperCollins.

Primo, Cassandra. 2018. Balancing Gender and Power: How Disney's Hercules Fails to Go the Distance. *Social Sciences* 7: 240. [CrossRef]

Pulver, Andrew. 2016. How Disney's Princesses Got Tough. Available online: https://www.theguardian.com/film/2016/may/26/has-disney-finally-given-up-on-princesses (accessed on 10 April 2017).

Ramadan, Nada. 2015. Aging With Disney and the Gendering of Evil. *Journal of Literature and Art Studies* 5: 114–27. [CrossRef]

Riff, Daniel, Stephen Lacy, and Frederick Fico. 2014. *Analyzing Media Messages: Using Quantitative Content Analysis in Research*. New York: Routledge.

Rudy, Rena M., Lucy Popova, and Daniel G. Linz. 2010a. Content Analysis [Special Issue]. *Sex Roles* 62: 705–847. [CrossRef] [PubMed]

Rudy, Rena M., Lucy Popova, and Daniel G. Linz. 2010b. The context of current content analysis of gender roles: An introduction to a special issue. *Sex Roles* 62: 705–20. [CrossRef] [PubMed]

Saladino, Caitlin J. 2014. Long May She Reign: A Rhetorical Analysis of Gender Expectations in Disney's Tangled and Disney/Pixar's Brave. Unpublished Bachelor's thesis, University of Nevada, Reno, NV, USA.

Signorielli, Nancy. 1990. Children, television, and gender roles: Messages and impact. *Journal of Adolescent Health Care* 11: 50–58. [CrossRef]

Signorielli, Nancy. 2001. Television's gender-role images and contribution to stereotyping: Past, present, and future. In *Handbook of Children and the Media*. Edited by Dorothy G. Singer and Jerome L. Singer. Thousand Oaks: Sage, pp. 341–58.

Signorielli, Nancy, George Gerbner, and Michael Morgan. 1995. Violence on television: The cultural indicators project. *Journal of Broadcasting & Electronic Media* 39: 278–83. [CrossRef]

Steyer, Isabella. 2014. Gender representations in children's media and their influence. *Campus-Wide Information Systems* 31: 171–80. [CrossRef]

Stover, Cassandra. 2013. Damsels and heroines: The conundrum of the post-feminist Disney princess. *LUX: A Journal of Trandisciplinary Writing and Research from Claremont Graduate University* 2: 29. [CrossRef]

Streiff, Madeline, and Lauren Dundes. 2017a. From shapeshifter to lava monster: Gender stereotypes in Disney's Moana. *Social Sciences* 6: 91. [CrossRef]

Streiff, Madeline, and Lauren Dundes. 2017b. Frozen in Time: How Disney Gender-Stereotypes Its Most Powerful Princess. *Social Sciences* 6: 38. [CrossRef]

Tangled. 2010. Directed by Nathan Greno and Byron Howard. Burbank: Walt Disney Studios Motion Pictures.

The Princess and the Frog. 2009. Directed by Ron Clements and John Musker. Burbank: Walt Disney Studios Motion Pictures.

The Walt Disney Company. 2016. Dream Big Princess. Available online: https://partners.disney.com/dream-big-princess-photo-campaign (accessed on 29 October 2018).

The Walt Disney Company. 2017. The Walt Disney Company Reports Fourth Quarter and Full Year Earnings for Fiscal 2017. Available online: https://www.thewaltdisneycompany.com/walt-disney-company-reports-fourth-quarter-full-year-earnings-fiscal-2017/ (accessed on 15 February 2018).

Thompson, Teresa, and Eugenia Zerbinos. 1995. Gender roles in animated cartoons: Has the picture changed in 20 years? *Sex Roles* 32: 651–73. [CrossRef]

To, Benjamin. 2016. Dance, Storytelling and the Art of Wayfinding: Behind the Scenes of Disney's Moana. Available online: http://www.nbcnews.com/news/asian-america/dance-storytelling-art-wayfinding-behind-scenes-disney-s-moana-n672141 (accessed on 19 April 2018).

Towbin, Mia A., Shelley A. Haddock, Toni S. Zimmerman, Lori K. Lund, and Litsa R. Tanner. 2004. Images of gender, race, age, and sexual orientation in Disney feature-length animated films. *Journal of Feminist Family Therapy* 15: 19–44. [CrossRef]

Wiersma, Beth A. 2001. The gendered world of Disney: A content analysis of gender themes in full-length animated Disney feature films [Abstract]. *Dissertation Abstracts International* 61: 4973.

Williams, Tannis M. 1981. How and what do children learn from television? *Human Communication Research* 7: 180–92. [CrossRef]

Wohlwend, Karen E. 2009. Damsels in discourse: Girls consuming and producing identity texts through Disney princess play. *Reading Research Quarterly* 44: 57–83. [CrossRef]

social sciences

Article

"I've Got to Succeed, So She Can Succeed, So We Can Succeed": Empowered Mothering, Role Fluidity, and Competition in *Incredible* Parenting

Suzan G. Brydon

Independent Researcher, Denver, CO, USA; suzanbrydon@gmail.com; Tel.: +1-314-691-4445

Received: 5 October 2018; Accepted: 23 October 2018; Published: 30 October 2018

Abstract: The social influence of Disney discourse is difficult to ignore, as is their repetitive matricide and positioning of the patriarchal and heteronormative family model in their blockbuster animated films. Yet, through its Pixar Animation Studios subsidiary, Disney has pushed progressively at the boundaries, not only in terms of animation artistry but also through the social topics explored. This study builds on previous research of male mothering in *Finding Nemo* by visiting the subsequent 11 Pixar animated films, with in-depth exploration of their most recent release, *Incredibles 2*. Ultimately, I argue that Pixar has once again opened space by embracing empowered and collaborative parenting.

Keywords: Disney; gender; motherhood; media criticism; family roles; masculinity; empowered mothering; Pixar

---

"Done properly, parenting is a heroic act.

Done properly.

I'm fortunate that it has never afflicted me." (Edna Mode, *Incredibles 2*)

1. Introduction

In 2003, Walt Disney Pictures via its Pixar Animation Studios subsidiary released *Finding Nemo*, a movie that as of 2018 has grossed one billion dollars worldwide (IMDB) and garnered the studio multiple awards, including four Academy Award nominations and an Oscar win for Best Animated Feature Film. Not only did this film entertain millions and significantly increase Disney accolades and profitability, it also became part of larger media and culture analyses of the Disney animated repertoire. In addition to the many media discussions of its creative vision and astounding box-office success, scholarly analyses abounded, ranging in topic from the beauty and finesse of the animated visual artistry (Cohen 2003) through the social and ecological impacts of anthropomorphizing animals, (Tidwell 2009; Militz and Foale 2015) to its representations of disability (Baxondale 2004; Preston 2010).

In previous research, I explored what I considered to be important about *Finding Nemo:* that for the first time in its discourse, Disney opened up space for a male character to mother (Brydon 2009). After complimenting Disney for stretching the boundaries of what mothering could look like and who could perform it, I ended my exploration by lamenting what appeared to have been a step backward in mothering representation with their 2004 release of *The Incredibles*. Creative and progressive in some ways, *The Incredibles* (2004) also relied on long-standing stereotypes about gender and family roles, with father, Bob Parr/Mr. Incredible, as a career-driven and hyper-masculine superhero focused on his breadwinning abilities and led astray by another woman, and mother, Helen/Elastigirl, as a stay at home mom who literally stretches herself thin to save her family and her marriage. In addition to their pre-verbal infant, they were joined by elementary-age son Dash Parr, whose super speed means he never sits still (epitomizing the modern ADHD-afflicted boy), and teen daughter Violet Parr, whose superpower was her ability to become invisible, especially around boys. Echoing some of my concerns, McMillan (2012) echoed many of my concerns in her analysis of the problems at the core of *The Incredibles*:

> While Bob gets his superhero groove back and Dash learns that sometimes you have to hold back in order to make the little people feel okay about themselves, Helen frets about the stability of the family and Violet gains enough confidence to ensure that she can wear more colorful clothes—a pink shirt, of course, because she's a girl—and talk to the cute boy in school. (par. 11)

Despite the impressive strength and abilities exhibited by the female superheroes in *The Incredibles*, ultimately the film emphasized the same old patriarchal, heteronormative structure we have seen in family films again and again.

It has been nearly a decade since *Finding Nemo* was released and Pixar's (therefore, Disney's) influence has only increased. Since 2000, Pixar alone has generated over $1.6 billion in gross box-office revenue for the Disney Corporation (Lynch 2018). Its financial success (via theatre sales, digital content, and merchandising) positions it as a leading cultural orator, as having the power to not only change movie history (Zorthian 2015) but to change what it means to be a person (Munkittrick 2011). As a key creator of our cultural texts of gender and family, Disney texts, generally, and Pixar's, specifically, deserve close and recurrent reflection. It is with that in mind that I explore Disney's portrayal of mothering in the years since *Finding Nemo* and of who performs it, with particular attention to its current bloc.kbuster: *Incredibles 2* (2018). What reveals itself is, in fact, a slow shift into the complexities of modern parenting and a recent embrace of empowered mothering.

Motherhood and Disney Discourse

American cultural texts (read broadly as social norms, books, media, etc.) and their consumption and utilization serve as evidence that "one is indeed not born, but must become a mother" (Coats and Fraustino 2015, p. 108). In broad cultural strokes, motherhood can be described as a state of gendered (historically female) action rooted in physical, time-consuming, hands-on care for children. This begins for many women at pregnancy, birth, and/or breastfeeding, but extends beyond that to long-term, daily nurturance and caregiving. This differs from notions of fatherhood, which Ruddick (1997) argues is rooted in three key elements: distant provision (acquiring the means to buy goods), protection (willing to show physical strength and toughness), and authority (rule-making and consequence creation). Both motherhood and fatherhood fall under the cultural concept of parenting, holistically described as the "complex, ongoing work of responding to children's needs in particular economic and social circumstances" (p. 206).

As women are not always or automatically mothers and men are not always or automatically fathers, we can think of mothering or fathering, like any stereotypically gendered behavior, as cultural performance (Butler 1990). Viewed through a feminist lens, this allows for us to separate motherhood from gender. In that way, women do not have to assume a mother identity, and men can be allowed to engage in mothering performance. This perspective differentiates mothering performance from motherhood or maternalism as a cultural construct, the latter more rooted in mother as a specific, gendered entity born to be "intuitively more empathetic, less exploitive, and more closely attuned to relational ambience than men" (Tucker, as cited by (O'Reilly 2016, loc. 209)). By separating mothering from motherhood, we make it easier to see mothering as "work that is valuable to society ... [but that] is not, and should not be, the sole responsibility and duty of mothers" (loc. 243). Taking a more performance-based approach allows us to identify a set of parameters to define what mothering could mean in a culture or specific discourse, who is performing it, and what constitutes "good" or "bad" mothering.

Western media representations of good mothering are rooted in privilege. They are narrow in scope, heteronormative, white, and upper/middle class in expectations of what successful or good appears to be. Due to the enormous impact of the Walt Disney Corporation's position as primary cultural storyteller for families and children, its representations of mothering are arguably some of the most important to explore. Not only is Disney's impact on American families significant, but as Zipes (1999) notes, families in Disney films are portrayed as models of behavior to be emulated and their storytelling "colonizes other national audiences" (p. 352). The fairy tale has long been "used . . . to comment on the civilizing process and socialization" (p. 337) of a culture and most commonly "reinforced patriarchal symbolic order based on rigid notions of sexuality and gender" (p. 338), and it is on these storytelling origins that the Disney empire stands. Fraustino (2015) takes that claim further by emphasizing the increase in power Disney has begun to wield now that their stories are truly timeless via digital formats that can be bought, streamed, purchased, and replayed by children for decades while parents are busy in the other room—the modern day "Mommy's little helpers" (p. 141). Suffice it to say, it seems impossible to overstate the impact of the Disney discourse, which is why so much scholarship exists there.

For more than half a century, Disney tales were fairy tales; however, the original tales written by the Grimm brothers, Hans Christian Andersen, and others, upon whose bones the Disney stories were fully fleshed, did not perpetuate the WWII American Dream patriarchy seen in most Disney films. The original stories were nearly always altered by Walt Disney Studios to kill off caregivers (mothers much more than fathers) under the guise of narrative plot development, and most were sanitized to eliminate any excessive violence or transgression that conservative Western families might find unpalatable. In terms of family formation, Disney has preferred the stork method of infant delivery and the firm positioning of women as love interests, first, and mothers, a close second. Young Disney heroines are "twitterpatt[ed] . . . into idealizing the romance that leads to the making of the patriarchal family" (Fraustino 2015, p. 129) but are not shown engaging in the "real cycle of life—of menstruation, sex, pregnancy, and parenting (because we all know how little mothering Disney heroines get)" (pp. 131–32). Although this sanitization may have originally developed as a response to constraints by the Motion Picture Production Code of what could be shown on the screen, those constraints expired in 1968, yet the sanitization remained far beyond that expiration date. Intentional or not, these widely consumed cultural texts have played a part in preserving the patriarchal order of power. (p. 131) against which women have struggled for decades. This proffered perspective—that Disney cinematic messaging is powerful and patriarchal—is certainly not new, nor is the backlash that feminist critiques of Disney films have prompted. Understandably, our culture learned to see the world through the Disney lens for so long that "such scrutiny isn't easy for parents and grandparents who grew up internalizing the same messages, including the mothering ideology that reproduces not only itself but also male dominance in society" (Fraustino 2015, p. 144). Yet, decades of analyses of Disney texts by scores of scholars from all disciplines support the stance that little changed with mothering representation between its first full-length animated film release in 1937 and *Finding Nemo* (2003).

Disney mothers have been consistently portrayed, when they are portrayed at all. Mothers in the last decade of the Disney repertoire remain nearly invisible, as matricide (or, more generously, mother absence) has long been a fairy tale action device and remains Disney's modus operandi for character development and audience bonding with the protagonist. Killing the parent (usually the mother) allows the young hero(ine) to mature through the precarious position it places the orphaned children in. There has been an historical dearth of mothers in Disney's animated fare and mothers with integral story roles in the last ten years remaining limited. As of 2006, only 10 of Disney's 39 animated films with sustained plots featured living mothers, and all of those mothers were either killed during the film or incapable "of protecting their offspring from harm" (Davis 2006, p. 102). When featured, though, Disney mothers have traditionally been written as hyper-feminine, in their texts (e.g., use of relational language, emotional and timid nonverbals such as crying and gasping, engaging in selfless and service-focused actions) and their somatexts, or texts of the body (e.g., drawn diminutively with graceful gestures and hourglass figures, excessive makeup, stereotypically feminine clothing, interacting through touch and dance). To quote the Disney definition verbatim:

"Well, a mother, a real mother is the most wonderful person in the world. She's the angel voice that bids you goodnight, kisses your cheek, whispers, 'Sleep tight' . . . The helping hand that guides you along, whether you're right, whether you're wrong . . . Your mother and mine." ('Your Mother and Mine', sung by Wendy (Peter Pan 1953))

Before *Nemo,* I argued that Disney films retaining mothers as part of the story often fell into one of four types: the animalistic mother (e.g., *Dumbo* (1941); *Bambi* (1942); *The AristoCats* (1970); *Tarzan* (1999)) who performs mothering instinctually and stereotypically; the anthropomorphized mother (e.g., *Beauty and the Beast* (1991); *Pocahontas* (1995)) who is often older and immobilized by her current position; the fragmented mother (e.g., *Lady and the Tramp* (1955); *The Rescuers Down Under* (1990); *Toy Story* (1995)) who is an incomplete, disembodied person with no literal voice; and the mother of color (e.g., *Mulan* (1998)). Regardless of type, however, "Disney characters engaged in mothering . . . have been required to be women and to desire an existence in/around the home" (Brydon 2009, p. 136). With *Finding Nemo,* however, I proffered there was a disruption, less so to the mothering norms as to the allowance of who could perform it. In *Nemo,* not only was the father, Marlin, allowed to live—which was not completely unheard of in Disney discourse (per Davis (2006), through 2006, 19 out of 39 films feature a father)—he was also different. As Disney defined it, Marlin was allowed to mother. Marlin shared food, groomed, nurtured, and taught. He tucked Nemo in, displayed emotions previously assigned on screen only to women like fear and worry, and was drawn with a feminine somatext (smaller body shape, timid movements, emotional gestures). Even better than previous Disney mothers, there was no romantic build up in Marlin's storyline. He was a dedicated, solely-focused caregiver. Nemo came first; all else came second. Perhaps most importantly, Marlin performed mothering as a part of unremarkable daily life. No one, himself included, mentioned it as unusual or anything other than expected. He was simply the primary nurturer. In this way, Marlin performed as mother within the Disney discourse.

Since *Finding Nemo,* the Walt Disney Company has increased the number of films released featuring young protagonists with living, loving mothers (even if briefly), such as *The Princess and the Frog* (2009); *Tangled* (2010); *Frozen* (2013); *Inside Out* (2015); *Finding Dory* (2016); *Moana* (2016); and *Coco* (2012). Unfortunately, in each case mother's love is sparing as the child spends most of the film separated from the mother and battling the adversities that accompany that separation. Explorations of Disney films by Holcomb et al. (2015) support the finding that there have been advancements in the nurturing and caregiving behaviors engaged in by parents, men in particular, in Disney's animated films, especially in the area of emotional nurturing and protection. Yet, they also confirm the continuing absence of strong mother roles. Importantly, they label much of this masculine caregiving in Disney animation as being performed by created kin and othermothers (communal and/or foster caregivers) and not by traditional, biological fathers. Arguably, widespread distribution of blockbuster films that allow communal childrearing is positive and progressive. The catch is, when a father is present in the film, shifting the nurturance to an othermother implies the father is unable or unwilling to perform that function. For example, positioning Bambi's father as overarching protector of the forest and Bambi within it shows some level of involvement, yet visually drawing him as distant and removed from Bambi's day-to-day life remains problematic. And, a nice as it may be to hear Jasmine's father, the Sultan, in *Aladdin* articulate interest in his daughter's happiness, he spends most the movie in his chambers playing with toys and attempting to transfer his responsibility of her caregiving by finding her a spouse (Åström 2017).

Within the Disney realm, the Pixar Animation Studio films have arguably driven the most progressive gender and family narratives. As Gillam and Wooden (2008) noted, Pixar has helped reshape animated images of masculinity in films such as *Toy Story* and *The Incredibles* (and I would add *Up* (2009)) by emasculating alpha-males, allowing them to engage in emotional sharing, vulnerability, and nurturing same-sex male bonding. That progressive brush stroke was taken a step further in *Finding Nemo,* as Pixar illustrated widescreen space for a man to specifically perform mothering. Marlin's mothering performance in his environment was indicative of what Gatens (1999) positioned as key to mothering: physical and emotional labor, domesticity, and nurture. Although his actions while his wife was alive were traditional and heteronormative, including acting as breadwinner ("Did your man deliver, or did your man deliver?") and seeking sexual play as a way to "win back [his] partner's attention" (Gatrell 2004, p. 131), through the majority of the film he performs mother. Marlin's performance remains distinct even from Sully's in *Monsters* (2001) or, later, from Mr. Fredrickson's in *Up*. Despite Sully exhibiting many of the same maternal behaviors, as he cuddles and nurtures the human baby, Boo, who gets stranded in Monstropolis, Sully's love may be permanent, but his caregiving is temporary. Here, he serves as created kin. He is not father to Boo; instead, he serves as protector for the child until she can be returned to her family. In this way, like Mr. Fredrickson in *Up*, who is forced to serve as temporary caregiver for Russell when the boy is inadvertently dragged along on Mr. Fredrickson's escape from the city, the caregiving, albeit protective and necessary, is short-lived.

Since 2009 when I last explored the Disney film repertoire, Disney's Pixar division has released 11 full-length, animated feature films. Of those, several feature young children or adolescent protagonists receiving parenting without resorting to matricide or patricide: *Up*, *Brave* (2012), *Inside Out*, *Finding Dory*, *Coco*, and *Incredibles 2*. Of these surviving parents, Russell's mother in *Up* has less than 30 seconds of screen time and no dialogue; his father is never seen but is mentioned several times as uninvolved. In *Brave*, we see an emotionally close father-daughter relationship between Merida and her father, Fergus, rooted in a shared love for archery, outdoor activities, and eating; yet, in no way does Fergus perform Disney mothering. What Fergus seems to appreciate most about his daughter is her stereotypically masculine behavior; in other words, he loves those elements of himself that he sees in her. His screen time is, instead, spent in hyper-masculine behaviors such as fighting, excessive overeating, singing about mounting heads to walls, bucking socially finessed behaviors, and, eventually, trying to kill the mother for Merida. The movie should be commended for the complexities of the mother-daughter relationship it represents and the amount of time the mother is allowed to parent. Yet, the mother spends half of the movie as a bear and several times is physically threatening to her daughter.

Family is a key theme in *Coco*, and intergenerational, communal caregiving is prominent. Miguel's mother and father are present in the film and live and work with him (the family runs a shoe-making business), yet they interact with him in ways equal to his interaction with his grandfather and extended family members. It is Miguel's abuelita, or grandmother, who performs as primary caregiver in the film. She engages in food sharing, emotional nurturance, and primary daily decision-making and discipline in the household. Miguel's mother is virtually silent in the film, his father repeats directives from the matriarch abuelita, and Miguel spends most of the film searching for the absent father (figure), his great-great-grandfather, Ernesto de la Cruz. In *Finding Dory*, the majority of the film is focused on Dory as adult, with occasional flashbacks of her childhood and parents. And, notably, the reason Dory gets separated from her family is because she attempted to make her mother feel better after she heard her crying in an open emotional display.

2. Mothering *Incredible* Children

Disney challenged that previous discourse, however, with *Incredibles 2*. The societal influence of "family-adventure movies" like *Incredibles 2* continues to expand as "the traditional children's or family film has been upgraded with a heavy injection of spectacular adventure to appeal to teenagers and young adults as well as their parents" (Ebrahim 2014, p. 5). Unlike the previously mentioned Disney feature films, *Incredibles 2* focuses once more on the intact, white, heteronormative, nuclear family, which we've surprisingly seen very little of (the intact part, anyway, as typically both parents are not allowed to be present). In the film, Helen (Elastigirl) is given the opportunity to work (illegally) as a superhero full-time (more out of necessity than desire, as the film begins with both parents unemployed) while Bob (Mr. Incredible) serves as primary caretaker for the children. Both parents maintain relationships with the children throughout; however, Helen's screen time is primarily spent fighting the villain (notably, another woman) and protecting the city while Bob's screen time is primarily spent feeding, teaching, ensuring safety, and providing emotional nurturance. She's a motorcycle-riding, previously mohawk-sporting, fully-engaged mom who feels in many ways far superior to the men around her. With Helen at the helm, the family begins and ends the movie unified, stronger in their communal support (from each other and their superhero community) than their separation. For these reasons and more, we can view *Incredibles 2* as rooted in refreshing elements of a third-wave mothering paradigm initiated with *Finding Nemo*. This time, their progressive narrative allows for empowered mothering and role fluidity, as well as an embrace of the complexities and competitive nature of collaborative parenting.

2.1. Empowered Mothering

As in the original *Incredibles* film, each independent family member—Dash Parr (the son), Helen Parr (Elastigirl, the mother), Bob Parr (Mr. Incredible, the father), and Violet Parr (the daughter)—serves as a co-protagonist, with particular partnership between mother and father (I am excluding the baby, Jack-Jack, from the list of co-protagonists, as he is given far less screen time and, although his power comes in handy, he is primarily present when being cared for by another family member). Whether or not the children have no superhero identities because they have underdeveloped human identities or because during their lifetime superheroes have been banned is up for debate. Bob and Helen share equitably in terms of screen time and fall into what Ebrahim (2014) describes as Pixar's repetitive pattern of co-protagonist films where "two central characters . . . embark on a psychological and/or physical journey together or who are part of some kind of twosome in which their interaction is key to the characters' growth" (p. 6). However, their collaboration to save the family and the world is premised on gender role fluidity: Helen is able to fight the villain and reclaim rights for supers because Bob is at home caring for and nurturing the children.

O'Reilly (2016) denotes that "[f]eminist mothering differs from empowered mothering in so far as the mother identifies as a feminist and practices from a feminist perspective or consciousness," whereas empowered mothers "resist patriarchal motherhood simply to make the experience of mothering more rewarding for themselves and their children" (loc. 2504). Helen's Elastigirl does not act in a common, second-wave feminist way of calling for a woman to act as a "self-interested, fully realized, and autonomous unit[]" (Takševa 2018, p. 182), but instead acts as an empowered mother. In fact, although Helen embraces empowerment she seems to question any prominent discourse that would relegate her to one group or another. In both *The Incredibles* and *Incredibles 2* we are shown the same video clip of her sharing her views on patriarchal power in her pre-marriage youth: "Leave the saving of the world to the men? I don't think so." When given an updated, flashier suit with embedded technology, she voices concern about it changing her identity: "I'm not dark and angsty. I'm . . . Elastigirl!"

Repeatedly throughout the film, the villain, Evelyn, challenges Helen's perspectives on female empowerment. Evelyn seems intent on creating division between independence and interdependency. Helen, however, refuses to embrace the division. When Evelyn accuses her of having spent too much time in her husband's shadow ("Must be nice for you, being out front after all this time . . . .But, you have the stage to yourself now. People have to pay attention"), Helen, lightly mocks the accusation ("What? Like, it's a man's world and all that?"). At another point, Evelyn tries to coax a reaction after a disastrous encounter with another villain ("I'm just saying, if you had handled The Underminer alone, things would have been different."), yet Helen literally shrugs off the comment. Once Helen ultimately realizes that Evelyn is a villain, Evelyn chides her for being so bound to her interdependency ("If it wasn't for your core beliefs, we could have been friends") while Helen stands her ground ("At least I have core beliefs."). These pivotal interactions can be seen as a microcosm of the long-standing debate between third-wave and matricentric feminists, strength in self versus strength in the village. Instead of claiming a particular feminist paradigm, Helen articulates strength (and weakness) through confidence in herself and interconnectivity, through being in-relation. She successfully fights crime and captures villains alone, but importantly, she maximizes the effectiveness of her power through communal support. She moves through and experiences strength through relational support. Yet, Helen is empowered mother but not feminist mother, the first "demanding more involvement from fathers and insisting on a life outside of motherhood" but the second owning "a larger awareness of, and challenge to . . . inequities of patriarchal culture" (O'Reilly 2016, loc. 2519).

Helen never indicates she sees caregiving as her sole and primary responsibility and positions it as simply one more thing in her life. In fact, she has arguably raised her kids to believe this, as well. Violet babysits multiple times and complains to her parents about being relegated to do this "while you guys did the important stuff," yet later acknowledges the benefits of being with Jack-Jack and his extensive powers. At one point or another, each family member refers to caring for the baby as a burden (albeit obviously one of love), but they also praise him and brag about his powers. In the second half of the movie, Mr. Incredible begins to embrace his role as primary caregiver and is shown patiently and methodically teaching him, redirecting him, and praising him. At the end of the film, after catching the villain and saving the city, Helen takes the baby from Bob and says to him and Frozone, "you guys got the next shift . . . I'm beat," thus perceiving caregiving as a break from her new "day job" but also as a moment in time, not an identity.

2.2. Role Fluidity

It is not unusual for speculative fiction, one type of which is superhero fiction, to demonstrate gender fluidity. More commonly, that gender fluidity is unidirectional and more behavioral than appearance-based. Female characters are much more likely to be shown engaging in stereotypically masculine behaviors like athleticism, strength, fighting abilities, and use of weaponry (think Wonder Woman, Storm, and Gamora) than male characters are to be showing exhibiting stereotypically feminine behaviors. It is difficult to name even a few instances of this in widespread superhero films, due to our cultural "effeminophobia" (Bray 2015). "The kind of gender fluidity that allows boys to consider the possibilities of male mothering is far more likely to be stigmatized than that which allows girls to take on more masculine roles and activities" (p. 161) which "privileges hegemonically masculine gender expression in all characters, male or female" (p. 161).

In some ways, the same goes for the fluidity in *Incredibles 2*, which occurs less through blatant physical appearance fluidity than it does through the bodies-in-action. Helen kicks, fights, and punches her way through each scene, but is obviously tiny in comparison to the men and sports perfectly coifed hair and thigh-high heeled boots while she kicks butt. Of interest, Disney chose not to "queer" Elastigirl's performance while allowing her to exude strength and power; they did not de-feminize her and they did not overtly sexualize her (despite the thigh-high boots). Disney also does not take Bob's caregiving role to the point of "dragging" him into motherhood, putting him in feminine clothing as he performs traditional mothering functions, as we see when Buzz Lightyear becomes Mrs. Nesbit before he can display emotional vulnerability. Instead, Bob's giant hands are gentle when he lays the baby in the crib to sleep and his exhaustion at providing full-time care for the baby shows up via the repetitive wearing of a brown robe and a 5 o'clock shadow. When Violet, at least two feet and 150 pounds smaller than her father, exhibits fury over one of his action, Bob stands in terror in the kitchen clutching a milk container, withering before this physically diminutive girl. With physical appearance alone and bodies in situ, most heteronormative physical appearance norms remain fully intact in *Incredibles 2*.

However, role fluidity is prominent. Physical protection, strength, and breadwinning (for Helen) and physical caregiving, vulnerability, and nurturance (for Bob) are key themes. Bob expresses sincere and repeated emotional concern for his daughter when she gets stood up for her date. He also shows vulnerability with his friend after finding primary caregiving difficult: "I broke my daughter. They changed math. I was supposed to get double A batteries; I got triple A." Finally, he articulates his parenting insecurities to his daughter: "I don't know what the right thing to do is anymore. I just wanna be . . . a good dad." Later in the movie, after serving as primary caregiver through most scenes, Bob is summoned (by the villain, as it turns out) to assist his wife who is acting erratically. His first move when he greets her is not to fight or strike, as he would have historically, but instead to communicate, to listen, to understand his wife, who is under mind-control by the villain. When that does not work, he tries to block and defend himself from her attacks but does not fight back. The villain ultimately notices the traditional approach is not working, so using mind-control she has Helen distract him with a kiss (which he happily accepts). His openness to his wife's affection allows her to force a mind-control device onto him, as well. It is not until he is under the control of the villain that he reverts to his hyper-masculine, crash-and-bash ways. With his newly honed, emotional awareness, he prefers communication to confrontation.

2.3. Collaborative and Competitive Caregiving

Åström's 2017 exploration of fathers in recent animated films concludes matricide was still required in order for men to serve as successful caregivers and nurturers, noting "participatory fathers in animated films are [still] not prepared to share their children with the mothers" (p. 254). It has taken another year beyond her analysis, but it appears Disney has opted to embrace collaborative parenting. Although the opening action sequence puts initial burden on Helen for childcare—Helen first comes onscreen holding the baby and providing direction to the children about how to keep themselves and the city safe—when viewing the film as a whole, their parenting is collaborative. Both Helen and Bob engage in food sharing, teaching, disciplining, general domestic duties, and emotional and physical nurturing. Helen orders dinner for the family. Bob makes giant stacks of homemade waffles for the kids before school and does not allow them to eat "sugar bombs" for breakfast. Helen provides direction to the older kids as to how best to help protect the crowd during an attack. Bob stays up all night to learn "new math," so he can help Dash complete his homework. Bob cleans spilled cereal off the floor and sets curfews for his daughter's date. Helen insists Dash eats his vegetables before watching TV. Bob coddles the baby, reads to him, and changes diapers. Helen hugs the kids regularly and spoon-feeds the baby. Although, most scenes show them performing parenting separately, what they perform is equitable and they work collaboratively to ensure tasks are accomplished.

However, with that collaboration comes a healthy dose of competition. Helen initially voices concerns that Bob can perform equally as a parent. When deciding whether or not she should take the new superhero job, Bob encouraged her: "I'll watch the kids. No problem. It'll be easy." In response, Helen replies: "Easy, huh? You're adorable." During her first night away, he mentions Jack-Jack's name and before he can share a milestone with her, Helen leaps to the conclusion that something is wrong. When Bob gets defensive, she chides: "So, things haven't spiraled out of control the moment I left?" When Dash responds to difficulty with his math assignments with, "I'll just wait for mom," Bob replies with frustration: "What? She won't be able to help any better than I can!"Bob seems frustrated and disinterested in Helen serving as relationship liaison between him and his children and despite her initial chidings and his initial stumbles, he proves a competent caregiver. His frustration and exhaustion with what appears to be a competition builds up and ultimately spills over in a manic outburst just before he connects with his best friend: "I'm doing the math, fixing the boyfriend, and keeping the baby from turning into a monster! I'm rolling with the punches, baby!"

Interestingly, Bob's frustration over bonding and performance has emerged in real-life interviews performed with fathers who engaged in traditional mothering work, such as grooming, food sharing, emotional nurturing, and daily care:

> "The issue of relationships with children and who should mediate theses is linked with a sense of power within the parental relationship, and this might provide part of the explanation for why, once they had gained this, fathers were keen to maintain their involved status, even if this made life difficult for them at times." (Gatrell 2004, p. 145)

Yet, Gatrell (2004) notes that there is a power struggle at play in many co-parenting relationships:

> "While some women saw the practical involvement of fathers as purely positive change (often meaning that both partners could work, minimizing the amount of time spent by children with paid carers), others were territorial about their role as mother and principal carer, and did not wish to see this threatened by the father." (p. 147)

This competition glides alternatively across the public-private dichotomy. Both parents want to be successful as parents, but, both want to be successful in their careers, as well. When The Incredibles parents review the opportunity in bed and Helen balks at taking the new job, Bob persuades her on behalf of their mutual success; "You've got to, so I . . . so we can be supers again." He then jokes with her before she hits him with a pillow: "Do it, so I can do it better." As she leaves the house on her custom superbike, their conversation is caring but has traces of envy:

> Bob: "You will be great."
>
> Helen: "I WILL be great. And you will too."
>
> Bob: "We will both be great." (standing stiffly, holding the baby)

Even when Bob breaks down and experiences a manic meltdown with his friend, he remains focused on on mastering parenthood while also opening career doors for them all: "I've got to succeed, so she can succeed, so WE can succeed." And, although his desire for a successful career position is not surprising, as "the provider role is an assumption, a given" (Blankenhorn, as cited by (Ruddick 1997, p. 208)) for men in heteronormative, white middle-class families, his desire to be a successful caregiver so both he and Helen can maximize their potential is.

3. Discussion

There are glimpses of communal caregiving in *Incredibles 2*, with care provided in varying degrees by Lucius, Bob's crime fighting sidekick, Frozone, and Edna Mode, the family's superhero costume designer who ultimately serves as "auntie" and passes along caregiver training to Bob. However, the blatant family structure is traditional, heteronormative, and nuclear, defined by "a strong sense of the separation of the unit of parents and children from both a more extended kinship network and from such non-kin-related persons as servants" and "marked by a norm of partnership between husband and wife and by the special role of the mother in shaping the character of her children" (Nicholson 1997, p. 31). In several scenes, both mother and father perform to those somewhat archaic role expectations. Bob does not fully embrace caregiving until Helen is required to leave. Helen, reluctant to leave home, constantly frets over the children's well-being while she is at work. When together as a family, Helen is visually represented as the primary caregiver until the final fight sequences and closure. In that way, we could read this text as proof that Disney, yet again, required removal of the mother in order to allow Mr. Incredible, as postmodern father, to care for and bond with the children (Åström 2017), and for that matter, to allow baby Jack-Jack to realize his full powers.

For me, this interpretation is too superficial. We could just as easily read this as an acknowledgement that many mothers who remain in nuclear, heteronormative family structures also share caregiving while working outside the home in order to meet the family's financial needs. As Feasey (2013) notes, economic burden increases "with rising numbers of stay-at-home mothers who have internalized the ideology of intensive mothering demanded of the 'good' mother" (p. 28), and Disney films have traditionally romanticized stay at home mothering. Allowing Helen to fully embrace both career and mothering—and perform successfully at both—is admirable, particularly in comparison to mother representation in the previous 80 years of Disney discourse. Additionally, the fact that mothering, as performance, is embraced and engaged in by a stereotypically gendered man in *Incredibles 2* is, to me, "incredible." I recognize, of course, that this opinion, in and of itself, is troublesome. One might argue what there is to celebrate in the fact that Pixar has not allowed this to occur in over nearly a decade since the release of *Finding Nemo*. I make no apologies for finding pleasure in positive change, however minor.

Of course, by praising cinematic images of men mothering and/or fluidly exchange nurturing tasks with female parents in widespread family films, I also run the risk of perpetuating what seems to be a cinematic obsession with fathers (Bruzzi 2005). A valid point, but one that decreases the value to be gained in removing mothering as a female assignment. Takševa (2018) summarizes:

"Dominant feminist theory and the imaginary boundaries established around the field of women and gender studies are still constructed upon the assumed link between women's oppression in relation to larger social and political structures—including the assumed normative presence of the nuclear family and the public-private dichotomy—and mothering". (p. 179)

Although this film most definitely is premised on a nuclear family, we are ultimately left with the understanding that, moving forward both mom and dad will likely "shift" fluidly in and out of their public and private responsibilities equally, as the children—and the arm of justice—require.

Since the focal point of discussion here has been Disney discourse and mothering, my analysis would be incomplete if I did not mention the short film that precedes *Incredibles 2*. For years, Pixar has made it a habit of placing an animated short before their full-length animated film. Those shorts are frequently as talked about as the movie itself, and several have won Oscars for Best Animated Short Film (*Tin Toy* (1988); *For the Birdsn* (2000); *Piper* (2016)). The short film preceding *Incredibles 2* is titled *Bao* (2018) and is focused on an overprotective mother who is so desperate to maintain her control over her child (shown as a dumpling she created) and his safety that she literally eats him (or the representation of him) to keep him from leaving her. As the first Pixar short film to be created by a female Chinese–Canadian director and writer, the painstaking efforts that went in to making this film as authentic as possible to Asian-American audiences are commendable. Shi's mother even came to Pixar twice to give the crew dumpling-making lessons (Sandoval 2018). Yet, the film also serves as another chapter in the Disney women tradition, where identity is created through child nurturing and food sharing, and depression and anguish over children are common emotions.

I will, however, not resort to labeling the beautifully created short film as a step backwards. As Takševa (2018) is quick to point out: "Just as the category of woman is not universal—a stance for which academic feminism has fought long and hard to establish—the practice and experience of motherhood is not universal either, nor are the ways mothers may acquiesce to or may resist oppressive structures" (p. 183). There is benefit in continuing to explore men mothering, as well as allowing space for a broad spectrum of mothering performance, be that successful career mother, intensive mothering mother, or father mother. If, as third-wave feminist scholars postulate, mothering is one of many identities up for selection, we can allow room for an emotionally hyper-invested mother in *Bao* as much as we can allow Bob to serve as primary mother in *Incredibles 2*. That is a benefit of a matricentric perspective: it creates space for all of us to mother *Incredible* children.

Funding: This research received no external funding.

Conflicts of Interest: The author declares no conflict of interest.

References

Åström, Berit. 2017. Marginalizing Motherhood: Postfeminist Fathers and Dead Mothers in Animated Film. In *The Absent Mother in the Cultural Imagination*. Edited by Berit Åström. London: Palgrave Macmillan, pp. 241–58.

Bambi. 1942. Directed by David Hand. Burbank: Walt Disney Productions.

Bao. 2018. Directed by Domee Shi. Emeryville: Pixar Animation Studios.

Baxondale, Sallie. 2004. Memories aren't made of this: Amnesia at the movies. *British Medical Journal* 329: 18–25. [CrossRef] [PubMed]

Beauty and the Beast. 1991. Directed by Gary Trousdale, and Kirk Wise. New York: Silver Screen Partners IV.

Brave. 2012. Directed by Mark Andrews, and Brenda Chapman. Burbank: Walt Disney Studios Motion Pictures.

Bray, Danielle Bienvenue. 2015. Sissy boy mothering: Male child mother figures in middle-grade fantasy literature. *Children's Literature in Education* 46: 160–74. [CrossRef]

Bruzzi, Stella. 2005. *Bringing up Daddy: Fatherhood and Masculinity in Hollywood*. London: BFI Publishing.

Brydon, Suzan. 2009. Men at the Heart of Mothering: Finding Mother in *Finding Nemo*. *International Journal of Gender Studies* 18: 131–46. [CrossRef]

Butler, Judith. 1990. *Gender Trouble: Feminism and the Subversion of Identity*. New York: Routledge.

Coats, Karen, and Lisa Rowe Fraustino. 2015. Performing Motherhood: Introduction to a Special Issue on Mothering in Children's and Young Adult Literature. *Children's Literature in Education* 46: 107–9. [CrossRef]

Coco. 2012. Directed by John Lasseter. Emeryville: Pixar Animation Studios.

Cohen, Karl. 2003. Finding the Right CG Water and Fish in 'Nemo'. Animation World Network. Available online: https://www.awn.com/animationworld/finding-right-cg-water-and-fish-nemo (accessed on 30 September 2018).

Davis, Amy M. 2006. *Good Girls and Wicked Witches: Women in Disney's Feature Animation*. Bloomington: Indiana University Press.

Dumbo. 1941. Directed by Ben Sharpsteen. Burbank: Walt Disney Productions.

Ebrahim, Haseenah. 2014. Are the "Boys" at Pixar Afraid of Little Girls? *Journal of Film and Video* 66: 43–56. [CrossRef]

Feasey, Rebecca. 2013. From Soap Opera to Reality Programming: Examining Motherhood, Motherwork and the Maternal Role on Popular Television. *Imaginations* 4: 25–46. [CrossRef]

Finding Nemo. 2003. Directed by Andrew Stanton, and Lee Unkrich. Emeryville: Pixar Animation Studios.

Finding Dory. 2016. Directed by Andrew Stanton, and Angus MacLane. Emeryville: Pixar Animation Studios.

For the Birds. 2000. Directed by Ralph Eggelston. Emeryville: Pixar Animation Studios.

Fraustino, Lisa Rowe. 2015. "Nearly Everybody Gets Twitterpated": The Disney Version of Mothering. *Children's Literature in Education* 46: 127–44. [CrossRef]

Frozen. 2013. Directed by Chris Buck, and Jennifer Lee. Burbank: Walt Disney Studios Motion Pictures.

Gatens, Moira. 1999. Power, Bodies and Difference. In *Feminist Theory and the Body: A Reader*. Edited by Janet Price and Margrit Shildrick. New York: Routledge, pp. 227–34.

Gatrell, Caroline. 2004. *Hard Labour: The Sociology of Parenthood*. Maidenhead: McGraw-Hill Education.

Gillam, Ken, and Shannon Wooden. 2008. Post-Princess Models of Gender: The New Man in Disney/Pixar. *Journal of Popular Film and Television* 36: 2–8. [CrossRef]

Incredibles 2. 2018. Directed by Brad Bird. Emeryville: Pixar Animation Studios.

Inside Out. 2015. Directed by Peter Docter, and Ronnie Del Carmen. Emeryville: Pixar Animation Studios.

Holcomb, Jeanne, Latham Kenzie, and Fernandez-Baca Daniel. 2015. Who Cares for the Kids? Caregiving and Parenting in Disney Films. *Journal of Family Issues* 36: 1957–81. [CrossRef]

Lady and the Tramp. 1955. Directed by Clyde Geronimi, Wilfred Jackson, and Hamilton Luske. Burbank: Walt Disney Productions.

Lynch, John. 2018. Pixar's Most Successful Movies at the Box Office, Including Record-Breaking 'Incredibles 2'. *Business Insider*. Available online: https://www.businessinsider.com/pixar-most-successful-film-2016-6#1-incredibles-2-2018-9648-million-20 (accessed on 30 September 2018).

McMillan, Graeme. 2012. Brave Old Worlds: Does Pixar Have a Problem with Stereotypes? *Time*. Available online: http://entertainment.time.com/2012/06/20/brave-old-worlds-pixars-stereotype-problem/ (accessed on 30 September 2018).

Militz, Thane A., and Simon Foale. 2015. The "Nemo Effect": Perception and Reality of *Finding Nemo's* Impact on Marine Aquarium Fisheries. *Fish and Fisheries* 18: 596–606. [CrossRef]

Moana. 2016. Directed by Ron Clements, and John Musker. North Hollywood: Hurwitz Creative.

Monsters. 2001. Directed by Pete Docter, David Silverman, and Lee Unkrich. Emeryville: Pixar Animation Studios.

Mulan. 1998. Directed by Tony Bancroft, and Barry Cook. Burbank: Walt Disney Feature Animation.

Munkittrick, Kyle. 2011. The Hidden Message in Pixar's Films. *Discover*. May 14. Available online: http://blogs.discovermagazine.com/sciencenotfiction/2011/05/14/the-hidden-message-in-pixars-films/#.W7Ev_GhKjD4 (accessed on 30 September 2018).

Nicholson, Linda. 1997. The Myth of the Traditional Family. In *Feminism and Families*. Edited by Hilde Lindemann Nelson. New York: Routledge, pp. 27–42.

O'Reilly, Andrea. 2016. *Matricentric Feminism: Theory, Activism, Practice*. Toronto: Demeter Press.

Peter Pan. 1953. Directed by Clyde Geronimi, Wilfred Jackson, and Hamilton Luske. Burbank: Walt Disney Productions.

Piper. 2016. Directed by Alan Barillaro. Emeryville: Pixar Animation Studios.

Pocahontas. 1995. Directed by Mike Gabriel, and Eric Goldberg. Burbank: Walt Disney Feature Animation.

Preston, Daniel L. 2010. Finding difference: Nemo and friends opening the door to disability theory. *The English Journal* 100: 56–60.

Ruddick, Sara. 1997. The Idea of Fatherhood. In *Feminism and Families*. Edited by Hilde Lindemann Nelson. New York: Routledge, pp. 205–20.

Sandoval, Cat. 2018. Food, Family Inspired Pixar's First Female-Directed Animated Short Film, *Bao. Newsy.* June 22. Available online: https://www.newsy.com/stories/food-culture-family-inspired-pixar-s-short-film-bao/ (accessed on 30 September 2018).

Takševa, Tatjana. 2018. Motherhood Studies and Feminist Theory: Elisions and Intersections. *Journal of the Motherhood Initiative* 9: 177–94.

Tangled. 2010. Directed by Nathan Greno, and Brian Howard. Burbank: Walt Disney Animation Studios.

Tarzan. 1999. Directed by Chris Buck, and Kevin Lima. Burbank: Walt Disney Pictures.

Tidwell, Christy. 2009. 'Fish Are Just like People, Only Flakier': Environmental Practice and Theory in *Finding Nemo. Americana: The Journal of American Popular Culture* 8. Available online: http://americanpopularculture. com/journal/articles/spring_2009/tidwell.htm (accessed on 29 September 2018).

The AristoCats. 1970. Directed by Wolfgang Reitherman. Burbank: Walt Disney Productions.

The Incredibles. 2004. Directed by Brad Bird. Burbank: Walt Disney Pictures.

The Princess and the Frog. 2009. Directed by Ron Clements, and John Musker. Burbank: Walt Disney Animation Studios.

The Rescuers Down Under. 1990. Directed by Hendel Butoy, and Mike Gabriel. Burbank: Walt Disney Pictures.

Tin Toy. 1988. Directed by John Lasseter. Emeryville: Pixar Animation Studios.

Toy Story. 1995. Directed by John Lasseter. Burbank: Walt Disney Pictures.

Up. 2009. Directed by Pete Docter, and Rob Peterson. Emeryville: Pixar Animation Studios.

Zipes, Jack. 1999. Breaking the Disney Spell. In *The Classic Fairy Tales.* Edited by Maria Tatar. New York: WW Norton, pp. 333–52.

Zorthian, Julia. 2015. How *Toy Story* Changed Movie History. *Time.* Available online: http://time.com/4118006/ 20-years-toy-story-pixar/ (accessed on 30 September 2018).

social sciences

MDPI

Article
Postfeminist Masculinity: The New Disney Norm?

Michael Macaluso

Institute for Educational Initiatives, University of Notre Dame, Notre Dame, IN 46556, USA;
mmacaluso@nd.edu; Tel: +1-574-631-2737

Received: 30 September 2018; Accepted: 30 October 2018; Published: 5 November 2018

Abstract: A recent trend in Disney scholarship attends to postfeminist readings of Disney film and media. This paper contributes to that conversation by focusing on the representations of *masculinity* that accompany postfeminist sensibilities in and through Disney media and its reception. With a sociological focus on postfeminist masculinity, this article reviews several Disney characters to argue for a new model of postfeminist masculinity advanced in recent Disney films, with a particular focus on the *Incredibles* films, and examines how this representation has been received in popular media.

Keywords: Disney; postfeminism; masculinity; gender; cultural studies

---

1. Introduction

A recent trend in Disney scholarship, in the wake of the blockbuster animated film *Frozen*, attends to postfeminist readings of Disney film and media (e.g., Frasl 2018; Macaluso 2016; Stover 2013) and public reception of these films. Because of Disney's questionable history of perpetuating dangerous gender stereotypes on film (e.g., Bell et al. 1995; Giroux and Pollock 2010)—and perhaps because of its implicit acknowledgement of this history, as evidenced by a recent string of movies with female leads—this postfeminist line of inquiry seems especially apt.

This paper contributes to that burgeoning conversation but focuses mainly on the representations of *masculinity* that accompany postfeminist sensibilities in and through Disney media and its reception. Though much work has been done to examine cinematic depictions of postfeminist masculinities in general (e.g., Abele and Gronbeck-Tedesco 2016; Gwyne and Muller 2013), this paper looks specifically at Disney and Pixar (hereafter, only "Disney") films' constructions of this concept, as previous conversations have typically concentrated on the portrayal of women and girls. As traditional or stereotypical versions of masculinity and masculine power continue to be supported and reaffirmed (through political and sports figures, superhero movies, and a plethora of gendered cultural practices and representations) but also challenged and dismantled (with such cultural movements like #MeToo), many have begun to wonder as to the criteria of and for masculine success. What role models might young boys—and adolescent and adult men—aspire to? With this question in mind, recent scholarship examines Disney films to offer more productive critical discourse around masculinity (e.g., Davis 2013; Wooden and Gillam 2014). Towards that same effort, I ask: How are recent Disney men discursively positioned through and by discourse? More specifically, how do Disney movies, as important texts of cultural production, reinforce a model of postfeminist masculinity? To answer these questions, I review several Disney characters to push back against simplistic categories of Disney men and to argue for a vision of masculinity that Disney seems to promulgate in its most recent films. Then, I illuminate the discourses and inherent meanings in and around *Incredibles 2* and its popular reception. In the process, I will argue that a postfeminist masculinity sensibility pervades these Disney cultural texts, signaling a new era—and yet another troubling model—of Disney masculinity. With a sociological focus on masculinity in particular, this paper responds to Rumens (2017) call for "more engaged research in the complicated ways in which discourses of postfeminist masculinities are historically patterned and intermingle with cultural . . . discourses" (p. 245).

2. Postfeminism and Postfeminist Masculinity

Before I discuss the conceptual tools that guide this paper, I find it necessary to briefly revisit the broad construct of postfeminism, as it can be employed and mis/used in a variety of ways. As I understand and use it, postfeminism (e.g., McRobbie 2007; Tasker and Negra 2007; Butler 2013; Munford and Waters 2013) refers to a range of contradictory gender discourses generally tied to, reified in, and arising from cultural and contemporary media. Postfeminism, in general, highlights narratives of achieved gender equity and sentiments that the goals of feminism and feminist equality and representation have been achieved or actualized or are no longer necessary. These "success narratives" tend to take cultural shape in media as "instances of typically heterosexual, white, middle-class [female] achievement in male-dominated workplaces, women's ability to treat men as sexual objects and the seemingly unfettered freedoms women enjoy in respect to career choice, parenting and domesticity" (Rumens 2017, p. 247). As a result, these narratives signify or indicate the end, fulfillment, or passing of feminism—and hence, an era of post-feminism where traditional feminist goals of gender equality, equal rights, and collective action are replaced by discourses and depictions of female empowerment, choice, and independence. Part of its contradiction stems from the inherent link or entanglement (McRobbie 2007) between postfeminist and feminist discourses: Postfeminism celebrates the perceived successes of feminism. Further, because of its perception of feminist actualization, postfeminism can also perpetuate a general backlash against feminism, by men and women, because of its—again, perceived—threatening, extreme, or difficult expectations for both men and women (Tasker and Negra 2007).

As postfeminism is linked more broadly with gender, culture, and power (Tasker 2008), it also employs its own discourse of and around masculinity. Tasker and Negra (2007) theorized postfeminist masculinity, the focus of this paper, as a discourse that "celebrates women's strength while lightly critiquing or gently ridiculing straight masculinity" (p. 21). In other words, postfeminist masculinity represents straight masculinity as foolish or comedic, perhaps even immature or incapable, in order to highlight capable, independent women. As Gill (2014) describes it, postfeminist masculinity is personified "in the repeated depiction of men as somewhat hapless, bumbling 'victims' or 'losers' in the 'sex wars,' alongside the presentation of feminism as extreme, old-fashioned and unnecessary/superfluous" (p. 191). The classic example of this trope can be seen in Ray Romano, the character from the popular television series *Everybody Loves Raymond*. On the show, Ray's wife regularly refers to him as an "idiot" while she is portrayed as strong, confident, capable, and demanding. More often than not, the comedic timing of the show comes at Ray's expense, as his words and actions—sometimes tied to his understanding of what it means to be a man or dad—tend to get him in trouble. This trope portrays the gendered-opposite formula of the classic television sitcom *I Love Lucy*—rather than Lucy and Ethel's antics, it's Ray's; and he, his brother, and his father seem to be the butt or subject of the show's jokes. Postfeminist masculinity can take on other forms, including vulnerable men in crisis, supportive husbands, and/or caring and inclusive male-figures, but the ridiculed depiction of masculinity seems most prevalent in Disney films of late.

3. Models of Disney Masculinity

It seems that Disney, as a producer of knowledge and culture, (implicitly or explicitly) recognizes certain traits and types—or fixed attributes—of masculinity in many of its male protagonists. For example, Davis (2013) has analyzed a broad swath of films to posit three broad depictions of Disney men—boys, heroes (both princes and non-aristocratic), and villains. But discussions around Disney masculinity problematically tend to stop here and attempt to pigeonhole characters into one category. In this section, I expand upon these categories—what I call "models of masculinity" (Table 1)—and offer a new model based upon recent Disney films.

Table 1. Models of Disney Masculinity.

Boy	Hero/Prince	Villain
Pinocchio Miguel	Prince Charming Prince Phillip Prince Eric Tarzan Hercules	Gaston Ratcliffe Judge Frollo Shan Yu Jafar Dr. Facilier
Aladdin Peter Pan John Smith Quasimodo		

The traditional depiction of Disney masculinity comes in the form of a dashing prince or hero. For example, early films like *Snow White and the Seven Dwarfs* and *Cinderella* depicted relatively passive princes (the nameless "Prince Charming") who served as secondary characters and objects of affection for the despondent or trialed female protagonists. Once these female characters were free of their wicked stepmother, they were able to escape to a "happily ever after" with this prince. The trope of the sidelined prince changed with movies like *Sleeping Beauty* and *The Little Mermaid* with named princes Phillip and Eric, respectively, who, though still an object of affection, played a vital role in heroically vanquishing the villain and, thus, more actively saving the princess in distress. The brave actions of these princely heroes essentially superseded those of both Aurora and Ariel—princesses in their own right by birth. Other non-prince characters also serve as heroes in Disney movies, including Tarzan, Hercules, and Aladdin.

Aside from heroes, Disney also tends to advance the trope of the boy-turned-man by way of some attainment of knowledge and/or personal understanding (i.e., moving from innocence to experience). This is classically personified in Pinocchio who learns what it means to be a "real boy" after a series of shameful and sinful associations with the likes of Lampwick, Honest John, Stromboli, and even Monstro the whale. In the end, Pinocchio learns that nothing can replace the value of family. Other Disney boys who experience some type of coming of age or bildungsroman include Miguel from *Coco*, who comes to much the same conclusion as Pinocchio, and even Peter Pan and, again, Aladdin. Though Peter could also fall into the hero category, he does come to realize the importance of the Darling children and their safe return to London. Aladdin, too, by the end of the film, understands the importance of being honest to himself and others about who he really is. In the words of the Blue Fairy, all of these characters prove themselves to be "brave, truthful, and unselfish" as they come to their personal understandings over the course of their respective films. Other "boy" archetypes may include characters like John Smith (*Pocahontas*) and Quasimodo (*The Hunchback of Notre Dame*).

Finally, Disney's memorable line-up of male villains constitutes another category. More often than not, these villains tend to take on a position of masculine authority—or, in more nuanced terms, hegemonic masculinity (Woloshyn et al. 2013)—until they are defeated, usually by the Hero/Prince who takes on a lesser or more acceptable form of hegemonic masculinity. Hegemonic masculinity is a type of masculinity where men dominate and subject other men and women. Because of this subjugation, hegemonic masculinity is strongly linked to heterosexuality and a hyper-masculine presence. This depiction of masculinity is classically characterized in Gaston from *Beauty and the Beast*. He is strong, tough, handsome, and dominates every scene he is in, most clearly by subjugating those around him, as evidenced by his treatment of his sidekick LeFou (more on this below). The song "Gaston" (Ashman and Menken 1991) further highlights the hegemonic and masculine features of Gaston the character: He has a thick neck and cleft chin, no one is as "burly and brawny," he has "biceps to spare," and, of course, "every last inch of me's covered with hair." Aside from the song, Gaston narcissistically and readily points out these features to Belle, accented by his suave smile and perfect hair, throughout the movie. The rest of the song notes that he's "intimidating" and "a man among men" who uses "antlers in all of my decorating." These "manly man" features are associated with traditional—and even stereotypical and dated—aspects of masculinity. In short, "no one says no to Gaston," which is indicative of a typical response to hegemonic masculinity. Similar villains of this type may include Shan Yu (*Mulan*), Jafar (*Aladdin*), Ratcliff (*Pocahontas*), Frollo (*The Hunchback of Notre Dame*), and Dr. Facilier (*The Princess and the Frog*). Though some of these villains may not have many of Gaston's stereotypical, "manly" attributes (like burly, brawny muscle), the way they act and treat others seems indicative of their intention to rule, dominate, or maintain power over others.

Certainly other depictions and versions of masculinity exist in the Disney universe, as postmodern theory acknowledges that masculinity may take many forms and exist in relation to other subject positions (i.e., that which is not masculine), but these versions seem to be outliers rather than recurring representations or tropes. Or, they tend to be overlooked for one of the categories detailed above. For example, Dundes and Streiff (2016) have analyzed the character Chi Fu from Disney's *Mulan* for his masculinity tropes and specifically as the antithesis of hegemonic masculinity—a man who, like LeFou, is indicative of effeminate, homosexual, or even hyposexual masculinity. But I would like to offer another category or model that I argue is recently recurring: That of post-feminist hero, whose features fall somewhere in between these versions of hegemonic masculinity and the effeminate or absence of masculinity. Or, perhaps rather, whose features index the man who fails to perform, inhabit, or actualize a hegemonic masculinity.

More specifically, the postfeminist version of masculinity is a Disney man who experiences some type of crisis or vulnerability, usually in relation to his understanding or performance of masculinity connected to work, family, partner, expectation, etc. In the first *The Incredibles* movie, Mr. Incredible, having been forced to conceal his superhero identity, takes on the trope of the worn-down masculine businessman who hates his job. This portrayal of the struggling Bob Parr (Mr. Incredible's alter-ego) indicates a postfeminist sentimentality, where men are depicted "as clinging on by a thread to their tenuous 'careers.' They are usually doing something boring for which they are overqualified" (Gill 2014, p. 193). In *The Incredibles*, this portrayal is further exaggerated by Bob's relationship with his boss, a literally diminutive but overbearing, strong, and seemingly more successful insurance businessman. Bob's revival comes through a renewal of his "primitive" masculinity (Ashcraft and Flores 2003)—through an invitation from a mysterious stranger to don his Mr. Incredible persona once again, use his super-strength, tone up his physique, and take down a villain. In this sense, his crisis of masculinity is resolved by reverting to a stereotypical, normalized version of manhood and masculinity—brute strength and physicality.

In *Incredibles 2*, Mrs. Incredible—under her previous and un-wedded identity (that is, her identity without a male/masculine attachment) as Elastigirl—accepts an offer from a corporation to fight crime in order to rebuild the public's trust in superheroes. The leaders of the corporation make it clear that they want Elastigirl specifically for this job because she, unlike her husband, creates less of a mess in collateral damage, hence her disassociation from her Mrs. Incredible title—an important post/feminist message, for sure. She, simply put, has not messed up enough or created as much collateral damage (literally and figuratively) as her husband. (On a side note here: The ease with which Elastigirl attains this position—without barriers or structures—and the success and ease with which she carries out the job also speak to the postfeminist nature of the film as a whole.) To support this endeavor, Mr. Incredible takes on the role of stay-at-home dad. In some of the funnier scenes of the movie, Mr. Incredible reaches breaking points when he cannot figure out Dash's new methods for completing his math homework, and the only way he knows how to manage the erratic behavior of his youngest son Jack-Jack, who is in the process of developing his own superpowers, is to feed him cookies. Because of his sheer exhaustion at one point, he quickly and desperately passes off Jack-Jack to a babysitter.

Even from this short description, the postfeminist themes are clear, as Elastigirl, the successful, independent, and empowered woman-at-work, literally saves the day on a daily basis, while Mr. Incredible struggles at home. A simple binary is established between the empowered, successful woman (who succeeds perhaps at the expense of a man/men) and the vulnerable, downtrodden male.

This role reversal marks an important cultural change from the first *Incredibles* movie fourteen years prior, when Mrs. Incredible/Elastigirl gave up her superhero career to care for the house and kids while Mr. Incredible performed his superhero duties to satisfy his mid-life crisis. The difference now, though, is that Mr. Incredible is gently ridiculed for his inability to parent and domesticate whereas Mrs. Incredible handled these duties perfectly fine in the first movie—and even managed to rescue Mr. Incredible at one point.

There are other, recent Disney movies that seem to reify the post-feminist hero. Wooden and Gillam (2014) have noted *Brave*'s "animal to imbecile . . . depiction of men as buffoonish thugs, amid its supposedly bold stride forward toward gender equality in children's film" (p. xii). I have written before about the ways in which both Hans and Kristoff from the enormously popular and critically respected *Frozen* abide by the tropes of postfeminist masculinity (Macaluso 2016). Both characters are portrayed as immature or offer some comic relief in the film in ways similar to Flynn Rider from *Tangled* and Prince Naveen from *The Princess and the Frog*. In fulfilling many of the same postfeminist tropes, Flynn and Naveen are often portrayed as the butt of jokes (with frying pans to the face, in Flynn's case) and as the female protagonists' unwilling and unwittingly travel partners who eventually fall for her charm and charisma. Even Héctor from *Coco*—a film which I admit has mostly positive and generative depictions of its characters overall—seems naïve and hapless, the bumbling victim of a cruel plot, who is only redeemed once the truth about his disappearance is revealed. Upon that reveal, he is welcomed back into his family, which is comprised of many strong women who have largely driven the plot of the movie. Without a postfeminist understanding, these characters may be hastily categorized as a hero or sidelined/passive prince, but Table 2 takes into account this new model of Disney masculinity, which seems to be indicative of Disney films of late (again, perhaps to compensate for its history of passive female heroes).

Table 2. Revised Models of Disney Masculinity.

Boy	Hero/Prince	Post-Feminist Hero	Villain
Pinocchio Miguel	Prince Charming Prince Phillip Prince Eric Tarzan Hercules	Mr. Incredible Kristoff Héctor Prince Naveen Flynn Rider	Gaston Ratcliffe Judge Frollo Shan Yu Jafar Dr. Facilier
	Aladdin Peter Pan John Smith Quasimodo	Prince Hans	
	Ralph Kuzco Maui		
	The Beast		

One interesting exception, as noted in the chart, is the Beast from *Beauty and the Beast*. He could potentially blend across all of these models, as he gains new knowledge and understanding over the course of the film, he makes the ultimate sacrifice in defeating the villain, and he shows authoritative and domineering behaviors, all while being gently ridiculed and chastised for these behaviors in generally comedic ways (e.g., he is groomed with bows and curls, he is shown how to properly eat soup and dance, he is hit with snowballs, etc.). In short, the Beast character "helps to forward the image of unloved and unhappy white men who need kindness and affection, rather than criticism and reform, in order to become their 'true' selves again" (Jeffords 1995, p. 165). This depiction proves that a post-feminist hero need not be confined to its own box or set of traits—just like Ralph (*Wreck-It Ralph*), Kuzco (*The Emperor's New Groove*), and Maui (*Moana*).

While postfeminist masculinity marks a relative change in the overall representations of men and masculinity in Disney films, it should not necessarily be thought of as a new, temporal masculinity that has displaced older or other versions of masculinity. I rely on notions of postfeminist masculinity as a sensibility (Gill 2014, 2007), allowing for an analysis of its discursive constructions and structure of feeling (Gill 2014) as one of many models of masculinity. However, it is interesting that the models of the postfeminist hero tend to come later in the Disney canon (the earliest in 2000 and most after 2009)—perhaps indicative of "the time and place" in which these films were created and produced.

In considering the postfeminist work that these movies, and especially the most recent *Incredibles* movies, do and perform, one must remember that a cultural text like a Disney movie shapes the social imagination and can, thus, "articulate gendered possibilities for social actors" (Rumens 2017, p. 251). Therefore, one must ask about the apparent affect, effect, or uptake of these postfeminist themes—what ideological work around masculinity does this movie and overall sensibility do? On the one hand, this brief analysis of Disney men affirms that "Disney's male characters have been affected and shaped by the discourse surrounding feminism and 'post-feminism' just as much as their female characters" (Davis 2013, p. 13). On the other hand, postfeminist masculinity must also implicitly reinforce or challenge male power or do something else entirely. In other words, ideology indeed "does" something. The next section of this paper considers this point and the potential effects these discourses have on viewers and how those discourses may interpellate male and female subjects. To do this, I briefly examine popular online media—through movies reviews and the social discussion website Reddit—for its popular reception around *Incredibles 2*, specifically, to see how average viewers negotiate the film's messages and postfeminist sensibilities.

4. Postfeminist Uptake of *Incredibles 2*

Naturally, "everyday critics" and average movie-goers alike picked up on the perceived feminist themes of the film, noting the active and independent role Elastigirl carries this time around, and as a result, reviews were and have been mixed (and generally along gendered lines). For example, several critics touted and celebrated its feminist message. Paige (2018) argues, "feel free to yell from the rooftops that *Incredibles 2* is hella feminist ... It's simply a reflection of our changing times and work ... " (para. 4). Smith (2018) from *The Guardian* calls the film "a feminist triumph" (para. 1) in the post-Weinstein era. Rey (2018) of the online women's magazine *Bustle* agrees, noting that the film's "premise had a sense of female empowerment [that] couldn't be more timely" (para. 1). Though these soundbites hearken to postfeminist discourses (such as the empowered, feminine yet feminist, white woman), these critics see the elevation of Elastigirl as the featured protagonist as incredibly significant in contemporary times. What seems to be somewhat lost in these reviews is the important—and similarly elevated—role this character played in the first film by actually saving Mr. Incredible from death and a formidable villain—in addition to being a good mom. This is not to say that one film does a better job than the other but to point out how (post)feminism can be easily reduced to simply having a strong female-lead.

Others critics, even while praising the film, expressed their frustrations with the "political" (i.e., perceived feminist) messaging of the film. For example, one critic (Adams 2018) from the online magazine *Slate* notes, "Bob Parr stays at home and plays bumbling househusband, fumbling Violet's adolescent emotional crises, furrowing his brow at Dash's math homework, and frowning at Jack-Jack's superpoopy diapers" (para. 3). Another critic (Knowles 2018) from opinion website *The Daily Wire*, in critiquing this representation, actually compared the film to *Everybody Loves Raymond*, sarcastically noting that Mr. Incredible "hilariously bungles" his parenting duties because "wives are just so much more competent than their idiot husbands" (para. 5). But what he calls "fashionable feminism" (para. 5) is, in actuality, indicative of a postfeminist—and specifically a postfeminist masculinity—sensibility. These reviews that do focus on the portrayal of the male characters see that portrayal as problematic, and rightly so. Fatherhood-on-film has been linked to postfeminist masculinities for decades now (Hamad 2013), and *Incredibles 2* is no exception, as these reviews critique Mr. Incredible's struggles to juggle and manage the parenting demands of his three children, accounting for much of the movie's comic relief.

But, importantly, the cultural reception around the "feminist" message of the film has extended to "everyday critics" of the internet as well. For example, Reddit can be a good data site for analyzing public reception because it acts as a moderated, digital bulletin board of important topics and discussions for registered users. These users, or members, can post content on various themed pages—or subreddits—of interest to them. One user, KC_weeden (2018) on the "Men Going Their Own Way" subreddit, a forum dedicated to men "forging their own identities and paths to self-defined success," posted the following about *Incredibles 2*: " … it was chock full of feminist ideology and tropes that all movies/shows seem to have these days. I swear, it's not hard to make a good movie without a political agenda" (n.p.). Of the 22 comments that follow, 18 of them focus on the "feminist political agenda" of contemporary movies, with comments like, "It seems every movie is really pushing this feminist, misandric, pro woman bullshit" (ConstantChinner 2018, n.p.) or "It's a sad thing that everything nowadays has to be politically driven. Music, movies, videogames, paintings, theatre. everything has to have a 'deep'—i.e., feminism—meaning, or else it's not up to par...". Only two of these comments mention the representation of masculinity. One user only mentioned that "they changed the male characters for no reason, to be dumb assholes, completely different from the first movie, while they kept the female characters the same", while the other commented positively on the portrayal of Mr. Incredible, saying, "it was at least balanced with a father (Mr. Incredible) bonding with his kids and supporting them, and men playing the roles they play anyway, as involved responsible men rather than overgrown children". Aside from the one positive comment, these reviewers overall seemed more frustrated with the—again—strong, female protagonist than with the specific representation of the main male character and the implications for masculinity and fatherhood that come with it. As a result, they blame the "political" construct of feminism.

This backlash appeared on other subreddits as well, though to a lesser degree. For example, similar messages were posted on the "Pixar" subreddit, where user 16coxk (2018) asked, "I've heard people calling The Incredibles 2 [sic] 'feminist propaganda.' What do you think?" (n.p.). Of the ten responses, only one of them seemed to think so, by saying, "To be fair there was a lot more impact by the female characters in this movie. Elasti-girl, Evelyn, Violet, Edna, the Senator. Mr. Incredible, Dash, Frozone and the other males felt like supporting characters" (LajiDwayem 2018, n.p.). In this more generic subreddit (one about all Pixar films compared to one about men and men's issues), the responses seemed more generic and open-ended.

What's interesting to me across all of these cases—from both critics and everyday critics/users—is that the apparent feminism/feminist ideology incurs misguided praise or criticism. On the one hand, some seem to be more angry at the depiction of a strong female lead than at the ridiculed male subject; on the other, some seem to celebrate shallow versions of feminism. In either case, "feminism" is celebrated for portraying "girl power" in the form of a strong female character paired with a weak or foolish male character—the very definition of a postfeminist sensibility. In the end, these Disney cultural texts serve no one because popular reception seems, at most, to reinforce traditional male power as a backlash against perceived feminism, and at the least, to repudiate feminism and further divide the sexes. In either case, postfeminism as a construct or sensibility is reaffirmed and lauded under the guise of feminism.

5. Implications

This paper began by asking: How are Disney men discursively positioned through and by (postfeminist) discourses? How do Disney texts, as important sites of cultural production, reinforce postfeminist masculinity sensibilities? I have attempted to show how recent Disney men, with a particular focus on the recent *Incredibles* films as representative of current examples, have been represented and how that representation has been received or taken-up in popular media with film critics and average consumers of texts (i.e., Redditors). Overall, the striking "finding" here is that

Soc. Sci. **2018**, *7*, 221

postfeminism exists, and it extends itself across texts and media by men and women. While I agree with Giroux (1999); Giroux and Pollock (2010) that popular texts, and especially Disney texts, act as teaching machines and serve as producers of ideological, cultural knowledge, I also acknowledge that today's abundant digital discourse plays that role as well. Disney is not necessarily solely to blame for the proliferation of these discourses—they did not create them, and they will not be the last to proliferate them. Rather, Disney produces *and* recycles and reinforces the sensibilities that we create and are created by. We, in other words, live in an era of postfeminist discourses because we are the producers of postfeminist sensibilities. Postfeminism—in its various forms, discourses, and sensibilities—is all around us, whether we see it or not.

On a much more practical level, any type of media runs the risk of intentionally or unintentionally, implicitly or explicitly, reifying cultural messages. In the case of some of the most recent Disney films, there seems to be a message that men must be weak in order for women to thrive. This message is dangerous to both sexes, as it subtly suggests that women and men cannot successfully coexist as strong, independent individuals together. Moreover, the *Incredibles* films further imply that two successful working parents simply do not and cannot exist; one parent must sacrifice a career or gendered expectations for the other to thrive. This is the real work of postfeminism. Moving forward, I do wonder if a *positive* postfeminist representation of men and masculinity can exist in the Disney universe or what that model would even look like. For example, could Disney produce a film that portrays positive depictions of men and women in pursuit of common goals and desires, or does that lead to bland storytelling and movie-making? Might a hypothetical *Incredibles 3* feature the family united in their fight against the villain the Underminer, building off of each other's strengths and weaknesses and finding comedic timing in just being a not-so-average family?

Finally, this paper offered a new model of Disney masculinity, the idea or trope of the postfeminist hero, as a potential new norm. The intention in proposing this model is, again, not necessarily to criticize Disney for their representations of men, women, and masculinity—though representations *do* matter, whether fiction or not, and especially those with and from a corporate and cultural producer like Disney, with its emphasis on family and children's entertainment. Rather, I propose the model as a new norm of Disney masculinity, and, thus, as a way to recognize and—importantly—to resist postfeminism in one of its many forms. If we are the cause for the circulation of these postfeminist discourses, then we must be ever present in heading them off and challenging the ways in which they call us to be and believe in the real world.

Funding: This research received no external funding.

Conflicts of Interest: The authors declare no conflicts of interest.

References

16coxk. 2018. I've Heard People Calling the Incredibles 2 'Feminist Propaganda'. What Do you Think? [Reddit Comment]. Available online: https://www.reddit.com/r/Pixar/comments/8yygnv/ive_heard_people_calling_the_incredbles_2/ (accessed on 28 August 2018).

Abele, Elizabeth, and John A. Gronbeck-Tedesco, eds. 2016. *Screening Images of American Masculinity in the Age of Postfeminism*. London: Lexington Books.

Adams, Sam. 2018. Incredibles 2 Has Incredible Action: If Only the Ideas Were Incredible, Too. Available online: https://slate.com/culture/2018/06/incredibles-2-reviewed.html (accessed on 15 August 2018).

Ashcraft, Karen Lee, and Lisa A. Flores. 2003. 'Slaves with white collars': Decoding a contemporary crisis of masculinity. *Text and Performance Quarterly* 23: 1–29. [CrossRef]

Ashman, Howard E., and Alan Menken. 1991. Gaston. In *Beauty and the Beast*. Recorded by R. White. New York: Walt Disney Records.

Bell, Elizabeth, Lynda Haas, and Laura Sells, eds. 1995. *From Mouse to Mermaid: The Politics of Film, Gender, and Culture*. Bloomington: Indiana University Press.

Butler, Judith. 2013. For white girls only? Postfeminism and the politics of inclusion. *Feminist Formations* 25: 35–58. [CrossRef]

ConstantChinner. 2018. Just Watched Incredibles 2. [Reddit Comment]. Available online: https://www.reddit.com/r/MGTOW/comments/8s5d5i/just_watched_incredibles_2/ (accessed on 28 August 2018).

Davis, A. 2013. *Handsome Heroes and Vile Villains: Men in Disney's Feature Animation*. New Barnet, Herts: John Libby.

Dundes, Lauren, and Madeline Streiff. 2016. Reel royal diversity? The glass ceiling in Disney's mulan and princess and the frog. *Societies* 6: 35. [CrossRef]

Frasl, Beatrice. 2018. Bright young women, sick of swimmin', ready to … consume? The construction of postfeminist femininity in Disney's The Little Mermaid. *European Journal of Women's Studies* 25: 341–54. [CrossRef]

Gill, Rosalind. 2007. Postfeminist media culture: Elements of a sensibility. *European Journal of Cultural Studies* 10: 147–66. [CrossRef]

Gill, Rosalind. 2014. Powerful women, vulnerable men and post-feminist masculinity in men's popular fiction. *Gender and Language* 8: 185–204. [CrossRef]

Giroux, Henry A. 1999. *The Mouse that Roared: Disney and the End of Innocence*. New York: Rowan & Littlefield Publications.

Giroux, Henry A., and Grace Pollock. 2010. *The Mouse that Roared: Disney and the End of Innocence*. New York: Rowman & Littlefield Publishers.

Gwyne, Joel, and Nadine Muller, eds. 2013. *Postfeminism and Contemporary Hollywood Cinema*. New York: Palgrave Macmillian.

Hamad, Hannah. 2013. Hollywood fatherhood: Postfeminist discourses of ageing in contemporary hollywood. In *Postfeminism and Contemporary Hollywood Cinema*. Edited by Joel Gwyne and Nadine Muller. New York: Palgrave Macmillian, pp. 99–115.

Jeffords, Susuan. 1995. The curse of masculinity: Disney's beauty and the beast. In *From Mouse to Mermaid: The Politics of Film, Gender, and Culture*. Edited by Elizabeth Bell, Lynda Haas and Laura Sells. Bloomington: Indiana University Press, pp. 161–74.

KC_weeden. 2018. Just Watched Incredibles 2. [Reddit Comment]. Available online: https://www.reddit.com/r/MGTOW/comments/8s5d5i/just_watched_incredibles_2/klim_milk (accessed on 28 August 2018).

Knowles, M. J. 2018. Review: An 'Incredible'-y Feminist Letdown. Available online: https://www.dailywire.com/news/32234/review-incredible-y-feministletdown-michael-j-knowles (accessed on 15 August 2018).

LajiDwayem. 2018. I've Heard People Calling the Incredibles 2 'Feminist Propaganda'. What Do You Think? [Reddit Comment]. Available online: https://www.reddit.com/r/Pixar/comments/8yygnv/ive_heard_people_calling_the_incredbles_2/ (accessed on 28 August 2018).

Macaluso, Michael. 2016. The postfeminist princess: Disney's curricular guide to feminism. In *Disney, Culture, and Curriculum*. Edited by Jennifer. A. Sandlin and Julie. C. Garlen. New York: Routledge, pp. 73–86.

McRobbie, Angela. 2007. Postfeminism and popular culture. In *Interrogating Postfeminism: Gender and the Politics of Popular Culture*. Edited by Yvonne Tasker and Diane Negra. Durham: Duke University Press, pp. 27–39.

Munford, Rebecca, and Melanie Waters. 2013. *Feminism and Popular Culture: Investigating the Postfeminist Mystique*. London: I.B. Tauris.

Paige, Rachel. 2018. Brad Bird Doesn't Want to Call Incredibles 2 Feminist—But that Doesn't Mean You Can't. Available online: https://hellogiggles.com/news/incredibles-2-feminist/ (accessed on 15 August 2018).

Rey, Ashley. 2018. Incredibles 2 had a Feminist Message that Couldn't Be More Timely. Available online: https://www.bustle.com/p/incredibles-2-has-a-feminist-message-thatcouldnt-be-more-timely-9317729 (accessed on 15 August 2018).

Rumens, Nick. 2017. Postfeminism, men, masculinities and work: A research agenda for gender and organization studies scholars. *Gender, Work and Organization* 24: 245–59. [CrossRef]

Smith, Anna. 2018. How Incredibles 2 Goes to Work for the Feminist Superhero. Available online: https://www.theguardian.com/film/2018/jun/28/incredibles-2feminism-animation (accessed on 15 August 2018).

Stover, Cassandra. 2013. Damsels and heroines: The conundrum of the post-feminist Disney princess. *LUX: A Journal of Transdisciplinary Writing and Research* 2: 29. [CrossRef]

Tasker, Yvonne. 2008. Practically perfect people: Postfeminism, masculinity and male parenting in contemporary cinema. In *A Family Affair: Cinema Calls Home*. Edited by Murray Pomerance. London: Wallflower.

Tasker, Yvonne, and Diane Negra. 2007. Feminist politics and postfeminist culture. In *Interrogating Postfeminism: Gender and the Politics of Popular Culture*. Edited by Yvonne Tasker and Diane Negra. Durham: Duke University Press, pp. 27–39.

Woloshyn, Vera, Nancy Taber, and Laura Lane. 2013. Discourses of masculinity and femininity in The Hunger Games: Scarred, bloody, and stunning. *International Journal of Social Science Studies* 1: 150–60. [CrossRef]

Wooden, Shannon R., and Ken Gillam. 2014. *Pixar's Boy Stories: Masculinity in a Postmodern Age.* Lanham: Rowman & Littlefield.

social sciences

MDPI

Essay

Storm Power, an Icy Tower and Elsa's Bower: The Winds of Change in Disney's *Frozen*

Lauren Dundes [1,*], Madeline Streiff [2] and Zachary Streiff [3]

[1] Department of Sociology, McDaniel College, Westminster, MD 21157, USA
[2] Hastings College of the Law, University of California, 200 McAllister St, San Francisco, CA 94102, USA; madeline.streiff@gmail.com
[3] Member of the State Bar of California, Monterey, CA 93940, USA; ZachAlanS@gmail.com
* Correspondence: ldundes@mcdaniel.edu; Tel.: +1-410-857-2534

Received: 8 May 2018; Accepted: 25 May 2018; Published: 31 May 2018

Abstract: In Disney's box office sensation *Frozen* (2013), Elsa conjures powers rivaling those of Zeus, which is an echo of the shifting gender dynamics at the time of the film's release. By independently creating offspring Olaf and Marshmallow through whirlwinds, Elsa's parthenogenesis (virgin birth) evokes wind-driven pollination, allowing her to circumvent any male role in creation. However, Elsa's autonomy clashes with the traditional gender hierarchy, which is reinforced by a cultural context replete with latent symbolic meanings. Examples include both carrots and carats as phallic symbols, eggs as representations of the procreative potential that is appropriated by men and devalued in women, gender bias in perceptions of magic and enchantment, and the value of the nubile nymph over the tempestuous termagant. The normalcy of male dominance likely drives the resolution of the plot, in which Elsa learns to wield power in a non-threatening manner. In addition to having implications for gender roles, *Frozen* also portrays a mélange of gender symbolism through Elsa's snowmen creations, which function as an expression of the storm of controversy surrounding the subversion of binary conceptions of gender. In the end, *Frozen* serves as a cautionary tale about the dangers inherent in an unattached female as the ultimate potentate. This content analysis suggests that the film reflects fears surrounding the maelstrom of societal changes including expanding fertility options and the re-conceptualization of gender identity–pressing issues likely to sustain *Frozen*'s relevance.

Keywords: Elsa; Kristoff; Olaf; Marshmallow; Let it Go; enchantment; applause; engagement ring; diamond; gender; snowmen; wedding toast; bullroarer; fireworks; witches; magic; standing ovation; fertility; parthenogenesis; gender nonconformity; non-binary; storms; family jewels; snowflake; feminism

1. Introduction

Among Disney's blockbusters, Frozen (2013) has achieved resounding success as its most popular animated feature yet. Earnings exceeded a billion United States (US) dollars (Hibberd 2017) and YouTube views of just one version of its musical chart-topping hit, 'Let it Go', approached the 1.5 billion mark within five years of the film's debut (YouTube 2018). In the years subsequent to its release, interest in the movie has prompted plans for a *Frozen* sequel (due out in 2019 (Gander 2018)), as brisk sales of *Frozen* merchandise continue to drive this "cultural behemoth" (Perry 2017). with influence that has been compared to Shakespeare (Dockterman 2018). The term "Disneyfication" encapsulates Disney films' putative ability to inculcate a commodified utopian vision of society (Bryman 2004; Fjellman 1992; Giroux 1995; Giroux and Pollock 2010; Griffin et al. 2018; Rojek 1993; Wills 2017) that persuades audiences to "long nostalgically for neatly ordered patriarchal realms" (Zipes 1995, p. 40). According to Zipes (2011), "The telos of all Disney's fairy-tale films is to shape the vision of spectators so that they are convinced and believe that they share in the values and accomplishments of the narrative, thus obviating any or all contradictions ... through the systematic dissemination of images in books, advertising, toys, clothing, houseware articles, posters, postcards, radio, and other artifacts that have mesmerized us" (pp. 25–26). Yet despite delivering an "annexed" version of family entertainment based on pre-existing fairy tales (Schickel 1997), *Frozen* has struck a chord in audiences, resulting in cultural tintinnabulation at a deep—and likely unconscious—level. Although the *de facto* star of *Frozen*, Queen Elsa, is endowed with magical powers that she struggles to control, she has been heralded as empowering to women.[1] Indeed, some analysts suggest that her lack of romantic interests and her avoidance of the "male gaze" (Macaluso 2016) constitute a welcome departure from stereotypical gender roles (Law 2014), while the sisterly love portrayed in the film purportedly aligns with "traditional notions of family" (Wills 2017, p. 105).

However, this essay presents a critical content analysis of the film, complementing literature that demonstrates how Disney films provide a window into the cultural landscape of their era including such issues as the valorization of the white heteropatriarchal family (Dundes and Dundes 2005; Garlen and Sandlin 2017; Streiff and Dundes 2017b; Zurcher et al. 2018) and allegedly anachronistic but entrenched gender roles (e.g., Coyne et al. 2016; Dundes and Streiff 2016; England et al. 2011; Hoerrner 1996; Rowe 1979; Rudloff 2016; Sellers 2001; Zipes 2007, 2012). Even though Elsa is in some sense a castrating woman socialized to become more conventionally feminine and nurturing (Streiff and Dundes 2017a), she is nevertheless marketed as *au courant* with modern gender roles (Dockterman 2018), as relayed in the following movie trailer tagline for *Frozen*: "Who will save the day? The ice guy, the nice guy, the snowman, or no man?" (see Wilde 2014, p. 146 for an insightful analysis of this tagline). The premise of the tagline is that it is simply shocking or inconceivable that "no man" is the answer. Furthermore, when Elsa "saves the day", it is at the end of the movie rather than during the iconic song 'Let it Go' (Vincent 2016), at which time she does not exhibit the full array of her powers. In fact, at the film's conclusion, when the lesson of the film emerges, she has become nurturing, demonstrating that the force she must defeat consists primarily of her own internal demons.

At the center of *Frozen*'s plot is Elsa's harmful unleashing of emotional turmoil in the form of storms. Her redemption comes when she scales back her use of power and supernatural abilities, suggesting that restrained power is apropos for a woman, and brings serenity to those around her. These same powers allow her to conceive without male input. She produces two non-human sons, Olaf and Marshmallow, through parthenogenesis (from Greek *parthenos* "virgin" + *genesis* "creation"). Elsa draws this procreative potential from the male-associated domain of wind and storms, weather conditions that she touts in the song, 'Let it Go'.

When Elsa initially harnesses the seminal power of the weather and parthenogenesis, her independence from men is depicted as anomalous, which is consistent with her original conception as a villain (and as a brainchild of males) in early pre-release plans (Acuna 2014; Solomon 2013). These early plans involved a jilted Elsa left at the altar (Hibberd 2017). Thus, it is not surprising that Elsa conceives without a male—although this act of subversion results in her having fatherless, gender non-conforming sons. Despite that her snowman son Olaf clearly is a male character, there is overt queer coding, from his pronouncement that he likes "warm hugs" to jokes about being impaled and asking Anna's love interest, Kristoff, to "grab his butt"(see Streiff and Dundes 2017a). Elsa's other son, Marshmallow, mixes truculence with the underlying meaning of his name, traits culminating in *sub rosa* cross-dressing after the credits roll. These themes that reflect anxieties that are prevalent at the time of the film's 2013 release are part of its titular message—*Frozen*—that is, the consequences of an eternal winter that is tied to threats to the gender hierarchy.

---

[1] Elsa's traits are not unique, as her powers resemble those of Storm, a black character who first appeared in 1975 as a member of the Marvel Comics X-Men, a group of mutant heroes. When Storm cannot control her emotions or succumbs to a fit of rage, violent weather can ensue, a characterization based on a Yoruba deity linked to "lightning and gale force winds, radical change, and sudden retribution that verges on the unmanageable" (Scott 2006, p. 310).

In this paper, we present a mythopoetic analysis of *Frozen* given the film's recapitulation of themes of Greek mythology. Myths are known for their adaptability and ability to "encapsulate cultural patterns ... [and] projections of basic human dilemmas or impulses" (Dundes 1984, p. 3). In fact, archetypes from Greek mythology arguably bridge millennia with lasting resonance. Since popular Disney films tap into an "era's complex and evolving" mores, they capture cultural shifts, especially gender-related conflicts (Davis 2007, p. 17). Our methodology involves content analysis with an unconventional emphasis on the symbolic and lexicographic manifestations of masculinity and effeminacy. Our analysis includes an examination of the portrayal of Olaf and Marshmallow, the snowflake emblem of Elsa's ice palace, and storm symbolism. A major theme explored is Elsa's command of storms as representative of her subversion of male power, which is imitative of the symbolism of Zeus, the Olympian king. As the Snow Queen, Elsa emulates Zeus in his position at the top of the social hierarchy in a cloud palace above Mount Olympus; Elsa lives in her palace atop the North Mountain, complete with a soaring steeple mounted on a phallic spire. Elsa conjures storm power associated with Zeus that denotes his consummate manhood (as symbolized by his phallic thunderbolt insignia). In taking on the role of Zeus, Elsa bucks the seemingly entrenched social order that defines males as the ultimate creators, with females as secondary.

Elsa's lack of romantic interest in men, her parthenogenesis, and her gender non-conforming sons portray a female that can dispense with men, especially in contrast to her romantically-inclined sister. Related anxieties about male expendability are consonant with the perspective of prominent feminist philosopher Sara Ruddick, who suggested that women's ability to give birth "inspires in men a fear that women will do it virtually without them and [that women could] exploit the real powers they would get if they were not socially dominated (and until recently, dominated by a reproductive body which they could not harness to their own uses)" (Kittay 1984, citing personal communication with Ruddick).

Gilmore (2010) echoes Ruddick's assessment, arguing that misogynistic practices reflect entrenched male anxieties surrounding men's simultaneous dependence on women and their loathing for how these needs are seen as degrading to their masculinity. Nevertheless, men's pride in their role in conception may sometimes supersede concerns about their manhood, resulting in the declaration, "We're pregnant." However, in *Frozen*, female parthenogenesis presents an interesting reversal of men's so-called 'womb envy', which plays out at an unconscious level, revealing the complexity of gender dynamics. Indeed, were such thoughts conscious, they could not sublimate unacceptable anxieties coinciding with the film's zeitgeist.

This paper elucidates these motifs that reflect the film's social context, specifically how Elsa challenges and terrorizes her people, hers by virtue of succeeding her father, when she usurps the domain of Zeus—specifically, control over the weather and fertility. Georg Simmel (1858–1918), one of the German 'fathers' of sociology, discusses related themes surrounding gender dynamics. Simmel posits that "the will of the *pater familias* ... imposed upon the home appears as 'authority' endowing men with a 'logical superiority'" (Simmel and Oakes 1984, p. 24). However, a gradual shift away from this model of male dominance may create "nostalgia for the past, a sort of eschatology in which the present is subject to a *wind* of total destruction" (Elliott and Turner 2012, p. 20, emphasis added), a nostalgia that may fuel angst about revised gender roles.

2. Images of Conception: the Fireworks of When the Sperm Meet the Egg

Storms represent divine power manifested in a variety of sounds including simulated gunfire and other explosions. Storms' visual effects include firework-like lightning bolts (such as Harry Potter's lightning bolt forehead scar). *Frozen* opens with the "iconic Disney castle" (Do Rozario 2004) with fireworks erupting over its phallic minarets (that connote creation reminiscent of the Biblical fiat, "Let there be light"). This imagery suggests conception, which is a phenomenon long associated with fireworks with good reason: "Human life begins in a bright flash of light as a sperm meets an egg, [which] scientists have shown for the first time, after capturing the astonishing 'fireworks' on film. [... as] an explosion of tiny sparks erupts from the egg at the exact moment of conception" (Knapton

2016, para. 1–2 regarding Duncan et al. 2016). Note that firework displays and explosions tend to be the dominion of males, including firecrackers that explode in blasts (Keller 2014), simulating lightning and thunder.[2] These audiovisuals reminiscent of Independence Day set the stage for other related themes in *Frozen*, including how control over the weather is associated with masculinity.

3. The Bullroarer and the Wind–Fertility Link

The links between storms, wind, and gender dynamics found in *Frozen* are also exemplified in an ancient and sacred male instrument, the bullroarer. It is a device that is whirled in a circle as part of a male-only ritual associated with thunder and wind (Dundes 1976), which is consistent with the multiple Greek gods of the wind (such as Aeolus and the Anemoi, or The Winds), all of whom are male. The sound made by the bullroarer is considered a form of thunder that represents the voice of a deity during a ritual in which boys become men through rebirth. However, this rebirth entails being born from men, not women.[3] Since the origin of the bullroarer is ascribed to women, male appropriation of the device may reflect male jealousy of female parturition (Dundes 1976). The reconceptualization of male identity through male rebirth erases the connotations of a mama's boy, as the absence of the term 'mama's man' implies that becoming a man entails effectuating freedom from maternal influence, and downplays women's procreative power. Thus, to create men symbolically, men (and exclusively men) are required; women can create only boys.

Males mimic female procreativity in symbolic form through the making of noise, wind, thunder, etc. (Dundes 1976). That is, blowing (breath, wind) is a critical act that is parallel to the fertilizing power of wind, simulating plants' pollination (see Motif T 524, Conception from Wind, e.g., Hera's impregnation by wind to conceive Hephaistos (Dundes 1976).[4] Similarly, so-called extending party 'blowout noisemakers' link blowing, noise, and erections (necessary for fertilization), while the well-known celebration emoji shows sperm-like confetti spewing from a horn (that is blown to commemorate victory). This is a variant of a cornucopia or horn of plenty marking conception as celebratory. It is also within the context of the horn's etymology as "an erection of the penis" (Horn 2018), which is part of the constellation of male power, blowing, and fertility that is commandeered by Elsa.

4. Wind and the Soul

At the close of the song 'Let it Go', Elsa invokes her power over the weather, singing, "Let the Storm Rage On". The origins of the word rage are "spirit and passion" (as in a fashion that is all the rage). Rage is also linked etymologically to hydrophobia (Rage 2018), which contextualizes the term 'raging storm'.

Psyche is also connected to the weather in its meaning of life in the sense of breath formed—from *psycho*, "to blow" (in Greek) as well as spirit, soul, ghost, and self (Psyche 2018). This same fundamental connection between life and breath is found in *pneuma*, an ancient Greek word for breath with a religious meaning of spirit or soul, while in Hebrew, *ruach* means wind, breath, and spirit (likely related to the significance of the shofar, a traditional Jewish trumpet made from a ram's horn). Similarly, spirit and breath are also found in the Chinese character for spirit and soul (hún), combining (ytextgreekún) and

---

[2]   *Son et lumière* (French: sound and light shows) recreate weather-related phenomena, especially those that include pyrotechnics at French châteaux.

[3]   The psychology of the bullroarer may explain the appeal of roaring leaf blowers as well as why male flatulence and the removal of mufflers on vehicles are markers of masculinity (Dundes 1976). 'Breaking wind' (also known as pumping) as a form of anal creation is connected to conceptions of male anal birth, connoted in the term 'thunderbox', a makeshift toilet. For more on anal birth, see Dundes (1984).

[4]   Weather vanes show the direction of the wind, traditionally fashioned as a cock with a penetrative arrow given that the wind is an agent of fertilization. Dundes (1994) notes that the cock's reputation for resurrection explains its placement atop penile architectural constructions such as church towers. In addition, a number of idioms connect wind and fertility, e.g., how "shooting blanks" can "take the wind out of [a man's] sails" (Szadek 2017, para. 17).

(gui) and related to the word for clouds as well as breath in expressions denoting smoking or vaping (François 2008).[5]

On a smaller (human) scale, the connection between wind and breath is manifested in the term to be winded, meaning out of breath. The words *inspiration* (breathing in air), *mind blowing*, and *afflatus* (a divine creative impulse, from Latin: *afflare*: to blow) are also related to wind power (that is, air as opposed to liquid, as in creative juices). In fact, the idiom 'brainstorm' in Spanish reveals these interconnections in the form of *lluvia de ideas*, a rainstorm of ideas, while the word idea is represented by a light bulb emoji as well, which is consistent with metaphors about inspiration that involve light bulbs (that simulate lightning), and show how conceptions of the weather permeate the everyday English lexicon.

Connections between spirit and breath were developed independently by disparate cultures (Liddell and Scott 1897), showing the cross-cultural resonance of the power of weather phenomena. Wind is personified in the word window (from Old Norse) wind + *auga* "eye" (Window 2018), which is akin to the eye of a storm. The wind in the sense of a spirit or ghost channeling male power helps explain why lesbians and spinsters are associated with these supernatural phenomena, since neither group accedes to men's domination, explaining why the connection in women is stigmatized (see the conceptualization of "ghostly and witchy lesbians" and "spinster witch[es]" in Cuomo 1995, p. 222). In other words, unmarried women have the freedom to appropriate male power, but must bear the social costs associated with this independence as old maids or queer women.

5. Wind as Fertilizing and Gender

Historically, the wind as a fecundating agent explains the role of the Holy Ghost (or spirit) in the pregnancy of the Virgin Mary (see Jones 1951; Zirkle 1936). *Geist* (ghost) is related to spirit, breath, or wind, given the belief in wind-eggs (Zirkle 1936). *Spiritus* meant either breath or ghost with the "consistent element that men seek to live without recourse to women" (Dundes 1976, p. 234). In *Genesis*, a wind moved over the waters (v1:2), after which God animated Adam by breathing life into his nostrils (v2:7).[6] The conflation of breath and soul lends meaning to a newborn's initial breath that allows the spirit into the body while a person's last breath (or rattle) signals the spirit's exit from the body (Ryrie 1997). Wind power is also evident in the notion of fanning the flames (of passion or anger), as well as the expression "as the spirit moves me", denoting when a person feels a sort of supernatural motivation that is beyond logic or consciousness.

Critical to this analysis is the portrayal of Elsa's various special powers derived through wind and storms as a curse. According to *Frozen* co-director Jennifer Lee, "One sister [has] a superpower—or an *affliction*—and one [is] ignored because her sister's taking up all the energy in the room" (Solomon 2013, emphasis added).[7] Her power serves as an apparently frightening reversal of traditional gender hierarchy in which a woman controls procreation in the context of a *Frozen* atmosphere, given that the title serves as a constant reminder that Elsa's "affliction" resulted in an "eternal winter", as Anna says (56:52), which is notable since creating something everlasting is normally enviable.

---

[5] Smoking makes the breath visible, creating a cloud of smoke that may give the smoker a feeling of power and creation, as when Mushu (in Disney's *Mulan*) blows smoke rings around the emasculated falcon of the villain, before riding him as an act of dominance (*Mulan* 1998, 1:13:45).

[6] Adam was "animated" by the breath of life just as (mostly) male Disney animators create life, especially given that the characters may seem real to children.

[7] Jennifer Lee, the only woman to direct a Disney animated feature film, went from screenwriter to co-director, increasing her role in *Frozen's* story. Born as Jennifer Rebecchi, she took her mother's name (Lee) after her parents' divorce. Her only daughter (with her ex-husband), Agatha Lee Monn, sings the middle verse of 'Do You Want to Build a Snowman?' a song celebrating Elsa's childhood magical powers. As Lee is also the voice of Elsa and Anna's mother, the story could reflect Lee's worldview about gender. A final sign that Lee's life may have influenced the story was the traumatic death of her boyfriend in a boating accident her junior year of college (reminiscent of the death by shipwreck of Elsa and Anna's parents) (UNH 2014). These factors illustrate the proverbial connection between art and life.

Elsa's power is clearly an affliction, because she initially abuses it to the detriment of the whole society, selfishly inviting the storm to "rage" on while she grapples with the consequences of her emotional lability (in defiance of the expectation of women's self-sacrifice and altruism (Dundes 2001)); at one point, when she and Anna talk in her ice palace, she confesses to her sister, "I can't control the curse" (57:16–18). Shortly thereafter, in a soliloquy, she watches in frustration as sharp icicles[8] emerge from the walls of her palace, as she chants in vain, "Control it. Don't feel—don't feel—don't feel." In the film's representation of the 2013 zeitgeist (the ghost or spirit of the time), anxieties about rising female power (reflected in Elsa's selfishness and lack of control) may have been conflated[9] with growing concerns that storms presage anthropogenic climate anomalies, especially during the "boreal" cold season (Cohen et al. 2009; Cohen et al. 2018), with boreal derived from Boreas, the god of the north wind.

6. The Hand as Surrogate Phallus

Elsa's manipulation of the weather occurs manually. However, this power is not unleashed until she frees herself of her father's order to metaphorically repress her sexuality, which had been accomplished by covering her hands with gloves (Streiff and Dundes 2017a).[10] After Anna accidentally pulls off one of Elsa's gloves at the coronation ball, an act that wreaks havoc, Elsa removes the second glove during the song 'Let it Go'. Elsa is then capable of female parthenogenesis since earlier, until the gloves come off, her sexuality is stifled.[11] This symbolism is clear in the popular saying "no glove, no love", which refers to condoms as metaphorical sheaths given the phallic association of hands. Indeed, the word man is cognate with manual meaning managing by using the hands (Hempl 1901). "The figurative use of the hand for the whole man is very natural and appears in almost every language. It refers to the hand as the skillful *member* and generally designates a laborer or a skillful person. Thus, deckhand, farmhand" (Hempl 1901, p. 426, emphasis added). The word *hand* is a metonym for authority with phallic connotations, as revealed in the name Benjamin, as *ben* means "son of" + *yamin* "right hand". "Ben" as the son of the right hand also connotes the celestial power of gods, as the word "ben" also means "mountain peak".

When Elsa executes parthenogenesis using her ungloved hands, she reveals them not only as phallic, but also as capable of magic, which is also known as prestidigitation, meaning fast fingers, or legerdemain, from French, *léger de main*, meaning literally "light (weight) of hand" (Legerdemain 2018). She accomplishes these feats without the use of a *hand*book, but rather as a so-called "phallic woman" (Steele 2001, p. 76).

7. Let it Go—Bucking the Trend of Songs as Evoking Romantic Enchantment

Elsa's first act of parthenogenesis occurs during 'Let it Go'. As a song, it is a form of incantation or en-*chant*-ment (see *chanter*, *cantar*, or *cantor*, related to singing). Typically, songs in Disney princess movies promote the heterosexual coupling of a female with a dominant male that can cause relative strangers to fall in love, especially in a magically short period of time; this phenomenon is parodied in *Frozen's* song 'Love is an Open Door', which precipitates the engagement of Hans and Anna the same day they met. 'Love is an Open Door' mocks characters such as *Sleeping Beauty's* Aurora, who

---

[8] Icicle is slang for penis, according to both male and female college students (see Cameron 1992, p. 381). Other penile pet names relevant to this essay include: thunder-log; thunder-stick; love horn; love wand; leaning tower of please-her; as well as firearms such as guns, rifles, and pistols (Cameron 1992, pp. 379–81).

[9] *Conflare*: from *con*- "together" + *flare* "to blow," is linked to the word afflatus or divine inspiration.

[10] Likewise, the ageless (and childless) Mickey Mouse always wears gloves and has a high-pitched voice, revealing that he has not gone through puberty and that gloves may symbolize repressed sexuality.

[11] Elsa's parthenogenesis is castrating because she usurps the putative role of men: "to father" a son means to provide the sperm, whereas the term "to mother" a son means to bring up a child with solicitude and affection. This then puts the emphasis on the men's role in ensuring their DNA is passed on (given doubts of paternity: see Horn 2004, p. 49) rather than input in the day-to-day care, which in the context of *Frozen* implies that Elsa's parthenogenesis calls into question the need for men.

falls for Prince Philip during a song in which they dance in the woods, and most classically Cinderella, who loves Prince "Charming" after their ballroom dance, which is accompanied by singing. Why the prince is "charming" is related to both the word's etymology from Latin *carmen* ("song, incantation") and to Old French *charme* ("chant, magic, spell") (Charm 2018). Thus, the magic of singing is related to its ability to magically 'charm' a person (or 'charm' a snake in the case of blowing a phallic wind instrument called a *pungi*). The result is a person who might say he is *enchanté* (enchanted) by a woman who makes him feel spellbound. This is a fundamental concept in Disney princess movies, given the ubiquity of enchantment, a phenomenon linked to wind in the sense that the word 'air' is a synonym for song. Moreover, it indicates how the magic associated with men is charming, whereas magic performed by women is chilling (discussed below).

However, Elsa and her propensity for inducing freezing are the antithesis of an enchantress that mesmerizes men. At her coronation ball, Elsa tells Anna, "No one is getting married" (26:22–23) after Anna and Hans tell her of their nuptial plans. Note that she does not say, "It's too soon to get married" or "You must ensure you've found the right person". Instead, she implies permanent restrictions on sexual behavior for both her sister and herself, suggesting her own lack of interest in bewitching a man. In fact, Anna criticizes Elsa's tendency "to shut people out" (26:41–43).

8. The Powerful Woman as Castrating Witch

Women who do not aim to please in social situations may feel marginalized, as shown in Elsa's coronation party, where she clearly does not have a ball. She refuses to dance with anyone and offers her sister as an alternative dance partner to the bloviating Duke of Weselton, since it seems to be impolite to 'stiff' a man, even one who is clearly undesirable–a "man in heels," as Anna calls the duke derisively (22:03–04). Elsa's discomfort intensifies when she loses one of her gloves, fearing what her bare hand will unleash. She ends the ball, decreeing, "The party [ball] is over. Close the gates" (26:54–57) (two sentences that are uttered consecutively with good [symbolic] reason). At this point, she is quite literally a ball-buster, with a metaphorical meaning of "a dominating or threatening woman who destroys a man's self-confidence" (Ball-buster 2018). Note that a dominating woman destroys (rather than just shakes) a man's confidence, since power shifts are a zero sum game—women apparently gain power at the expense of men. Shortly thereafter, Elsa loses her master status as queen when the duke accuses her of sorcery (27:31–32), and later refers to her powers as a "curse" (29:39–45). At this point, Elsa's power elicits fear as she is portrayed as a type of witch who flies off the (broom?) handle, bringing to mind witches' incantations and chanting[12] over a boiling cauldron (with cauldrons connoting a situation characterized by instability and strong emotions). Elsa is an echo of witches of the Middle Ages, many of whom were killed as they were perceived as too threatening according to the witchhunting manual, the *Malleus Malficarum*.[13] The manual describes witches' penis envy as they straddled broomsticks and castrated men, storing the phalluses in a bird's nest. Thus, the phalluses were a nest egg of sorts in lieu of actual eggs since witches coveted the power of phalluses rather than ova, helping them displace men. These images were invented to express male fears stemming from

---

[12] When fans or cheerleaders chant, there may be an unconscious connection between chanting and the power of en-chant-ment to bring good fortune to the preferred team (analogous to protestors that chant). On a similar note, in the Disney ride *It's a Small World*, "three hundred audio-animatronic children chant the ride's title song ... [which was] crafted in response to the Cuba Missile Crisis" (Wills 2017, p. 52), illustrating how 'chanting' is a form of enchantment with prayer-like qualities. It is a mantra of sorts that reflects belief in the magic of the 'omnipotence of thought' (see Pumpian-Mindlin 1969; and Dundes 2003b for how some individuals believe that their decision to bring—or not to bring—an umbrella will affect the weather).

[13] In the *Malleus Malficarum*, "the field of masculine magic is dramatically limited and male magicians are pointedly marginalized" (Broedel 2003, p. 175). The book targeted women, revealed by the titular use of 'maleficarum,' versus 'maleficorum', a spelling that denoted a feminine gender and "hostility toward women" (see Pavlac 2009, p. 57). This hostility is evident in the rarely used full title of the *Malleus Malficarum*: "The Hammer of Witches which destroyeth Witches and their heresy as with a two-edged sword," with a sword bringing to mind the need to re-feminize these usurpers of male-associated power.

societal shifts in which women were scapegoats (Ben-Yehuda 1980; Zika 1989), and have parallels to how Elsa's community reacts to her phallic powers.

Not surprisingly, the special powers of men were seen differently, as the word magic derives from *magos* and is the basis of the word magi meaning men, specifically the Wise Men *and* "māga", magicians, from Old Persian *magush*, possibly from the root magh- "to have power" (Magic 2018). Yet the word *māg* means not only "relative or kinsman", but also means "son" (Hempl 1901, p. 427). With these etymologies, then, we can understand a classic magic trick as an expression of womb envy: pulling a live rabbit out of a hat.[14] Thus, the magic and enchantment that is part of Disney's male-associated 'Magic' *King*dom can be seen within the context of male creation fantasy.

Elsa's use of her hands to create is the usurpation of male power associated with the 'stroke' of a magic wand and the phallic power of pens, a form of handiwork reflected in the creation of holy scripture (writing).[15] This phenomenon relates to the term pen name and the import of signing ceremonies (Mayer 2002) with multiple ballpoint or fountain pens (with a font of ink) that are given out as phallic trophies after the signer has issued his John Hancock. Pencils, which are etymologically "little penises", have lower status, as the province of pusillanimous pencil-pushers (see Pencil 2018).

The phallic use of hands—and specifically pens—links to the weather given that a stroke of a pen also means a stroke in the sense of striking someone or something: a blow, e.g., a stroke of genius (related to "inspiration" from wind), or a stroke or blow of a cane (Stroke 2018). As such, a *strike* of lightning or winds that *blow* connote storm power and fertility; similar to the stroke of (phallic) pens, they are part of unconscious gendered symbolism as when Elsa eventually uses her hands to defrost Arendelle, first looking down at them (1:27:53) before ending her rebellion against paternal pressure to be the perfect daughter, which entailed concealing her power (Streiff and Dundes 2017a) to be stereotypically ladylike.

9. Son (Sown) Versus Daughter and Conception Via Whirlwinds

Elsa's status as a daughter is a key element of the plot. The word daughter is etymologically associated with the adjectives "mild; gentle; meek", while the word son (*sōn*) is related to procreative powers as in "to bear; give birth" (Son 2018). Specifically, to sow or to "scatter, disperse, or plant" (seeds) is related to semen "seed", which is a suffixed form of the root *sē- "to sow" (Seed 2018). Sow is also commonly invoked in common parlance: "You reap what you sow", or "sowing wild oats". Thus, sons are etymologically imbued with hopes for fertility. Sowing is also linked to the wind as reproductive. For example, in *Hosea* 8:7: "They have sown the wind, and they shall reap the whirlwind." Thus, the act of sowing (fertilizing) results in a whirlwind (a mini-tornado), which is linked to creation.

However, Elsa as a daughter independently produces two snowmen sons by using her ungloved hands to create whirlwinds and sparkles (i.e., sparks) that transform into Olaf and Marshmallow, without male input (see Figure 1). The twinkling that emanates from her hands as they create snowflakes and Olaf are reminiscent of the billions of zinc sparks that occur when a sperm connects with an egg during a successful egg-to-embryo transition (Que et al. 2015). Without gloves, Elsa can procreate, using wind power. In fact, the movement of wind was central enough to *Frozen* to spawn a whole article devoted to techniques used to simulate wind effects in the film (Wilson et al. 2014).

---

[14] This trick requires (1) pulling, which connotes the delivery of a child at birth; (2) the use of rabbits, which are fertility symbols; and (3) hats (Rabbit hat 2018) that are slang for vagina in German (Borneman 1971) and conceptually related to the infamous 'pussy hats' as vaginas or uteruses (see Brewer and Dundes 2018 for the controversy over these hats as an appropriate feminist symbol). Finally, when a female performs a trick, prostitution is implied, as opposed to men who are encouraged to 'wear many hats'.

[15] Hand idioms are ubiquitous. For example, the word hand is mentioned in the Bible over 1000 times, and those with manifold skills (factotums) are called handymen, to provide just one example.

Figure 1. The creation of Olaf.

Elsa's act of conception shows her as a "tempestress" of sorts, reflecting her ability to conjure storms and make herself seemingly an object of desire. Her swagger in her form-fitting dress signals her temptress capabilities that remind the audience of women's power to entice men. Her makeover includes stiletto heels, connoting danger and sexuality symbolized by stilettos as pumps, but also as daggers (Praz 1970; Steele 2001) (33:07–09; see 1:02:33 for a close up of Elsa's stiletto spike). Thus, her foot, along with her hands, allows her to express her creative power in a way that combines male *and* female aspects that are usually involved in creation. Elsa stomps on ice as the first "step" in making her castle (33:22), a *mise-en-scène* in which her sexual appeal and ability to create are striking. This mix of Elsa's power with creation is likely related to fears about controlling women's sexuality, especially the role of a woman's eggs. Due to conflicted feelings about women's power in this regard, men's integral role, including in conception, is normally emphasized.

Historical sociology provides some perspective on this age-old tension. Vromen (1987) explains how sociologist Georg Simmel viewed gender dynamics: "Women are expected to please, serve and complement men . . . Outside of their relationship to men, Simmel insisted, women are seen as *nothing*" (Vromen 1987, p. 570, emphasis added). Simmel's proposed solution to gender inequality is ironic in light of our analysis: "There is room for cultural creativity by women only 'if they accomplish something that *men cannot do*' (Simmel's emphasis) . . . eliminat[ing] women as competitors against men" (Vromen 1987, p. 571). Simmel suggests that women reduce the competition over "creativity" by both presiding over the home and socializing men since "only to the extent that woman differs from man is her autonomy assured" (Vromen 1987, p. 575); this assessment omits women's unique procreative abilities. The idea that women are seen as "nothing" outside of their relationship with men, or as a metaphorical zero, raises the question of whether women's indispensable role in conception is devalued to avoid acknowledging men's dependence on women for procreation (that is, men's lack of worth without women).

10. The Devaluation of Women's Eggs and Fertility

When Elsa creates independently (without men), she symbolically contributes an egg without a complementary male fertilizing agent (besides the wind)—a zero of sorts, with a distinct egg shape in certain cultures: ٥ : the Arabic zero. This implies that an egg, similar to a zero, has no value by itself (until another numeral is added in the case of a zero). The connection between female eggs and zeroes is seen in the term goose egg, which applies to games that feminize those shut out from scoring (a blow out).[16]

---

[16] The custom of egging houses humiliates the target through feminization, just like having egg on one's face connotes humiliation. Breaking eggs, however, can also be propitious as in Mexico, when *cascarones*—hollowed eggshells filled with confetti—are crushed on people's heads, bringing good luck (specifically fertility) (Contreras et al. 2015), which is likely due to the sperm-like associations of confetti (that are paired with eggs penetrated by sperm as part of conception).

While the term goose egg is an insult, the link between a zero and an egg could be examined within the context of how the time in utero prior to birth is not typically counted. In other words, when babies are born, they are not considered to be nine months old (if they are full term). This both empowers and demeans women. Prior to the baby's birth, when the fetus is in utero, the woman has virtually complete control over the growing being (which is empowering). However, the fact that the pre-natal time in utero is *not* counted in a child's age in the US could be construed as demeaning, since this time when women do have complete control over the fetus is not credited as the beginning of life. As such, we pose the following question regarding a hypothetical Father Gander instead of Mother Goose: if men were associated with fictional pseudo-birds that incubated fertilized eggs, would the newborn still be age zero at birth? Perhaps what happens before birth is a metaphorical goose egg, not because of any biological realities, but rather because following fertilization, men are not involved in pregnancy (and may even be unaware that they have fathered a child). In other words, personhood seems to require independence from the mother, akin to "oppositional self-assertion and separation ... of the toddler or adolescent male vis-à-vis the parent, usually the mother" (Eurich-Rascoe and Kemp 1997, p. 12). The separation is also interpreted as respect for patriarchy (Creed 1993). Thus, the term goose egg likely reflects androcentrism in the English lexicon as well as in larger society. Just as zeroes (metaphorical eggs) have no value without another numeral attached to them, women ostensibly need male input for their eggs to be viable—unless that woman is Elsa running amuck with snowmen spawn. These assertions are consistent with calling someone a bad egg if they misbehave, an expression that implicitly attributes flaws entirely to the woman. In other words, it is her fault if the rapscallion is 'rotten', since the female provides the egg.

11. Women as Nubile

Elsa's lack of interest in males in any capacity stands in sharp contradistinction to her sister, Anna. Elsa is more termagant than nubile nymph; she is the storm, raging on (as she sings in 'Let it Go').[17] She has no interest in assuming the passive female role in a union with a man who penetrates the female to fertilize her. Instead, similar to Zeus, she is capable of parthenogenesis, while wielding power that intimidates, and indeed emasculates men such as the unemployed icemen that describe Elsa as an "icy force" in the first line of the film (in *The Frozen Heart: Ice Worker's Song*) and who see her as sexually inaccessible (see Streiff and Dundes 2017a). She not only prevents them from working, but also usurps their role, as we see when Anna knocks on the doors of Elsa's ice palace. The doors open for her, but Kristoff is told not to enter. Anna is nervous about how Elsa will react to him and thus instructs him not to come inside, prompting him to stammer with frustration, "But, but ... come on! It's a palace made of ice. Ice is my life" (53:36–38). Thus, Anna goes in alone (initially), showing that Elsa has both eclipsed the male role of ice harvester and has no desire for males to enter her (ice palace).

This scene cues the audience to see Elsa as hostile to men, tempestuous rather than nubile (meaning not just like a cloud, but also like a young, sexually mature woman that is suitable for marriage). Nubile women are highly prized, and even likely to incite envy. We see ritualized protection against invidious reactions to their desirability in wedding 'toasts' that connote metaphorical drying, perhaps related to the evil eye in which enviable situations risk inviting desiccation committed by those who (often inadvertently) covet another person's good fortune (e.g., presumed impending fertility for newlyweds).[18] Note that nubile women are young (not older, presumably infertile women). As cloudlike, they augur marital bliss of ascendance to the mythical cloud nine.

---

[17] Similarly, colds have been popularly associated with frigid temperatures, while the idiom catching a cold hints at the airborne spread of viruses via wind-like manifestations of illness. These symptoms, such as "blowing" one's nose, coughing, and sneezing, may cause others to feel dis-ease, while among children, avoidance is played out in the game tag in which youth flee con-*tag*-ion, the game's etymological derivation (Contagion 2018).

[18] The best man typically gives a wedding toast that makes fun of the groom, as a public performance meant to both convey knowledge of the groom based on friendship but also as a means to present a façade that implies that the groom is not worthy of envy.

As nubile (that is, cloudlike), these ostensibly fertile women are similar to water vapor that condenses, preventing dryness. Yet because a toast is metaphorically drying, there is a compensatory need for fluids to counteract any drying associated with envy (that is, the evil eye). As such, it is strictly socially mandated that all wedding guests drink following a toast. An empty glass or refusal to join in the toast is taboo; all guests must imbibe fluid that is dedicated to the hydration and thus fertility of the couple (Sakkas et al. 2015) traditionally mandated to be fruitful and multiply. Wine (or *spark*ling wine) is the drink of choice, which is likely because Dionysus, the god of wine who was born from Zeus' thigh, promotes fertility. It is perhaps because of Zeus's parthenogenesis of the god, also known as Bacchus, that this begotten[19] son became the eponymous facilitator of intoxication-fueled ecstasy. The loud popping of a champagne cork exiting a bottle prefigures the male climax that is traditionally expected on the wedding night.

12. Alcohol as Spirits that Reinforce Conventional Masculinity

The latent gender implications of Bacchus's origins and the underlying meaning of wedding toasts are hardly isolated examples of how beverages evoke the gender hierarchy, albeit unconsciously. Elsa is powerful because her conflicts are no tempest in a teapot, as befits a woman (cf. *Beauty and the Beast*'s even-keeled Mrs. Potts). Likewise, the analogous term storm in a cream bowl (Bartlett 1891) implies that women's volatility is normally less consequential than that of males, as cream is from milk; even drinking coffee with milk is arguably a form of feminizing it, versus drinking an espresso "black" with a double shot. A tempest in a teapot differs from the storm power associated with concoctions such as Hurricanes as well as Dark n' Stormy 'cocktails'. Distilled liquor (rum, brandy, whiskey, gin, and vodka), so-called spirits, are hard liquor that contrast with soft drinks (that is, soda). Moonshine, which was originally a slang term for high-proof distilled spirits, was known as white lightning. Pressure for men to imbibe hard liquor is manifested in men competing in taking shots, as in taking bullets from a gunshot (since the idiom is not drinking a shot). Males who take shots competitively show their ability to be symbolically impaled by a projectile and survive; the man who stops drinking or passes out is feminized. In this regard, it is notable that the term abstinence applies both to restraint in alcohol consumption and sex. When Zeus or Thor releases the power of a storm, no restraint is expected (as Zeus is not a drop in the bucket kind of being).[20] Male drinkers are encouraged to get blasted or smashed, words that can be used to describe storm damage. This is why excessive alcohol is commonly part of fraternity hazing in which establishing masculinity is central (see Dundes and Dundes 2002 for more on this topic). The term aspirational blackout (Carrick 2016) from binge drinking is as if the drinker unconsciously invokes the power of lightning strikes.

Frozen includes a gender-coded drink in its provocative beach scene in which Elsa's gender non-conforming son, Olaf, imagines luxuriating on a beach under an umbrella, with a pink drink in hand, garnished with an orange slice on a straw, and diluted with ice cubes. It is clearly not a stiff drink that is served straight up, but rather more of a fruity drink (a descriptor with queer coding as the word fruit is a derogatory term for gay males). This fantasy beach scene (47:52–53) is celebrated in products such as Disney's "*Frozen* Tablecloth featuring Summer Olaf" and the "*Frozen* Olaf Loves Heat Bath Towel" (available on Amazon.com). Although we have no way of knowing if Olaf's pink drink had value-added masculinity by being "spiked", as an effeminate male, Olaf was under no pressure to

---

[19] By definition, beget (or begotten) may imply parthenogenesis: "typically of a man, sometimes of a man and a woman: bring (a child) into existence by the process of reproduction" (Begotten 2018).

[20] Elsa's control of the weather conjures Zeus's unparalleled power, as reflected in his Roman name, Jupiter. The planet Jupiter is 2.5 times the size of all of the other planets in the solar system combined. It is made primarily of gases, and thus is a gas giant (Rogers 1995). It is perhaps related conceptually to thunder, which is compressed air (wind) that powerfully explodes, connoting the metaphor of the Big Bang believed to mark the beginning of the universe, with sexual overtones that hint at male sexual release (and guns as phallic). In the case of Thor, as the god of thunder, storms, and wind (for whom Thursday is named), it is significant that he is also a fertility god, linking control of the weather and fertility, likely because of the role of the wind in plant fertilization (Violatti 2014).

prove himself by consuming a macho beverage. This is consistent with research showing that men drink more when their masculinity is threatened by shifting gender roles. According to Lyons et al. (2006), "Young men who feel that their identity is threatened [by] changes and [that] their traditional roles are being challenged take up masculine values more strongly than previously [and display] stronger versions of masculinity [that] distinguish men's drinking from women's" (p. 230).

13. Kristoff and Sven as Masculine

Olaf's open effeminacy is a useful foil to bolster Kristoff's masculinity, especially as Kristoff is an iceman emasculated by Elsa's eternal winter, which puts him out of work (Streiff and Dundes 2017a). In addition, Kristoff benefits from compensatory virility when he is compared to his competitor, Hans. Hans woos Anna only because he craves power; he is a classic "false hero" (in line with the *dramatis personae* articulated by Propp (1958)). As a false hero slated for deportation back to his country of origin (1:29:41–42), he exemplifies the 2013-era "solutions" for dealing with *persona non gratae* in the wake of immigration concerns. Kristoff, a name that is a form of Christopher (bearer of Christ), burnishes his masculinity by playing a stereotypically important role (although not the sole role) in aiding the damsel in distress, as he rushes a deathly-ill Anna back to Arendelle atop a galloping Sven.

Since Kristoff is not hypermasculine, it is critical that his sidekick Sven be unambiguously masculine in his traits. In fact, Sven is Kristoff's equal and *not* truly his sidekick. This is because Sven (Old Norse for young warrior) enhances Kristoff's machismo as a big animal well endowed with impressive, multi-pointed antlers (a masculinity-affirming trophy often mounted for display in man caves (Dundes 1997b)).

14. Elsa's Snowflake

The points (or spikes) that are characteristic of the antlers or horns of such beasts as Sven are also salient in Elsa's snowflake emblem—and with good (symbolic) reason. The snowflake is on frequent display, but most noticeably on Elsa's ice palace ceiling, which is featured for a full five seconds of the film (53:57–54:01). It is a non-standard form, a shape that was distinct by design, since *Frozen's* artists wanted Elsa to have an extraordinary snowflake: "Elsa [has] a signature snowflake shape. If you saw it anywhere in the movie, you'd know it wasn't nature, it was her" (Solomon 2013) (see Figure 2).

Figure 2. Elsa's signature snowflake.

Her emblem is also featured as a phallic-shaped, spiked snowflake chandelier hanging impressively from the ceiling of her ice palace (33:53–55) (in a design that departs from the conventional spider of lights–*araña de luces*–style). In "How to Draw Elsa's Snowflake" (Draw 2018), a how-to video depicts how the snowflake resembles a flower surrounded by arrows. Hence, symbolically, Elsa is deep down a delicate flower, but one with petals that extrude manifold barbs and arrowheads with clearly depicted *diamond*-shaped arrowheads—a shape that is specifically identified as a "diamond" in the aforementioned how-to video.

15. Elsa's Snowflake and "Ice" as a Substitute Diamond Engagement Ring

The diamonds that are salient in Elsa's snowflake are highly significant, albeit at an unconscious level. Like the points on antlers that represent threatening masculinity, angularly cut diamonds on engagement rings carry an important latent meaning that helps elucidate the symbolism of snowflakes in the plot. A rock is a metonym of the engagement ring due to its hardness (hard as a rock) and its use as a primordial tool of male dominance, as connoted in its selection as the moniker of the 2016 Sexiest Man Alive winner, Dwayne Johnson, "The Rock" (and voice of the hypermasculine Maui in *Moana* (see Streiff and Dundes 2017b)). The expression "diamonds are forever" perhaps is more about diamonds' reputation as a hard substance rather than relationships, which clearly have questionable longevity (as divorce rates indicate). Investment in this custom of diamond engagement rings is so deeply rooted that despite publicity about conflict diamonds, couples remain wedded to this choice of gem.

The traditional rules of engagement (rings) require that a man give the ring to a woman to indicate his claim on her virginity. Its shininess (and size) reflect the male's masculinity, while its reputation for hardness—given the etymology of carat as a 'horn'—wards off and intimidates rivals that threaten the woman's virginity. Similar to the classic red rose, with buds ready to open but protected by spikes that threaten to draw blood to protect the flower, the engagement ring also has 'points', which are a symbol of phallic masculinity. When discussing diamonds, points refer not to the number facets in a diamond, but rather to its weight: e.g., a 10-point diamond weighs 1/10th of a carat, and a 50-point stone weighs one-half of a carat. Thus, diamond rings have a carat that is etymologically related to horns (that are phallic), while the word point (from Latin *punctum*) is related to puncturing or pricking connoting phallic aggression with sexual innuendo (see Figure 3).

Figure 3. The elements of an engagement ring.

An engagement ring is broached in *Frozen* in the scene in which the trolls (Kristoff's surrogate family) try unsuccessfully to rush Anna and Kristoff through a marriage ceremony. When Kristoff informs them that Anna is engaged (to Hans), a troll questions Anna's availability, noting, "I don't see no ring" (1:07:15–17). Yet we would not expect Hans, a false hero, to have given Anna a ring, due to its symbolism. As the trolls intuit, "This quote 'engagement' is a flex arrangement", meaning that the engagement is not a firm commitment. These allusions to questionable masculinity are consistent with a pattern in which the Disney villain is feminized (Li-Vollmer and LaPointe 2003; Putnam 2015; Thompson and Zerbinos 1995; McLeod 2016; Towbin et al. 2004; Patterson and Spencer 2017). This trope is relevant to Hans, who at the end is humiliated when Anna punches him in front of a gallery of men (1:29:16–22), whose ensuing laughter effectively completes his emasculation (Abedinifard 2016). Anna's lack of an engagement ring indicates that Hans is only using her to gain power, and is not concerned with fending off suitors from Anna. Thus, the unconscious symbolic value of an engagement ring is not relevant for Hans. However, the symbolism of engagement rings is relevant to Elsa, whose self-created snowflake emblem embodies her singular independence, which is most notably defined by her refusal to be dominated by a male.

Elsa's ice palace has a number of parallels with diamonds. Her palace has "frozen fractals all around", (according to her narration in 'Let it Go'). *Frozen's* lighting director designed the palace to be "all refractive" (Solomon 2013, p. 121), akin to diamonds that have the highest refractive index amongst natural minerals (Zaitsev 2001). In fact, according to *Frozen's* assistant art director Lisa Keene, the ice is "like a roomful of diamonds" (Solomon 2013, p. 122). In addition, Elsa says in the song that her thoughts "crystallize", which is of note since diamonds are a crystal. There is nothing before*hand*, that is, all is created with only the use of her ungloved hands, releasing their procreative power as manifested in sharp ice shards and icicles that resemble crystals.

Elsa has no need for ice (slang for diamonds) from a man. Her sparkling snowflake emblem is an enhanced version of an engagement ring, but does not carry with it the connotation that a male controls or dominates her. Her surrogate diamond wards off all suitors (from the Latin *sequi*: to follow, or pursue). Notably, her ice palace is an artistic creation, and not a place that is inviting (for example, it lacks a kitchen or other rooms denoting conventional female duties). Her palace is almost dream-like in representing Elsa's soul rather than a home with stereotypical connotations of warmth and nurturing. In fact, her new home is more of a bower: a woman's private quarters, especially in a medieval castle, with privacy implied when she unceremoniously shuts out the audience at the end of 'Let it Go'. This is consistent with her bower as boudoir (from French: *bouder*, to sulk or pout), which is a place to retreat. In some sense, Elsa's whole ice palace is her bower, since she has no interest in entertaining guests and even creates her son Marshmallow as a guard to fend off anyone that attempts to storm her private retreat.

Her spikey snowflake with its ice (metaphorical and literal) seems effective in deterring male suitors, given a total dearth of male interest in the attractive, even seductive Elsa. Despite this absence of romantic entanglements, Disney markets a diamond engagement ring, the "Enchanted Disney Elsa's Snowflake Diamond Engagement Ring" with a diamond that has "the resemblance of a snowflake" (for $4499; Reeds 2018), supporting the interpretation of Elsa's "ice" or snowflake as a symbolic diamond.

It is important within the context of Elsa producing her own diamond to note that it usually represents the male, and *not* the female. This assertion is consistent with Disney's prior portrayal of Aladdin as "a diamond in the rough". In its non-shiny state, a diamond is just a hard surface with the ability to cut, but that lacks the shininess that makes a man an appropriate suitor for a woman, since Aladdin has work to do before he is a suitable mate—or a knight in shining armor or otherwise metaphorically shiny—for Princess Jasmine. Thus, the sparkling diamond (and not a pearl or other stone) signifies that a male has made a claim on a woman, and as such, the conspicuousness of the ring deters male rivals.

Yet another indication that a diamond is symbolic of a male with impressive metaphorical antlers or points that show off manhood and threaten competitors is the well-known term "family jewels":

> When "gonads are equated with expensive gems, male heterosexuality turns into a cost-effective experience in need of a tally sheet and maybe even insurance. The overwhelming emphasis on performance and the portrayal of the penis as a mechanical device, whether tool or weapon, [creates a] heteronormative discourse on masculinity wherein men control the behavior of other men . . . and rely on this misogynist discourse." (Murphy 2001, p. 122).

In addition to the gonads as an instrument of aggression and control, the term family jewels also "place[s] significant value on the reproductive function of the male[21] [without] any comparable slang term for ovaries" (Murphy 2001, p. 35). Furthermore, the term implies that men are "irreplaceable", which could be a form of "womb envy" (Murphy 2001, p. 36): "Men may refer to their gonads as jewels to compensate for their latent realization that the testicles do not hold the same significance in reproduction as does the uterus. That is, men's value in work as in reproduction remains in question and thus a phrase like 'family jewels' is required to assert men's worth" (Murphy 2001, p. 37). Specifically, the "family" jewels denote a man's ability to create a family, that is, offspring that provide a legacy of possible genetic immortality, which is an aspiration modeled by Zeus.

---

[21] In the expression son of a gun, guns as phalluses (Trnka 1995) minimize women's procreative role.

We assert that the flashy diamond on display is thus part of the *man's* jewel collection on loan, presumably on permanent loan, to the female of interest. While wedding bands imply sexual exclusivity for both partners, the diamond engagement ring uses a phallic threat as a sometimes ostentatious means of promulgating the man's sole rights of entry. This interpretation is dependent on the custom of the man giving a woman an engagement ring, but never vice versa. Yet in reality, not only is the tradition of engagement rings unidirectional, but it is also culturally proscribed for a woman to pick out and buy the engagement ring herself. This tradition is so inculcated that the man normally presents the ring to his prospective fiancée, sometimes publicly, in a display of masculinity that marks his proposal. The ring even has a special, designated finger where it must be displayed to avoid ambiguity in its symbolic significance, which clarifies that it was given to the woman by her suitor and is not part of her collection of gems.

These underlying factors explain the tradition of giving back the ring if the engagement does not culminate in marriage. While women sometimes do keep the ring, it is recognized as counter to custom. Returning the ring restores the man's family jewels. This makes sense given that when couples break up, other jewelry is usually not returned (even if it is given away or sold by the woman). In fact, mothers may give their engagement ring to their sons to give to their future wives, but they usually will not give it to their prospective sons-in-law to give to their daughters, in accordance with traditional rules of family lineage in which the same last name carries on as an unspoken mandate inherent in a male's family jewels. The custom of returning the engagement ring to the man if the wedding is called off acknowledges that it ultimately belongs to him—a part of him that is displayed on 'his' woman to show her status relative to him.[22]

16. Clapping: Sounds of Weather Equals Power

In reality, while women cannot engage in parthenogenesis, they are at least seemingly closer to it than men, as the ones who experience pregnancy and whose role is perforce more extended than a single brief encounter, but rather lasts nine months. Perhaps to compensate for women's more visible role in creation, it is male gods that control the weather or that may independently procreate. However, beyond the symbolic level, compensatory substitutes have emerged, in particular, applause in its simulation of a rainstorm. While light applause (or snapping) sounds like falling rain (a point explained by audio experts (Zhang and Kuo 2013, p. 113)), more enthusiastic applause sounds even more like a storm. We surmise that the power of applause: *ad* 'to' + *plaudere* "to strike, clap" is based on a lightning "strike" and a "clap" of thunder. The connection between the sounds of weather and human-made sounds shows respect for the power of phenomena such as storms (associated with Thor and Zeus). Furthermore, verbal cheers, chants, and shouts may sound similar to rushing water heard from a distance.

In the case of a curtain call, continued applause is a request for performers to return to the stage at the end of a show to acknowledge plaudits. The lights are turned off and then on again; these actions are often accompanied by thunderous applause. Performers presumably feel a rush from being empowered to see effects resembling lightning elicit the sounds of a storm—a stagecraft technique called "fast blackout/lights up cues" (Glossary 2018). In contemporary times, flashing cell phone flashlights replicate this function for concert-goers. This theory is corroborated by alternatives to clapping: stomping of feet or rapping of fists or hands on a table, which also are storm-like sounds. Sometimes, a thunderous burst of applause can "bring down the house", implying a storm. In addition, applause accompanied by whistling resembles whistling wind that enhances storm simulation and

---

[22] The symbolism of the family jewel is a serious matter that may require court intervention. For example, in New York, "once a marriage proposal is extended and accepted—once the promise is made—no matter what day of the year, that ring is no longer considered a gift. It's a contract to enter into marriage" and must be returned (Julien 2018). Thus, while the ring is ostensibly a gift and a purported expression of love and commitment, it apparently possesses enough deep-rooted meaning to be the equivalent of a penned signature in a legal agreement.

connotes power (just as whistleblowers wield power).[23] The use of body percussion-like clapping to simulate rain (e.g., Poole 2016) is remarkable (and available in auditory form in a number of sites on YouTube under keywords body percussion rainstorm). 'Snap to it' is a command reflecting weather-related cause and effect given that the sound of snapping resembles both applause and rain (and is the usual sound that signals the start of a tempest as simulated in a body percussion storm).

17. Ova and Standing Ovation

The assertion that applause is traditional because it sounds like a storm and thus connotes power can be augmented by an analysis of the term 'standing ovation'. First, we note that the word ova means eggs (related to oval, ovoid, or ovate, which pertain to eggs). An ovation, from the Latin word *ovare*, means to lay eggs or to impregnate, but it also means to rejoice (Ovare 2018). Since ova is plural for eggs and *ovada* means pregnant (in Spanish, said of birds) (Roberts 2014, p. 288), then ova + "tion" might combine rejoicing with laying eggs and pregnancy. The original meaning of ovation was the honor accorded to Roman army generals after great victories. Thus, we speculate that their honor may have been linked to fertility-related prowess.

In other words, a standing ovation is applause that sounds like a storm *and* is associated with laying eggs, that is, a type of creation (that occurs when birds are in a standing position). This symbolism was evident when *Frozen* animator John Ripa pitched the climax of the movie in which Anna thwarted Hans' efforts to kill Elsa: the ecstatic production team reportedly gave him "a standing ovation" (Solomon 2013). This connection seems to have been recognized already by a fertility company, *Ovation Fertility*, which specializes in "removing the obstacles that prevent conception" (that as of 2015 offers services similar to Carrot—see footnote 35). However, the connection between applause as it relates to male parthenogenesis does not seem to have been previously suggested—although it is not unusual for creation myths to have an egg theme (see Stith Thompson's *Motif-Index of Folk Literature* (1955–1958): Motif A641: Universe brought forth from an egg, and Motif A1222: Mankind originates from eggs (noted by Dundes 1997a)), a link also conveyed by the Latin dictum: *Omne vivum ex ovo*: All life from an egg.

This connection between males, eggs, and procreativity is also manifested in the Easter Bunny, a male with eggs analogous to a male stork, which is said to use a chimney (birth canal) to 'deliver' babies (Dundes 1980, 2007). These males associated with eggs and fertility unconsciously usurp female powers. Not coincidentally, the term couvade,[24] in which men take on the role of the parturient, is from French *couver*, 'to hatch' (Dundes 2003a). In this regard, the word '*ovada*', which is said of birds, makes sense when applied to humans (men, in this case). This is not to say that a standing ovation means that the audience is consciously invoking powers associated with female fertility, but rather shows that so many elements of the cultural milieu reinforce various subtle as well as blatant patterns that recapitulate historical gender politics. The word innovation, with '*nova*' meaning new, may also connote creativity and newness, but with more gender neutrality in the absence of the implications of a returning Roman army rejoicing in triumph in association with laying eggs or impregnation.

18. Elsa's Parthenogenesis in 'Let it Go'

In a reversal of male womb envy, Elsa circumvents any male control as she explains in 'Let it Go'. She describes a howling wind and "a swirling storm inside" as she lets loose her creative potential in the birth of Olaf (32:09–10), which is marked by a swirly gust (including a whooshing sound simulating

---

[23] The Wizard of Oz creates a display of power by simulating the sounds of a storm, including flashes of lightning and crashes of thunder, which is consistent with the meaning behind the wizard's request that Dorothy bring him the wicked witch's broomstick: to keep males atop the power hierarchy.

[24] Couvade involves men participating in rituals as if they themselves were giving birth to their child (Dundes 2003a). *Faire la couvade* means in French to sit doing nothing, which shows the ambivalence toward the female role in that they are seen as not doing anything (from a male perspective).

wind that is blowing snow). Shortly thereafter, she uses her ungloved hands to send out gusts and release sparks that create a swirling whirlwind that morphs into Marshmallow (accompanied by the sound effects of a breath/small gust of wind) (58:12–15). The power of wind is also manifested in the terms 'whirlwind romance' and 'windfall', which are phenomena that suggest a supernatural element. Parthenogenesis through wind is an ancient concept: "Most classical and medieval philosophers believed that certain mammals and birds could be impregnated by wind"; the wind's breath allowed conception "without copulation" attributable to anemophily or wind pollination (Zirkle 1936, p. 95). The wind that Elsa conjures is similar to the Holy Spirit (or breath) responsible for Christ's virgin birth, and many other examples of impregnation by the wind in myths (Zirkle 1936).

In 'Let it Go', Elsa says that her power "flurries" (i.e., blows) through the air, while her mental energy "crystallizes like an icy blast [wind]", indicating phallic imagery of sharp crystals that work in tandem with the wind. These images suggest that she is usurping the male role in conception. Her use of male power is more visually obvious when she sings, "Let the storm [wind] rage on", and then proceeds to use her hands to command clearly phallic icicle-like projections to rise up to become her castle, which is later decorated with a phallic snowflake (see Figure 2) with menacing sharp spokes (33:32–37).

Elsa conceives but does not carry her progeny in utero; she skips pregnancy, calling into question her ability to be a good mother. This point is demonstrated in an exchange occurring when Elsa is finally reunited with Olaf in her ice castle, where significantly more of her effort has gone (i.e., in her castle, not her children)—perhaps since it is 'a man's' home that is his castle, rather than a woman who should preside over such a lofty structure. The following scene poignantly exposes Elsa's maternal deficits:

Olaf (shyly): You built me. You remember that?

Elsa (surprised): And you're alive?

Olaf (unsure): Um . . . I think so? (55:03–10)

Elsa then looks down at her hands, presumably contemplating their power to give life to the non-animated pre-pubescent version of the snowman in spite of her being a cold ice princess who lacks maternal warmth.[25] In her capacity as a Snow Queen or a queen in a surrogate parent role, she fails, as her subjects suffer under her rule. Even at the end of the film in her reformed state, she gives Olaf a protective flurry, bestowing coldness, not warmth, that ensures his ability to stay erect, much to his delight.

19. Olaf and His Phallic Carrot Nose

In accordance with his status as a male, Olaf is preoccupied with his carrot, a phallic symbol (Hines 1999) that is a recurring theme in *Frozen* (Streiff and Dundes 2017a). Its symbolic meaning perhaps suggests why it serves as motivation, that is, a carrot as enticement (as in the carrot or the stick). Similarly, sticks as symbolic phalluses (as when men are upset to "get the short end of the stick") can express phallic punishment, as in "stick it to the man", in which feminization results in condign retribution. When Anna first inserts the carrot into Olaf, bestowing him with a nose, she jams it in forcefully (since as a virginal woman, she does not know much about carrots and their correct positioning).[26] This act causes Kristoff to visibly cringe. Olaf nevertheless responds saying that he "always wanted a nose" and refers to it as a "little baby unicorn" (46:21–22), before Anna re-positions it to make it bigger (prompting Olaf to say, "I love it even more" (46:24–25)). The word corn in unicorn is cognate with horn, with a variety of phallic connotations such as with Sven's antlers, candy corn

---

[25] The expression colder than a witch's tit (in a brass bra) serves as a reminder that powerful women that wield magic are not only castrating, but also unable to nurture or nurse.

[26] Even in writing, a carat ^ is a symbol that text has been inserted.

(horn) witch costumes, and also a car horn that conveys aggression with an overlay of sexual innuendo (as in "honk if you're horny").[27] However, because Olaf has been isolated from any male influence, he is effeminate.

Olaf loves warm hugs, but without the presence of a father, warm hugs and his desire for a warm climate would be his undoing (causing loss of masculinity through melting). Olaf needs male guidance, yet has no one to teach him how to be a man, which is socialization that often occurs in gender-exclusive "boundaried collectivities" (Thorne 1993, p. 117). In fact, in his capacity as a sidekick, a type of character that is almost always a male that can be feminized for comic relief, he is the butt of jokes about his deviation from traditional masculinity, such as when he talks about his lack of bones, which is code for boner (1:01:17–19).

20. Marshmallow

Marshmallow is gender-ambiguous because despite his ferocity, he is a marshmallow made out of a delicate sweet, who in the end reveals his true nature. After the credits roll, the audience watches as he ensures that he is alone, and then withdraws his menacing spikes and teeth. Next, he dons Elsa's tiny crown, which he finds sexually gratifying (as revealed in his grunts and body language) and the fact that this is the only time he smiles (a toothless smile).[28] As a male wearing a tiara, he ceases to be a threat (just like a law or rule with no teeth). It turns out that Marshmallow is all bark and no bite (as he fails to penetrate anyone in the course of the film). The crown scene is a surprise moment once the movie seems to be over, allowing viewers to laugh at their realization that his ferocity was just a front that hid his desire to act feminine. Elsa had thrown away her tiara, saying, "The past is in the past", apparently referring to her conformity to femininity among other societal norms. Thus, it is interesting that Marshmallow wants to wear this same crown.

Originally, marshmallows were derived from a swamp (marsh) plant with sticky white sap with roots used as lozenges for sore throats, called suckets (Foster and Johnson 2008, p. 244–45), which may have created a connection between marshmallows and breasts, given sucking as a means of gratification in the oral stage. Although marshmallow breasts denote small breasts, marshmallow root, an herb that typically comes in a pill form, is believed to make breasts grow faster (see e.g., Organicfacts 2018), especially if taken following a milk thistle cleanse (Milk thistle 2018). Despite the lack of scientific testing of these herbal treatments, people believe that the remedies will work, likely due to latent psychological reasons.

As Elsa's son and thus an extension of Elsa that is made out of marshmallows, he represents a giant breast, but one that is cold and threatening, not warm and nurturing. However, Marshmallow is a combination of both male and female stereotypical traits: he symbolizes a large breast but also possesses phallic traits; he has sharp teeth and spikes that emerge when he is threatened. He suffers downward displacement symbolic castration when Hans dramatically severs his foot, causing him to plunge into an abyss (1:10:55–1:11:06).[29] He thus falls outside of the gender binary, as neither nurturing nor an effective protector (as Elsa is knocked out and taken hostage despite his role as palace guard).

---

[27] To get angry or blow up is related to the word inflate (Blow up 2018). This lexical connection helps explain why letting the air out of a car's tires is emasculating. Similarly, keying a car is a phallic affront (cf. the word play: a key that opens many locks is a master key while a lock opened by many keys is a cheap lock).

[28] Similarly, in *Rudolf the Rednosed Reindeer* (1964), a nerdy misfit dentist symbolically castrates the Abominable Snowman by pulling his teeth. The snowman becomes docile and performs chores as ordered (perhaps reinforcing latent castration-related odontophobia, fears exacerbated by dentists' penetrating drills). In contrast, Rudolf eventually affirms masculinity, complete with his shiny nose, an echo of the reindeer Sven's machismo.

[29] The foot as phallic equivalent is part of the story of Cinderella, whose foot fits perfectly inside a slipper that may be made out of glass (that can only be broken once—akin to virginity) or fur (a more patent vaginal reference) (Dundes 1989a, p. 139). The best-known version of the tale (AT 510A) was published by Charles Perrault in 1697 as "Contes de Ma Mère l'Oye,", or Tales of My Mother Goose (Dundes 1988, p. 14). The foot as phallus is often part of Jewish weddings when the groom breaks the glass with his foot to prefigure the bride's loss of virginity. A light bulb in a velvet bag advertised as making a loud pop when crushed may be substituted to ensure that the glass breaks (Jewish Wedding 2018).

While both Marshmallow and especially Olaf are likeable, Disney still has not portrayed animated gay characters that are open about their sexuality, and even in *Frozen*, the gender ambiguity characterizes snow beings, not humans. Although both provide comical and somewhat positive portrayals of gender non-conforming characters, they are also quite daft at times, prompting the audience to laugh at their expense (and oftentimes because of their gender nonconforming traits). Furthermore, while neither of them is the real hero, they nevertheless serve as evidence of Elsa's creative powers sans men.

21. The Significance of Gender Non-Conforming Sons

At the end, similar to a pampered son or mama's boy (Coyle et al. 2016), Olaf receives his own personal flurry from Elsa, a salient gift that will protect him against the very-real male fears of (metaphorical) melting, but that also emasculates him, since males are supposed to take care of themselves and take risks. The need for the flurry reiterates that without men, the powerful woman's child is being reared in a way in which he will never be a real man. Although Marshmallow is a menacing palace guard, when he dons Elsa's crown, as Patterson and Spencer (2017) note, Marshmallow's cross-dressing is supposed to bring a laugh. The fact that this is a hidden scene that many viewers miss (because most people do not watch all of the credits) is a parting reminder to the audience that males who self-feminize are funny, and a means to leave audiences with a feel-good moment of superiority. A key part of this post-script is its sense of voyeurism in which Marshmallow hides his sexuality, as he furtively looks around to make sure no one sees his 'deviance' before he dons the crown. This contrasts with Olaf, who is more open about his sexuality as expressed in the carrot as phallus, including scenes of his carrot sagging due to melting, signaling a loss of a metaphorical erection (a fear known as medomalacuphobia).[30] In any case, both snowmen escape the threat of melting, allowing them to retain a modicum of masculinity, and model different types of gender non-conformity.

22. Vehicles as a Means to Display Conventional Masculinity

Although both snowmen reflect shifting gender roles, Kristoff does not stray far from traditional masculinity. After Kristoff's macho, boot-stomping entrance into Oaken's Trading Post, he is later unceremoniously tossed out by Oaken, landing in a sexually vulnerable position (face down in the snow with this rear end in the air) (38:08–10). To reclaim his masculinity, he identifies strongly with his vehicle (a sled that is destroyed but then restored at the film's conclusion). Vehicles can convey "masculine strength, virility and prowess [through males'] technical ability to control a performance motor vehicle at high speed and [men's] courage and daring through risk-taking" (Walker et al. 2000, p. 162) (symbolism that is less subtly conveyed in so-called "truck nuts" (see Lamoureux 2015)).

Early in the film, there is a sled scene involving Kristoff, his reindeer Sven, and Anna. Kristoff must contend with dangerous nighttime driving, due to challenges from the forces of nature that include hard-to-maneuver icy roads and then a dramatic, high-speed flight from marauding wolves (tough sledding of sorts). Wolves are a worthy adversary, as they symbolize masculinity (see Dundes 1989b), as reflected in the gendered connotations of a lone wolf or a wolf whistle, which conveys sexual intent by blowing air through a small opening; similarly, female wolves must be designated as she-wolves.[31]

---

[30] There is a fertility benefit service called *Carrot*, which is likely based on reports that carrots enhance sperm motility. Yet news coverage of carrots' link to fertility ignores the highlighted study's single mention of carrots as just one of multiple foods rich in beta-carotene (Zareba et al. 2013), which is evidence of the psychological component of carrots' association with virility.

[31] Similar to wolves, dogs are "presumed" male and cats are "presumed" to be female (Leach 2000, p. 334). 'Salty dogs' can land in the doghouse, while women may be catty or be deemed sex kittens subject to catcalls from men with their tongues hanging out. The expression, "Cat got your tongue?" endows cats with the "canine" power to castrate, given that tongues are symbolically phallic (cf. Disney's *Little Mermaid* (Dundes and Dundes 2000)). A homely woman is a 'dog', while an

Kristoff's machismo is also evidenced in his care for his vehicle, which reveals his masculinity.[32] When Anna puts her feet up on the "dashboard" (a word used in the official Disney book version of *Frozen* (Rudnick 2015)), Kristoff is offended: "Whoa, who! Whoa, whoa, whoa! Get your feet down." He then pushes Anna's feet down, adding, "This is fresh lacquer. Seriously, were you raised in a barn?" Kristoff then spits on the dash to clean it, resulting in some of his spit flying back into Anna's face (40:18–24).[33] Kristoff clearly holds the reins of his reindeer and reminds Anna that only he gives orders to Sven in Sven's capacity as a metaphorical motor of sorts to his vehicle. Many men insist on being the (French-derived word) *chauffeur* or driver, a word with the syllable '*chau*', meaning hot[34] (part of their desire to be hot stuff or sexually attractive).

23. Elsa as Zeus' Daughter?

Anna's character develops in part within the context of her relationships with men and relatively mundane interactions. Yet it is hard to imagine Elsa in similar scenarios, even though the two women are sisters. We speculate that Elsa represents a daughter of Zeus, metaphorically, as intimated in the first line of the film, in the song 'The Frozen Heart (Ice Worker's Song)'. When the macho ice harvesters sing about Elsa (as suggested by Streiff and Dundes 2017a), their lyrics describe her as: "Born of cold and winter air and mountain rain combining". As discussed in this essay, someone "born" from winter "air" coupled with hydrating fluid from a mountain (where Zeus lives) suggests a supernatural birth (and the promiscuous Zeus was indeed the father of another Disney character, Hercules). Elsa's parents do not understand her power (and there is no family history of her "condition"); they must consult with a non-human being, a troll, about this "condition". Elsa's father is determined to quash her power, forcing her into a pariah existence because he sees her power as stigmatized rather than as a divine gift (that defies mortal origins). Her parents die due to a storm that appears to combine the powers of Zeus (with lightning striking the parents' ship) with the powers of Zeus' brother Poseidon, the god of the sea, as the ship is disabled by the storm and then swallowed by the sea (10:01–15).

Yet Elsa is no Zeus replacement: in a defining moment in the film, Elsa inadvertently 'strikes' her sister with ice, prompting Anna's senescence. In other words, because Elsa, the castrating, termagant sister, cannot properly wield power, her nubile sister sees her hair begin to turn white, which is reminiscent of the hoary tresses of a crone (from carcass, meaning too thin—and old—to procreate (Crone 2018)). Anna's distress is a harbinger of her near-death by freezing at her sister's hand. Elsa's salvation comes in the form of stereotypically feminine tears that reverse her magic malfunction. Her weeping and empathy restore her humanity—or more specifically, her femininity—that replaces her masculine, castrating persona, propelling the story to an anachronistic happy ending.

24. Conclusions

We hope that by bringing attention to the complexities of meaning embedded in *Frozen* and its breathtaking success that we can elucidate contemporary societal struggles at a time when long-standing male dominance and traditional concepts of masculinity are changing. For example, according to *Carrot*, LGBTQ employees have, in many cases, been shut out of family planning coverage due to different fertility needs (O'Connor 2017), which is a manifestation of the challenges

---

effeminate male is disparaged as a 'pussy'. Male dogs are sires (denoting procreation), but female dogs are bitches, revealing a gender hierarchy ascribed to the animal 'kingdom', including how 'raining cats and dogs' hints at gendered competition over weather-driven power.

[32] Kristoff's anxiety about his sled's shininess from its fresh lacquer (wax) is consistent with male preoccupation about shininess (symbolic of a lubricated phallus ready to penetrate), akin to when knights in 'shining' armor ride their steeds (Old English *stead*: stallion, stud). Sex wax for surfboards (sticks) and male-dominated car waxing rituals also appertain.

[33] Spit is equivalent to sperm, as in spitten image (see Dundes 1991), the male counterpart to Elsa's parthenogenesis.

[34] Male *chau*vinism may have the same etymology, as in men who are hot and predisposed to exert their dominance in battle and well as sexually. While the word is reportedly derived from Nicolas Chauvin, who was allegedly a solider in Napoleon's army, this story is considered apocryphal, as there is no evidence that Chauvin existed (see De Puymège 1997).

at the crossroads of sexuality and reproduction.[35] Contemporary controversies include IVF (in vitro fertilization) treatment, which in at least one case resulted in a biological father paying child support for a son born without his permission post-divorce (Pearson 2018). With Elsa's snowmen progeny, Disney has sidestepped a procreation dilemma that they faced in their rendition of the mythical story of Hercules. In the original Hercules story, Zeus procreated with Alcmene, whose mortal husband fathered Hercules' other twin in an act of heteropaternal superfecundation. Yet in Disney's version of *Hercules* (1997), Hera and Zeus were presented as Hercules' parents, eliminating not only Zeus's infidelity, but also issues surrounding alternative methods of procreation. This means of reproduction also resulted in the Gemini astrological twins, when Zeus fathered Pollux but not his mortal twin Castor, yet another example of heteropaternal superfecundation.

Despite these options showcased in mythology long ago and increasingly available today through technological advances, Elsa's procreation is limited to snowmen that are not heteronormative. This suggests societal struggles with accepting a non-conventional means of reproduction, which is associated with gay couples. The snowmen's gender fluidity could show concerns about the possible outcomes of women procreating without male input, as *Frozen*'s 2013 release coincided with debates and changing opinions on gay marriage and transgender rights that were indubitably among the most visible and contentious social issues at the time.

Shortly after *Frozen*'s production, a *Time* cover story aptly encapsulated the socio-historical context for *Frozen* in its discussion of greater openness in discussing people who are transgender, and new policies reflecting efforts to enact "changes in schools, hospitals, workplaces, prisons and the military" (Steinmetz 2014, para. 2) (see Drum 2016 for how the movement to install gender-neutral bathrooms began in 2012–2013).[36] This relates to Elsa because she usurped Zeus' role at a time when trans men (born female) were seen as encroaching on men's bathrooms simultaneous with resistance to more unisex bathrooms that would detract from men's exclusive spheres, in the absence of any sound reason for the continued binary separation (Molotch and Noren 2010), even though in the first public bathrooms (latrines) in Rome, men and women sat side by side (Michaels 2016).

Elsa's virgin birth is a reversal of inveterate male creation aspirations that are so culturally inculcated that they are overlooked as normal. Elsa's appropriation of storms associated with virgin birth concludes 'happily' in her wielding power in a more gender-stereotypical manner: making ice sculptures, a skating rink, and snow confetti as she mingles with the commoners. Our concern is that Elsa's storm wielding and procreative powers were presented as a societal challenge that needed redress. At the end, when Elsa becomes nurturing and less castrating, her snowflake as a symbol that could ward off suitors becomes less central to her identity. As such, once rehabilitated, she conjures a giant signature snowflake in the sky (1:28:38), and then proceeds to obliterate it (1:28:40). This suggests that she is now available and open to suitors' advances, which qualifies as a happy ending for those partial to reinforcing gender stereotypes. Her tendency to slam doors, with connotations regarding restricted sexual access (Streiff and Dundes 2017a), changes in the finale when she embraces open gates, telling Anna, "We are never closing [the gates] again" (1:31:56–57). Notably, she uses the pronoun we, but probably is not referring to Anna, who lacks power and never shut the gates in the first place. Instead, Elsa implies that she is relinquishing her status as a one-woman phenomenon and is perhaps open to the influence of a partner.

In addition, Elsa's lack of interest in men (see Streiff and Dundes 2017a) coupled with her father-absent births might reflect latent concerns about women balancing career, marriage, and children.

---

[35] The article title, "Carrot Fertility Raises $3.6 M to Help Take IVF, Egg *Freezing* Benefits *Mainstream*" (emphasis added) reveals growing fertility options (Buhr 2017). In fact, women's ability to defy their biological clock is increasingly relevant because egg freezing has become "all the rage" (Weller 2017). Perhaps oocyte cryopreservation—egg-freezing technology—and its growing availability to women helped spawn the anxieties underlying Elsa's parthenogenesis using frozen matter.

[36] The Boy Scouts mirror social shifts such as their 2017 decision to begin accepting members based on the gender listed on their application, which allowed transgender boys to join (Chokshijan 2017). Furthermore, beginning in 2018, the Boy Scouts decided to permit younger girls to join Cub Scouts and older girls to earn the rank of Eagle Scout (Hosking 2017).

There is still the notion that marriage and children go hand-in-hand. In fact, the term "Disney Princesses" has a proprietary, creationist nuance, as Walt Disney is the father of the company. It is through this lens that we can view her atypical motherhood, which is a twist on Mother Nature. The spirited discussion in the media about Elsa's sexuality (for example, Gander 2018) shows that viewers see the movie as a vehicle to discuss and advance causes related to sexuality.

The film also reflects women's rising power and their growing ability to perform in formerly all-male professions. These changes were highly visible in female inroads in both major political parties, notably in 2008, when Hilary Clinton competed against Barack Obama in the Democratic primary and Sarah Palin was the Republican Vice Presidential candidate, John McCain's running mate. While both women were disparaged, Clinton earned the chilling moniker "wicked witch of the left" (Miller 2018).

Elsa, however, discards her stigma as a sorcerer at the end of *Frozen*, because she is no longer wreaking havoc, but rather promoting a sense of community. She first saves her sister with love expressed as a tearful hug, literally a 'heartwarming' moment that stands in contradistinction to her acts of freezing. Yet her powers are to remain subdued and apparently should not emphasize that she is more powerful than the common villagers. This is the desired outcome, since the storms that Elsa conjures are a powerful force that is the dominion of men, with symbolic implications for fertility. Thus, Elsa's usurpation and misuse of the weather as well as her parthenogenesis present a crisis that must end in either her reform or her destruction. Fortunately, for the sake of *Frozen 2*, it is the former.

These tropes are longstanding in Disney movies, and are commonly recapitulated, including in *Frozen*, whose modern heroine still follows certain rules that do not subvert male dominance: that is, her independence from men means that she should not threaten a man's status as the metaphorical person in the driver's seat of a relationship. Without a male driver, her parthenogenesis results in gender non-conforming sons that deviate from conventional masculinity. Yet Elsa's fatherless progeny are non-humans, making the lack of paternity moot. Furthermore, as non-heteronormative males, Elsa's sons are less likely to wield power in society or threaten the gender hierarchy.

The famed sociologist Georg Simmel "posed a unique cultural dilemma for women, the problem of creativity" (Vromen 1987, p. 576) as distinct from procreativity, in Simmel's theoretical considerations. Simmel did not see nor could he "resolve the tension between equality and difference (a tension perhaps not resolvable)" (Vromen 1987, p. 576) due to "his inability to transcend a biological model of womanhood" (Vromen 1987, p. 577). The movement to "transcend" this model appears to be a latent theme of *Frozen*. Simmel also proposed that, "The artist is capable of doing what the logician is not: to extend a concept without it losing content" (Swedberg and Reich 2010, p. 33). In the end, the artists that produced *Frozen* present a cautionary tale about how a female imperils the status quo. The inexorable changes of the future, such as expanding fertility options and the re-conceptualization of the gender binary, make *Frozen* relevant to cultural shifts that engender ambivalence about a growing number of women who steal the thunder of men.

Author Contributions: All authors contributed equally to this essay.

Acknowledgments: We are grateful for the illustrations by Hsun-yuan Hsu https://www.hsunyuanart.com/. We also wish to thank Sander Buitelaar and Michael B. Streiff for their helpful suggestions.

Conflicts of Interest: The authors declare no conflict of interest.

References

Abedinifard, Mostafa. 2016. Ridicule, Gender Hegemony, and the Disciplinary Function of Mainstream Gender Humour. *Social Semiotics* 26: 234–49. [CrossRef]

Acuna, Kirsten. 2014. One Huge Change In The 'Frozen' Storyline Helped Make It A Billion-Dollar Movie. Available online: http://www.businessinsider.com/frozen-elsa-originally-villain-2014-9 (accessed on 30 March 2018).

Ball-buster. 2018. Available online: https://en.oxforddictionaries.com/definition/us/ball-breaker (accessed on 2 April 2018).

Bartlett, John. 1891. *Familiar Quotations: A Collection of Passages, Phrases, and Proverbs Traced to Their Sources in Ancient and Modern Literature*. Boston: Little, Brown, and Company.

Begotten. 2018. New Oxford American Dictionary. Available online: https://en.oxforddictionaries.com/definition/beget (accessed on 2 April 2018).

Ben-Yehuda, Nachman. 1980. The European Witch Craze of the 14th to 17th Centuries: A Sociologist's Perspective. *American Journal of Sociology* 86: 1–31. [CrossRef]

Blow up. 2018. Available online: https://en.wiktionary.org/wiki/blow_up (accessed on 5 March 2018).

Borneman, Ernest. 1971. *Sex Im Volksmund*. Reinbek Bei Hamburg: Rowohlt Verlag.

Brewer, Sierra, and Lauren Dundes. 2018. Concerned, Meet Terrified: Intersectional Feminism and the Women's March. *Women's Studies International Forum* 69: 49–55. [CrossRef]

Broedel, Hans Peter. 2003. *The Malleus Maleficarum and the Construction of Witchcraft: Theology and Popular Belief*. Manchester: Manchester University Press, ISBN 9780719064418.

Bryman, Alan E. 2004. *The Disneyization of Society*. Thousand Oaks: Sage Publications.

Buhr, Sarah. 2017. Fertility Startup Carrot Raises $3.6 million to Make IVF and Egg-Freezing More Affordable. TechCrunch.com. Available online: https://techcrunch.com/2017/09/14/fertility-startup-carrot-raises-3-6-million-to-make-ivf-and-egg-freezing-more-affordable/ (accessed on 10 April 2018).

Cameron, Deborah. 1992. Naming of Parts: Gender, Culture, and Terms for the Penis among American College Students. *American Speech* 67: 367–82. [CrossRef]

Carrick, Ashton Katherine. 2016. Drinking to Blackout. *New York Times*, September 19. Available online: https://www.nytimes.com/2016/09/19/opinion/drinking-to-blackout.html (accessed on 17 April 2018).

Charm. 2018. Available online: https://en.wiktionary.org/wiki/charm#English (accessed on 3 April 2018).

Chokshijan, Niraj. 2017. Boy Scouts, Reversing Century-Old Stance, Will Allow Transgender Boys. *New York Times*, January 30. Available online: https://www.nytimes.com/2017/01/30/us/boy-scouts-reversing-century-old-stance-will-allow-transgender-boys.html (accessed on 30 March 2018).

Cohen, Judah, Mathew Barlow, and Kazuyuki Saito. 2009. Decadal Fluctuations in Planetary Wave Forcing Modulate Global Warming in Late Boreal Winter. *Journal of Climate* 22: 4418–26. [CrossRef]

Cohen, Judah, Karl Pfeiffer, and Jennifer A. Francis. 2018. Warm Arctic Episodes Linked with Increased Frequency of Extreme Winter Weather in the United States. *Nature Communications* 9: 869. [CrossRef] [PubMed]

Contagion. 2018. Available online: https://www.etymonline.com/word/contagion (accessed on 4 April 2018).

Contreras, Cuevas, Tomás Jesús, and Isabel Zizaldra Hernández. 2015. A Holiday Celebration in a Binational Context: Easter Experiences at the US–Mexico Border. *Journal of Heritage Tourism* 10: 296–301. [CrossRef]

Coyle, Emily F., Megan Fulcher, and Darinka Trubutschek. 2016. Sissies, Mama's Boys, and Tomboys: Is Children's Gender Nonconformity More Acceptable When Nonconforming Traits Are Positive? *Archives of Sexual Behavior* 45: 1827–38. [CrossRef] [PubMed]

Coyne, Sarah M., Jennifer Ruh Linder, Eric E. Rasmussen, David A. Nelson, and Victoria Birkbeck. 2016. Pretty as a Princess: Longitudinal Effects of Engagement with Disney Princesses on Gender Stereotypes, Body Esteem, and Prosocial Behavior in Children. *Child Development* 87: 1909–25. [CrossRef] [PubMed]

Creed, Barbara. 1993. *The Monstrous-Feminine: Film, Feminism, Psychoanalysis*. London and New York: Routledge.

Crone. 2018. Available online: https://en.oxforddictionaries.com/definition/us/crone (accessed on 6 April 2018).

Cuomo, Chris. 1995. Spinsters in Sensible Shoes. In *From Mouse to Mermaid: The Politics of Film, Gender, and Culture*. Edited by Elizabeth Bell, Lynda Haas and Laura Sells. Bloomington: Indiana University Press, pp. 212–23.

Davis, Amy M. 2007. *Good Girls and Wicked Witches: Changing Representations of Women in Disney's Feature Animation, 1937–2001*. Bloomington: Indiana University Press.

De Puymège, Gérard. 1997. The Good Soldier Chauvin. In *Realms of Memory*. Edited by Pierre Nora. New York: Columbia University Press.

Do Rozario, Rebecca-Anne C. 2004. The Prince and the Magic Kingdom: Beyond Nostalgia, the Function of the Disney Princess. *Women's Studies in Communication* 27: 34–59. [CrossRef]

Dockterman, Eliana. 2018. The Ice Queen's New Kingdom. *Time*, March 19, pp. 58–61.

Draw. 2018. How to Draw Elsa's Snowflake, Drawing Tutorial. Available online: https://www.youtube.com/watch?v=M39LnEEfl1s (accessed on 1 April 2018).

Drum, Kevin. 2016. A Very Brief Timeline of the Bathroom Wars. *Mother Jones*, May 14. Available online: https: //www.motherjones.com/kevin-drum/2016/05/timeline-bathroom-wars/ (accessed on 3 April 2018).

Duncan, Francesca E., Emily L. Que, Nan Zhang, Eve C. Feinberg, Thomas V. O'Halloran, and Teresa K. Woodruff. 2016. The Zinc Spark is an Inorganic Signature of Human Egg Activation. *Scientific Reports* 6: 24737. [CrossRef] [PubMed]

Dundes, Alan. 1976. A Psychoanalytic Study of the Bullroarer. *Man* 11: 220–38. [CrossRef]

Dundes, Alan. 1980. The Crowing Hen and the Easter Bunny: Male Chauvinism in American Folklore. In *Interpreting Folklore*. Bloomington: Indiana University Press, pp. 160–75.

Dundes, Alan. 1984. Earth-diver: Creation of the Mythopoeic Male. In *Sacred Narrative*. Edited by Alan Dundes. Berkeley: University of California Press, pp. 270–94.

Dundes, Alan. 1988. Headnote on Cinderella, or the Little Glass Slipper (by Charles Perrault). In *Cinderella: A Casebook*. Edited by Alan Dundes. Madison: University of Wisconsin Press, vol. 3, pp. 14–15.

Dundes, Alan. 1989a. The Psychoanalytic Study of the Grimms' Tales: "The Maiden Without Hands" (AT 706). In *Folklore Matters*. Edited by Alan Dundes. Knoxville: University of Tennessee Press, pp. 112–50.

Dundes, Alan. 1989b. Interpreting "Little Red Riding Hood" Psychoanalytically. In *Little Red Riding Hood: A Casebook*. Madison: University of Wisconsin Press, pp. 192–236.

Dundes, Alan. 1991. The 1991 Archer Taylor Memorial Lecture. The Apple-Shot: Interpreting the Legend of William Tell. *Western Folklore* 50: 327–60. [CrossRef]

Dundes, Alan. 1994. Gallus as Phallus: A Psychoanalytic Cross-Cultural Consideration of the Cockfight as Fowl Play. In *The Cockfight: A Casebook*. Edited by Alan Dundes. Madison: University of Wisconsin Press, pp. 241–82.

Dundes, Alan. 1997a. The Flood as Male Myth of Creation. In *From Game to War and Other Psychoanalytic Essays on Folklore*. Lexington: University Press of Kentucky, pp. 78–91.

Dundes, Alan. 1997b. Traditional Male combat: From Game to War. In *From Game to War and Other Psychoanalytic Essays on Folklore*. Lexington: University Press of Kentucky, pp. 25–45.

Dundes, Lauren. 2001. Disney's Modern Heroine Pocahontas: Revealing Age-Old Gender Stereotypes and Role Discontinuity under a Façade of Liberation. *The Social Science Journal* 38: 353–65. [CrossRef]

Dundes, Alan. 2003a. Couvade in Genesis. In *Parsing Through Customs*. Madison: University of Wisconsin Press, pp. 145–86.

Dundes, Alan. 2003b. Response: Better Late than Never: The case for Psychoanalytic Folkloristics. *Journal of Folklore Research* 40: 95–99. [CrossRef]

Dundes, Alan. 2007. Structuralism and Folklore. In *The Meaning of Folklore: The Analytical Essays of Alan Dundes*. Edited by Simon J. Bronner. Logan: University Press of Colorado, pp. 123–53.

Dundes, Lauren, and Alan Dundes. 2000. The Trident and the Fork: Disney's 'The Little Mermaid' as a Male Construction of an Electral Fantasy. *Psychoanalytic Studies* 2: 117–30. [CrossRef]

Dundes, Alan, and Lauren Dundes. 2002. The Elephant Walk and Other Amazing Hazing: Male Fraternity Initiation through Infantilization and Feminization. In *Bloody Mary in the Mirror: Essays in Psychoanalytic Folkloristics*. Edited by Alan Dundes. Jackson: University Press of Mississippi, pp. 95–121.

Dundes, Lauren, and Alan Dundes. 2005. Young Hero Simba Defeats Old Villain Scar: Oedipus Wrecks the Lyin' King. *The Social Science Journal* 43: 479–85. [CrossRef]

Dundes, Lauren, and Madeline Streiff. 2016. Reel Royal Diversity? The Glass Ceiling in Disney's Mulan and Princess and the Frog. *Societies* 6: 35. [CrossRef]

Elliott, Anthony, and Brian S. Turner. 2012. Debating "The Social": Towards a Critique of Sociological Nostalgia. *Societies* 2: 14–26. [CrossRef]

England, Dawn Elizabeth, Lara Descartes, and Melissa A. Collier-Meek. 2011. Gender Role Portrayal and the Disney Princesses. *Sex Roles* 64: 555–67. [CrossRef]

Eurich-Rascoe, Barbara L., and Hendrika Vande Kemp. 1997. *Femininity and Shame: Women, Men, and Giving Voice to the Feminine*. Lanham: University Press of America.

Fjellman, Stephen. 1992. *Vinyl Leaves: Walt Disney World and America*. Boulder: Westview.

Foster, Steven, and Rebecca L. Johnson. 2008. *National Geographic Desk Reference to Nature's Medicine*. Washington: National Geographic Society.

François, Alexandre. 2008. Semantic Maps and the Typology of Colexification: Intertwining Polysemous Networks across Languages. In *From Polysemy to Semantic Change: Towards a Typology of Lexical Semantic Associations*. Edited by Martine Vanhove. Studies in Language Companion Series, 106. New York: Benjamins, pp. 163–215.

Frozen. 2013. Directed by Chris Buck and Jennifer Lee. Produced by Peter Del Vecho. Screenplay by Jennifer Lee. Story by Chris Buck, Jennifer Lee and Shane Morris. Burbank: Walt Disney Pictures.

Gander, Kashmira. 2018. Frozen 2: Disney's Elsa Shouldn't be a Lesbian Say Thousands of Backers in Anti-Gay Petition. Newsweek.com. Available online: http://www.newsweek.com/frozen-2-disneys-elsa-shouldnt-be-lesbian-sequel-say-thousands-backers-anti-846112 (accessed on 30 March 2018).

Garlen, Julie C., and Jennifer A. Sandlin. 2017. Happily (N)ever After: The Cruel Optimism of Disney's Romantic Ideal. *Feminist Media Studies* 17: 957–71. [CrossRef]

Gilmore, David D. 2010. *Misogyny: The Male Malady*. Philadelphia: University of Pennsylvania Press.

Giroux, Henry. 1995. *From Mouse to Mermaid: The Politics of Film, Gender, and Culture*. Edited by Elizabeth Bell, Lynda Haas and Laura Sells. Bloomington: Indiana University Press, pp. 43–61.

Giroux, Henry A., and Grace Pollock. 2010. *The Mouse that Roared: Disney and the End of Innocence*. Lanham: Rowman & Littlefield Publishers.

Glossary. 2018. Theatrecrafts.com. Available online: http://www.theatrecrafts.com/pages/home/topics/stage-management/glossary/ (accessed on 2 April 2018).

Griffin, Martyn, Mark Learmonth, and Nick Piper. 2018. Organizational Readiness: Culturally Mediated Learning through Disney Animation. *Academy of Management Learning & Education* 17: 4–23.

Hempl, George. 1901. Etymologies. *The American Journal of Philology* 22: 426–31. [CrossRef]

Hercules. 1997. Directed by John Musker and Ron Clements. Produced by Alice Dewey, John Musker and Ron Clements. Screenplay by Ron Clements, John Musker, Donald McEnery, Bob Shaw and Irene Mecchi. Burbank: Walt Disney Pictures.

Hibberd, James. 2017. Frozen Original Ending Revealed for the First Time. EW.com. Available online: http://ew.com/movies/2017/03/29/frozen-original-ending/ (accessed on 5 April 2018).

Hines, Caitlin. 1999. Foxy Chicks and Playboy Bunnies: A Case Study in Metaphorical Lexicalization. *Amsterdam Studies in the Theory and History of Linguistic Science Series* 4: 9–24.

Hoerrner, Keisha L. 1996. Gender Roles in Disney Films: Analyzing Behaviors from Snow White to Simba. *Women's Studies in Communication* 19: 213–28. [CrossRef]

Horn, Laurence R. 2004. Spitten Image: Etymythology and Fluid Dynamics. *American Speech* 79: 33–58. [CrossRef]

Horn. 2018. Available online: https://en.wiktionary.org/wiki/horn (accessed on 2 April 2018).

Hosking, Taylor. 2017. Why do the Boy Scouts Want to Include Girls? *The Atlantic*. October 12. Available online: https://www.theatlantic.com/politics/archive/2017/10/why-did-the-boy-scouts-decide-to-accept-girls/542769/ (accessed on 2 April 2018).

Jewish Wedding. 2018. Jewish Wedding: Breaking of the Glass Kit: Lightbulb in Purple Bag with Flowers. Available online: https://www.amazon.com/dp/B000PGE0C8/ref=as_li_ss_tl?ie=UTF8&tag=justprofit-20 (accessed on 10 April 2018).

Jones, Ernest. 1951. *Essays in Applied Psychoanalysis, Volume 2: Essays in Folklore, Anthropology and Religion*. London: The Hogarth Press.

Julien, Jane Gordon. 2018. Should You Give the Engagement Ring Back? *New York Times*, January 18. Available online: https://www.nytimes.com/2018/01/18/fashion/weddings/should-you-give-the-engagement-ring-back.html (accessed on 7 April 2018).

Keller, Evelyn Fox. 2014. *Secrets of Life, Secrets of Death: Essays on Science and Culture*. New York: Routledge.

Kittay, Eva F. 1984. Rereading Freud on "Femininity" or Why Not Womb Envy? *Women's Studies International Forum* 7: 385–91. [CrossRef]

Knapton, Sarah. 2016. Bright Flash of Light Marks Incredible Moment Life Begins When Sperm Meets Egg. *The Telegraph*, April 26. Available online: https://www.telegraph.co.uk/science/2016/04/26/bright-flash-of-light-marks-incredible-moment-life-begins-when-s/ (accessed on 2 April 2018).

Lamoureux, Mack. 2015. Balls Out: The Weird Story of the Great Truck Nuts War. Vice.com. Available online: https://www.vice.com/en_ca/article/8gkqbg/balls-out-the-weird-story-of-the-great-truck-nuts-war (accessed on 10 March 2018).

Law, Michelle. 2014. Sisters Doin' it For Themselves: Frozen and the Evolution of the Disney Heroine. *Screen Education* 74: 16–25. Available online: https://issuu.com/atompublications/docs/law_frozen (accessed on 14 March 2018).

Leach, Edmund Ronald. 2000. *The Essential Edmund Leach: Culture and Human Nature*. New Haven: Yale University Press, vol. 2.

Legerdemain. 2018. Available online: https://en.wiktionary.org/wiki/legerdemain (accessed on 1 April 2018).

Liddell, Henry George, and Robert Scott. 1897. *A Greek-English Lexicon*. New York: American Book Company.

Li-Vollmer, Meredith, and Mark E. LaPointe. 2003. Gender Transgression and Villainy in Animated Film. *Popular Communication* 1: 89–109. [CrossRef]

Lyons, Antonia C., Sue I. Dalton, and Anna Hoy. 2006. 'Hardcore Drinking' Portrayals of Alcohol Consumption in Young Women's and Men's Magazines. *Journal of Health Psychology* 11: 223–32. [CrossRef] [PubMed]

Macaluso, Michael. 2016. The Postfeminist Princess: Public Discourse and Disney's Curricular Guide to Feminism. In *Disney, Culture, and Curriculum*. Edited by Jennifer A. Sandlin and Julie C. Garlen. Studies in Curriculum Theory Series. New York: Routledge.

Magic. 2018. Available online: https://www.etymonline.com/word/magic (accessed on 4 April 2018).

Mayer, Kenneth. 2002. *With the Stroke of a Pen: Executive Orders and Presidential Power*. Princeton: Princeton University Press.

McLeod, Dion Sheridan. 2016. Unmasking the Quillain: Queerness and Villainy in Animated Disney Films. Doctor of Philosophy thesis, School of the Arts, English and Media, University of Wollongong, Wollongong, Australia. Available online: http://ro.uow.edu.au/theses/4802 (accessed on 15 February 2018).

Michaels, Samantha. 2016. N.C.'s Transgender Skirmish Is Just the Latest in a Long History of Bathroom Freakouts. *Mother Jones*, May 11. Available online: https://www.motherjones.com/politics/2016/05/north-carolina-transgender-history-bathrooms-freakouts-timeline/ (accessed on 4 April 2018).

Milk thistle. 2018. Milk thistle cleanse for NBE. Grow Breasts Naturally. Available online: http://www.growbreastsnaturally.com/milk-thistle-cleanse-for-nbe.html (accessed on 8 February 2018).

Miller, Madeline. 2018. From Circe to Clinton: Why Powerful Women are Cast as Witches. *The Guardian*, April 7. Available online: https://www.theguardian.com/books/2018/apr/07/cursed-from-circe-to-clinton-why-women-are-cast-as-witches?CMP=fb_gu (accessed on 6 April 2018).

Molotch, Harvey, and Laura Noren, eds. 2010. *Toilet: Public Restrooms and the Politics of Sharing*. New York: NYU Press.

Mulan. 1998. Directed by Tony Bancroft and Barry Cook. Produced by Pam Coats. Screenplay by Rita Hsiao, Philip LaZebnik, Chris Sanders, Eugenia Bostwick-Singer, and Raymond Singer. Burbank: Walt Disney Pictures.

Murphy, Peter F. 2001. *Studs, Tools, and the Family Jewels: Metaphors Men Live By*. Madison: University of Wisconsin Press.

O'Connor. 2017. Carrot Fertility Raises $3.6M to Help Take IVF, Egg Freezing Benefits Mainstream. *Forbes*. Available online: https://www.forbes.com/sites/clareoconnor/2017/09/14/carrot-fertility-raises-3-6m-to-help-take-ivf-egg-freezing-benefits-mainstream/#8716455517ef (accessed on 3 April 2018).

Organicfacts. 2018. Available online: https://www.organicfacts.net/home-remedies/breast-enlargement.html (accessed on 15 March 2018).

Ovare. 2018. Available online: https://www.etymonline.com/search?q=ovare&source=ds_search (accessed on 18 March 2018).

Patterson, Paul G., and Leland G. Spencer. 2017. What's So Funny about a Snowman in a Tiara? Exploring Gender Identity and Gender Nonconformity in Children's Animated Films. *Queer Studies in Media & Popular Culture* 2: 73–93.

Pavlac, Brian. 2009. *Witch Hunts in the Western World: Persecution and Punishment from the Inquisition through the Salem Trials: Persecution and Punishment from the Inquisition through the Salem Trials*. Santa Barbara: ABC-CLIO.

Pearson, Alexander. 2018. German Man Ordered to Pay Child Support After Ex-Wife Forges Signature for IVF Pregnancy. *USA Today*, May 3. Available online: https://www.usatoday.com/story/news/world/2018/05/03/german-man-child-support-ivf/576077002/ (accessed on 5 May 2018).

Pencil. 2018. Available online: https://www.etymonline.com/word/pencil (accessed on 20 March 2018).

Perry, Spencer. 2017. *Frozen 2* Details: Everything We Know About the Sequel. ComingSoon.net. Available online: http://www.comingsoon.net/movies/features/905423-frozen-2-details#Sbc3HrqVuGQwSfZ6.99 (accessed on 20 March 2018).

Poole, Harrison Grant. 2016. Rainstorm Activities for Early Childhood Music Lessons Inspired by Teachable Moments. *General Music Today* 30: 11–15. [CrossRef]

Praz, Mario. 1970. *The Romantic Agony*. New York: Oxford University Press.

Propp, Vladimir. 1958. *Morphology of the Folktale*. Bloomington: Indiana Univ. Research Center in Anthropology, Folklore and Linguistics, Publication 10.

Psyche. 2018. Available online: https://www.etymonline.com/word/psyche (accessed on 22 March 2018).

Pumpian-Mindlin, Eugene. 1969. Vicissitudes of Infantile Omnipotence. *The Psychoanalytic Study of the Child* 24: 213–26. [CrossRef] [PubMed]

Putnam, Amanda. 2015. Mean Ladies: Transgendered Villains in Disney Films. In *Diversity in Disney Films: Critical Essays on Race, Ethnicity, Gender, Sexuality and Disability*. Jefferson: McFarland & Company, pp. 147–62.

Que, Emily L., Reiner Bleher, Francesca E. Duncan, Betty Y. Kong, Sophie C. Gleber, Stefan Vogt, Si Chen, Seth A. Garwin, Amanda R. Bayer, Vinayak P. Dravid, and et al. 2015. Quantitative Mapping of Zinc Fluxes in the Mammalian Egg Reveals the Origin of Fertilization-Induced Zinc Sparks. *Nature Chemistry* 7: 130–39. [CrossRef] [PubMed]

Rabbit hat. 2018. Available online: https://idioms.thefreedictionary.com/pull+a+rabbit+out+of+hat (accessed on 13 March 2018).

Rage. 2018. Available online: https://www.etymonline.com/word/rage (accessed on 22 March 2018).

Reeds, Jewelers. 2018. Enchanted Disney Elsa Snowflake Diamond Engagement Ring. Available online: https://www.reeds.com/enchanted-disney-elsa-s-snowflake-diamond-engagement-ring-1ctw-plurgo4871-w4cw-dsin.html (accessed on 2 April 2018).

Roberts, Edward A. 2014. *A Comprehensive Etymological Dictionary of the Spanish Language with Families of Words Based on Indo-European Roots*. Bloomington: Xlibris Corporation.

Rogers, John H. 1995. *The Giant Planet Jupiter*. Cambridge: Cambridge University Press, vol. 6.

Rojek, Chris. 1993. Disney Culture. *Leisure Studies* 12: 121–35. [CrossRef]

Rowe, Karen E. 1979. Feminism and Fairy Tales. In *Don't Bet On The Prince. Contemporary Feminist Fairy Tales in America and England*. Edited by Jack Zipes. New York: Routledge, pp. 209–23.

Rudloff, Maja. 2016. (Post)feminist Paradoxes: The Sensibilities of Gender Representation in Disney's *Frozen*. *Outskirts: Feminisms Along the Edge* 35: 1–20.

Rudnick, Elizabeth. 2015. *A Frozen Heart*. Los Angeles: Disney Press.

Rudolf the Rednosed Reindeer. 1964. Directed by Larry Roemer. Written by Romeo Muller and Robert May. Produced by Jules Bass and Arthur Rankin, Jr. New York: Rankin/Bass Productions.

Ryrie, Charles C. 1997. *The Holy Spirit, Revised & Expanded*. Chicago: Moody Publishers.

Sakkas, Denny, Mythili Ramalingam, Nicolas Garrido, and Christopher L. R. Barratt. 2015. Sperm Selection in Natural Conception: What Can We Learn from Mother Nature to Improve Assisted Reproduction Outcomes? *Human Reproduction Update* 21: 711–26. [CrossRef] [PubMed]

Schickel, Richard. 1997. *The Disney Version: The Life, Times, Art and Commerce of Walt Disney*, 3rd ed. Chicago: Ivan R. Dee.

Scott, Anna Beatrice. 2006. Superpower vs Supernatural: Black Superheroes and the Quest for a Mutant Reality. *Journal of Visual Culture* 5: 295–314. [CrossRef]

Seed. 2018. Available online: https://en.wiktionary.org/wiki/seed (accessed on 2 March 2018).

Sellers, Susan. 2001. *Myth and Fairy Tale in Contemporary Women's Fiction*. New York: Palgrave.

Simmel, Georg, and Guy Oakes. 1984. *Georg Simmel: On Women, Sexuality and Love*. New Haven: Yale University Press.

Solomon, Charles. 2013. *The Art of Frozen*. San Francisco: Chronicle Books.

Son. 2018. Wiktionary. Available online: https://en.wiktionary.org/wiki/son (accessed on 2 March 2018).

Steele, Valerie. 2001. Fashion, Fetish, Fantasy. In *Masquerade and Identities: Essays on Gender, Sexuality and Marginality*. Edited by Efrat Tseëlon. New York: Routledge, pp. 73–82.

Steinmetz, Katy. 2014. The Transgender Tipping Point. *Time*, May 29, 38–46.

Streiff, Madeline, and Lauren Dundes. 2017a. Frozen in Time: How Disney Gender-Stereotypes Its Most Powerful Princess. *Social Sciences* 6: 38. [CrossRef]

Streiff, Madeline, and Lauren Dundes. 2017b. From Shapeshifter to Lava Monster: Gender Stereotypes in Disney's *Moana*. *Social Sciences* 6: 91. [CrossRef]

Stroke. 2018. Available online: https://en.oxforddictionaries.com/definition/us/stroke (accessed on 6 March 2018).

Swedberg, Richard, and Wendelin Reich. 2010. Georg Simmel's Aphorisms. *Theory, Culture & Society* 27: 24–51.

Szadek, Max. 2017. 'The Great Silence': Diabetes & Erectile Dysfunction. Divabetic.org. Available online: http://divabetic.org/2017/06/09/great-silence-diabetes-erectile-dysfunction-divabetics-spaghetti-western-themed-fathers-day-celebration/ (accessed on 28 March 2018).

Thompson, Teresa L., and Eugenia Zerbinos. 1995. Gender Roles in Animated Cartoons: Has the Picture Changed in 20 Years? *Sex Roles* 32: 651–73. [CrossRef]

Thorne, Barrie. 1993. *Gender Play: Girls and Boys in School*. New Bruswick: Rutgers University Press.

Towbin, Mia Adessa, Shelley A. Haddock, Toni Schindler Zimmerman, Lori K. Lund, and Litsa Renee Tanner. 2004. Images of Gender, Race, Age, and Sexual Orientation in Disney Feature-Length Animated Films. *Journal of Feminist Family Therapy* 15: 19–44. [CrossRef]

Trnka, Susanna. 1995. Living a Life of Sex and Danger: Women, Warfare, and Sex in Military Folk Rhymes. *Western Folklore* 54: 232–41. [CrossRef]

UNH. 2014. University of New Hampshire. "Frozen" Screenwriter/Director Jennifer Lee '92 speech from the 2014 University of New Hampshire Commencement. Available online: https://www.youtube.com/watch?v=TLwsrVVgeQs (accessed on 3 April 2018).

Vincent, Alice. 2016. Why Frozen's Let it Go is so Darn Catchy—According to Science. *The Telegraph*. December 25. Available online: https://www.telegraph.co.uk/music/artists/frozens-let-go-darn-catchy-according-science/ (accessed on 2 February 2018).

Violatti, Cristian. 2014. Thor. *Ancient History Encyclopedia*. Available online: https://www.ancient.eu/Thor/ (accessed on 5 February 2018).

Vromen, Suzanne. 1987. Georg Simmel and the Cultural Dilemma of Women. *History of European Ideas* 8: 563–79. [CrossRef]

Walker, Linley, Dianne Butland, and Robert W. Connell. 2000. Boys on the Road: Masculinities, Car Culture, and Road Safety Education. *The Journal of Men's Studies* 8: 153–69. [CrossRef]

Weller, Chris. 2017. What You Need to Know about Egg-Freezing, the Hot New Perk at Google, Apple, and Facebook. *Newsweek*, September 17. Available online: http://www.businessinsider.com/egg-freezing-at-facebook-apple-google-hot-new-perk-2017-9 (accessed on 28 March 2018).

Wilde, Sarah. 2014. Repackaging the Disney Princess: A Post-Feminist Reading of Modern Day Fairy Tales. *Journal of Promotional Communications* 2: 132–53.

Wills, John. 2017. *Disney Culture*. New Brunswick: Rutgers University Press.

Wilson, Keith, Aleka McAdams, Hubert Leo, and Maryann Simmons. 2014. Simulating Wind Effects on Cloth and Hair in Disney's *Frozen*. In *SIGGRAPH Talks*. New York: ACM SIGGRAPH, article 48.

Window. 2018. New Oxford American Dictionary. Available online: https://en.oxforddictionaries.com/definition/window (accessed on 14 March 2018).

YouTube. 2018. *Frozen: Let It Go* Sing-along. Official Disney UK. Available online: https://www.youtube.com/watch?v=L0MK7qz13bU (accessed on 2 May 2018).

Zaitsev, Alexander M. 2001. *Optical Properties of Diamonds: A Data Handbook*. Berlin: Springer Science & Business Media.

Zareba, Piotr, Daniela S. Colaci, Myriam Afeiche, Audrey J. Gaskins, Niels Jørgensen, Jaime Mendiola, Shanna H. Swan, and Jorge E. Chavarro. 2013. Semen Quality in Relation to Antioxidant Intake in a Healthy Male Population. *Fertility and Sterility* 100: 1572–79. [CrossRef] [PubMed]

Zhang, Tong, and C. C. Jay Kuo. 2013. *Content-based Audio Classification and Retrieval for Audiovisual Data Parsing*. Berlin: Springer Science & Business Media, vol. 606.

Zika, Charles. 1989. Fears of Flying: Representations of Witchcraft and Sexuality in Early Sixteenth-Century Germany. *Australian Journal of Art* 8: 19–47.

Zipes, Jack. 1995. Breaking the Disney Spell. In *From Mouse to Mermaid: The Politics of Film, Gender, and Culture*. Edited by Elizabeth Bell, Lynda Haas and Laura Sells. Bloomington: Indiana University Press, pp. 21–42.

Zipes, Jack. 2007. *Fairy Tales and the Art of Subversion*. New York: Routledge.

Zipes, Jack. 2011. *The Enchanted Screen: The Unknown History of Fairy-Tale Films*. New York: Routledge.

Zipes, Jack. 2012. *The Irresistible Fairy Tale: The Cultural and Social History of a Genre*. Princeton: Princeton University Press.

Zirkle, Conway. 1936. Animals Impregnated by the Wind. *Isis: A Journal of the History of Science Society* 25: 95–130. [CrossRef]

Zurcher, Jessica D., Sarah M. Webb, and Tom Robinson. 2018. The Portrayal of Families across Generations in Disney Animated Films. *Social Sciences* 7: 47. [CrossRef]

MDPI

St. Alban-Anlage 66

4052 Basel

Switzerland

Tel. +41 61 683 77 34

Fax +41 61 302 89 18

www.mdpi.com

Social Sciences Editorial Office

E-mail: socsci@mdpi.com

www.mdpi.com/journal/socsci

www.ingramcontent.com/pod-product-compliance
Lightning Source LLC
Chambersburg PA
CBHW051313020426

42333CB00028B/3321